Fifty Miles and a Fight

Fifty Miles and a Fight

Major Samuel Peter Heintzelman's

Journal of Texas and

the Cortina War

EDITED AND WITH AN INTRODUCTION BY

JERRY THOMPSON

TEXAS STATE HISTORICAL ASSOCIATION

AUSTIN

Library of Congress Cataloging-in-Publication Data

Heintzelman, Samuel Peter, 1805–1880.
  Fifty miles and a fight : Major Samuel Heintzelman's journal of Texas and the Cortina war / edited and with an introduction by Jerry Thompson
    p. cm.
  Includes bibliographical references and index.
  ISBN 0-87611-160-6 (alk. paper)
  1. Cortina, Juan N. (Juan Nepomuceno), 1824–1894. 2. Lower Rio Grande Valley (Tex.)—History. 3. Mexican-American Border Region—History. 4. Heintzelman, Samuel Peter, 1805–1880—Diaries. 5. Soldiers—Texas—Diaries. I. Thompson, Jerry D.
    F391.C77H45 1998
    972 ' .014—dc21

                 98-40366
                 CIP

5 4 3 2 1   98 99 00 01 02

Book design by David Timmons. Tinting and dustjacket design by David Timmons.

Published by the Texas State Historical Association in cooperation with the Center for Studies in Texas History at the University of Texas at Austin.

∞ The paper used in this book meets the minimum requirements of the American National Standard for Permanence of Paper for Printed Library Materials, z39.48–1984.

Frontispiece: *Samuel Peter Heintzelman, a small and slender thirty-three-year veteran of the United States Army, defeated the Cortinistas at El Ebonal on December 14, 1859, and crushed Juan Cortina and his five-hundred-man army at Rio Grande City on December 27.* Courtesy Library of Congress.

Contents

Introduction

———◆·❧·◆———

EARLY ON SUNDAY MORNING, APRIL 24, 1859, a small and slender thirty-three-year veteran of the U.S. Army stepped from the gangplank of the steamship *Switzerland* at Indianola, Texas. With his wife and two children, the well-dressed fifty-three-year-old major in the 1st U.S. Infantry made his way to the Hotel Casimir where he inquired about a room for the evening and passage to San Antonio. Five months later, just as he was settling in as commander at Camp Verde in the heart of the picturesque Texas Hill Country, Samuel Peter Heintzelman received orders placing him in command of the Brownsville Expedition and sending him scurrying for the Mexican border.[1] With seventy-five raiders, a practically illiterate thirty-five-year-old Tejano *ranchero* named Juan Nepomuceno Cortina had ridden into Brownsville, shot up the town, killed five men, and left a vicious border war in his wake. Heintzelman's role as commander of the U.S. Army in the Lower Rio Grande Valley during what was known as the Cortina War, was crucial in helping to bring peace to the area while at the same time preventing a widening of the violence that threatened to drag the United States and Mexico into war. Moreover, during the five months Heintzelman spent on the border, he religiously maintained his habit of recording his thoughts in a daily journal, a practice he had begun as a young cadet at West Point some thirty-seven years earlier.

Heintzelman's journals, pocket diaries, assorted papers and military records provide a rare glimpse into the nineteenth-century history of the United States, and of Texas in particular. They offer a look not only at the day-to-day activities but also the private life of one of the most cultured, dedicated, and well-respected (although often vain) officers of the antebellum frontier

---

[1] Journal of Samuel Peter Heintzelman, Nov. 13, 1859, Manuscript Division, Library of Congress, Washington, D.C. Hereafter referred to as HJ.

army. His pocket diaries and journals alone total over 15,500 handwritten pages and several million words. They begin with the innocent and idealistic thoughts of a young and determined Pennsylvania-German boy at West Point in 1822 and end in 1872 with the somewhat embittered recollections of an aged and physically broken old general. Except for a six-week lapse in 1844, following his marriage, and another five-week omission, after being wounded at the Battle of First Bull Run, the journals are continuous from 1825 to 1872. Daily entries vary from a few sentences to several hundred words.

Before his death, Heintzelman bound the journals for 1825–1841 in three volumes. Later, the remaining journals were also bound, thereby creating a total of ten volumes of daily events covering forty-seven years. In 1913–1914, these ten volumes, along with six boxes of army orders, maps, and correspondence, were given to the Library of Congress by Mary Lathrop Heintzelman, the general's only daughter, and by a grandson and West Point graduate, Capt. Stuart Heintzelman.[2] Unfortunately, none of the lengthy personal letters, perhaps a thousand or more, from Heintzelman to his wife appear to have survived, nor did the correspondence from Margaret Heintzelman to her husband-soldier.

A serious deterrent to any scholarly study of the Heintzelman journals and papers has been the inability of scholars to read Heintzelman's difficult handwriting. Although his penmanship was legible at the time he entered West Point, it grew progressively worse in the decades that followed and at times became almost unreadable, especially during periods of fatigue or stress. While attempting to read portions of his journals in 1865, Heintzelman himself complained that "the writing is so bad that I can't immediately make out the words. I have left out letters, syl[l]ables & words & frequently spelled words wrong. I should have each day read off what I wrote & corrected it."[3]

Creola Blackwell, who transcribed Heintzelman's Fort Yuma journals from January 1, 1851, to December 31, 1853, complained of the "tedious undertaking" and said that reading Heintzelman's writing was "akin to translating a foreign language."[4] Discouraged by the difficult and time-consuming

---

[2] Introduction to the "Papers of Samuel Peter Heintzelman" (Manuscript Division, Library of Congress, Washington, D.C.)

[3] HJ, Dec. 8, 1865. Except for a brief period in early 1849, while he was at sea on his way to California, the journals are, with considerable patience, readable. This particular portion of the journals is difficult if not impossible to read since Heintzelman wrote in pen on both sides of thin paper and the ink bled through the paper.

[4] Creola Blackwell (trans.), *Samuel P. Heintzelman's Journal: 1851–1853, Fort Yuma* (Yuma, Ariz.: Yuma County Historical Society, 1989), v.

task of trying to read the journals, a number of scholars appear to have turned away. One exception was the Arizona physician and historian Benjamin Sacks, who mined Heintzelman's Civil War journals for his study of the creation of the Territory of Arizona. Sacks, who hoped to translate and annotate Heintzelman's Arizona journal, was one of the first to realize the historical value of the day-to-day accounts. What Heintzelman's writing lacked in "literacy luster" was "more than compensated for by the precise information it supplies," Sacks concluded.[5] Certainly some of Heintzelman's most valuable journal entries recall his twenty months with the frontier army in Texas in 1859 and 1860. Undeniably, the most exciting portion of Heintzelman's Texas journal is the five months he spent on the border during the tumultuous days of the Cortina War.

With an objectivity not evident in other contemporary accounts of the Cortina War, Heintzelman details events not mentioned in other sources. Along with John S. Ford's widely read and frequently quoted memoirs and three congressional reports, Heintzelman's journal is pivotal in developing an understanding of this often misunderstood episode of Texas history. Of particular interest is Heintzelman's account of his attack on Cortina's forces at El Ebonal, upriver from Brownsville, on December 14, 1859, and his crushing defeat of the *Cortinistas* at Rio Grande City two weeks later.

Heintzelman's journal also magnifies the brutal nature of the Texas Rangers, a portrayal not readily evident in other sources. Not only does Heintzelman record his disdain and distrust of the Rangers but also their indiscriminate killing of *Mexicanos* and *Tejanos*. In reality, Heintzelman saw the Texas Rangers as worrisome allies and as a serious distraction to peace. Heintzelman came to realize that the Rangers, who had cowered in the early weeks of the war, were little more than an organized horde of undisciplined marauders. Additionally, Heintzelman's journal provides glimpses into the filibustering activities of the shadowy Knights of the Golden Circle, who were hoping to expand the Cortina War into a larger conflict that would lead to war, the eventual annexation of Mexico, and the creation of a slave empire south of the Rio Grande. In the midst of the border conflict, Heintzelman also details his rather imprudent visit to the mines at Vallecillo, Nuevo León. His impressions of his senior commander, Col. Robert E. Lee, who arrived on the border in March 1860, are also noteworthy.

Fifty-five years before coming to Texas, Heintzelman was born in Manheim, Pennsylvania, in the early morning hours of September 30, 1805,

---

[5] B. Sacks, *Be it Enacted: The Creation of the Territory of Arizona* (Phoenix: Arizona Historical Foundation, 1964), 90.

the son of Peter H. Heintzelman and Ann Grubb Heintzelman.[6] The young Samuel Peter received a limited education from private tutors and the parochial school of the Manheim Lutheran Church. In 1822, after presenting U.S. Representative James Buchanan of Lancaster with a letter from a local teacher certifying that he was competent in English grammar, arithmetic, and algebra, he was able to obtain the obligatory congressional recommendation necessary for appointment to West Point.[7] Buchanan wrote Secretary of War John C. Calhoun that the seventeen-year-old was the son of a "very respectable German," and "intelligent beyond what I would have expected from a boy of his age."[8] Ten prominent Manheim citizens, including Samuel Peter's father, also wrote Calhoun to say that the young man had an "unblemished moral character" and a "strong and healthful constitution." Receiving the news of his acceptance, Samuel Peter wrote the customary acknowledgement to Calhoun to say that he was "highly honored."[9] On July 1, 1822, Heintzelman entered the United States Military Academy at West Point, New York.

At West Point, Heintzelman struggled academically, especially with chemistry and philosophy. Driven by the dream of a career in the military, he placed a blanket over his window at night so the lamp would not reveal he was

---

[6] George L. Heiges, "Gen. S. P. Heintzelman Visits His Hometown of Manheim," *Journal of Lancaster County Historical Society*, 68 (1964), 88; HJ, Dec. 29, 1831; A. K. Hostetter, "Major Samuel Peter Heintzelman," *Historical Papers and Addresses of the Lancaster County Historical Society*, 17 (1913), 58. Also see Eleanor Jane Fulton and Barbara Kendig Mylin (comps.), *An Index to the Will Books and Interstate Records, Lancaster County Pennsylvania 1729–1850*, book 5, vol. 1, (1936). In 1810 Manheim had a population of 1,282, including eight free persons of color. United States Third Census (1810), Lancaster County, Pennsylvania (National Archives, Washington, D.C.; hereafter referred to as NA). Heintzelman was always close to his two older sisters—Maria, who was born on July 25, 1800, and Juliana, who was born on May 24, 1802. A brother, H. Wagner, came into the world on July 30, 1804, but died three months later. Another brother, Henry was born on December 8, 1807 and died at the age of twenty in 1826. A younger sister, Ann Elizabeth, named after her mother, was born in 1810. Yet another sister, Susan, who was born during the War of 1812, lived for only four weeks.
[7] James Buchanan to J. C. Calhoun, Feb. 27, 1822, West Point Application Papers of Samuel Peter Heintzelman, Adjutant General's Office (referred to hereafter as AGO), Record Group 94 (NA).
[8] Ibid.
[9] David May, et al., to Calhoun, Jan. 17, 1822; Samuel P. Heintzelman to Calhoun, Apr. 9, 1822; both in ibid. See also Calhoun to Heintzelman, Mar. 23, 1822, Heintzelman Papers (Manuscript Division, Library of Congress, Washington, D.C.; cited hereafter as HP).

studying well past "lights out."[10] He did not do well in mineralogy either, but he was fascinated by the subject and often roamed the rugged hillsides around West Point and along the banks of the Hudson River in search of rocks and minerals. Despite his studiousness, there was time at West Point for sketching, skating, dancing, and a class in fencing. He also joined the school lyceum, played chess, practiced on a flute he purchased for $4, and began recording daily temperatures.[11] Through hard work and dedication, traits that would characterize his lengthy military career, he graduated a respectable seventeenth in a class of forty-one in 1826.[12]

It was in Buffalo, New York, in April 1843, while commanding Company D of the 3d Infantry, that Heintzelman, by this time a captain, met a slender and petite Albany socialite named Margaret Stuart. In his journal Heintzelman noted seeing "Miss Margaret," who was "quite handsome," and that they had spent a "couple of hours . . . very agreeably."[13]

Three months later, on July 4, 1844, the couple attended the customary salute at the garrison and a dance in the evening. Two days later he was with Margaret at the theater to hear Edwin Forrest "rant as usual" in *Othello*.[14] But it was in October 1844, following an incident in which she took the arm of another officer during a "beautiful moonlight night," that he was seized by a fit of jealousy and mustered the courage to propose. "I saw Miss Margaret . . . & offered myself & after proper maidenly reflection was accepted. I have to ask her mother, but have no doubt she will give her consent," he wrote.[15] On December 5, 1844, Margaret Stuart and Samuel Peter Heintzelman were married in Buffalo. He was thirty-eight, she was twenty-five.

---

[10] A. I. Measonton to S. G. Blunt, June 3, 1880, Cullum Collection (Archives, United States Military Academy, West Point, New York); HJ, Feb. 18, 1825.

[11] HJ, Jan. 8, Feb. 5, Apr. 13, July 6, 1825.

[12] George W. Cullum, *Biographical Register of the Officers and Graduates of the U.S. Military Academy at West Point, N.Y. From its Establishment in 1802 to 1890* (Cambridge, Mass.: Riverside Press, 1891), 372–374.

[13] HJ, Oct. 20, 1843.

[14] HJ, July 6, 1844.

[15] HJ, Oct. 15, 1844. The 1850 San Diego County, California, census lists Margaret Heintzelman as twenty-five, which would indicate that she was probably born in 1825. North indicates that she was born on December 1, 1819. The date on the 1850 census is suspect since Charles, age five, is listed as being born in New York, whereas he was born in Detroit, Michigan. Diane M. T. North, *Samuel Peter Heintzelman and the Sonora Exploring & Mining Company* (Tucson: University of Arizona Press, 1980), 190. Margaret's vanity may help explain the census discrepancy in her age. Her tombstone in Forest Lawn Cemetery does not give her birthdate.

In June 1845 the Buffalo press reported that Mexico had invaded the newly acquired state of Texas. Within days the captain and Margaret had departed for Fort Gratiot, Michigan, where Heintzelman was to continue as assistant quartermaster and company commander.[16] At Fort Gratiot he learned that Mexico had declared war on the United States, but the news had been expected, he said, and did not create "much excitement." The war, he also realized, meant he was certain to be transferred, although exactly where he did not know. Margaret, who was pregnant, would not be able to accompany him, and he did not want her to return to Buffalo. "I want to get her away from her family & teach her to depend upon herself," he confessed.[17] He later learned, much to his delight, that he was being sent to Detroit. Although the post was a "miserable place," the couple was able to rent a comfortable house in town and it was here that their first child was born. "Yesterday at 20 minutes past 4, I was made a father," he recorded on December 29, 1845. "Margaret has a son. He is a fine healthy child & weighs 8½ pounds. Both are doing well."[18] The child was Charles Stuart, who was to share many of his father's adventures in Texas, graduate from West Point in 1867, and serve in the U.S. Army in the trans-Mississippi.

In early May 1846 even more exciting news arrived from Texas. On April 24, 1846, a company of U.S. dragoons had been surrounded and either killed or captured by the Mexican Army not far from the banks of the Rio Grande. When the United States declared war three weeks later, there was "great excitement throughout the country," Heintzelman recorded.[19] Receiving orders to report to Louisville, Kentucky, he was certain he was to be part of an expedition to be sent across the Great Plains to Santa Fe, New Mexico.

Leaving Margaret and their newborn son in Detroit, he arrived in Louisville to find the town a beehive of activity. A local company was turning out twenty army tents a day and agents scurried about contracting steamboats for use on the Gulf of Mexico and the Rio Grande.[20] Indiana, Ohio, and Kentucky volunteers were arriving daily and recruiting officers hurried east to enlist more men. More sobering realities of war came when the badly wounded began to arrive on steamboats from New Orleans and the Rio Grande.[21] In

---

[16] HJ, Sept. 12, 1845; Regimental Returns (referred to hereafter as RR), 2d Infantry, July–September 1845, AGO, RG 94.

[17] HJ, Sept. 14, 1845.

[18] HJ, Dec. 29, 1845.

[19] HJ, May 14, 1846.

[20] HJ, June 9, 1846; RR, 2d Infantry, June–July 1846, AGO, RG 94. See also "Heintzelman Letter Book," June 10, 1846–Oct. 31, 1846, HP.

[21] HJ, June 14, 1846.

September 1846, word arrived that Gen. Stephen W. Kearny had seized Santa Fe and that the Bear Flag Revolt had put most of California in American hands.

Within days, he departed for Washington, where he arrived in time to see the captured, bullet-riddled battle flag of the Tampico Battalion displayed at the Adjutant General's Office. After less than two weeks in the capital, he hurried west again by train and stage, past Harper's Ferry and Wheeling, Virginia, and down the Ohio River to Guyanadotte, Virginia, where several volunteer companies were preparing to depart for Mexico. Reflecting on the war, he commented, "No one to thank but Mr. Polk & the an[n]exation of Texas. It has changed the fate of many & will that of many more."[22] Later, after reading Polk's "Declaration of War," however, he commented, "I begin to think we are not so much in the wrong as I once believed."[23] Expecting orders that would take him to Mexico, he purchased two books on Mexico and began studying Spanish.

Back in Washington, he watched as crowds gathered daily on street corners to hear the latest news read from the pages of the New Orleans *Picayune*. Gen. Zachary Taylor had won a great victory at Buena Vista southwest of Saltillo, Mexico, the newspapers said, and by early April 1847, Gen. Winfield Scott had landed at Vera Cruz.

Sent to Worcester, Massachusetts, on recruiting duty, he found the town to be "a great anti-slavery, anti-war, anti-everything" place and after several days he was able to recruit only a single Irishman.[24] In Worcester on the first anniversary of the Battle of Palo Alto, he learned that General Scott had defeated a large Mexican Army under Gen. Antonio Lopez de Santa Anna at Cerro Gordo on the road to Mexico City and that the U.S. Army was continuing to push toward the Mexican capital.

Heintzelman arrived in New York City on July 29, 1847, and a few days later, along with 300 recruits of the 2d Infantry, he finally sailed for Mexico. Landing in Vera Cruz, he managed a quick visit to the city and the historic castle of San Juan de Ulloa, before setting out with the four companies of the 2d Infantry along the National Road for Jalapa and Mexico City. A week later, five miles from the National Bridge and halfway to Jalapa, the column went into camp at a small village. At 2 A.M. on September 14, 1847, just as he had retired to his tent for the evening, a band of guerrillas who were concealed in a graveyard on a nearby hill, fired into the camp. While running barefoot

---

[22] HJ, Dec. 7, 1846.
[23] HJ, Dec. 11, 1846.
[24] HJ, Apr. 11, 13, 1847.

from his tent in the darkness he struck his foot on a tent peg and was slightly injured. Although the sniping continued until morning, only one American was killed in the attack, all of which he speculated had been in retaliation for the army having plundered and burned several nearby ranches.[25]

Continuing toward Jalapa, the devastation from the war became more evident. Every house along the road had been burned and the countryside was in ruin. With his men exhausted and some further weakened from yellow fever and scurvy, he arrived in Jalapa on September 19, 1847.

Ascending through the mist-shrouded Sierra Madres in early October, the small U.S. Army reached the Mexican central plateau. Crossing a large cultivated plain rich in corn and barley, Heintzelman and the men of the 2d Infantry looked up to see the American flag floating over the colonial fortress of Perote. Perote brought bitter memories, for it was here that many of the men of the ill-fated 1842 Texas-Mier Expedition had been imprisoned. The captain took time to ride out to the "castle" to see "the bones of the Texans shot there."[26]

Leaving Perote, he was less than a mile from the picturesque town of Humantla on October 9, 1847, when a courier raced up to say that some 3,000 green-clad Mexican lancers had overrun the town and that Capt. Samuel Walker, legendary Texas Ranger, had been killed by a sniper. Ordering his men to "double quick" into the town, Heintzelman found Walker lying on the plaza, "shot above the eye & in the right breast."[27] Seeing the dead captain, the Americans went into a frenzy and "killed every Mexican they saw," he confessed. The "beautiful town" was plundered and "dead Mexicans [lay] about in every direction."[28] Such a "drunken lot I never saw . . . . I could do nothing with them," he confessed.[29] Homes were robbed and the goods given to the poor women of the town. "We are a strange people," he concluded.[30]

---

[25] HJ, Sept. 14, 1847. The soldier was buried in a shallow grave in a garden the next day.

[26] HJ, Oct. 4, 1847. Heintzelman confused the execution of the Mier prisoners at Salado in the "black bean episode" on March 25, 1843, with the death of other Mier prisoners at Perote of typhus in the winter of 1843–1844.

[27] HJ, Oct. 10, 1847. See also Walter Prescott Webb, *The Texas Rangers* (Austin: University of Texas Press, 1977), 118; Robert W. Johannsen, *To the Halls of the Montezumas: The Mexican War in the American Imagination* (New York: Oxford University Press, 1985), 135–136.

[28] HJ, Oct. 10, 1847. See also, K. Jack Bauer, *The Mexican War: 1846–1848* (New York: Macmillan, 1974), 331.

[29] HJ, Oct. 10, 1847.

[30] Ibid.

Although his role in the Battle of Humantla, the last of the war, was slight, Heintzelman was later breveted a major for the battle. With the passage of time, the battle would be magnified in his imagination into a much larger event. For years to come, every October 9 would be celebrated with a joyous toast.

Three days after leaving camp near Humantla, Heintzelman helped to raise the American flag over the old colonial city of Puebla. Although Puebla had fallen to General Scott's Army of Occupation on its march to Mexico City, one company, upon nearing the city, had been fired on by Mexican guerrillas concealed in a cornfield. Entering the city, the sight of seven bodies of men from a Pennsylvania regiment who had been hacked to pieces by the guerrillas sent the Americans into a rage. Although white flags were everywhere, Heintzelman watched helplessly as the Americans ran wild, sacking every house and business, well into the night. Even a number of churches were desecrated. "From the little respect we paid their saints & images, I do not wonder they call us barbarians," he wrote.[31]

Heintzelman remained at Puebla for two weeks. Besides constantly trying to keep his men sober, he found time to attend a fandango, and he sat helplessly as two minor earthquakes shook the city. He also recorded how an American teamster, who had murdered a wagonmaster, was hanged in the central plaza. The Mexicans "looked on in wonder" while "our people laughed & joked," he wrote.[32] He also rode out to the ancient ruins of Cholula where he spurred his horse to the top of a giant pyramid for a magnificent view of the Mexican countryside. Never, he wrote, had he seen "anything to compare with it."[33]

Frustrated with his inability to freely converse in Spanish, he spent several hours each night studying. Reminders of home came in a letter from Margaret containing a lock of Charles' hair, "fair, fine, soft & silky."[34] Leaving Puebla in early December 1847, he was in Mexico City less than a week later. With the war all but over, he took quarters in the quaint village of Tacuba, just south of the city. Evenings were spent writing lengthy letters to Margaret, studying Spanish, and reading William H. Prescott's *Conquest of Mexico*. Each day he rode into Mexico City to the theater, the "largest & finest" he had ever seen.[35] At Contreras, Churubusco, and Chapultepec, he walked over the bloodied earth where the U.S. Army had swept the Mexicans from the field

---

[31] HJ, Oct. 12, 1847.
[32] HJ, Oct. 19, 1847.
[33] HJ, Oct. 22, 1847.
[34] HJ, Dec. 3, 1847.
[35] HJ, Dec. 9, 1847; RR, 2d Infantry, Dec. 1847, AGO, RG 94.

and brought the war to an end. At San Cosme, at the gates of Mexico City, a young lieutenant named Ulysses S. Grant showed him where the Mexican artillery had tried in vain to defend the capital.[36] After the signing of the Treaty of Guadalupe-Hidalgo on February 2, 1848, he moved into the city and rented a large house from a wealthy Mexican widow.

In Mexico City, exciting news arrived from Buffalo. "My daughter was born on the evening of 27 Feb. & all doing well . . . I got a lock of hair," he recorded in early April 1848.[37] Neither mother nor father realized at the time that the newborn, christened Mary Lathrop, had been born with a slight deformity in one of her legs and that the child was slightly crippled. Mary, nevertheless, was to become an important part of her father's life, especially in old age when she would be a constant companion.

Heintzelman departed Mexico City on June 6, 1848, in a mile-long column of bluecoats. Four days later, with "drums beating & colors flying," the column passed through Puebla.[38] Ill, he continued past Perote, through the Tierra Caliente, and into the sweltering tropical heat of Vera Cruz on July 2, where he departed for New Orleans. Still sick, he arrived at Algiers, opposite New Orleans, four days after leaving Vera Cruz. "The first human being I saw on shore this morning in this land of liberty was a slave," he sarcastically commented.[39]

After spending a few days at Camp Jeff Davis at East Pascagoula, Mississippi, he was back in New Orleans where he left on the ill-fated *Sultana* for St. Louis.[40] At Jefferson Barracks, plans were already underway for the departure of the 2d Infantry for California. After considerable debate, it was decided that the regiment would depart by ship in the fall from New York rather than travel overland.

In early September 1848, after crossing Lake Erie, he arrived at Buffalo where it was agreed that Margaret and the children, along with Margaret's sister, Caroline Stuart, would accompany him to California. It was an exciting time for the family, for the lengthy trip around Cape Horn was certain to be one of the great adventures of their lives.

In October 1848, Heintzelman rushed ahead to New York to make final arrangements for the departure of the 2d Infantry. Margaret, Caroline, and

---

[36] HJ, Jan. 29, 1848.
[37] HJ, Apr. 2, 1848.
[38] HJ, June 10, 1848.
[39] HJ, July 11, 1848.
[40] HJ, July 30, 1848; RR, 2d Infantry, July 1848, AGO, RG 94. On April 27, 1865, the *Sultana* sank on the Mississippi River about ninety miles south of Memphis when its boilers exploded. Over six hundred Union prisoners of war who were returning to their homes drowned in the disaster.

the children followed a few days later. In the brisk morning air of November 8, 1848, the *Rome*, with Companies D and H of the 2d Infantry on board, weighed anchor and set sail for California.[41]

On April 6, 1849, after five months at sea, the *Rome* reached Monterey, California. Three days later, the ship's crew defiantly struck out for the gold fields as the captain of the ship fired several shots from his "six shooter at the deserters."[42] Caught up in the excitement of the time, Heintzelman hoped that somehow he might be stationed in the gold country but orders arrived sending him to San Diego instead. After a pleasant trip down the coast, the Heintzelmans arrived in the small community on April 20, 1849, just in time for a Mexican fandango.[43] Life on the Pacific included picnics at the old mission of San Diego de Alcala, some five miles east of Old Town. In the afternoon there were quiet buggy rides to the top of a hill to watch the Pacific surf breaking on the shore and whales at play in the harbor. There were also quail, duck, and rabbit hunts, and long walks along the beach with the children.

While he was at San Diego, Heintzelman received orders directing him to "establish your command in the most eligible position in the vicinity of the junction of the Gila and Colorado rivers . . . as early as possible in order to give protection to the emigrants and to repress any hostile disposition on the part of the Indians."[44]

After leaving Margaret and the children to later depart for New York, Heintzelman set out on the exhausting 240-mile trek across the desert, ninety miles of which was difficult sand, for the Colorado River. Finally reaching the river on November 27, 1850, tents were pitched and the captain set out to make life as bearable as possible. Brush arbors and picket fences made of reeds were placed around the tents for protection from the sun and the wind. Despite the harshness of life at Fort Yuma, Heintzelman would always remain attracted to the beauties of the desert and the natural world around him. His naturalistic instincts notwithstanding, Heintzelman's main concern was the day-to-day operation of the post.

---

[41] HJ, Nov. 6, 8, 1848. Companies C, G, and I with Col. Bennett Riley, sailed on the *Iowa* while Companies A and F embarked on the *Mary* and *Adeline*. RR, 2d Infantry, Nov. 1848, AGO, RG 94; Battalion Returns, Cos. D & H, 2d Infantry, Dec. 1848, in RR, AGO, RG 94; Arthur Woodward (ed.), *Journal of Lt. Thomas W. Sweeny, 1849–1853* (Los Angeles, Westerlore Press, 1956), 23.

[42] HJ, Apr. 10, 1849.

[43] HJ, Apr. 20, 1849.

[44] Edward Canby to Heintzelman, July 4, 1850, HP. See also Heintzelman to W. H. Emory, Aug. 6, 1850, HP; Battalion Returns, Cos. D & H, 2d Infantry, in Post Returns, Fort Yuma, Oct. 1850, AGO, RG 94.

Heintzelman's future would be directly influenced by a party of miners who reached the Yuma crossing in June 1854 that included a young Kentucky adventurer named Charles Debriell Poston and a German mining engineer, Hermann Vollrath Ehrenberg. After prospecting for four months in the Sonoran Desert, they had located several rich veins of silver in the mountains west of Tubac, and had specimens of ore to prove it. At the crossing, Poston and Ehrenberg began surveying a townsite called "Colorado City," a precursor of present-day Yuma.[45] At the time, important news arrived from the east. The United States, in hopes of building a Pacific Railroad, had purchased some 29,640 square miles of territory south of the Gila River in present-day Arizona and New Mexico for $10 million.

After three years at the post, word arrived in June 1854 that he was being relieved by Bvt. Maj. George H. Thomas of the 3d Artillery. A month later, he rode west across the desert with a drunken escort to San Diego, and in early July departed for San Pedro, Monterey, and the ship-jammed foggy harbor of San Francisco.

After returning to the East Coast by way of Panama, Heintzelman was appointed superintendent of the Western Recruiting Department in the summer of 1855 and sent to Newport Barracks, Kentucky, on the south bank of the Ohio River opposite Cincinnati. In Cincinnati, Heintzelman invested $1,000 in the Texas Western Railroad with Andrew Gray, whom he had come to know at Fort Yuma.[46] He also began to spend a lot of time with Charles Poston, who brought more "information as to the silver mines in the Purchase."[47] Heintzelman introduced Poston to Thomas and William Wrightson, brothers who edited the *Railroad Record*, a publication advocating the building of western railroads. Encouraged by the meeting, Heintzelman and Poston made plans to establish a mining company.[48] Able to persuade the Wrightsons and other Cincinnati businessmen to invest in the company, Heintzelman subsequently was made president on May 24, 1856, and plans were made to send Poston with a party of men back to Arizona, where he would meet Ehrenberg, the mining engineer, and begin mining. In August 1857, the Sonora Exploring and Mining Company was incorporated in Ohio with capital stock listed at $2 million.[49]

---

[45] HJ, July 11, 1854; Douglas D. Martin, *Yuma Crossing* (Albuquerque: University of New Mexico Press, 1954), 179; Sacks, *Be It Enacted*, 9.

[46] North, *Samuel Peter Heintzelman*, 14.

[47] HJ, Mar. 7, 1856.

[48] HJ, Mar. 24, 1856; North, *Samuel Peter Heintzelman*, 22.

[49] North, *Samuel Peter Heintzelman*, 22.

Poston, who was heading west to Arizona, paused to write encouraging letters from El Paso, Texas, and from Las Cruces and Mesilla, New Mexico Territory, where he proposed a scheme to buy the Hugh Stevenson Mine in the Organ Mountains, east of Las Cruces, along with a tract of land in the Mesilla Valley for $20,000.[50] By January 1857, Poston wrote that he had reached Arizona and despite the fact that his party, due to death and illness, was reduced to four, he had taken possession of "17 veins of silver within 10 miles of Tubac" and that ten Mexican miners were already at work.[51] Poston also expected to acquire the nearby silver-rich Arivaca Ranch. In February 1857, Frederick Brucknow and Charles Schuchard, who were hired as mining engineers, were reporting sixteen veins of silver, some of them two to four feet thick, within a mile of Cerro Colorado, west of Tubac. Heintzelman also began corresponding with Sylvester Mowry, a young and ambitious lieutenant who was stationed at Fort Yuma, who was also promoting mining in the Gadsden Purchase; in addition, Heintzelman sent Mowry several reports of the Sonora Mining and Exploring Company.[52]

His interests in the Arizona mines were overshadowed on August 25, 1857, by the birth of the Heintzelman's second son, Henry Summers. Heintzelman recorded that the infant was not well and did not breathe correctly. A month later the child remained ill "from pain in the bow[e]ls."[53] The child's frail condition would remain a major concern of the family and in January 1858, the child died in Buffalo of whooping cough.

Back in Washington, Heintzelman received a letter from Hermann Ehrenberg, who wrote encouragingly about the Arizona mines and sent a map he had made of the Gadsden Purchase and Sonora. Mowry, who had resigned from the army to promote his own Sopori Mining Company, wrote regularly to say that he was coming to Washington to lobby in person for the creation of a Territory of Arizona, separate from New Mexico. Mowry wanted to see Sen. Jefferson Davis, who had served as secretary of war during the Franklin Pierce administration, and hoped Heintzelman would accompany him. Poston wrote to say that the main shafts at Cerro Colorado, named the Heintzelman Mine, were reported to be "quite rich."[54]

---

[50] HJ, Aug. 10, 13, 17, 27, Sept. 1, 1856.

[51] HJ, Jan. 31, 1857. See also *Sonora and the Value of Its Silver Mines: Report of the Sonora Exploring and Mining Co., Made to the Stockholders, Dec., 1856* (Cincinnati: Railroad Record Print, 1857).

[52] HJ, Mar. 1, 1857.

[53] HJ, Aug. 25, 26, 1857.

[54] HJ, Sept. 26, 1857.

In Washington, Heintzelman met with Maj. William W. Chapman, army quartermaster and a stockholder in the lead and silver mines at Vallecillo, Nuevo León, Mexico. Chapman gave Heintzelman several copies of a brochure describing the Mexican mines and proposed that his company and the Sonora Mining and Exploring Company exchange stock.[55] Major Chapman also took Heintzelman to see Samuel Colt, the "pistol man." Colt appeared interested in the Arizona mines, but Heintzelman was fearful that Mowry would persuade him to invest in the Sopori Mining Company instead.

In February 1858, Heintzelman was in Washington at Willard's Hotel where he began to seriously lobby for the creation of an Arizona Territory. On February 25, 1858, he visited with Sen. William M. Gwin of California who had just introduced a bill to organize the territory. Mowry and Colt were there to help and they called on Stephen A. Douglas, influential senator from Illinois and chairman of the Committee of Territories, and showed him reports from the Sonora Exploring and Mining Company.[56]

In late March 1858, Heintzelman was back in Cincinnati for a meeting of the Sonora Mining and Exploring Company where it was suggested he obtain a year's leave and go to Arizona.[57] Late in May 1858, upon hearing that his leave had been granted, Heintzelman said good-bye to his family and left for New York where he met with Major Chapman to continue discussion of the Arizona and Mexican mines.

Arriving in Panama, he caught the newly completed Panama Railroad which sped travelers through the isthmus rain forest in less than five hours. After another two weeks at sea, he arrived in San Diego for a prearranged meeting with Solon Lathrop, a close friend who was married to his wife's sister, Elizabeth. On July 14, 1858, after spending the night in a dirty room in filthy beds, the two men left in a mule-drawn wagon for Fort Yuma. Crossing the desert in the scorching summer heat, they arrived on the Colorado River ten days later. Halting only to walk over the parade ground and inspect some of the newer buildings at the post, the two men crossed the river and headed east along the Gila Trail. Pausing at Oatman Flats, they pushed on to the Pima villages and Maricopa Wells, where they purchased forage and melons before setting out across the eighty-mile "Great Desert," past giant saguaro cactus and the naked spire of Picacho Peak, for Tucson. With good grass, ample water, and a cooling summer rain, they reached the desolate village of

---

[55] HJ, Dec. 10, 21, 1857.

[56] HJ, Mar. 1, 1858; Sacks, *Be It Enacted*, 15.

[57] HJ, Mar. 28, 1858.

weathered adobe on August 14, 1858.[58] Two days later they took the road south past the mission of San Xavier del Bac to Tubac where they found Poston waiting. Here amid the ruins of the old Spanish presidio, on the west back of the Santa Cruz River, Poston had established the headquarters of the Sonora Exploring & Mining Company. A few weeks later, after returning to Tucson briefly, Heintzelman left in a four-mule wagon over a rough, makeshift road past forests of ocotillos and through the rugged Tumacacori Mountains to the Heintzelman Mine beneath the barren south face of Cerro Colorado, some seventeen miles west of Tubac.

Except for brief visits to Fort Buchanan, Tucson, and Tubac, Heintzelman would remain isolated at Cerro Colorado for the next four and one-half months, living in an uncomfortable tent, although on one occasion he does mention sleeping in the corner of the "carpenter's shop, on a broken cot, with a keg of powder under the side."[59] Arising every morning before daybreak, he set an example of hard work and self-sacrifice for everyone at the mine.

At Cerro Colorado, Heintzelman's initial optimism quickly turned sour. Poston had estimated that ten men could mine over $2 million dollars in silver in one year. Mining engineers thought the mine would yield at least $700 a week. The mine, however, as Heintzelman learned, rarely yielded enough money to pay expenses.

In late November 1859, as workers reached one of the richest veins at Cerro Colorado, Heintzelman's mood heightened and he reported "getting out the richest and most abundant" ore. One day later, the "fine looking ore" turned out to be mostly copper and yielded only $400 a ton in silver.[60] A month later, with much work still to be done, he admitted he was homesick and "disheartened." Furthermore, the company's debt in San Francisco was at $6,292 and there was only $1,000 to pay it. Although anxious to join his family at Newport Barracks, he was hesitant to leave until the arrival of William Wrightson, who was heading west with a large train of supplies and machinery, as well as the type and press for the *Weekly Arizonian*, the first newspaper to be established in what is today Arizona. Wrightson had pushed west from Texas into the Mesilla Valley in New Mexico and struck out through the heart of Apache country for Tucson only to be slowed by two feet of snow at Apache Pass.[61]

---

[58] North, *Samuel Peter Heintzelman*, 53.
[59] Ibid., 107. See also, Jay Wagoner, *Early Arizona: Prehistory to Civil War* (Tucson: University of Arizona Press, 1977), 386.
[60] North, *Samuel Peter Heintzelman*, 132–133; HJ, Nov. 24, 25, 1858.
[61] North, *Samuel Peter Heintzelman*, 162; HJ, Jan. 5, 1859.

With a sack of ore as samples for eastern investors, along with shells and a dead snake for the Smithsonian Institution, Heintzelman departed Tubac in an ambulance with one of the mining engineers, Charles Schuchard, only one day after Wrightson arrived.[62] In Tucson three days later, the two men bought seats on the Butterfield Overland Stage with some "rather hard looking characters" including a common gambler, a "broken down" New York City political boss, and an Arkansas farmer.[63] Spotting a few Apaches and slowed by ice and snow at Apache Pass, they sped east past the towering spire of Cooke's Peak, and through rain and snow to the Rio Grande at Mesilla. After pausing at Franklin, the stage rattled east beneath the naked limestone face of El Captain and the summit of Guadalupe Peak, through scrubby mesquite to the Pecos River, and across the Llano Estacado in the night. After passing Forts Chadbourne and Belknap, Texas, Heintzelman reached Fort Smith, Arkansas, where the stage continued through the Ozarks past Fayetteville in terrible cold to Springfield, Missouri. The mercury dropped to five degrees below zero, Heintzelman reported, and in the unprotected stage, several apples he was carrying in his coat pockets froze solid.[64] For weeks he would complain of frostbite. At Springfield, the owner of the line, John Butterfield, came aboard for the final leg of the trip to St. Louis. After a jolting and tiring journey across much of the continent, Heintzelman arrived at Newport Barracks where he was joyously welcomed by Margaret and the children.[65] Although he would never return to Arizona, the mines of the Sonora Exploring and Mining Company would continue to dominate his entrepreneurial interests and most of his life.

At Newport Barracks, there were visits to the garrison to see old friends, shopping in Cincinnati, and meeting with Thomas Wrightson. Heintzelman had been at Newport Barracks for less than a month when he set out for Washington where he continued to lobby for the creation of a Territory of Arizona. After two hour-long meetings with Secretary of War John B. Floyd, he reported a "pleasant talk . . . about Arizona & Sonora."[66] In Washington, he also learned that along with the 1st Infantry and the 2d Cavalry, he was being sent to Texas.

In the early spring of 1859, the family began to pack for the long journey to the distant Southwest. Margaret and the children seemed excited about going to the Lone Star State, and Margaret in particular was hoping the Texas

---

[62] HJ, Jan. 1, Mar. 8, 1859.
[63] HJ, Jan. 26, 1859.
[64] Ibid.
[65] Ibid.
[66] HJ, Feb. 17, 1859.

sun would help ease her rheumatic pains. When Heintzelman placed an ad in a Cincinnati newspaper for a male servant, several individuals applied and Zachary Jackson, a free man of color, was hired for one year at $15 a month.[67] In early April 1859, with two wagon loads of household goods and personal belongings, the Heintzelmans went aboard the paddle-wheeler *Switzerland* and steamed for New Orleans.[68] Two days later, they were at Cairo, Illinois, and into a flooded Mississippi River that swept them rapidly downriver. After stopping briefly at Vicksburg, the *Switzerland* put in beneath the bluffs at Natchez where the family walked ashore to clip roses. Arriving in a crowded New Orleans on April 16, 1859, they made their way to the elegant St. Charles Hotel.[69] They were on their way to Texas and one of the great adventures of their lives.

During the twenty months Heintzelman spent in Texas, he would serve first at Fort Duncan, a remote post on the Rio Grande at what is today Eagle Pass, and later at Camp Verde in the heart of the Texas Hill Country. With the outbreak of violence on the border in late 1859, he was dispatched to the Rio Grande, this time to Brownsville and the Lower Rio Grande Valley. Back at Camp Verde, he also watched and agonized as the secession crisis engulfed the Lone Star State.

It was while Heintzelman was stationed at Camp Verde on September 28, 1859, that a daring thirty-five-year-old illiterate *ranchero* named Juan Nepomuceno Cortina sent shockwaves throughout Texas by brazenly leading seventy-five angry raiders into the dung-splattered streets of Brownsville. Tired of a clique of Brownsville attorneys, resentful of men he accused of killing *Tejanos* with impunity, and determined to settle a blood feud with a bitter enemy, Adolphus Glavecke, Cortina initiated a war that would reverberate north to Austin and beyond to the halls of Washington and Mexico City.

Born only a stone's throw from the banks of the Rio San Juan at Camargo, Tamaulipas, on May 16, 1824, Cortina had served as a corporal in the *Defensores de la Patria*, a company of the *Guardia Nacional de Tamaulipas*, and in 1846 fought with the Mexican Army at Palo Alto and Resaca de la Palma.[70] After the war he settled on his mother's ranch nine miles upriver from Brownsville where he became active in the rough-and-tumble politics of Cameron County, while at the same time maintaining his status in the Mexican militia. In the twisted and tangled web of Cameron County politics,

---

[67] HJ, Mar. 31, 1859.

[68] HJ, Apr. 9, 1859.

[69] HJ, Apr. 6, 1859.

[70] Jerry Thompson, *Juan Cortina and the Texas-Mexico Frontier, 1859–1877* (El Paso: Texas Western Press, 1994), 1–2.

Cortina learned that intimidation was an accepted political tactic. Clearly, the party with the most money, guns, alcohol, and promises of spoils was destined to control Brownsville and Cameron County. He also watched as Mexican Texans were abruptly relegated to second-class status. Although *Tejanos* were a clear majority in the county, they were rarely elected to office, and when they were, they were always subservient to the dominant Anglo entrepreneurial elite. Only in 1853, when two *Tejanos* were selected as county commissioners, did the Mexican American majority come close to comprising a meaningful political minority in county government. Petit and grand juries, highly politicized and instruments of oppression and intimidation, rarely included *Tejanos*.

In Cameron County politics, Cortina was remembered as a "striker," someone who was hired to lead the lower-class *Tejanos* to the polls and show them how to vote. At one time, he was said to have served briefly as deputy sheriff and controlled from forty to fifty votes. Five-feet, six-inches tall, with green eyes, a ruddy complexion, and a reddish-brown beard and hair, Cortina in time came to be deeply admired by many of the poorer Mexicans on both sides of the border.[71] Politicians admitted that he was a "political factor of some importance."[72] One Brownsville resident remembered him as "an influential man in elections" and someone who was "treated with a great deal of leniency."[73]

But it was the controversy over land that pushed Cortina toward revolution. Although his mother, Maria Estefana Goseascochea de Cortina, was able to retain a third of the large Espíritu Santo Grant, which she had inherited, she was forced to sacrifice thousands of acres to lawyers to defend her land titles.[74] Cortina was also furious that Adolphus Glavecke (married to a widow of Cortina's first cousin), along with Cameron County Judge Elisha Basse, mishandled and squandered the estate of a deceased aunt, Feliciana

---

[71] Milo Kearney and Anthony Knopp, *The Historical Cycles of Matamoros and Brownsville* (Austin: Eakin Press, 1991), 108.

[72] Stephen B. Oates (ed.), *Rip Ford's Texas*, (Austin: University of Texas Press, 1963), 364. For Cortina being a deputy sheriff, see A. M. Cook to Acting Assistant Adjutant General, Apr. 4, 1872, LR, AGO, RG 94.

[73] W. W. Nelson, Indictments by the 12th District Court (Brownsville), Spring, 1859, Sam Houston Papers (Texas State Archives, Austin, Texas; hereafter referred to as TSA).

[74] "Impeachment of Judge Watrous," vol. 2, 1856–1857, no. 913 (Washington, D.C: Cornelius Wendell, 1857), 34th Cong., 3d Sess., no. 175, 1–6; James Heaven Thompson, "Nineteenth Century History of Cameron County, Texas," (M.A. thesis, University of Texas at Austin, 1965), 36; Ruby A. Woolridge, "Espíritu Santo Grant," in *Studies in Brownsville History* ed. Milo Kearney (Brownsville: Pan American University at Brownsville, n.d.), 114–119.

Juan Nepomuceno Cortina, Texas folklorist J. Frank Dobie wrote, was the "most striking, the most powerful, the most insolent, and the most daring as well as the most elusive Mexican bandit, not even excepting Pancho Villa, that ever wet his horses in the muddy waters of the Rio Grande." In recent years, historians have tended to view Cortina more as a frontier caudillo and "social bandit" than as a ruthless outlaw. Photograph by Louis DePlanque, Matamoros. Courtesy Jerry Thompson.

Goseascochea.[75] This growing mistrust came to a head in the cattle-rustling incident in 1858, in which Glavecke followed Cortina across the river into Mexico to recover livestock stolen in Cameron County. Although both men were indicted in the incident, Cortina swore revenge. By 1859, he was determined to kill Glavecke on sight.[76]

Another contributing factor that made possible the Cortina War was the 1859 decision of Gen. David E. Twiggs, the aging and infirm commander of the 8th Military Department, to abandon Fort Brown at Brownsville and transfer Company L of the 1st Artillery to Fort Duncan at Eagle Pass. With the acquiescence of the War Department, General Twiggs also closed Ringgold Barracks at Rio Grande City and Fort McIntosh at Laredo, and sent the troops to Camp Hudson on the Devils River to guard the San Antonio–El Paso Road.[77] Ninety-three of Brownsville's merchant-elite and entrepreneurs from as far away as Corpus Christi and San Patricio immediately protested Twiggs's decision to abandon Fort Brown. Unprotected by the military, the capitalists warned, "Mexican armed soldiers, highwaymen, and Indians" would invade the border.[78] Twiggs bluntly replied, however, that there never had been "any danger of the Mexicans . . . crossing the river to plunder or disturb the inhabitants and the outcry on [the Rio Grande] for troops is solely to have an expenditure of the public money."[79]

The incident that more clearly sparked the Cortina War came on a hot and humid July 13, 1859, as Cortina spurred his pinto into the dusty streets of Brownsville. With indictments pending against him in the district court for cattle stealing, he now came to town heavily armed. In Brownsville, he slid down from his horse in front of Gabriel Catsel's small bar and coffee house on the east side of Market Plaza where he frequently came to sit and drink with friends. Unknown to Cortina was the fact that Stephen Powers, county judge and major of the town at the time, had given newly appointed City Marshal

---

[75] Commissioner's Court Minutes (1853–1862), Cameron County (County Clerk's Office, Brownsville), 123, 346–347. See also, United States Seventh Census (1850), Cameron County (NA); and *Antonio Tijerina vs. Adolphus Glaevecke*, Cause no. 549, Minutebook B (District Clerk's Office, Brownsville), 577–579. After the Civil War, the Glaevecke family somehow dropped the first "e" in their name.

[76] Adolphus Glarvke [*sic*] Affidavit, Jan. 16, 1860, *Difficulties on the Southwestern Frontier*, 36 Cong., 1st Sess., no. 52, 65 (hereafter referred to as *DSF*). See also W. W. Nelson, Indictments by the 12th District Court, Spring 1859, Houston Papers (TSA); Oates (ed.), *Rip Ford's Texas*, 262–263.

[77] D. E. Twiggs to L. Thomas, Jan. 11, 1859, and General Order no. 1, Feb. 5, 1859, 8, both in *DSF*.

[78] F. W. Latham, et al., to John B. Floyd, Mar. 9, 1859, *DSF*, 12–14.

[79] Twiggs to S. Cooper, Mar. 28, 1859, *DSF*, 14–15.

In command of the Third Corps of the Army of the Potomac, Samuel Peter Heintzelman became a major general of volunteers during the Civil War. He was wounded at First Bull Run and fought bravely at Yorktown, Williamsburg, the Seven Days, and Second Bull Run. After commanding the defenses of Washington, D.C., he was placed in charge of the Northern Department (Ohio, Indiana, Illinois, and Michigan) and finished the war at a minor post in Wheeling, West Virginia. Photograph by Mathew Brady. Courtesy Library of Congress.

Robert Shears a warrant for the arrest of a *Tejano* who had once worked for Cortina and his mother. As Cortina watched through the window of Catsel's small coffee house, Marshal Shears attempted to arrest the *vaquero*, who some witnesses said was drunk. When the *vaquero* resisted, Shears began a vicious pistol whipping, whereupon Cortina strode forth to intervene. "Why do you ill-treat this man?" Cortina remembered saying years later.[80] When Shears answered —"insolently," Cortina bragged—"I punished his insolence and avenged my countrymen by shooting him with a pistol and stretching him at my feet."[81] Shears claimed that his back was turned when Cortina first shot at him and missed. When the marshal wheeled about, Cortina fired a second shot that hit him in the left shoulder, the bullet coming out his back.[82] While Shears lay bleeding in the street, Cortina swung his *vaquero* friend up behind him on his horse and galloped out of town "amidst the stupor of the Yankees and the enthusiastic hurrahs of the Mexicans."[83]

With Shears badly wounded, Sheriff James G. Browne gathered a posse of twenty-five to thirty men to pursue Cortina. When the time came to ride out of town, however, only four or five men had retained enough courage to do so and the pursuit had to be called off.[84] As the hot Brownsville summer passed into fall and Heintzelman remained comfortably at Camp Verde with his family, Cortina was seen frequently across the river in Matamoros. Tired of the racism in Brownsville and the discriminatory world of Cameron County politics, and fearful of being arrested, Cortina appears to have given up hope of remaining in Texas. Largely through the influence of his first cousin, Col. Miguel Tijerina, who commanded the Federal cavalry in Matamoros, Cortina obtained a captain's commission to recruit a company of men to reinforce the Federal Army of Tampico.[85]

---

[80] Juan N. Cortina to the Public, Sept. 8, 1875, *Texas Frontier Troubles*, 44th Cong., 1st Sess., no. 343, 117–118 (hereafter referred to as *TFT*).

[81] Ibid., 118.

[82] Robert Shears, Affidavit, Jan. 14, 1860, *Hostilities on the Rio Grande*, 44th Cong. 1st Sess., no. 343, 117–118 (hereafter referred to as *HRG*). The Brownsville attorney and civil rights activist J. T. Canales, who hoped someday to write a biography of Cortina, said the shooting was at the corner of Washington and 12th Streets. J. T. Canales, *Bandit or Patriot: An Address by J. T. Canales before the Lower Rio Grande Valley Historical Society at San Benito, Texas, October 25, 1951* (San Antonio: Artes Graficas, 1951), 10.

[83] Cortina to the Public, Sept. 8, 1875, *TFT*, 118.

[84] Affidavit [Jeremiah Galvan?], n.d. HP.

[85] Glavecke Affidavit, Jan. 17, 1860, *HRG*, 13, Most of the documents reprinted in the Congressional Records are found in the Adjutant General's Records, RG 94 (NA).

But in early September 1859, Cortina made a fateful decision, one that would influence the history of the Lower Valley well into the next century. Before leaving for Tampico, he would exact revenge on Glavecke and several other men in Brownsville whom he had come to despise for their racism and lawlessness. At four o'clock on the morning of Wednesday, September 28, 1859, Cortina led seventy-five raiders into the darkened streets of the border town. The sharp crack of pistol and rifle fire, residents recalled, echoed through the streets as shouts of *"Viva Cheno Cortina," "Viva la Republica Mexicana,"* and *"Mueran los Gringos"* rang out.[86] Several citizens who were returning from a belated *Dies y Seis* celebration in Matamoros were shocked to see bands of heavily armed horsemen racing toward them firing their pistols in the air. "No man could have appeared in the streets with arms without being shot down," one observer recalled.[87] "Organized resistance," said the French priest P. F. Pariot, "was out of the question," for the Americans were "terror-stricken [and] had only time to look for hiding places."[88]

Leading his men down Elizabeth Street, Cortina placed sentinels on several street corners and gave orders to shoot anyone attempting to resist. Continuing on to the two-story Miller Hotel, he divided his raiders into small parties of four each. Each squad was given the task of finding and killing a particular person on Cortina's death list. Placing Tomás Cabrera, his chief lieutenant, in command of the men along Elizabeth Street, Cortina rode on to Fort Brown, where he had hoped to raise the Mexican flag on the parade ground but was unable to do so because he could not find a rope.

Men killed in the raid included a blacksmith named George Morris, whom Cortina said had "perpetrated many Mexican murders."[89] Another victim, William Peter Neale, had killed a Mexican in Matamoros in a fit of jealousy and a second Mexican in Brownsville two months later for the same reason.[90] Others who perished include Robert J. Johnston, the town jailer who died when the raiders attacked the town jail, and Viviano García, a small merchant who tried in vain to defend Johnston.[91] A fifth victim, an innocent

---

[86] Ibid.

[87] Unsigned letter, New Orleans *Picayune*, Oct. 10, 1859, quoted in *DSF*, 39–40.

[88] P. F. Parisot, *The Reminiscences of a Texas Missionary* (San Antonio: Johnson Brothers, 1899), 97.

[89] W. P. Rayburn to F. A. Hatch, Nov. 21, 1859, *DSF*, 65.

[90] Ibid.

[91] R. Fitzpatrick to Lewis Cass, Oct. 1, 1859. Despatches from United States Consuls in Matamoros, 1826–1906, General Records of the Department of State, RG 59 (NA). See also Heintzelman to Robert E. Lee, Mar. 1, 1860, *TFT*, 3–4; *State of Texas vs. Jua:: Nepomuceno Cortina*, et al., Nov. 1859, Washington Daniel Miller Papers (TSA).

Mexican *carretero* named Clemente Reyes, died under uncertain circumstances.[92] In all, six men, including one of Cortina's raiders, Alejos Vela, died
in the attack. Those on Cortina's death list who managed to escape included
Red Thomas, Peter Collins, Henry Kahn, Adolphus Glavecke, and Marshal
Shears, who hid in an oven. Although Cortina's men seized guns, ammunition, and liquor and stole a number of horses, there was never an attempt
during the raid at indiscriminate plunder or violence. In fact, several times
Cortina told citizens not to fear him, that he had come to Brownsville only to
kill what he called the "bad" Americans.

Shortly after daybreak, just as the first rays of a new day broke over the
Gulf to the east, José María Jesús Carbajal, one of the most influential and
powerful men on the border, crossed from Matamoros and appeared on the
levee near the Rio Grande, offering to stop the violence. Joined by Col.
Miguel Tijerina, Cortina's cousin, along with Capt. Agapito Longoria, and
the Mexican consul, Manuel Treviño, the party convinced Cortina that he
must leave Brownsville. At about 7:30 A.M., with many of the Brownsville
poor following him on foot and on horseback, Cortina rode slowly out of
town toward his mother's Rancho del Carmen, some nine miles upriver.[93]
Brownsville, a town of about 2,500 citizens, Heintzelman later told Col.
Robert E. Lee, had been "occupied by a band of armed bandits, something
unheard of in these United States."[94]

From Rancho del Carmen on September 30, 1859, Cortina, very much in
the Mexican tradition, issued a *pronunciamiento* explaining and attempting to
rationalize the reasons for his deadly raid. Printed in English and Spanish and
distributed on both sides of the river, the proclamation was addressed to the
"inhabitants of the State of Texas, and especially of those of the city of
Brownsville."[95]

With Cortina safely at Rancho del Carmen, Brownsville fell into a state
of panic. Several citizens, including Mayor Powers, Mifflin Kenedy, and José
San Ramón, hastily formed a Committee of Safety. Fearing a second attack,
citizens stretched chains across the main streets and constructed barricades

---

[92] Adolphus Glavecke, "The Story of Old Times," W. H. Chatfield, *Twin Cities of the Border and the Country of the Lower Rio Grande* (New Orleans: E. P. Brandao, 1893), 23.

[93] A. Werbeskie, Affidavit, Jan. 10, 1860, *HRG*, 12.

[94] Heintzelman to Lee, Mar. 1, 1860, *TFT*, 3–4.

[95] Matamoros *El Jayne*, Oct. 12, 1859, quoted in *Reports of the Committee of Investigations Sent in 1873 by the Mexican Government to the Frontier of Texas* (New York: Baker & Godwin, 1875), 136; Cortina Proclamation, Sept. 30, 1859, RG 94, AGO (NA). See also Thompson, *Juan Cortina*, 14–18.

from 80,000 bricks. Sentinels were posted day and night. Desperate for assistance, the Committee of Safety sent an urgent plea to General Carbajal in Matamoros. In response, Carbajal dispatched a poorly armed company of fifty Matamoros militia across the river to help defend the town.[96] Several citizens watched in awe as the Mexican infantry crossed the Rio Grande to Texas to protect U.S. citizens from an irregular army of *Mexicanos* and *Tejanos* led by a man who once considered himself a U.S. citizen and who had once been a member of the Matamoros militia that now came to protect his enemies. In Austin and Washington it all seemed very confusing.

The Committee of Safety pleaded with Gov. Richard Hardin Runnels for protection.[97] Urgent requests were also sent to General Twiggs and President James Buchanan. In Austin, U.S. Sen. John Hemphill could not believe what he was hearing from Brownsville. How could an illiterate Mexican bandit capture an entire town? But then General Twiggs had left the border defenseless, he remembered. Hemphill warned President Buchanan that assistance must be provided to the helpless citizens of Brownsville.[98]

Before General Twiggs could hear from the Committee of Safety, he received a letter from Frank W. Latham, collector of customs at Brownsville and Brazos Santiago. Brownsville had been raided, Latham reported, by a "well armed . . . crowd of banditti" from Mexico. Moreover, the town was in "perfect turmoil" and many of the families had fled to Matamoros for protection.[99] Although Latham made it clear that the raiders were a "dangerous class of [the] Mexican population," Twiggs somehow came to believe the town had been attacked by Indians.[100] Surprisingly, the general ordered one company of soldiers into the area of the upper Frio River, southwest of San Antonio, and another company into camp on the Rio Grande between Fort Duncan and Fort McIntosh. Yet a third company was sent to scout the area between Fort Duncan and Fort Clark.[101] Despite the desperate situation in Brownsville, no bluecoats, with the exception of ten men on Brazos Santiago, were still within 225 miles of Brownsville.

In early October, Cortina, who had rallied as many as 250 men to his cause, crossed the river into Mexico. Jeremiah Galvan, a Brownsville merchant who became a friend and confidant of Heintzelman, reported that in so doing, Cortina not only took "his own stock and a friend's stock but all the

[96] Latham to Twiggs, Sept. 28, 1859, *DSF*, 32.
[97] Henry Webb, et al., to Hardin Runnels, Oct. 2, 1859, *DSF*, 21–22.
[98] Ibid.
[99] Latham to Twiggs, Sept. 28, 1859, *DSF*, 32.
[100] Twiggs to Cooper, Oct. 7, 1859, *DSF*, 67.
[101] Ibid.

other stock in the neighborhood."[102] In the weeks that followed, Cortina was frequently seen, along with a number of his men, casually strolling the streets of Matamoros where he was greeted as a conquering hero, someone who had struck a fatal blow at the powerful and arrogant *gringo* elite across the river.

With Cortina in Matamoros and Brownsville appearing safe, the Committee of Safety agreed that the Mexican militia could return to Mexico. Thus, on October 8, 1859, with the Committee of Safety and Mexican officials exchanging *abrazos*, the militia was escorted to the ferry where they crossed to Matamoros.[103]

With Cortina no longer a threat, the critical situation on the border might well have faded into the footnotes of history had not another incident stoked the coals of the valley's smoldering racial tensions. Early on the morning of October 12, 1859, a posse headed by Sheriff Browne rode upriver toward Rancho del Carmen where they captured the elderly Tomás Cabrera, Cortina's lieutenant who lived at San José near Rancho del Carmen. From Matamoros, Cortina angrily warned that Cabrera must be released or he and his men would burn Brownsville to the ground.[104] When Cameron County officials refused, Cortina defiantly splashed across the river with forty of his men and again went into camp at Rancho del Carmen.

Cortinistas appeared on the outskirts of Brownsville, firing shots into town every night, causing panic again to grip the populace. Still Cortina promised that if Cabrera were released, he "would withdraw his men and leave the country."[105] Instead, Mayor Powers obtained a four-pounder howitzer from one of Mifflin Kenedy's steamboats and again asked Matamoros for help. Consequently, on October 22, 1859, the Matamoros guardsmen were back in Brownsville.

Moreover, the Committee of Safety concluded that peace could never be restored to the valley until Cortina was driven into Mexico. Expelling Cortina, whose stature continued to grow on both sides of the border, fell to twenty volunteer militia calling themselves the "Brownsville Tigers," along with forty Mexican American *rancheros*, all mounted but poorly armed, from the ranches between Brownsville and the gulf. Pulling Kenedy's four-pounder howitzer, the Brownsville Tigers, led by William B. Thompson, and the

---

[102] Affidavit [Galvan?], n.d. HP.

[103] "Cortina, the Leader, and his Character," New Orleans *Picayune*, Oct. 10, 1859, *DSF*, 39–40.

[104] Heintzelman to John Withers, Mar. 1, 1860, *TFT*, 4.

[105] Israel B. Bigelow, letter, Oct. 23, 1859, in Galveston *News*, quoted in *DSF*, 47–48.

Tejano *rancheros*, headed by Antonio Portillo, both reinforced by seventy-five Matamoros militia, moved cautiously upriver.

On October 24, 1859, the small army encountered about twenty of Cortina's pickets on the river road, two miles downriver from Rancho del Carmen. As the *Cortinistas* fell back into the dense chaparral, the overconfident Thompson, fearing that Cortina would escape into Mexico, sent Portillo's mounted *rancheros* in a flanking movement to secure several boats that had been spotted on the river. At the same time he ordered his remaining force forward on foot along the road. In the process, the Mexican artillery became stuck in the mud and when the gun was finally fired, it became dislodged from its carriage and had to be abandoned.[106] Kenedy's small gun was brought forward, but it too became unserviceable and was also abandoned. After considerable effort, several of the *rancheros* dragged the gun to the river bank and pushed it into the muddy waters of the Rio Grande. More confusion came when Thompson's men found their muskets would not fire in the misty weather. Furthermore, many of the cartridges provided the men were too large for their muskets.[107]

With the loss of both guns and darkness rapidly approaching, Thompson's men faltered, fell back, and then fled in panic. "Our retreat was in the utmost confusion," Thompson admitted.[108] "Our men commenced arriving in town, some on foot, others on horses, mules, and asses, mostly double, and many of them without arms," one observer recalled.[109] In the fight at Rancho del Carmen, Thompson lost one man killed and several wounded, while Cortina lost two men, both killed by the Mexican guardsmen.

Two days later, Cortina sent a letter in Spanish with "wretched spelling and grammar" into Brownsville from his forward camp at Villanueva, a mile downriver from Rancho del Carmen.[110] Cortina said that he did not want to attack Brownsville for fear of injuring "many persons who are faultless."[111] To avoid further bloodshed, however, Glavecke and Marshal Shears, whom Cortina called the "Squinting Sheriff," along with a number of others, must be turned over to him. With Cortina's men visible from the town's barricades and the reverberations from the captured cannon, which Cortina had managed to drag from the river and remount, audible every morning at six

---

[106] W.B. Thompson to Stephen Powers and J.G. Brown[e], Oct. 25, 1859, *DSF*, 69. See also *American Flag* (Brownsville), extra, Oct. 29, 1859, in *DSF*, 68–69.

[107] *American Flag* (Brownsville), extra, Oct. 25, 1859, in *DSF*, 44–45.

[108] Bigelow, letter, Nov. 1, 1859, in *Galveston News*, quoted in *DSF*, 48–49.

[109] *American Flag* (Brownsville), extra, Oct. 25, 1859, in *DSF*, 44–45.

[110] Cortina to Estevan Powers, Oct. 31, 1859, HP.

[111] Ibid.

o'clock, a chilling, somewhat unnerving atmosphere again settled over the border town.

With Cortina's reputation growing, reinforcements continued to pour into his camp until he had a formidable army. Many recruits came from Mexico, while others arrived from the small ranches and villages on the north bank of the river. A ruffian from Starr County named Santos Cadena rode into camp with forty men from Agualeguas. Sixty men broke out of prison in Ciudad Victoria, capital of Tamaulipas, and made their way to the border to join Cortina.[112] A band of thinly clad Tampacaus Indians from near Reynosa also reached his camp.[113] By the latter part of October, Cortina's men were in the process of ravaging many of the larger farms and ranches in the Lower Valley and were raiding as far north as the Arroyo Colorado.

Still in a state of panic, Mayor Powers sent James B. Thomas to Washington by steamer with a letter for President Buchanan. Stopping in New Orleans, Thomas persuaded forty-four of the Crescent City's leading citizens, most with close commercial ties to Brownsville and Matamoros, to petition Secretary of War John Floyd for troops.[114] The most alarming news from Brownsville, however, came from a citizen named W. J. Miller. Fearing that Cortina was about to attack the town, Miller swam his horse across the river to Matamoros where he fled through the night to the mouth of the river in order to make his way to Corpus Christi by way of Padre Island.[115] Miller's sworn affidavit, which appeared in Texas newspapers such as the San Antonio *Herald*, Corpus Christi *Ranchero*, Galveston *Daily Civilian*, and the Indianola *Commercial Bulletin*, revealed that after a bitter five-hour, hand-to-hand battle, in which every defender had been killed or executed, 400 of Cortina's men, crying "death to all Americans" and "no quarter," had overrun Brownsville.[116] At the head of 1,500 men, Cortina was reported to be within fifteen miles of Goliad. Some said he was determined to push the *gringos* back to the Colorado River while others speculated that he would stop only at the Sabine.[117]

---

[112] Heintzelman notes from *American Flag* (Brownsville), extra, Oct. 25, 1859, HP.

[113] Grand Jury Report, Jan. 8, 1860, Miller Papers. Also, Heintzelman's notes from *American Flag* (Brownsville), Oct. 15, 1859.

[114] Stephen Powers to James Buchanan, Oct. 18, 1859; J.C. Harris, et al., to Buchanan, Oct. 25, 1859; Harris to the Secretary of War, Oct. 24, 1859; all in *DSF*, 34–37.

[115] Corpus Christi *Ranchero*, Nov. 12, 1859; Affidavit, H.A. Miller, Nov. 7, 1859, *DSF*, 53. See also New Orleans *Daily Delta*, Oct. 26, 1859.

[116] San Antonio *Herald*, n.d., Corpus Christi *Ranchero*, Nov. 12, 1859; Galveston *Daily Civilian*, Nov. 11, 1859; Indianola *Commercial Bulletin*, Nov. 12, 1859; all in LR, AGO, RG 94.

Although Juan Nepomuceno Cortina is best remembered in Texas for his brazen and daring September 1859 raid on Brownsville, he rose to become a general in the army of Benito Juárez and govenor of Tamaulipas. He died at the village of Azcapotzalco near Mexico City on October 30, 1894 of pneumonia and was buried in the Panteón de Dolores. Courtesy Rose Collection, Western History Collections, University of Oklahoma.

Miller's fabricated story was reinforced by H. Clay Davis, a leading citizen of Rio Grande City, who rode north to San Antonio to say that "the whole Rio Grande country" was in "an uproar and that outrage and murder are the order of the day." With 600 red-eyed *"greaser pelados,"* Cortina was certain to have sacked Rio Grande City and was on the Arroyo Colorado and advancing toward the Nueces.[118] Throughout Texas, many citizens came to envision little brown-skinned, serape-clad, sombrero-crowned Mexicans riding north from the border, wielding machetes to seize a land that had once been theirs.

In Corpus Christi it was reported that "the entire Mexican population, on both sides of the Rio Grande, are up in arms," and that the *Cortinistas* were certain to "murder every white inhabitant and to reconquer our country as far as the Colorado River."[119] Henry A. Maltby, influential editor and owner of the Corpus Christi *Ranchero*, warned that "an idle, vicious, depraved, thievish, ignorant and fanatical population . . . being either escaped peons from the interior of Mexico, or desperadoes and escaped felons from that country as well as Texas" must be subdued.[120] This "class known as *pelados* or *labrones*" could only be governed "by an iron rod—by force or fear," Maltby further pontificated.[121] Although embarrassed by the falsity of the Miller affidavit, Maltby nevertheless proclaimed that "it matters not whether Brownsville be taken or not."[122]

A militia company, the Corpus Christi Guards, was hastily recruited and dispatched to detect any advance of Cortina's raiders. At the hamlet of Banquete, west of Corpus Christi, residents also formed a militia company and sent scouts into the chaparral.[123] In Live Oak County at Gussettville, similar plans were underway to resist the expected invasion from the border. Closer to the war, the *American Flag* (Brownsville) in an extra on October 25, 1859, wrote of Cortina, "He has good arms, and his men are under discipline, and fight with zeal. [He] certainly shows great skill as well as courage [and] he seems to wait his time and opportunity and this with a self-reliance and a firmness of purpose which may well give us pause."[124]

On November 12, 1859, General Twiggs telegraphed the War Department to say that Cortina had murdered 100 Americans and was on the

---

[117] Indianola *Courier*, Nov. 12, 1859, in LR, AGO, RG 94.
[118] San Antonio *Herald*, extra, n.d., in LR, AGO, RG 94.
[119] Corpus Christi *Ranchero*, Nov. 5, 1859.
[120] Ibid.
[121] Ibid.
[122] Ibid.
[123] Ibid.
[124] *American Flag* (Brownsville), extra, Oct. 25, 1859, in *DSF*, 44–45.

march for the Nueces River with 800 men. The next day, Major Heintzelman received orders at Camp Verde placing him in command of the Brownsville Expedition and sending him scurrying for the border. Besides Heintzelman's command of nine companies, two companies of light artillery and three of infantry from Fort Leavenworth, Kansas, along with six companies of infantry from as far away as Fort Monroe, Virginia, were to depart "with all speed to the Rio Grande."[125] Four days later, Twiggs wired Washington again to say that Cortina was certain to have from 800 to 1,500 men.[126] Nuevo León and Coahuila strongman Gov. Santiago Vidaurri, who was in San Antonio, told Twiggs that Cortina was thought to be backed by the "Priest Party" and that he was rumored to be paying his men a dollar a day for their services.[127]

Twiggs was especially concerned about the security of the large military warehouses on Brazos Santiago where two complete field batteries along with $125,000 in ammunition was stored. The 146 cannon, howitzers, and mortars (some of them thirty-two and twenty-four pounders), "had probably been taken . . . by Cortina," Twiggs told Washington on November 15, 1859.[128] Three days later, however, he again wired Washington, this time to say that he was "disposed to think the Cortina affair is greatly exaggerated."[129] Four days later he assured the War Department that the rumors from Brownsville were "mostly false."[130] Consequently, orders sending troops to the border were countermanded. Heintzelman, however, was still being sent to the border, but the size of his forces was to be scaled back.

By the time Heintzelman arrived in San Antonio to begin preparations for his long march to the Rio Grande, Texas Rangers were already on the move. On October 25, 1859, Capt. William G. Tobin rode out of San Antonio with sixty men. Recruiting another forty men along the way, Tobin paused only at the Santa Gertrudis Ranch of Richard King, where the Rangers exchanged horses before racing on for the border. Riding hard, the Rangers arrived on the outskirts of Brownsville late on the evening of November 15, sixteen days out of San Antonio.[131] With the Rangers' bugle

---

[125] Twiggs to the Secretary of War, Nov. 12, 1859, LR, AGO, RG 94. This same letter was published in *DSF*, 55.

[126] Twiggs to the Secretary of War, Nov. 16, 1859, LR, AGO, RG 94. Published in *DSF*, 58.

[127] Ibid.

[128] Twiggs endorsement, Nov. 15, 1859, on Abstract of Ordnance and Ordnance Stores on hand at Brazos Santiago, Sept. 30, 1859, LR, AGO, RG 94.

[129] Twiggs to the Secretary of War, Nov. 17, 1859, LR, AGO, RG 94.

[130] Twiggs to the Secretary of War, Nov. 21, 1859, LR, AGO, RG 94.

[131] W. G. Tobin to Runnels, Nov. 16, 1859, Sam Houston Papers, TSA.

blaring in the darkness, besieged and frightened citizens thought the town was being attacked by *Cortinistas* and fired a salvo of grapeshot at the Rangers. No one was seriously injured, but Adolphus Glavecke, who had ridden north to the Nueces to guide the Rangers to the border, had two pieces of shrapnel rip through his coat.[132]

The night after the Rangers arrived in Brownsville, Tomás Cabrera was dragged from the Brownsville jail and lynched by a frenzied mob in Market Square. It was a disgusting affair and an event that Cortina would not soon forget. "Who did it is not known," the Corpus Christi *Ranchero* announced.[133] Another source reported only that "an unknown and lawless mob" was responsible.[134] Judging by the timing of the lynching as well as their record during the Cortina War of indiscriminately killing *Mexicanos* and *Tejanos*, the Rangers were undeniably involved, if not responsible for the lynching. When Cortina received word of the death of his friend, he allegedly retaliated by lynching three captives, including a man by the name of McFadden.[135]

A few days after the Cabrera lynching, thirty Rangers commanded by the sheriff of Karnes County, John Littleton, who had also arrived on the border, were sent out to escort a second company of Rangers from Live Oak County, under John Donaldson, who were scheduled to arrive in Brownsville. In the confusion, the Live Oak Rangers took a different road and entered Brownsville without seeing the party that was sent to guide them. At noon the next day, while returning to Brownsville, Lieutenant Littleton spotted a band of *Cortinistas* about a mile from the Palo Alto House near the old Palo Alto battlefield, north of town. Pursuing Cortina's men into the chaparral, the Rangers dismounted, tied their horses to some scrubby mesquite, and charged into the dense brush. In a vicious fight that lasted for thirty minutes, three of the Rangers, William McKay, Thomas Grier, and Nicholas R. Milett, were killed while four others were badly wounded, including Lieutenant Littleton, who was shot in the arm.[136] Yet another wounded Ranger, John Fox, who surrendered to the *Cortinistas*, was allegedly executed.[137]

The day after the Palo Alto fight, Captain Tobin, along with Mat Nolan, sheriff of Nueces County, rode to the scene where they found the stripped and mutilated bodies of the dead Rangers.[138] After burying the men, Tobin

---

132   Corpus Christi *Ranchero*, Nov. 26, 1859.
133   Ibid.
134   W.P. Reyburn to F.A. Hatch, Nov. 22, 1859, *DSF*, 67.
135   Corpus Christi *Ranchero*, Nov. 26, 1859.
136   Tobin to Runnels, Nov. 27, 1859, Houston Papers (TSA).
137   Ibid.
138   Ibid.

rode to the village of Santa Rita, upriver from Brownsville and about two miles from Cortina's camp, where he was joined by a company of thirty-nine men from Atascosa County commanded by Capt. Peter Tumlinson, fourteen men from Indianola, Lt. Loomis Lyman Langdon of the 1st Artillery from Brazos Santiago, and the Brownsville Militia commanded by Mifflin Kenedy, who brought along a 24-pounder howitzer. Vengefully, they burned most of the small *jacales* in the village and in a council of war vowed they would attack Cortina as soon as possible.[139]

Leaving their cannon and sixty men at Santa Rita to protect his rear, Tobin moved upriver on the morning of November 22, 1859, to "exterminate Cortina." By noon the Rangers were past Rancho del Carmen and within a few hundred yards of Cortina's camp when they were met by a "galling fire of round shot, grape and canister."[140] Realizing that Cortina was "strongly entrenched and fortified," and fearful of being attacked on both flanks, Tobin retreated in confusion, "hotly pressed" by the *Cortinistas*.[141]

Back at Santa Rita, sixty of the Rangers refused to follow order and retreated to Brownsville. The next day, however, Tobin again marched upriver toward Cortina's camp. One mile above Rancho del Carmen near San José, again in sight of Cortina's camp, Tobin hesitated. Estimating the *Cortinistas* to number from 350 to 500, he concluded it would be "imprudent to attack the enemy in his fortifications."[142] Cortina was "strongly fortified in and surrounded by a dense chaparral on all sides," Tobin wrote Austin.[143] Back in Brownsville, as many as 100 of the Rangers decided they had had enough of the Cortina War and departed for the Nueces and home. "It was a wise decision," Heintzelman would later write, for in "their disorganized condition, an attack would have brought certain defeat."[144]

Inspired by his repulse of the Rangers, Cortina issued a second *pronunciamiento* from Rancho del Carmen on November 23, 1859. The loss of land by Mexicans, either through legal manipulation and chicanery or through threats and intimidation, must be avenged, he wrote. Moreover, the impunity with which Anglos had killed Mexicans in Brownsville and Cameron County must not go unanswered. Anglo-American racist treatment of Mexicans must

---

[139]   Ibid.

[140]   Corpus Christi *Ranchero*, Dec. 3, 1859.

[141]   Ibid.

[142]   Tobin to Runnels, Nov. 27, 1859, Houston Papers, TSA.

[143]   Ibid.

[144]   Heintzelman to Lee, Mar. 1, in *TTF*, 6.

stop, he further warned.[145] More confident than ever, Cortina now saw himself as the spokesman for all "Mexican inhabitants of the State of Texas."[146]

By this time Heintzelman was on the march. With units of the 1st Infantry, Heintzelman left San Antonio on November 17, 1859, and arrived at Fort Merrill on the Nueces River, four days later.[147] Although General Twiggs had scaled back the size of his command, he was still to proceed to the border and restore civil order as soon as possible.[148] At Fort Merrill, Heintzelman was joined by two companies of the 1st Artillery as well as a company of the 2d Cavalry under Capt. George Stoneman.[149] On the Nueces River, Heintzelman was also joined by Richard King, who accompanied the army downriver to San Patricio and south to his ranch on the Santa Gertrudis where the bluecoats arrived on November 29, 1859. South of the King Ranch, Heintzelman began to see abandoned ranches, evidence of the Cortina War. Continuing south through a bitterly cold blizzard and across the shifting sands of the Wild Horse Desert, the men crossed the Arroyo Colorado ferry on December 4, 1859. Pushing his men across the Palo Alto Prairie, Heintzelman entered Brownsville in the early morning darkness of December 5, 1859.

During the twenty months Heintzelman spent in Texas, especially during the Cortina War, he continued to keep his daily journal. Diane M. T. North, who transcribed, ably edited, and published Heintzelman's journal from August 3, 1858, to January 29, 1859, while Heintzelman was in Arizona as president of the Sonora Exploring and Mining Company, remarked that the Texas portion of his journal reads "like a Zane Grey thriller."[150] This rare and dramatic first-hand account provides a strikingly transparent window into one of the most volatile and traumatic events in the state's long history. Heintzelman's journal begins on a sunny and optimistic New Orleans day, April 17, 1859, with the Heintzelman family on their way to Texas, and ends on a depressingly cool and overcast December 31, 1860, also in the Crescent City, with the Cortina War behind him and secession fever sweeping the South and the nation on the verge of war.

---

[145] *American Flag* (Brownsville), Nov. 26, 1859. The *pronunciamiento* was also published in the Corpus Christi *Ranchero*, Dec. 3, 1859. See Thompson, *Juan Cortina*, 19–28.

[146] *American Flag* (Brownsville), Nov. 26, 1859.

[147] HJ, Nov. 15, 1859.

[148] HJ, Nov. 17, 1859.

[149] HJ, Nov. 19, 1859.

[150] North, *Samuel Peter Heintzelman*, 218.

Leaving Texas in December 1860, the fate of the Union occupied Heintzelman's every thought. Although South Carolina had left the Union by the time he reached New Orleans, Heintzelman remained optimistic that the "Cotton States will not prevent the Government's going on as usual." It was a pity, he thought, that "they did not go long ago. It is better to be rid of them."[151] Although he had never embraced the abolitionist cause, Heintzelman was a determined and uncompromising Unionist with little sympathy for the defiant South.

In Washington, with additional southern states seceding, the capital became a beehive of confusion and rumor; events were moving fast. A number of officers, including Col. J. K. F. Mansfield, arrived from Texas to report that the Lone Star State was certain to secede. In early March 1861, as President-elect Abraham Lincoln slipped into the capital incognito by train at dawn, Washington took on a somber but excited atmosphere. Heintzelman professed little enthusiasm for Lincoln and seemed surprised when large crowds gathered to gawk at the strange-sounding prairie lawyer from Illinois. With Margaret a few days later he was able to visit briefly with Mary Lincoln. Although pleased with the soon-to-be first lady's demeanor, he seemed surprised that she "had no glove on & put out her hand."[152]

The day after Lincoln's arrival in Washington, the telegraph was alive with news from Texas. Gen. David E. Twiggs, or Traitor Twiggs as he came to be known in the North, had "surrendered the arms & supplies . . . of the troops to the State of Texas," Heintzelman learned. "If I were with troops, I would not obey such an order. I cannot believe it," he wrote in disgust.[153]

While in Washington, Heintzelman conversed with several prominent politicians, including Louis T. Wigfall and John Hemphill, secessionist senators from Texas who were still in the capital, along with the pro-Southern delegate from New Mexico Territory, Miguel A. Otero. Heintzelman continued not only to lobby for the creation of a Territory of Arizona but also hoped that his commendable service during the Cortina War would warrant an additional brevet, as Gen. Winfield Scott had recommended. When Thomas Wrightson arrived with news of renewed Apache attacks in Arizona, the two men rushed to the capitol to ask that troops be sent to protect the Arizona mines.[154]

---

[151] HJ, Jan. 2, 1861.

[152] HJ, Mar. 1, 1861.

[153] HJ, Feb. 25, 1861. Heintzelman kept a copy of the orders dismissing Twiggs for "treachery to the flag of his country." General Orders no. 5, Mar. 1, 1861, HP. See also, *New York Times*, Mar. 5, 1861.

[154] HJ, Mar. 14, 1861.

On Inauguration Day, March 4, 1861, the rain started early but soon the day became cool and clear, as a large and excited crowd gathered on the streets of the capital. With Solon Lathrop and Margaret, Heintzelman made his way from Willard's Hotel down Pennsylvania Avenue past armed guards and sharpshooters on the roofs of many buildings to the capitol. After seeing Margaret to a seat in the balcony on the east portico, beneath the still unfinished capitol dome, Heintzelman was able to get "a good view of Lincoln."[155] Proclaiming that secession was the essence of anarchy and certain to lead to civil war, Lincoln's well-received address proved to be one of the most important in American history. A lady in the crowd put it best, Heintzelman thought, when she referred to Lincoln's conciliatory forthright remarks as "a steel hand in a soft glove."[156]

The day after Lincoln's inauguration, Heintzelman met Col. Robert E. Lee at General Scott's headquarters; Lee felt badly about secession and the prospect of war, Heintzelman wrote.[157] Two weeks later the Heintzelmans rode across the Potomac River for a social visit with the Lees at their Arlington mansion. While Mary Custis Lee, crippled with arthritis, showed Margaret the "old fashioned home" and its "beautiful view," their officer-husbands reminisced for over an hour about Texas, the Cortina War, and Twiggs's surrender.[158] Lee, who had been in San Antonio at the time of the one-sided negotiations, "gave me much information about the disgraceful surrender," Heintzelman wrote. Lee "told the commissioners they could not get the arms from the troops without fighting for them."[159] It was evident that had Colonel Lee been in command in Texas in February 1861, the Civil War would have begun in the Lone Star State and the entire course of events that followed, including Lee's resignation, would have been radically altered.

In early April 1861, Heintzelman was appointed superintendent of the Eastern Recruiting Department and ordered to Fort Columbus on Governor's Island, New York.[160] After a short visit to Buffalo, he was on a train to New York City when he learned that at 4:30 A.M., April 12, 1861, Confederate guns had fired on Fort Sumter in the harbor of Charleston, South Carolina. Six days later, on the anniversary of the Battle of Lexington, he read that a Baltimore mob had attacked several companies of the 6th

---

[155] HJ, Mar. 4, 1861; *New York Times*, Mar. 5, 1861.
[156] Ibid.
[157] HJ, Mar. 5, 1861.
[158] Ibid. Also, Mary H. Nelligan, *Custis-Lee Mansion: The Robert E. Lee Memorial* (Washington, D.C.: National Park Service, 1962), 20–25.
[159] HJ, Mar. 5, 1861.
[160] HJ, Apr. 16, 1861; Special Orders no. 98, Apr. 8, 1861, HP.

In the late summer of 1861, following the debacle at First Bull Run, Heintzelman poses on the steps of Robert E. Lee's Arlington House with members of his staff and family. Margaret Heintzelman is on the general's left and his good friend, the noted photographer Mathew Brady, is in the top hat on Heintzelman's right. Heintzelman had visited with Lee at Arlington House twice before Lee made his decision to pledge his allegiance to his native Virginia. Lee told Heintzelman that had he been in command of the Federal forces in Texas in February 1861, he never would have surrendered to the secessionists. Courtesy Library of Congress.

Massachusetts Regiment en route to Washington. When the melee was over, four soldiers and twelve Baltimore civilians lay dead. Heintzelman was still in New York when a reporter told him that four more southern states, including Lee's Virginia, had seceded. "These are stirring times," he wrote. "There never was such excitement in the country & such unanimity of feelings."[161]

On May 2, 1861, he was summoned back to Washington where he was appointed acting inspector general and placed under the command of Col. J. K. F. Mansfield in the newly created Department of Washington.[162] Surrounded by slave states, Washington was quickly taking on the look of an armed camp. Not long after his arrival, Heintzelman, along with a number of other officers, visited Lincoln at the White House. "The president shook my hand as if I was an old & particular friend," he recalled.[163]

Only days after assuming his duties as inspector general, he was promoted to colonel of the 17th Infantry.[164] Three days later he was placed in command of forces being sent to occupy Alexandria and Arlington Heights on the Virginia side of the Potomac River. At 2 A.M., May 24, 1861, "was commenced," Heintzelman would write, "the first operation against the rebels in front of Washington."[165] By using the Long Bridge, the Aqueduct, and a steamer, he led his men across the Potomac by torchlight to occupy Alexandria and capture a few rebel cavalry.[166] Some 700 rebel infantry, upon

---

[161] HJ, Apr. 19, 1861.

[162] General Orders no. 20, May 8, 1861; Simon Cameron to Heintzelman, May 27, 1861, both in HP. Also, HJ, May 2, 1861.

[163] HJ, May 9, 1861.

[164] Heintzelman to G. W. Cullum, Dec. 18, 1865, HP. The original of this letter and accompanying outline of Heintzelman's military career are in the archives at West Point.

[165] Heintzelman to L. Thomas, July 20, 1863, *The War of the Rebellion: A Compilation of the Official Records of the Union and Confederate Armies* (Washington: Government Printing Office, 1889), Ser. 2, Vol. 41. These voluminous records, all from the first series unless otherwise noted, will hereafter be referred to as *OR*, by volume, part, and page. Heintzelman outlined much of his Civil War career in a November 30, 1864, letter to Assistant Adjutant General E. D. Townsend, HP. For his career in the war, see: William C. Davis, *Battle at Bull Run, A History of the First Major Campaign of the Civil War* (Baton Rouge: Louisiana State University Press, 1977); Stephen W. Sears, *George B. McClellan: The Young Napoleon* (New York Ticknor & Fields, 1988); Stephen W. Sears, *To the Gates of Richmond: The Peninsula Campaign* (New York: Ticknor & Fields, 1992); William J. Miller (ed.), *The Peninsula Campaign of 1862: Yorktown to the Seven Days* (Campbell, Calif.: Savas Woodbury Publishers, 1995); John J. Hennessy, *Return to Bull Run: The Campaign and Battle of Second Manassas* (New York: Simon & Schuster, 1993).

[166] HJ, May 25, 1861. See also General Orders no. 1, May 28, 1861, HP.

learning of the approach of Federal troops, fled toward Richmond along the Orange and Alexandria Railroad, burning bridges behind them as they headed south.

Only days after crossing into Virginia, Heintzelman rode to Arlington House to find that Lee and his wife were gone. Lee, who had been offered command of the Federal Army, had resigned his commission to cast his fate with his native Virginia. Lee's overseer told Heintzelman that the mansion was vacant; the Lees, having removed most of their paintings and furniture, had gone south to Richmond where Lee had been given command of the Virginia militia.

Commanding a division, Heintzelman fought bravely at the Battle of First Bull Run on July 21, 1861, but while trying to rally his men late in the afternoon, he was hit in the right arm about two inches below the right elbow by a spent minie ball. Refusing to dismount or retreat, he remained on the field as Dr. William S. King, his friend from the Texas frontier, rode forward and successfully cut the minie ball from his arm.[167] He later learned that his uniform had also been pierced by a Rebel ball. After twenty-eight hours in the saddle, he arrived back in Washington where Margaret, apprehensive and frightened, sent for Dr. Eugene H. Abadie, whom they had known in Texas. After his wounds were properly dressed, he collapsed from exhaustion. For six weeks thereafter he would be unable to use his right arm, which was fractured and terribly swollen. In fact, he would never completely regain the use of the arm for the remainder of the war.[168]

Bull Run had been a humiliating defeat for President Lincoln, Generals Scott and Irvin McDowell, Col. Heintzelman, and the entire Federal Army. Still somehow the pieces of a shattered army had to be put back together. In time he would come to see Bull Run as the event around which a Northern consciousness was to emerge; out of defeat would emerge a better army, one capable of winning the war, he hoped.

Heintzelman was still at home recuperating from his wound when he learned that General McDowell had been replaced by thirty-four-year-old Gen. George B. McClellan and on August 2, 1861, with his arm in a sling, Heintzelman reported to his new commander. Three days later, largely

---

[167] HJ, Sept. 1, 1861. See also miscellaneous newspaper obituary, n.d., HP. Of the 470 Union soldiers who died at First Bull Run, 182 were from Heintzelman's division, including Lt. Douglas Ramsay, who had commanded a company during the Cortina War.

[168] HJ, Sept. 6, 1861.

through the efforts of the Pennsylvania congressional delegation, he was made a brigadier general of volunteers.[169]

During the pleasant days of fall, Heintzelman first heard his name mentioned as the possible commander of an expedition to Texas.[170] Texas Unionists, who had fled the state by the hundreds, were beginning to arrive in the capital pleading with Lincoln and anyone who would listen to send troops to the Lone Star State. In December 1861, Jeremiah Galvan, a Brownsville merchant-friend from the Cortina War, arrived in the capital and the two spent a pleasant evening together.[171] Galvan had crossed the Rio Grande to Matamoros following the Confederate occupation of the lower Rio Grande Valley. "He gave me much information about Texas," Heintzelman wrote. "There are no guns at Brazos, but Ft. Brown has been repaired. There were two companies on the Rio Grande when he left, but I understand they have dwindled down to 87 men."[172] Galvan also reported "few Secessionists in Brownsville & they [Unionists] want me to come with Union troops to relieve them. The Texans have not received a barrel of flour or a bag of corn from the Confederates . . . They are ripe for a revolt."[173] Although Heintzelman contemplated offering his services for the cause in Texas, the war in the east would soon be reaching a climax, he concluded, and if McClellan faltered, he would be in line to command the mighty Army of the Potomac. Any chance for greatness lay in Virginia, not on the Texas frontier.

As early as October 1861, Heintzelman learned that McClellan was proposing to divide the Army of the Potomac into corps. It was not until March 1862, however, that a presidential order made the decision official. Each of the five senior generals, including Heintzelman, would be assigned a corps; he would have the 3rd Corps, which consisted of three divisions of three brigades and a battery of artillery.[174]

In the 1862 attempt to seize Richmond, Virginia, during the Peninsula Campaign, Heintzelman led the 3rd Corps of the Army of the Potomac at the battles of Yorktown, Williamsburg, Oak Grove, Glendale, and Malvern Hill. He was on the Peninsula when he learned from Margaret that Texas Unionists, who had fled Texas for Mexico and eventually Washington and

---

[169] Special Orders no. 51, July 30, 1861; Special Orders no. 10, Aug. 4, 1861, both in HP; Special Orders no. 87, Oct. 3, 1861, *OR*, 51, 1:491; HJ, Sept. 6, 10, 1861.

[170] HJ, Nov. 30, 1861.

[171] HJ, Dec. 16, 1861.

[172] Ibid.

[173] Ibid.

[174] Frank J. Welcher, *Union Army, 1861–1865* (2 vols.; Bloomington: Indiana University Press, 1993), I, 802, 805, 813.

A fatigued and ruffled but resolute Major General Heintzelman and his officers sit for a group photograph on August 7, 1862 at Harrison's Landing, Virginia, following the bloodletting of the Seven Days. "Mr. Brady's artist [Alexander Gardner] called and took our photograph in a group—one large and the other carte de visite," Heintzelman recorded in his journal. Gardner's glass negative was later damaged. Courtesy Library of Congress.

New York, were continuing to urge the president to send an army to the Lone Star State to assist "Union men" and that they wanted him to command the expedition. "They say they don't believe the Texas Rangers would fight against me & all the Union men would join," he wrote. Although Heintzelman was honored by the confidence the Texans placed in his abilities, he did not care to go to Texas, for he remained convinced that the war would be won or lost in the east, not in the vast expanses of the distant Southwest.[175] It was also on the Peninsula that Heintzelman learned that he had been promoted to major general of volunteers and breveted a brigadier general in the regular army.[176]

It was after the Union retreat from the Virginia Peninsula at Second Bull Run on August 29 and 30, 1862, that Heintzelman's leadership came to be seriously called into question. In his own mind, however, he placed the blame for the Union disaster on Gen. John Pope, Union commander of the newly created Army of Virginia. Hearing that McClellan was riding out from Washington to take command of the retreating Federal Army, Heintzelman remarked that "whatever mistakes he has made he has the confidence of the troops . . . & he would be received with enthusiasm by the whole army."[177] However, to Heintzelman, "neither officers or men have the slightest confidence in Pope." Back in Washington, Heintzelman bluntly told Secretary of War Stanton what "had occurred & why" and he "did not spare Pope."[178]

It would be over six weeks before Heintzelman would write his official report of the Union disaster at Second Bull Run. Although he tried to put a good face on what was clearly a stunning Union reversal, there was no hiding the extend of the defeat.[179] Moreover, the 3rd Corps was now down to fewer than 5,000 effectives. Two of his divisions were "ruined from their heavy losses," he wrote. More importantly, the Union defeat at Second Bull Run had paved the way for Lee's invasion of Maryland.

But Heintzelman was also to be a victim of Second Bull Run. One historian would go as far as to compare his leadership in the battle to a "ninth-place finish in a horse race."[180] On September 5, 1862, he was in Washington when he learned that he was being relieved of command of the 3rd Corps. A

---

[175] HJ, June 22, 1862.

[176] HJ, July 5, 1862. See also Sears, *To the Gates of Richmond*, 226–27.

[177] HJ, Aug. 31, 1862.

[178] HJ, Sept. 4, 1862.

[179] Jeffry D. Wert, "Second Battle of Bull Run," in *Historical Times Illustrated Encyclopedia of the Civil War* (New York: Harper & Row, 1986), 93. Pope suffered 14,462 casualties while Confederate losses were placed at 9,474.

[180] Hennessy, *Return to Bull Run*, 464.

few days later he received notice that he was to assume command of the Department of Washington, with orders to defend the capital. Once again he set up his temporary headquarters at Fort Lyon, southeast of the capital, as Lee's Army of Northern Virginia waded across the Potomac River into Maryland.

Heintzelman remained in Washington when word came that Gen. Thomas "Stonewall" Jackson had taken Harper's Ferry. "They always out-general us," he complained.[181] On September 18, 1862, however, the news-papers were "full of good news from McClellan's army."[182] At Sharpsburg, Maryland, Lee had been turned back in the Battle of Antietam—the single bloodiest day in American history.

Realizing that he was unlikely ever to command the Army of the Potomac, Heintzelman now began to give more thought to the proposed expedition to Texas. In particular, Edmund J. Davis, antebellum district judge from South Texas whom he had learned to respect and trust during the Cortina War, was pushing for him to command the Texas Expedition. Davis, however, reported that Lincoln's cabinet had little interest in Texas and that the president was not willing to send troops to the Lone Star State until the war in the east had been largely decided.[183] Still he would "go if they make it an object," Heintzelman wrote.[184] His expectations rose in early November 1862, when he heard that Lincoln wanted to see him, thinking perhaps that a major command was in the offing, but the meeting turned out to be of minor importance. Meeting with Andrew J. Hamilton, antebellum congressman and leading Texas Unionist who had fled to Mexico and who had been commis-sioned a brigadier general and military governor of Texas, he learned that Gen. Nathaniel Banks was being considered for the Texas Expedition.[185] In early December 1862, Banks set sail, but his destination was a secret, although it was rumored that he was bound for South Carolina, not Texas.[186] Nevertheless, Heintzelman continued to meet with several leading senators, as well as Secretary of War Edwin M. Stanton, in hopes of obtaining a com-mand where he would redeem his waning military reputation.

In Washington, he also met with William Wrightson and the two contin-ued to lobby for the creation of a territory of Arizona. Poston was in Washington, too, but soon left for New York on his way to Europe in hopes of

[181] HJ, Sept. 16, 1862.
[182] HJ, Sept. 18, 1862.
[183] Edmund J. Davis to Heintzelman, Aug. 8, 1862, HP.
[184] HJ, Nov. 4, 1862.
[185] HJ, Nov. 9, 1862.
[186] HJ, Dec. 6, 1862.

selling the Arizona mines. "I am willing to sell them for almost anything," Heintzelman wrote.[187] At the same time, he maintained his interest in a Pacific railroad and the Vallecillo Mines in Northern Mexico, which he had visited during the Cortina War. He was hoping that the proposed expedition to Texas would help open the road "to our mines & get our silver-lead to market."[188]

After the traditional visit to the White House on New Year's Day, 1863, Heintzelman was with several politicians, including the handsome and wealthy governor of Rhode Island, William Sprague, the Mexican minister to the United States, Matías Romero, as well as Edmund J. Davis, now a colonel in the Union Army, when he learned that Lincoln had issued his Emancipation Proclamation. Most agreed that the proclamation was a "war measure" that would have "decided success."

With the capital safe, Heintzelman spent much of February 1863 lobbying for the Arizona Bill. Poston arrived early in the month and the two went to see Sen. Lyman Trumbull of New York and Sen. Benjamin F. Wade of Ohio. A few days later, William Wrightson arrived in the capital from Cincinnati and on February 17, Heintzelman held an "oyster supper . . . to talk Arizona."[189] The next day, Heintzelman, Poston, Wrightson, and Wade made their way through rain and muddy streets to see Rep. John A. Gurley, an advocate of territorial organization for Arizona and a principal candidate for governor of the proposed territory. After a lengthy meeting, they decided they would call on the president as soon as possible to push for the creation of the territory. Heintzelman felt that if a Territory of Arizona could be created, the chances of troops being sent to the desert Southwest would be greatly improved, and with troops in Arizona, the mines could be reopened. Stanton must be convinced, Heintzelman thought, that two regiments of troops, along with a third from California, would be needed to secure the territory.[190] Finally on February 20, 1863, Heintzelman learned that the Senate had passed the Arizona Bill by a vote of two to one; his persistent lobbying had at last brought results. In late February, he went with Wrightson to see Lincoln, who had signed the Arizona Bill four days earlier, in hopes of having Poston made Superintendent of Indian Affairs for the new territory. Well into March 1863, the Heintzelman residence continued to be a beehive of activity on behalf of Arizona.

---

[187] HJ, Oct. 6, 1862.
[188] HJ, Oct. 17, 1862.
[189] HJ, Feb. 16, 1863.
[190] HJ, Mar. 10, 11, 1863.

On July 11, 1863, he entertained Charles Poston and Thomas Wrightson and watched the next day as the newly appointed government of the Territory of Arizona departed for the desert Southwest.[191] Meeting with Col. Edmund J. Davis and his wife, Anne Britton Davis, at Willard's Hotel on the evening of July 15, 1863, Heintzelman listened, with a rainstorm pounding outside, as Anne Davis related how she had been badly treated in Texas and how her husband had almost been hanged by Rebels near Brownsville.[192] In early September Heintzelman learned from the War Department that as many as 25,000 men had been committed to the Texas Expedition. There was little doubt that such a force "should sweep Texas in a very short time," he thought. It would also "convince Louis Napoleon . . . not to interfere with us." To Heintzelman, whoever commanded the expedition must be "a man who has served in Texas & understands the country and its difficulties."[193] Although few men possessed such qualification, he suspected that Gen. Ulysses S. Grant, who had arrived in Washington, was to command the Texas Expedition. "I don't care to go to Texas much, but I want the command of a separate army," he wrote.[194] The only difficulty in such an expedition was "the scarcity of water" in Texas, he concluded. Later, when he learned that Grant was to assume a more exalted position, he speculated that either Gen. Nathaniel B. Banks or Gen. William B. Franklin would be in charge of the expedition, although neither, he felt, were "fit to command an army in Texas." The Union failure at Sabine Pass on September 8, 1863, was a direct result of the Federal commander not being familiar with Texas, he asserted. Anyone who would have "served in Texas . . . would have known better."[195]

By October 1863, not only did Heintzelman learn that he was not being sent to Texas, but he was being removed as commander of the Department of Washington. Hurt and angry, he struck out at Lincoln in his journal. The president "had better look out for the state of Penn. [that] would run me for president," he wrote.[196] Moreover, he was not even being told where he was being sent. Suspecting that he was deliberately being kept in the dark, he approached a reporter for the *New York Times*, who did not know, either.

In early November 1863, when General Banks with 7,000 Federals successfully landed on Brazos Island and took Brownsville, Heintzelman remarked that it was he who had recommended the plan to General-in-Chief

---

[191] HJ, July 11, 1863.
[192] HJ, July 15, 1863.
[193] HJ, Sept. 6, 1863.
[194] HJ, Sept. 7, 1863.
[195] HJ, Sept. 25, 1863.
[196] HJ, Oct. 6, 1863.

Henry W. Halleck. The expedition, however, "should have been made before McClellan went to the Peninsula," he felt.[197] With the Union Army now in control of the Lower Rio Grande Valley, Heintzelman took time to write to his friend, Jeremiah Galvan, who was back in Brownsville.

On January 2, 1864, Heintzelman, who was still uncertain about where he was to be sent, went to see Stanton but the secretary professed ignorance. "I have since been thinking the matter over & can think of nothing but Texas," Heintzelman confided to his journal.[198] One day later he heard that Lincoln was indeed sending him to the Rio Grande. "I am satisfied, thought I did not care to go to Texas," he recorded. A few days later he also heard that Seward and several New York politicians were pushing for him to command the army on the Mexican border; however, on January 12, 1864, he learned from Sen. John Sherman that he was being ordered to Ohio. "I had hoped it would be Texas," he wrote dejectedly.[199] One day later he received orders placing him in command of the Northern Department, which consisted of Ohio, Indiana, Illinois, and Michigan, with headquarters at Columbus, Ohio.[200]

With the health growing bad, Heintzelman spent most of his time in Ohio sparring with the Peace Democrats. Coughing up blood and lame from a foot he had injured in Texas before the war, he was disabled for weeks at a time. He also complained of rheumatism. But with Margaret and Mary visiting from Washington, his spirits were rejuvenated and he was able to assume, although temporarily, some semblance of family life. There was even the circus, complete with dogs, monkeys, and horses.

In October 1864, Gen. Joseph Hooker arrived in Columbus with orders sending Heintzelman to Wheeling in the new state of West Virginia. It was "as nice a piece of petty spite as I have seen," he recorded, as he packed his books and papers. Three days later he was in Wheeling, "a sort of Botany Bay" where there was "nothing to do."[201]

Bored and depressed in Wheeling, Heintzelman complained that his hair was falling out and that he was growing bald, "the first indication I have that I

---

[197] HJ, Nov. 25, 1863. For Heintzelman advising the War Department on Texas, see Heintzelman to Stanton, July 15, 1864; Heintzelman to [William] Dennison, Nov. 15, 1864, HP.

[198] HJ, Jan. 2, 1864.

[199] HJ, Jan. 12, 1864.

[200] E. D. Townsend to Heintzelman, Jan. 12, 1864, HP; General Orders no. 17, Jan. 12, 1864, HP; HJ, Jan. 13, 1864. See also Frank L. Klement, *The Copperheads in the Middle West* (Chicago: University of Chicago Press, 1960), 183–185; Heintzelman to Henry W. Halleck, Mar. 29, 1864, *OR*, 32, I, 629; and HJ, June 12, 1864.

[201] HJ, Oct. 1, 4, 1864.

am growing old." Continuing to blame Secretary of War Stanton, "a tyrant," for his West Virginia exile, he yearned to return to Washington to be with Margaret and Mary and where he could be closer to the war in Virginia. With Gen. Ulysses S. Grant at the gates of Petersburg and Gen William Tecumseh Sherman at Savannah, he felt the war could not last much longer. Sen. John Sherman promised to intervene with Lincoln, and Thomas Wrightson sent a petition to the president protesting Heintzelman's treatment, but all was to little avail.

Heintzelman was in Paducah, Kentucky, on court-martial duty when 100 guns were fired to commemorate Sherman's taking of Charleston, South Carolina, but he was back in Wheeling in early April when Petersburg and Richmond fell. Flags were flying, bands were marching, bells were ringing, and there was "great rejoicing in the city."[202] On April 15, 1865, however, tragic news arrived from Washington; President Lincoln was dead at the hands of a recreant assassin. Flags that had flown so high only days earlier were now draped in black and the bells that had tolled so joyfully now rang out a somber message; the "whole city was horrified."[203] After attending a eulogy for the slain president, Heintzelman was able to obtain a twenty days' leave and depart for Washington.

With the war successfully concluded, Texas again came to dominate his thoughts. He met with Matías Romero, Mexican minister to the United States, and a senator he failed to identify, who asked if he were interested in an "expedition to root out the French" in Mexico.[204] Declining the unofficial order to command an army, rumored to number as many as 70,000 that was to be sent to the Mexican border, Heintzelman, remembering the Cortina War, felt the real reason for such an army in Texas was to stop Americans from invading Mexico, not to expel the French. Besides, he argued, 10,000 men were more than enough to guard the Mexican border.

But despite his many ambitions, the Civil War would remain the pivotal event of his life. Strolling through the streets of the capital on the fourth anniversary of the First Battle of Bull Run, he was disappointed by his failure to meet a single individual who had been at the battle. While in the capital, he took time to remind Stanton that he was "unemployed and wanted to be put on duty."[205] He was willing to go to Texas, he said, if given a command inde-

---

[202] HJ, Apr. 3, 1865. For Heintzelman's views of ending the war, see Heintzelman to the editor, *New York Times*, Dec. 28, 1864, HP.

[203] HJ, Apr. 15, 1865.

[204] HJ, July 3, 1865.

[205] HJ, July 21, 1865. On being mustered out of volunteer service, see General Orders no. 135, Aug. 24, 1865, HP.

pendent of Gen. Philip Sheridan. On August 28, 1865, after hearing that he had been mustered out of volunteer service, he took a leisurely stroll by the White House for a baseball game and was so impressed that he returned again the next day to watch a second contest.

Hearing rumors that he might be sent to New Mexico Territory, he put in for a six months' leave to be with his family. In October, however, he learned that he would not be going to New Mexico but rather to Hart's Island in New York Harbor to join the 17th Infantry; then in November, when Margaret arrived in New York from Washington for a short visit, the couple hurried north to visit Charles who was following in his father's footsteps at West Point. Indian summer back in New York City proved to be a pleasant respite from the war years. With Margaret he was able to attend the theater and visit the various art galleries, one of which featured a "most vulgar" statue of Napoleon. But he realized, as did Margaret, that it was only a matter of time before he received an assignment in the West, far from the sights and sounds of New York and the city he had come to love so much.

By March 1866 he was back in Washington when he received orders sending him and the 17th Infantry to Texas. With Charles at West Point and Mary at school in West Chester, Pennsylvania, Margaret declined to go, but Solon Lathrop, now a captain in the regiment, along with his wife Elizabeth, would be making the long trip south and west. On April 8, with the regimental band playing in a light rain, Heintzelman departed by ship for Texas. Arriving in New Orleans, he was able to meet briefly with Gen. Philip Sheridan. In Galveston a few days later he quickly realized how affairs in Texas had changed when he watched a black regiment on parade. He also met briefly with General Lee's "Old Warhorse," James Longstreet, perhaps the most conciliatory of the Confederate generals. Two days after leaving the island city he was in Indianola at the Casimir Hotel. Except for the wharves that had been burned during the war, the town looked much the same as it had in 1860. Passing through Victoria, he arrived in San Antonio a week later and took a room at the Menger Hotel where, unpacking his personal belongings, he was horrified to discover that a box containing several of his journals and papers was badly water damaged. Over 100 prized photographs were covered with a black mold. The box, he learned, had fallen into the harbor at Indianola.

After assuming command of the Central District of Texas, he was able to visit with a number of old friends, including Frances and Ludovic Colquohn and Mary and Samuel Maverick.[206] As he had done before the war, he took a

---

[206] HJ, June 6, 1866. Heintzelman described Mary Maverick as a "pleasant middle aged woman."

leisure buggy ride down the San Antonio River to Mission Concepción and San José, "a miserable ruin though still used & with a few of the lowest class of Mexicans about."[207] Later at a picnic at San Pedro Springs celebrating emancipation he watched "an ex-rebel Capt. . . . dancing among'st the negroes." Colquohn was sure the man had to be a "Yankee abolitionist."[208]

On July 4, 1866, he listened attentively to a speech by Charles Anderson, a Texan Unionist he had known before the war. Although the German population of the city was in a festive mood, not one former secessionist "put out a flag or joined the celebration." A few days later, Policarpo Rodríguez, his old friend and guide from Camp Verde, rode into town to say that he still had a box of the Heintzelman's crockery which had been left at Camp Verde in December 1860. Two weeks later, Rodríguez again came into San Antonio to report that he had been on a scout "after Indians" and that he had found a road that would cut off 100 miles between San Antonio and El Paso. He also invited Heintzelman to his ranch northwest of San Antonio to "spend a few days."[209]

In early October 1866, Heintzelman, along with Sam Maverick, rode out into the Hill Country. Arriving at Zanzenberg or Center Point, where he had spent many pleasant evenings in 1859–1860, Virginia Ganahl, whose husband was in Brownsville, sent for Policarpo who rode through the night to see Heintzelman. After breakfast the next day, the three men set out on a fishing trip up the Guadalupe River. The following day they rode on to Rodriguez's ranch and then to Camp Verde, which Heintzelman found largely deserted and little more than a "cattle rancho."[210] Only an Irish family was living on the grounds and the buildings were badly dilapidated. The fences, sutler's store, and even Heintzelman's bath house were all gone. Before departing for San Antonio there was more fishing and a turkey hunt. "Polly is one of the best Mexicans I ever met with & I parted from him with regret," he wrote.[211]

Earlier he had received a letter from Gov. James Throckmorton inviting him to Austin and in early September, with cholera rearing its ugly head in San Antonio, he left for the capital. After spending the night at a "miserable house" in New Braunfels, he reached the Colorado River in darkness and rather than wait until morning to cross, waded the river in water up to his hips for a long talk with Throckmorton the next day.[212] Although most of the con-

---

[207] HJ, Apr. 12, 1866.
[208] HJ, June 9, 1866.
[209] HJ, July 25, 1866.
[210] HJ, Oct. 12, 1866.
[211] HJ, Oct. 13, 1866.
[212] HJ, Sept. 4, 5, 1866.

versation centered around Indian affairs, Heintzelman was suspicious of the governor, as he was of most Texas politicians. Throckmorton's request for a more vigorous pursuit of raiding Indians was really a thinly veiled plea for moving the Federal "troops out of the settlements."[213] Although he was invited to appear before the State Senate, he hurried back to San Antonio where the cholera was growing worse. In the rain and heat the army hospitals were full and as many as fourteen soldiers were dying each day. Within days he had all the army camps moved to a healthier location on the Medina River west of the city, and with cooler weather the cholera slowly subsided.

Earlier Heintzelman had learned that Gen. Horatio G. Wright, who had served as his chief engineer during the 1862 Peninsula Campaign, would be replacing him and that he was being assigned to the subdistrict of Galveston. In late October 1866, he left San Antonio and spent the eighty-sixth anniversary of the British surrender at Yorktown in 1781 at Yorktown, Texas, before going on to Indianola and finally to Galveston where he found the Lathrops—Solon, Elizabeth, and their daughter Maggie—sick, but anxiously awaiting his arrival.[214] Since Margaret was uncertain about coming to Texas, he decided that he should move in with the Lathrops. If Margaret "chooses to come, well & good & if not, I must get along," he recorded.[215] In November 1866, Heintzelman, too, came down with the chills and fever; everyone feared that he might have the cholera but he recovered quickly and was back on duty within a week.

Heintzelman had been in Galveston for only a few weeks when he learned that Gen. Charles Griffin would be arriving to relieve him. Griffin, he complained to anyone who would listen, had commanded a light battery of artillery in his Third Corps in 1862 and had not even been born when Heintzelman entered West Point. To General Sheridan, who commanded the Military Division of the Missouri (which included Texas), Heintzelman was simply too friendly and sympathetic to former Texas Confederates. Consequently when Heintzelman, who had never been comfortable with Reconstruction in Texas, returned some old cannon to the City of Galveston, Sheridan decided to remove him. Nevertheless, Heintzelman blamed his old adversary Stanton for his removal. His "long service & attention to duty weigh nothing against [Stanton's] ill will," Heintzelman dejectedly wrote.[216] He hastily wrote a number of senators and congressmen to protest his removal but there was little that could be done. In the rough and tumble

---

[213] HJ, Sept. 5, 1866.
[214] HJ, Oct. 23, 1866.
[215] HJ, Nov. 13, 1866.

world of Texas Reconstruction politics, he had simply been caught between former secessionists, who were trying to resume power, and an army controlled by Radical Republicans determined to reform a wayward South.

His Texas sojourn was further complicated when he learned in December 1866 that a state district judge in Seguin, John Ireland, whom Heintzelman claimed was "notoriously disloyal," had issued a warrant for his arrest. Earlier Capt. Samuel A. Craig, an agent of the Freedmen's Bureau, had freed a soldier arrested by civil authorities in Seguin for gambling. Subsequently Captain Craig was arrested by the Guadalupe County sheriff for allegedly destroying some court records. Heintzelman then ordered a company of soldiers to Seguin to secure Craig's release and help spirit him out of the state. He complained to Sen. Thaddeus Stevens, as well as the brash and uncompromising Sen. Benjamin Wade of Ohio, that in Texas "a horse thief is almost sure to be hung, but human life is considered of less value, if it is that of a Union man or Freedman." Heintzelman vowed not to submit to the warrant. "Texas must have a military governor," he proclaimed.[217]

He became involved in another potentially explosive incident in January 1867, when Ashbel Smith, a leader in the Texas Democratic Party, called on his way to New Orleans to say that he would be accompanying the remains of Gen. Albert Sidney Johnson back to Texas for reburial. Heintzelman, following General Sheridan's directions, made up his mind that he would not allow the remains of his old West Point classmate to be gloriously paraded through the streets of Galveston. He had never forgotten that when he first arrived in Galveston, the ladies of the coastal city, "a rebel town," had hissed when "Yankee Doodle" was played by an army band.[218] When the committee escorting Johnston's remains to Texas arrived in Galveston on its way to Austin a few weeks later, Heintzelman ordered the coffin taken directly to a boat waiting to take it to Houston. Admitting that he had created "quite an excitement," he finally agreed that Johnston's remains could be taken to a local church for services. Later he watched as several thousand somber citi-

---

[216] HJ, Nov. 30, 1866. See also Heintzelman to J. R. Doolittle, Dec. 12, 1866; Heintzelman to Geo. W. Schofield, Jan. 12, 1867; Heintzelman to Edgar Cowan, Jan. 28, 1867, all in HP.

[217] HJ, Dec. 8, 20, 1866. For the Seguin, Texas, incident, see: I. P. Hatch to A. A. General, Dec. 11, 1866; James Wilcox to the Sheriff of Galveston County, Dec. 11, 1866; Heintzelman to D. J. Baldwin, Dec. 26, 1866; Baldwin to Heintzelman, Dec. 29, 1866 (two letters on same date), all in HP. See also William L. Richter, *The Army in Texas during Reconstruction* (College Station: Texas A&M University Press, 1987), 79–80.

[218] HJ, Oct. 30, 1866.

zens of the seaside city marched bareheaded behind the coffin.[219] In March 1867, when the incumbent mayor was defeated simply because he had been too friendly to "officers and Yankees," Heintzelman had had enough of Galveston and Reconstruction in Texas.

A few days after Christmas 1866, Heintzelman was saddened to learn that his friend, Hermann Ehrenberg, "a true man," had been "murdered by Apaches." It was sad, he said, "to read [of] the deaths of one after another of our old Arizona friends."[220] Later Poston wrote to say that the Sonora Mining and Exploring Company had "been sold out by the sheriff" and Heintzelman realized that he had "lost all I had in it."[221] Only his interest in the Santa Rita Company remained of his once promising mining interests in Arizona.

Problems of a personal nature also complicated his stay in Texas. Lathrop was relieved of his staff position in Galveston and ordered to San Antonio in what Heintzelman called "vindictive rascality."[222] But he worried more about his sister-in-law Elizabeth than Solon. Elizabeth, irritable and moody, had been sick and at times lost "all self-control." Despite her insistence of a ridiculously lavish lifestyle and the fact that she was a malicious gossiper, there was little doubt that she was "one of the most kind hearted people in the world."[223] She wanted to return to Buffalo, but Heintzelman feared that if she did, Solon, who was known to drown himself in alcohol when lonely and depressed, would "soon go to the dogs." Realizing that a "single glass of ale upsets his mind," Heintzelman wrote Lathrop in San Antonio to "let every kind of liquor alone."[224]

Family relations were further strained when Margaret wrote Elizabeth asking her to repay a personal loan of $860. In a fit of anger, Elizabeth vowed to repay the loan, even if she had to sell her diamonds and jewels. It was no fun, Heintzelman remarked, living "in a house with a half crazed woman."[225] No sooner had Lathrop arrived in San Antonio, Heintzelman learned, than he had been arrested. From what Heintzelman could gather, Lathrop had taken a large dose of laudanum while consuming alcohol, became "quite beside himself" and abusive to his commanding officer, after which he was arrested and charges preferred.[226]

---

[219] HJ, Jan. 25, 1867.
[220] HJ, Dec. 28, 1866.
[221] HJ, Apr. 19, 1867.
[222] HJ, Jan. 6, 1867.
[223] HJ, Jan. 13, 1867.
[224] Ibid. See also HJ, Feb. 3, 1867.
[225] HJ, Jan. 14, 22, 1867.
[226] HJ, Jan. 26, 1867.

While in Galveston, Heintzelman read in the *Army and Navy Journal* that he was scheduled to be forcibly retired from the military. General Grant, who had never liked him, was undoubtedly to blame, he concluded. Complaining that he could not live on a "pittance . . . out of the army," he urged Margaret to see Grant personally, but when she did, Grant refused to change the order.[227] On April 30, 1867, in what he realized was probably his last muster, he symbolically ordered a "colored company put with the others & it was decidedly in the best order."[228] Six days later, Gen. Philip Sheridan arrived in Galveston and Heintzelman departed, first by boat to New Orleans and then by train north out of "rebeldom" to Cincinnati, where he managed a brief visit with Wrightson before going on to West Chester, Pennsylvania, to see sisters Juliana and Maria, both old and decrepit, and finally on to Germantown to see Mary, who was still in school there. He was still in Germantown when a messenger overtook him saying that Juliana was seriously ill and that he should return at once.[229] Rushing back to West Chester he found that his sister had died only hours earlier. After a hastily arranged funeral, he went on to Philadelphia to meet Margaret, whom he found tired but looking "very well." The couple then traveled on to West Point to attend Charles's graduation at West Point and subsequently journeyed west to Buffalo.[230]

Back in Washington in July 1867, Heintzelman met with Thaddeus Stevens, who inquired about the practicality of dividing Texas into two or more states. Heintzelman liked the idea and suggested the Brazos River as a boundary.[231] In Washington he also met with Benjamin Butler and Nathaniel Banks as well as General Grant, who said he was being considered for temporary duty in New York City. He was also able to see President Andrew Johnson, but the president professed to know little of what the army had planned for him.[232]

Heintzelman was in New York in September 1867 when a yellow fever epidemic raged out of control in Texas. Only hours after presiding over a meeting at the Cooper Institute, tragic news arrived from the Lone Star State. In a shocking telegram he learned that his life-long friend, Solon Lathrop, forty-four, had died on October 7 of yellow fever at Victoria, Texas.[233]

---

[227] HJ, Jan. 28, Apr. 21, 1867.
[228] Heintzelman to G. Maston, Jan. 29, 1867, HP; HJ, Apr. 30, 1867.
[229] HJ, June 3, 4, 5, 1867.
[230] HJ, June 7, 13, 14, 19, 1867.
[231] HJ, July 12, 1867.
[232] HJ, July 18, 19, 24, 1867.
[233] Heintzelman to E. D. Townsend, Oct. 11, 1867, HP; HJ, Oct. 10, 1867.

Worried about Elizabeth, he telegraphed Lt. Henry Norton, his wife's nephew who was stationed in Texas with the 17th Infantry, to hurry to her side and bring her "out of Texas."[234] Within days, Norton replied that he had arrived in Victoria but he too had been stricken with the dreaded disease. It was not until early December that Norton arrived in New York with Elizabeth and her daughter Maggie. Solon's remains would follow in March 1868 for interment in Buffalo's Oaklawn Cemetery.[235]

Heintzelman had always loved the sights and sounds of New York City and since the Retirement Board on which he was serving met infrequently, the winter of 1867–1868 proved to be a pleasant respite from the stress of military duty and Washington politics. There was "draw poker" with friends, lectures at the Cooper Institute with Margaret and Mary, visits to the city's numerous art galleries, the theater, and to church. He also had time to keep up with his investments that now included oil lands in Western Pennsylvania, the Southern Pacific Railroad, a chemical works in New Jersey, and, of course, the Vallecillo lead and silver mines in Mexico and what little was left of the silver mines in Arizona. At social events, Margaret and daughter Mary were frequent companions. The pampered Mary, whom he loved dearly, sometimes got on his nerves, however: "Mary is full of whims & . . . her mother yields to them," he wrote.[236] Margaret, he insisted, had "made a baby of her & it is hard for her to change."[237] Letters from Charles, who was stationed at Fort Kearny, Nebraska, told of pursuing Indians and the rigors of army life on the western frontier. Charles, however, had never liked the army and wrote of resigning and "going to a foreign land," an idea his father found asinine and ridiculous.[238]

Three weeks later Heintzelman met ex-governor James Throckmorton of Texas at the office of the Memphis & El Paso Railroad. Heintzelman's main interest, however, remained in mining, especially after he was elected president of the Defiance Silver Mining Company with holdings at Georgetown, Colorado. In Arizona, the Santa Rita Mining Company was $50,000 in debt and Poston and William Wrightson were unable to raise sufficient capital to keep the company in operation. Hearing that Gen. Joseph Hooker's wife had recently died and left a sizeable fortune, he approached Hooker about investing in the company but the old general was not interested.[239] He was still hoping to recover some of his investments since Poston was negotiating to sell the company to a Spanish corporation for as much as a million dollars.

---

234 Ibid.
235 HJ, Dec. 6, 1867; Mar. 14, 1868.
236 HJ, July 1, 1868.
237 HJ, July 18, 1868.
238 HJ, Oct. 3, 1868.
239 HJ, Apr. 12, 1870.

In Mexico, Lowry, whom he was coming to mistrust, was failing to turn a profit at the Vallecillo mines. Still he had no doubt that there was money to be made in mining. He insisted that his stock in the Vallecillo Company was worth $10,000, but Margaret defiantly argued that he could not get more than $500.[240]

Heintzelman yearned to find a permanent home "for the few remaining years I can expect to live."[241] More and more he was thinking of settling at San Diego, California, if the Southern Pacific Railroad ever became a reality. He had always liked the sunny and invigorating Southern California climate and had maintained his property in the oceanside town. His interest in the West was heightened after attending a stirring lecture on the "Colorado canons" by Maj. John Wesley Powell which was given at the Packer Institute in January, 1871.[242]

In Washington in February 1872, he was visited by a delegation from Texas that included ex-governor Edward Clark and the old Unionists John Hancock and George W. Pascual. They had a long talk about Texas politics, mining in Mexico, and "doings on the Rio Grande."[243] There were continued problems on the border with Juan N. Cortina, the Texans said, and as the commanding officer in the Cortina War, they hoped Heintzelman would testify before the Foreign Affairs Committee of the House of Representatives "about the troubles on the Rio Grande," Growing old and decrepit, Heintzelman could not keep his mind off Texas and the Southwest; hearing that Tucson now had a population of 3,000, he realized how the region was being transformed. In his leisure moments he read a book on the exploration of Yellowstone and although he was unable to invest, he remained interested in a copper mining company that had purchased 30,000 acres of land in Texas.[244]

He also concerned himself with family matters. Charles was offered a professorship in civil engineering at Cornell, but politely declined. Charles "don't fancy small western colleges," Heintzelman wrote.[245] But in Heintzelman's imagination there was always the lure of Texas and the West. He visited with the one-armed Major Powell and continued to attend lectures on the exploration of the Colorado River. Powell even gave him twenty to thirty stereoscopic views of the Grand Canyon of the Colorado. Heintzelman, who had first heard of the Grand Canyon when he was at the

---

[240] HJ, Apr. 19, 1870.
[241] HJ, Dec. 31, 1870.
[242] HJ, Jan. 14, 1871.
[243] HJ, Feb. 14, 1872.
[244] HJ, Apr. 3, 1872.
[245] HJ, Apr. 23, 1872.

Yuma Crossing some twenty years earlier, was so inspired that he dug out his journals covering his long sojourn at Fort Yuma and read the entries on a trip he had made down the river in 1851. He even copied and gave to Powell a portion of his journal that included his brief description of the journey. In the process, he became convinced that he was "probably the first white man [to have] ever descended" the river.[246] He also took time to reread his copies of the Treaty of Guadalupe-Hidalgo, the Gadsden Purchase, and William H. Emory's 1857 *Boundary Survey*. In June he visited with several Arizona Indians that Gen. Oliver Otis Howard, his brigade commander from First Bull Run, brought to Washington. The natives included Apaches, Pimas, Maricopas, Papagos, and his old friends, the Yumas. "The true way to deal with an Indian," he reflected, "is to tell him what he must do & what you will do & that if he don't you will make him. That was my policy and it was successful. I never promised an Indian only what I could perform & took care to do so."[247]

In Washington in December 1872, he thought again of moving to San Diego but instead he finally settled into a house on M Street in the capital.[248] Here old friends from Texas and comrades from the Civil War came to call. One was Francis W. Latham, the customs collector from Brazos Santiago whom he had met in Brownsville during the Cortina War.[249] He also met with Thomas P. Robb, who was heading a congressional commission to investigate problems on the Texas border, and Congressman John Hancock, who had arrived from Texas, and there was much talk of the Cortina War and the continuing problems on the border. Robb recalled having once discussed with Gen. George Thomas the possibility of having the U.S. Army follow Mexican raiders across the Rio Grande. To do so would mean war, Thomas warned Robb, but "Heintzelman did it."[250]

On December 31, 1872, Heintzelman made the last entry in his journal. In a cold Washington rain he had called on Congressman Hancock and the two "had a long talk [about] the situation on the Rio Grande." Reflecting the popular Texas attitude at the time, Hancock favored "the military occupation of the Mexican side of the river." In the final analysis, Hancock was "about right," Heintzelman concluded.[251]

---

[246] HJ, May 17, 1872. Heintzelman, of course, had no knowledge of Hernando de Alarcón's ascent and descent of the lower Colorado River as part of the Francisco Vásquez de Coronado expedition in 1540.

[247] HJ, June 25, 1872.

[248] HJ, Nov. 15, 19, 1872.

[249] HJ, Dec. 14, 1872.

[250] HJ, Dec. 30, 1872.

[251] HJ, Dec. 31, 1872.

In his waning years Heintzelman remained in Washington and never saw Texas again, although he was able to fulfill one lifelong desire in 1876 when he and Margaret traveled to Europe for a lengthy vacation.[252] Samuel Peter Heintzelman, a man of "intense nature" and "vehement action," died in Washington at his residence at 1123 Fourteenth Street in the early morning hours of May 1, 1880. With the Stars and Stripes in the capital at half-mast and after a small funeral at his residence, his body was accompanied by a military escort to Buffalo, New York, where it lay in state at the City Hall before burial with military honors in Forest Lawn Cemetery next to his infant son.[253] The old general was seventy-four.

---

[252] Heintzelman to Rufus Ingalls, Mar. 16, 1876, HP.

[253] *New York Times*, May 2, 4, 1880; Charles D. Poston, "In Memoriam: Major-General Samuel P. Heintzelman," *Arizona Weekly Star* (Tucson), May 13, 1880; "Maj. Gen. Samuel P. Heintzelman," miscellaneous newspaper obituary, n.d., HP; *Eleventh Annual Reunion of the Association of the Graduates of the U.S. Military Academy at West Point, New York June 17, 1880* (East Saginaw: E. W. Lyon, 1880), 103–104; *Twelfth Annual Return of the Graduates of the U.S. Military Academy, June 9, 1881* (East Saginaw: E.W. Lyon, 1881), 35–36; *Biographical Register of the Officers and Graduates of the U.S. Military Academy at West Point, N.Y.* (Boston: Riverside Press, 1891), 1:372–74.

Since he gave no indication that he was ending his journal on December 31, 1872, it appears likely that Heintzelman continued to maintain the journal and that subsequent writings were either lost or were never part of the Heintzelman collection that was given to the Library of Congress.

Margaret Stuart Heintzelman died on August 9, 1893, and was buried next to her husband in Buffalo's Forest Lawn Cemetery. Mary Heintzelman, their beloved semi-invalid daughter, who fought most of her life to defend her father's Civil War reputation, died on March 24, 1927, and was also buried in Buffalo next to her parents. North, *Samuel Peter Heintzelman*, 190; Tombstone data, Forest Lawn Cemetery, courtesy of Charles E. Chambers.

Capt. Charles Stuart Heintzelman, after serving in Texas and at various posts in Florida and the trans-Mississippi, died of disease only ten months after his father on February 17, 1881, at the age of thirty-five in Washington, D.C.

The Heintzelmans' grandson, Stuart (Tommy) Heintzelman, born in New York City in 1876 and educated abroad and at Groton, Connecticut, graduated from West Point in 1899. He served in the Philippines, the Boxer Rebellion, and as a military instructor at Princeton University in 1916. He fought with the A. E. F. at St. Mihiel during World War I and was an observer with the French Army and later on the Italian front in the winter of 1917. He received a number of French and Italian medals including the *Croix de Guerre* and the Order of the Crown. He was promoted to brigadier general in 1922 and major general in 1931. Gen. Stuart Heintzelman died at Hot Springs, Arkansas, July 6, 1935. *Sixty-Seventh Annual Report of the Association of Graduates of the United States Military Academy at West Point, New York, June 11, 1936* (Newburg, N.Y.: Moore Printing, 1936), 209–212.

❦ April 1859 ❦

"... part of the way over Hog wallow prairie."

New Orleans Sun. Apl. 17, 1859

A little cool to-day. We sat in the parlor awhile last evening, after we had been to supper. Major Harris of Washington came in & I introduced him to the ladies. He came down the river from Pittsburgh in a steam wheeler, to send to Tehuantapec. He didnt go any farther in her.

I went out this morning & took a look at the new Custom House. It is not finished. I then went on board the steamer Mexico. She is laid up for repairs. The Texas leaves next Thursday. In the afternoon we went to see the Cathedral & hear the music. It is Palm Sunday & we did not see much. The cathedral is a very ordinary building in side.[1] The square (Jackson) in front is beautiful. We also took a walk in the French parts of the town.

New Orleans Tues. Apl. 19, 1859

Yesterday was a little warmer & still rain to-day. I went yesterday & engaged my passage & went to-day & paid it & got my ticket. I went & called on Mrs. Col. Myers—went on board the Switzerland.[2] I also called & saw Dr. Abadie. In the evening we saw his wife & Mrs. Gen. Kearney.[3]

---

[1] Facing Jackson Square and the Mississippi River, St. Louis Cathedral had been completed in 1794 and was the third church on the site. The first had been destroyed by a hurricane in 1722 and the second by fire in 1794.

[2] Abraham C. Myers, West Point class of 1828, had been breveted a lieutenant colonel for gallantry at the Battle of Churubusco during the Mexican War. Myers had visited with the Heintzelmans at Newport Barracks, Kentucky, on his way downriver in May 1858. He resigned in January 1861 to become a colonel in the Confederate Army. Myers died in June 1899. HJ, May 20, 1858; Francis B. Heitman, *Historical Register and Dictionary of the United States Army, From its Organization, September 29, 1789, to March 2, 1903* (2 vols.; Washington, D.C.: Government Printing Office, 1903), I, 739.

[3] French-born Eugene Hilarian Abadie had served as a surgeon in the army since

This morning I was on board the steam ship & saw our state room. I stopped yesterday & saw Judge Walker & met him in the street this morning.

I went to get tickets to the Opera but could only get a whole box.[4] I sent after from the Hotel & got a box. I got a carriage & we rode out on the shell road to the lake & back & stopped in the Firemans cemetery.[5] It dont pay to ride out there. We waited till we were tired for some refreshments & then left.

New Orleans Wed. Apl. 20, 1859

We went last evening to the Opera. It had commenced when we got there. It looks like a small dingy affair after the splendid house in Cincinnati. The house was not half filled. The play was the Favorite.[6]

We went & finished our shopping & at 4 p.m. took Miss Hurd on board the Steamer Switzerland. After I got on board I learned that she would not leave until 5 p.m. next day. I left her there. We took dinner at 2 p.m. We busied ourselves at intervals all day packing.

4 p.m. Thurs. Apl. 21 1859 Off mouth of Mississippi

We had an early breakfast & went on board with our baggage a little before 8 a.m. At that hour the bell tapped & the boat left punctually. We have a great many passengers. The weather is beautiful & we had a delightful run to the mouth. We got a very fine dinner.

1836. Abadie was in San Antonio when Gen. David E. Twiggs surrendered the Department of Texas in February 1861. He was later breveted a colonel for meritorious service during the Civil War. Abadie died in December 1874. Heitman, *Historical Register*, 149; *Alamo Express* (San Antonio), Apr. 24, 1861.

Mary Radford Kearny, devoted wife of Gen. Stephen Watts Kearny and mother of eleven children, outlived her husband by more that half a century. General Kearny died on October 31, 1848, at the home of Meriwether Clark near St. Louis. Mary Kearny died in her eighty-eighth year at St. Louis on June 27, 1899. Dwight L. Clarke, *Stephen Watts Kearny: Soldier of the West* (Norman: University of Oklahoma Press, 1961), 386–389.

[4] New Orleans had two opera houses at this time—the Orleans Theater in the Vieux Carre and the St. Charles Theater located above Canal Street. Walter G. Cowan, et. al, *New Orleans, Yesterday and Today: A Guide to the City* (Baton Rouge: Louisiana State University Press, 1983), 193–194.

[5] Also known as Cypress Grove, the Fireman's Cemetery was established in 1840 at the end of Canal Street at what was then the edge of Metairie Bayou. Ibid., 75–76.

[6] Gaetano Donizetti's *La Favorite* was performed in New Orleans as early as 1843. A grand opera set in four acts, *La Favorite* was a tragic love story set in Santiago de Compostela, Spain. Leslie Orrey (ed.), *Encyclopedia of Opera* (New York: Charles Scribner's Sons, 1976), 123.

GALVESTON SAT. APL. 23, 1859 STEAM SHIP TEXAS

As we got to sea the wind was on shore, but before morning a Norther set in & we had a heavy blow that lasted till after night. Quite a number of the passengers were sick. Margaret & the children were. This morning after day-light we crossed the bar & when I got up we were at the wharf. We here left most of our passengers.

I left Charles to take care of his dogs & Margaret, Mary & I walked ashore. We got a carriage, took a drive on the beach & all over town & into the Cemetery. This [is] a pretty flourishing place, but suffers from the yellow fever. The horses were landed to give room to put our freight & I sent them to a livery stable. The weather is delightful. We leave at 5 P.M.

INDIANOLA TEXAS SUN. APL. 24, 1859

We got tired enough waiting for the boat to leave. It was a little after 5 & the sun set after we passed the light. The wind blew fresh & it was cool. Before day we made the bar & had to wait till near 7 before the tide reversed then we touched a few times. We got breakfast before we reached the wharf.

We got our baggage ashore & walked to the Hotel Casimir.[7] I got rooms & then hunted up Capt. Reynolds, the Qr. M.[8] He sent for a cart to haul up

---

[7] Only one block from where the New Orleans steamers docked on Lavaca Bay, the Casimir House offered luxurious accommodations that included game rooms and an elegant bar. Named after the owner, Casimir Villeneuve, the Casimir would accommodate 150 guests and was one of the most popular hotels in Texas. A "good fisherman is attached to the house who keeps it constantly supplied with the best fish," prospective guests were told. Returning to Texas in March 1866, Heintzelman again took lodging at the Casimir. Although Gen. John B. Magruder had ordered the wharves burned during the Civil War, "the house & town look as when I passed through before," Heintzelman recorded. Brownson Malsch, *Indianola: The Mother of Western Texas* (Austin: State House Press, 1988), 67, 70, 79; San Antonio *Daily Herald*, Feb. 8, 1859; HJ, Mar. 28, 1866.

[8] Alexander Welch Reynolds, a Virginian from the West Point class of 1838, had been promoted to captain in the 1st Infantry in 1848. Dismissed in 1855 for failure to explain discrepancies in his accounts, Reynolds was reinstated in 1858. In 1859, he was serving as assistant quartermaster at Indianola, the major supply depot for the Department of Texas. Dropped from the army in October 1861 after he remained in the South following the surrender of the Department of Texas, Reynolds became a brigadier general in the Confederate Army. After the war, Heintzelman tried repeatedly to collect money from Reynolds for the horses Heintzelman had left with Reynolds to sell when the Heintzelmans departed Texas in 1860. Along with his son, Frank, Reynolds later served in the Egyptian Army where he became involved in a feud with George H. Butler, counsul general in Alexandria and nephew of Benjamin Butler. Reynolds died in Alexandria, Egypt, in May 1876. Erza J. Warner, *Generals in Gray:*

our things. I put the horses in the Qr. M. stable & our goods. Reynolds is keeping batchelors hall & has his stepson with him. Lt. Shaaf is commissary.[9] We must get off tomorrow in our Ambulance & he will send up some of our things. I paid the freight this morning. It is $56.95 & it was but $10 on the river. Some of it I now find was left behind at Galveston. It is too provoking to pay such a price & have part of the freight left ashore. It will be here tomorrow. It is warm here, but a nice breeze. This is quiet a nice little town.

INDIANOLA TEXAS MON. APL. 25, 1859

We were up & had breakfast at 7. I send Charles & Jackson to see about getting the Ambulance & bale of our luggage up & Margaret & I packed, having to arrange to leave part of our trunks. The Texas left early & the other boat got in.

I got the Ambulance up & the horses out. The later is the smallest kind of mule & will not do for the horses. I tried to get others, but there is none in town. I have borrowed a couple of set & will let mine go up & either get mules or try changing in San Antonio. Capt. Reynolds lends me a set & will send my luggage. We leave immediately after dinner.

CHOCOLATE TEX.[10] MON. APL. 25, 1859

We got off at 3¼ & arrived here at 6½—15 miles, part of the way over the Hog wallow prairie.[11] It was very warm, but a good breeze. The tounge is too short for such large horses. They go well. We are a little crowded with bundles but can reduce them or rather stow them better.

Lives of the Confederate Commanders (Baton Rouge: Louisiana State University Press, 1959), 255; William B. Hesseltine and Hazel C. Wolf, *The Blue and the Gray on the Nile* (Chicago: University of Chicago Press, 1961), 71–75; J. K. F. Mansfield to Lorenzo Thomas, Sept. 27, 1860, LR, AGO, RG 94 (NA).

[9] John Thomas Shaaff, twenty-nine and from the West Point class of 1851, had transferred to the 2d Cavalry in March 1855. Reynolds had relieved Shaaff of command of the Indianola Depot in May 1859, only weeks after the Heintzelmans arrived in Texas. Along with his Kentucky-born wife, Helen, twenty-one, and a four-month old daughter, Shaaff was later stationed at Fort Mason. Resigning in February 1861, Shaaff served as a quartermaster in the Confederate Army and died in July 1877. Heitman, *Historical Register*, 875; 8th Census, Mason County.

[10] A favorite resting spot on the Indianola-San Antonio Road, Chocolate took its name from Chocolate Bayou, which flowed from northwestern Calhoun County some twelve miles to empty into Chocolate Bay, an inlet of Lavaca Bay, about a mile south of present-day Port Lavaca. Walter Prescott Webb, H. Bailey Carroll, and Stephen Branda (eds.), *Handbook of Texas* (3 vols.; Austin: Texas State Historical Association, 1952; 1976), I, 343.

[11] A nearly flat strip of wet lowlands along the Gulf Coast, sometimes only a few feet above sea level that ranges from three to twenty miles in width.

The house is not very promising, but we got a good supper.

HELENA TEXAS.12 FRI. APL. 29, 1859

Tuesday was very hot & we reached Victoria about 2 P.M. There was much Hog wallow & no place to stop. One of the horses, the one that was sick on the boat, did not pull much and the other got quite tired.

The hotel at Victoria is rather indifferent & the town small.[13] Wednesday we got off tolerably early & on outskirts of the town crossed the Guadalupe river. We then took the wrong road & missed going by Yorktown. There are no stopping places along the road. With much difficulty we got about 25 or 30 miles & stopped at a miserable place.

It rained & hailed in the night & some rain yesterday. When we got up I found the big horse sick & so stiff he could scarcely move. He is badly foundered. I tried to get another horse, but without success. We finally had to start with him & come in a walk, he pulling the sick one. We came about 20 miles yesterday & stopped on a small stream. Accommodations bad enough. I tried every where, but could not get a horse. At last I got a pair & came 5 or 6 miles this morning to this place & left Jackson to lead the other horses.[14]

We are here, but it is doubtful whether I can get horses. If I can we will go on this afternoon & if not I will take the stage & leave the rest to come on. It is very hot here & very little breeze.

---

[12] Helena, on the San Antonio River at the intersection of the Chihuahua Trail and the San Antonio Road, was a rowdy frontier town established in 1852 and named after Helena Owens, a friend of Thomas Ruckman, who had helped to organize the county. County seat of Karnes County, the small settlement consisted of a stage station, general store, grist mill, saw mill, and a hotel and blacksmith shop. In the late–1800s the community gained the reputation of being the "Toughest Town on Earth." Webb, Carroll, and Branda (eds.), *Handbook of Texas*, I: 793. See also Roy L. Swift, *Three Roads to Chihuahua: The Great Wagon Roads that Opened the Southwest, 1823–1883* (Austin: Eakin Press, 1988), 151–54.

[13] Established by the empresario Martin de León in 1824, Victoria was named after Guadalupe Victoria, the first president of the Republic of Mexico. In 1858, the community boasted of a population of 1,400. Heintzelman probably stayed at the Globe Hotel on the north side of Constitution (De León) Square. A modern brick structure with a bar, restaurant, elegant sleeping rooms (some with fireplaces), and an adjacent livery stable, the Globe was one of the more popular hotels in Texas. It was destroyed by fire in January 1861. In Victoria in March 1866, Heintzelman complained of "fleas, bed bugs, etc., & dirt" at a rebuilt Globe Hotel. Sidney R. Weisinger, "Globe House," *Victoria Advocate*, February 3, 10, 17, 1974. Articles courtesy of Charles Spurlin, Victoria College. See also HJ, March 28, 1866.

[14] A free man of color, Zachary Jackson was the family hired hand. HJ, Mar. 31, 1859.

☙ May 1859 ❧

"We had tolerable sup & break & plenty of fleas."

San Antonio Texas Sun. May 1st, 1859

I made a mistake. We got to Helena on the 29th. We came Wed. about 25 or 30 miles & stopped at a miserable place. The house had only one room finished & our Sup & break were coffee, without sugar, bacon & corn bread. The worst accommodations Margaret ever had. We left & by all of us walking by turns & the children driving we got to [a] creek (Cavesa) & there staid all night.[1] Our supper was better, but sleeping about the same. No sugar. We here got horses & in an hour were in Helena & in an hour more Jackson arrived with our horses.

The driver we got the day before yesterday at Helena was quite mean. They however yesterday gave us some lunch & fortunate it was for us, as yesterday we could not find a house to stop at & had to encamp about half way. Margaret & I slept in the wagon & the children under. We were almost eatin up [by] the fleas. The country through which we rode is beautiful, but very few inhabitants. Most of the corn has been killed by the frost.

Where we stopped I got a Mex. women to boil us a dozen eggs & this with what was left of our lunch sufficed for the children & us.

This morning they were half starved, but with the fragments of our lunch & couple of oranges got along. The house here is crowded, but we have a tolerable room. The dinner was indifferent. We got here about 12.[2]

---

[1] Located on the headwaters of Cabeza Creek in Western DeWitt County, Cabeza was another stage stop on the road to San Antonio. Webb, Carroll, and Branda (eds.), *Handbook of Texas*, I, 261

[2] Complaining of having been "detained by the sickness of a horse," Heintzelman reported his arrival in San Antonio on May 1, 1859, after six days on the road from Indianola. The San Antonio *Daily Herald* noted the arrival of "Maj. S.P. Heintzelman with family, USA," at the Menger Hotel on May 3, 1859. Heintzelman to S. Cooper, May 1, 1859, LR, AGO, RG 94 (NA).

Major Fitzgerald is here sick, to leave for N. Orleans in a couple of days.[3] The General is still confined to his bed.[4] I have not seen any others of the Officers yet. It rained a few drops at daylight & misted a little after we started.

The year from the date of my order expired on Friday, but I did not leave Washington until about the 4th of this month, waiting on the Sec. of War so I must not consider my leave out yet.

I have written my monthly Reports.

SAN ANTONIO TEXAS MON. MAY 2, 1859

It was warm last night. Got letters from Sister Maria, Solon.[5] They have

---

[3] Edward H. Fitzgerald had been breveted a major for gallantry at Chapultepec during the Mexican War. Heintzelman had known Fitzgerald when the two were stationed at Fort Yuma. Fitzgerald died on January 9, 1860. Heitman, *Historical Register*, 422; HJ, Feb. 26, Mar. 2, 6, 22, 26, July 1, 1852.

[4] Seventy-one-year-old David Emanuel Twiggs, or "Old Davey" as he was known in the frontier army, was in ill health as Heintzelman's journal indicates. Heintzelman had visited with Twiggs, a veteran of the War of 1812 and the Mexican War, at Jefferson Barracks, Missouri, in June 1855. After surrendering the Department of Texas in February 1861, Twiggs became known as "Traitor Twiggs." Despised in the North and dismissed from the army, he became the oldest officer of the antebellum army to declare for the Confederacy. Appointed a major general and placed in command of the District of Louisiana that included the defenses of New Orleans, he was never active in the Confederate cause and died in July 1862. Carolina Baldwin Darrow, "Recollections of the Twiggs Surrender," *Battles and Leaders of the Civil War* (4 vols.; New York: Yoseloff and Co., 1956), II: 33–39; Warner, *Generals in Gray*, 312; M. L. Crimmins, "An Episode in the Texas Career of General David E. Twiggs, " *SHQ*, 41 (Oct., 1937), 167–173; Robert M. Utley, *Frontiersmen in Blue: The United States Army and the Indian*, 1848–1865 (New York: Macmillan, 1962), 128. See also Jeanne Twiggs Heidler. "The Military Career of David Emanuel Twiggs" (Ph.D. diss., Texas Christian University, 1976).

[5] Throughout his military career, Heintzelman maintained a regular correspondence with his older sister. While living at Circleville, Ohio, Maria married a Colonel Keffer on August 28, 1842. Following the death of her husband, Maria moved to West Chester Pennsylvania, where she died on January 6, 1872. HJ, Aug. 22, 24, 28, 1842; Jan. 6, 1872; Heiges, "Heintzelman Visits his Hometown," 95.

Solon Huntington Lathrop, age thirty-four and one of Samuel Peter's closest friends, was married to Elizabeth Stuart, the younger sister of Margaret Heintzelman. The two had become friends during the winter of 1843–1844 while Heintzelman was stationed at Buffalo, New York. On July 27, 1847, only hours before he departed for Vera Cruz and the Mexican War, Heintzelman attended Elizabeth and Solon's wedding in Buffalo. The well-to-do Lathrop built a fine home on Johnson Park in the city. Newspaper publisher and son of a minister, it was Lathrop who first suggested that Heintzelman ask for a one year leave in 1856 and go to Arizona to supervise the mining operations of the Sonora Mining and

found a new vein near the H. Mine promises to be as rich or even richer than the H. mine.[6] Margaret got letters from Mrs. Norton & Caroline.[7]

I called & reported. I did not see the General. He recommends my going to Ft. Duncan & seeing Col. Morris.[8] If he goes on leave I will go to Duncan, if not to Camp Cooper. I saw Vinton, Dr. Jarvis, the latter called last evening & this morning Capt. Withers & Lt. Blake.[9] I also saw Capt. Blair the

---

Exploring Company. Lathrop, who had been elected treasurer of the company, met Heintzelman in San Francisco in July 1858, and the two crossed the desert from San Diego to Tubac together. After Heintzelman returned to duty in 1859, Lathrop became the acting director of the company's operations but joined the Heintzelmans at Camp Verde for the trip east in 1860. He went on to serve on Heintzelman's staff during the Civil War and rose to the rank of lieutenant colonel. Although Heintzelman and Lathrop were close, Heintzelman's journal indicates an occasional intolerance of his friend. In confronting ruffians in Arizona, Heintzelman hinted that Lathrop was less than courageous. On the steamboat *Chancellor* on the Mississippi River above Memphis in January 1861, Heintzelman rescued Lathrop from a riverboat gambler. Lathrop, who was drunk and playing cards, had lost all of his money and even a bar of silver. "I got up & brought him away," Heintzelman recorded, and reclaimed the Arizona silver. Heintzelman lived with Elizabeth and Solon Lathrop briefly in Galveston in 1866. While a captain in the 35th Infantry, Lathrop died on October 7, 1867, of yellow fever at the age of forty-four at Victoria, Texas. Lathrop is listed on the 1860 census at Tubac with real estate of $50,000 and personal property of $20,000. North, *Samuel Peter Heintzelman*, 41, 203; HJ, Dec. 31, 1843; Jan. 7, 26, June 2, 7, 1844; Nov. 23, 1846; Mar. 22, May 22, July 27, 1847; Apr. 22, June 16, 1849; Jan. 6, 1861; Heintzelman to E. D. Townsend, Oct. 11, 1867, HP; 8th Census, Arizona County, New Mexico Territory.

    6 The Heintzelman Mine was at Cerro Colorado, seventeen miles west of Tubac, Arizona. As president of the Sonora Mining & Exploring Company, Heintzelman lived at Cerro Colorado and supervised the mine operations for four and one-half months in 1858 and 1859. It was originally thought that $2 million in silver could be taken from the mine each year. In reality, the mine made little more than expenses and proved to be a disappointment. North, *Samuel Peter Heintzelman*, 89–162; HJ, Nov. 24, 25, 1858; Jan. 5, 1859.

    7 Mary Stuart Norton and Caroline Stuart were sisters of Margaret Heintzelman. Caroline had traveled with the Heintzelmans around Cape Horn to California in 1848–1849. On the trip she met and later married, in San Diego, Dr. John Edward Summers, a Virginian and assistant surgeon. See note 4, August 1859 chapter.

    8 Gouverneur Morris attended the U.S. Military Academy but had never graduated. After being breveted a major during the Mexican War, Morris was promoted to lieutenant colonel in the 1st Infantry in May 1857. Morris, whom Heintzelman mistrusted and disliked, retired in September 1861 and died in October 1868. Heitman, *Historical Register*, 727.

    9 San Antonio quartermaster David Hammond Vinton, fifty-five, a Rhode Islander, and 1822 West Point graduate, was promoted to major during the Mexican War. Heintzelman had met Vinton on a number of official and social occasions and as early as 1842 the two frequently corresponded. Heintzelman had dined with Vinton at

Commissary.[10] I will go to Duncan & see.

I sent off my monthly Reports & will leave in the next stage (Thursday) for Duncan.

I wrote to Dr. Tripler.[11]

Buffalo in June 1855 and again at Jefferson Barracks, Missouri, in May, June, and September, 1855. Heintzelman recorded the death of Vinton's first wife in January 1845 and his second marriage in New York three years later to a lady the "same age as his eldest daughter." In his usual frankness, Heintzelman would later note: "By his present wife he has three children. She [second wife] is not pretty." Vinton was breveted a major general during the Civil War and retired from the army in July 1866. He died in February 1873. Ibid., 988. See also 8th Census, Bexar County; HJ, Nov. 8, 14, 1842; Apr. 28, 1843, Feb. 21, 1845; Nov. 2, 1848; June 14, May 27, 28, June 14, September 19, 1855.

A New Yorker, Nathan Sturges Jarvis served as a surgeon during the Mexican War. Older brother of Samuel M. Jarvis, the Reconstruction mayor of Laredo, Texas, and the brother-in-law of Samuel Colt, he died in May 1862. A photograph of the surgeon is in the Foster Papers at the Webb County Heritage Foundation, Laredo, Texas. Numerous references to Dr. Jarvis can be found in Caleb Coker (ed.), *The News From Brownsville: Helen Chapman's Letters from the Texas Military Frontier, 1848–1852* (Austin: Texas State Historical Association, 1992). For Jarvis's account of the Battle of Monterrey see Jerry Thompson, *Sabers on the Rio Grande* (Austin: Presidial Press, 1974), 144–145.

John Withers, an 1848 West Point graduate and a brevet captain, was assistant adjutant general at department headquarters in San Antonio. Withers was married to Anita Dwyer in San Antonio in June 1859, after which he departed for New York on leave. From Tennessee, Withers resigned in March 1861 to serve as a lieutenant colonel in the Confederate Army. Withers died in February of 1892. Heitman, *Historical Register*, 1052; San Antonio *Daily Herald*, June 16, 1859.

First Lieutenant Edward D. Blake was an 1843 West Point graduate. Promoted to captain in October 1860, he resigned in June 1861 to become a lieutenant colonel in the Confederate Army. Blake died in November 1882. Heitman, *Historical Register*, 223.

[10] William B. Blair, a Virginian from the West Point class of 1838, had by 1859 become assistant commissary at department headquarters in San Antonio. He resigned shortly after the Twiggs surrender to enter the Confederate Army. Blair died in March of 1883. Heitman, *Historical Register*, 222. See also San Antonio *Daily Herald*, Apr. 24, 1861.

[11] Dr. Charles Stuart Tripler was an army surgeon from New York and a close friend of the Heintzelmans. Heintzelman had played chess and billiards and gone to parties with the physician. Tripler had lanced Margaret's breast and had led two other physicians in operating on Mary's leg at Newport Barracks, Kentucky, in 1858. Tripler's son, Stuart, attended Gambier College in Ohio along with Charles Heintzelman. Tripler, who organized the Medical Corps of the Army of the Potomac, was later breveted a brigadier general during the Civil War. Heintzelman was in Galveston in 1866 when he learned of Tripler's death in Cincinnati in October of that year. HJ, June 24, 1843; Jan. 27, 1846; Jan. 1, Feb. 7, Sept. 21, Oct. 21, Dec. 8, 1857; May 10, 27–29, 1858; Aug. 6, 1860; June 24, Nov. 3, 1866.

SAN ANTONIO TEX. WED. MAY 4, 1859

Hot & disagreeable yesterday. I was at the office & spent an hour with Vinton. He called in the forenoon & his wife & Mrs. Chilton in the afternoon.[12]

I went & saw Brucknow & saw his specimens of silver ore. He gave me an Arizonian.[13] A bar of silver (no 7) worth over $1,000 was sent to New York. He speaks in raptures of the mine. It now more that pays expenses. With two bbl we get $1,400 a week & by this time must have three bbl in operation. We have plenty of rich ore.

FORT DUNCAN TEXAS. SAT. MAY 7, 1859

A little before daylight Thursday morning it commenced raining & rained very hard till after six. I got up & had breakfast, but the stage did not leave till near 7. There was one passenger with me to Castroville, 26 miles.[14] On Wed. Jackson got back with the horses. I saw Capt. McLean the A.Q.M. & left orders to turn them out on grass with the Gov. animals. The foundered horse is still quite stiff.

The rain made the road quite heavy the first few miles. I got a poor dinner at Castroville & got to Dahanis at 5 P.M. 48 miles & there we staid all night.[15] It soon commenced raining. We had tolerable sup & break & plenty of fleas. The road was muddy & heavy & got along badly. After we changed mules it got better & we passed the Nueces, the old Mex. Boundary near sundown. There is but one watering place this side & one stretch of 35 miles without water. We had a little rain just after crossing the Frio. I got here at 6 A.M. & went to Lt. Thomas's quarters, knowing his father the Qr. M.[16]

---

[12] The wife of Robert Hall Chilton, a major and paymaster in the 2d Dragoons. Heitman, *Historical Register*, 299.

[13] First published at Tubac in 1859, and later at Tucson, the *Weekly Arizonian* was Arizona's first newspaper. The first publisher was Heintzelman's friend and business partner William Wrightson. Donald B. Sayner and Robert P. Hale (comps.), *Arizona's First Newspaper: "The Weekly Arizonian"* (Tucson: Arizona Historical Society, n.d.).

[14] On the west bank of the Medina River, Castroville was founded by Henri Castro in September 1844. The bustling Alsatian community boasted of a number of power plants and sawmills. Bobby D. Weaver, *Castro's Colony: Empresario Development in Texas, 1842–1865* (College Station: Texas A&M University Press, 1985), 40–56.

[15] D'Hanis, named after William D'Hanis, Antwerp manager of Henri Castro's colonization company, was established in the spring of 1847 by twenty-one Alsatian families. Webb, Carroll, and Branda (eds.), *Handbook of Texas*, I: 498.

[16] Charles William Thomas, an 1855 graduate of West Point, had transferred to the 1st Infantry and by June 1858 had become regimental quartermaster. In 1859,

The road is generally very good, but barren enough this side the Nueces. After breakfast I went to the office and saw all the officers but the Col. Lt. Thomas & I called & after a long talk I left him to consider the subject matter. Thomas saw him since & he thinks that he will leave. I like the appearance of the post. I called & saw Dr. King & his family & Capt. Caldwell & his & take tea at Lt. Mowers.[17] I take my meals with the men.

The ride was cool & pleasant & last night so cool I had to put on my cloak. It is pleasant here & not very warm—a fine breeze.

FORT DUNCAN SUN. MAY 8, 1859

Lt. Col. Morris sent for me the middle of the afternoon & told me that he will go on sick leave & that I can return as soon as I please & take command. I have hired his servant woman & her boy of about eleven for $15 per month. The wages are high, but then she is a good woman & it reassures us against any contingency. He will give me a list of his things for us to take what we want. He talked quite reasonably.

Lt. Thomas & I took tea with Lt. Mower & his wife. We were also invited to Capt. Caldwells. After tea we went there & stopped an hour.

Dr. King called & his daughter will go with me as far as Ft. Inge.[18] Capt.

Thomas was serving in Co. F of the 1st Infantry. In his journal, Heintzelman frequently complains of Thomas's constant procrastination and incompetence. Breveted a lieutenant-colonel during the Civil War, Thomas resigned from the army in May 1872 and died in 1882. Heitman, *Historical Register,* 953.

[17] William Shakespeare King had been a surgeon in the army since 1837. Heintzelman had met King in New Orleans in 1846 and in San Diego in 1852. It was King who cut the spent minie ball from Heintzelman's right arm on the field at First Bull Run on July 21, 1861. King retired from the Army in 1882 and died in August 1895. Heitman, *Historical Register,* 600; HJ, Dec. 30, 1846; Sept. 8, 24, 1852; Sept. 1, 1861.

A native of Ohio, James Nelson Caldwell was an 1836 West Point graduate and a captain in the 2d Infantry. During the Civil War, Caldwell was breveted a lieutenant colonel for gallantry at the Battle of Stone's River. He died in March 1886. Heitman, *Historical Register,* 273.

Joseph Anthony Mower had served as a private in the artillery during the Mexican War. By 1859 he had been promoted to 1st lieutenant in Co. A of the 1st Infantry. During the Civil War, he rose to the rank of major general of volunteers and was singled out for bravery at the battles of Farmington, Iuka, and Jackson, Mississippi; Fort de Russy, Louisiana; and Salkehatchie, Georgia. Heitman, *Historical Register,* 733.

[18] Established on March 13, 1849, on the left bank of the Leona River near Uvalde, Fort Inge helped to guard the San Antonio-El Paso Road or Lower Military Road. J. K. F. Mansfield to Lorenzo Thomas, Oct. 9, 1860, LR, AGO, RG 94 (NA); Thomas Tyree Smith, *Fort Inge: Sharps, Spurs, and Sabers on the Texas Frontier, 1849-1869* (Austin: Eakin Press, 1993), 115-128; Robert W. Frazer, *Forts of the West,*

McClay is there.[19]

We had a dust storm yesterday afternoon remaining me of Yuma.[20] It did not last long. We had a few drops of rain & some hail. The largest I ever saw. Two pieces were picked up were as [large as] hen's eggs. A calf got knocked down by one.

This morning is beautiful & not to[o] hot. The band is playing at guard mounting. It is a good one & makes it more pleasant here.

I will leave this evening for San Antonio.

San Antonio Texas Tues. May 10, 1859

I expected to leave Sun. eve. but there was every appearance of a storm & the driver came & proposed to wait for morning. As Miss King was going along I agreed. It soon blew some & looked threatening to the East. We called in at Dr. King's.

The driver called at daylight & I got up & sent to wake them at Dr. King's. I then went & took breakfast with Miss King & we were off at 20 min. of 5.

We had a delightful ride as far as the weather is concerned. It had rained hard along the road. There is now water at several more places & on the 35 mile [stretch]. We reached Ft. Inge at 1½ P.M—sixty miles. Miss King stopped there & I stayed & had breakfast with Capt. McClay & his wife. We reached the Sabinal at sunset & then stopped overnight.[21] I had a better place to sleep than at the other place on the road. Next morning we took breakfast & I got in there at sunset.

(Norman: University of Oklahoma Press, 1965), 152; Robert Wooster, *Soldiers, Sutlers, and Settlers: Garrison Life on the Texas Frontier* (College Station: Texas A&M University Press, 1987), 8–10.

[19] At Fort Inge, Robert P. Maclay commanded Company A of the 8th Infantry. Maclay, an 1840 West Point graduate, had fought in the Seminole War and was later wounded at Resaca de la Palma. He resigned in 1860, became a Louisiana planter, and eventually a Confederate brigadier general.

[20] While he was in the process of established Fort Yuma in 1850 and in the three years that followed, Heintzelman frequent wrote in his journal of the blistering heat and blinding dust storms, some of which flattened tents and made life miserable at the post. HJ, Mar. 28, 1852.

[21] Sabinal, on the east bank of the Sabinal River in eastern Uvalde Country, was originally named Patterson for John W. Patterson, who came to the area in 1852. In 1856, Capt. Albert Brackett established Camp Sabinal near the present town. Webb, Carroll, and Branda (eds.), *Handbook of Texas,*II: 523.

The stage left San Antonio early every Monday morning and arrived in Eagle Pass Wednesday afternoon. J. De Cordova, *Texas: Her Resources and Her Public Men* (Waco: Texian Press, 1969), 197.

I met the Camels encamped near the road, three miles this side Sabinal. They were packed ready to start—at 7 A.M.[22] I got a letter from Dr. Tripler. He has the wine & some from Clark.[23] He has shipped the balance of it & also sent the cavalry floats.

The weather was pleasant yesterday. On this trip I have not suffered either with heat or dust. It was quite pleasant this morning.

I got letters from Solon. He still writes about Mr. Wrightson.[24] He does not get along well.

Gen. Twiggs is not so well again. Margaret was going out to Mrs. Chilton's. At 9 P.M. Major Graham & I went for the Ladies.[25] Mrs. G. was sick in bed. The sniffels with sick head aches & neuralgia.

After breakfast I went out & called on Mrs. Barton & stopped to see my watch—called at the Adjt. Genl's, saw Capts. Blair & Vinton & rode with him to the General's & left my card & then went with V. to his house.[26] I called at Dr. Howard's.[27] My things have not left the coast yet. Capt. Reynolds has

---

[22] These were camels out of Camp Verde. See note 9, June 1859 chapter.

[23] In 1852, Fort Clark had been established on the west bank of Los Moros Creek at present-day Bracketville to guard the San Antonio–El Paso Road. Mansfield to Thomas, Dec. 1, 1860, LR, AGO, RG 94 (NA); Caleb Pirtle III and Michael F.Cussack, *The Lonely Sentinel, Fort Clark: On Texas's Western Frontier* (Austin: Eakin Press, 1985), 15–16; Dorman H. Winfrey, "Fort Clark," *Frontier Forts of Texas* (Waco: Texian Press, 1968), 173–184; Wooster, *Soldiers, Sutlers, and Settlers*, 8–10

[24] Thomas and William Wrightson were mining partners who published the *Railroad Record* that advocated western railroad expansion. Along with Heintzelman, William was an original incorporator of the Sonora Exploring and Mining Company, which had been incorporated under the laws of Ohio as a joint-stock company with capital stock listed at $2 million, divided into 20,000 shares of $100 each. In 1858, William became secretary of a subsidiary company, the Santa Rita Silver Mining Company, to develop the silver mines in the Santa Rita Mountains south of Tucson. Along with Heintzelman, Thomas served as a board member of the new company. From the time Heintzelman was elected president of the Sonora Exploring and Mining Company, his correspondence with the Wrightson became extensive. North, *Samuel Peter Heintzelman*, 28–29, 39, 44–47.

[25] From Washington, D.C., 1st Lt. William Montrose Graham commanded Co. M of the 1st Artillery. S. P. Heintzelman, "Return of the Troops of the Brownsville Expedition, Dec. 14, 1859, HP.

[26] This was the wife of Seth Maxwell Barton, 1849 West Point graduate and captain in the 1st Infantry.

[27] From Heintzelman's journal and other sources it appears that Dr. Howard was a civilian physician residing in San Antonio. Although seven males with the name of Howard were living in Bexar County in 1860, none are listed as physicians. The same is true of the six males with surnames of Howard listed on the census of 1850. Since he mentions "Dr. Howard" in reference to his baggage having not left the coast, the indi-

gone north as a witness. I wrote to Lt. Shaaf. I also received my orders and wrote to Col. Morris & sent him a list of the things we will take. The General says I can stay a month if I like. Vinton told him I wanted to stop a few days.

The weather was delightful this morn, but now is warm. I met Brucknow this morning.[28] Lathrop writes that he was drunk for the last three months & Methner too, only the latter could hold more.[29] I got a letter from Dennis Meade who lives near town.[30]

San Antonio Texas Thurs. May 12, 1859

Cool & pleasant in the morning, but hot in the middle of the day. We went & spent last evening at Dr. Jarvis's. They sent after the children. We called in the afternoon on Mrs. Williams & Mrs. Vinton & Mrs. Blair at the latters.

I saw Capt. McLean & he will let us have a pair of mules to drive whilst we stay here. The horse is still quite stiff.

I went to the offices, but everybody had left but Capt. Blair & I there met Dr. Jarvis.

Dr. Burns has been acquitted by the court, but the Sec. is very severe on him. Lt. Caleb Smith of the 2 Infy was dismissed, but restored.[31] He is Extra Billy Smith's nephew.

San Antonio Texas Fri. May 13, 1859

Tolerably pleasant. I got last night a letter from Mr. Wrightson enclosing

---

vidual may be George Thomas Howard, a leading San Antonio freight operator. 7th and 8th Census, Bexar County. See note 36, this chapter.

[28] Born in Berlin around 1830, Frederick Brunckow, thirty-nine and a graduate of the Royal Mining Academy at Freiburg, Saxony, was a mining engineer for the Sonora Exploring and Mining Company. Once a shingle maker in New Braunfels, Texas, it was Brunckow who named the Heintzelman Mine near Cerro Colorado after Samuel Peter and who became administrator of the mine. The Prussian is listed on the 1860 census at the San Pedro Mines near what became Tombstone, Arizona. Thrapp, *Frontier Biography*, I: 183–184; 8th Census, Arizona County, New Mexico Territory.

[29] Theodore Methner, an assistant of Brunckow, was in charge of smelting operations for the Sonora Exploring and Mining Company. North, *Samuel Peter Heintzelman*, 101.

[30] Dennis Meade, a resident of San Antonio, had been contacted by Charles Poston about the possibility of taking charge of the Stephenson Mine in the Organ Mountains near Las Cruces, New Mexico Territory. Meade, in turn, had contacted Heintzelman. A Deronis Mead, Irish-born and forty-two, is listed on the 1850 Bexar County census.

[31] Second Lt. Caleb Smith, a Virginian in the 2d Infantry, resigned in May 1861 to become a colonel in the Virginia Infantry. He died in December 1874.

copies of letters from Colt, Poston & Howe about a nefarious scheme of Colt's to absorb all ($800,000) of Sonora stock by him at a nominal price.[32] I wrote to Wrightson & Poston.[33] he matter is well understood & he will be prevented I hope. I met Schuchard, who came from New Braunfels to see me.[34] He tells me that the drafts of the company given him were returned— on the 17th Apl. Colt had agreed to attend to them. He has done all in his

---

[32] In Washington in December 1857, Capt. William W. Chapman introduced Heintzelman to Samuel Colt, the well-known firearms inventor and manufacturer. The two men had spent an entire evening together and Heintzelman persuaded Colt to invest $10,000 in the Sonora Exploring and Mining Company. He is "quite taken with our mining co.," Heintzelman confided in his journal. In early January 1858, Heintzelman accompanied Colt to his home in Hartford, Connecticut, to inspect the arms works. Colt later gave Heintzelman a small pistol that Samuel Peter carried with him to Arizona later in the year. Much to Heintzelman's regret, however, Colt became the largest stockholder in the company and was elected president in April 1859. See also HJ, Dec. 19–21, 1857; Jan. 1, 2, 3, 17, Apr. 6, 10, 12, 13, 1858.

[33] Charles Debrille Poston, thirty-nine, a Kentucky politician and adventurer, became known as the "Father of Arizona." Poston was instrumental in the location and development of Colorado City (present-day Yuma) when Samuel Peter was in command of Fort Yuma in 1854. Poston also assisted in organizing the Sonora Exploring and Mining Company. From May 1855 until late 1860, Heintzelman corresponded frequently with Poston. Later Poston leased the mines from the company for ten years for $25,000. At the beginning of the Civil War, Poston's brother, John, was killed by Mexican laborers, whereupon Charles fled to Fort Yuma, and the properties of both the Sonora Exploring and Mining Company and the Santa Rita Silver Mining Company were abandoned. After Colt's death in 1862, the mines and property were sold. In the meantime, Lincoln had appointed Poston as the territory's first superintendent of Indian affairs. He was also elected as Arizona's first delegate to Congress. Poston later held a number of jobs in the territory and died in poverty in a Phoenix hovel in 1902. 8th Census, Arizona County, New Mexico Territory; North *Samuel Peter Heintzelman*, 15–20, 32, 172–85; Sacks, *Be It Enacted*, 8–12, 47–61, 81–91, 104–109. Henry Howe was an Ohio investor in the Sonora Exploring and Mining Company.

[34] Charles Schuchard, German mining engineer and artist, along with Brunckow, had located the silver mines in the Santa Rita Mountains and at Cerro Colorado in 1857. In 1852, Schuchard had served as artist for Andrew B. Gray's survey for the prospective route along the thirty-second parallel for the Texas Western Railroad. In 1858, Schuchard, who had been in the California Gold Rush, was in charge of the Arenias Mine, one-half mile north of Arivaca. Schuchard traveled east with Heintzelman on the Butterfield Stage in January 1859 to settle in Texas and raise sheep near Fredericksburg. Still interested in mining, he was manager of the Corralitos Mining Company when he died in Mexico City on May 4, 1883. Thrapp, *Frontier Biography*, 3: 1277; Kathleen Doherty, "Carl Schuchard," in *New Handbook of Texas*, eds. Ron C. Tyler, et al., (6 vols.; Austin: Texas State Historical Association, 1997), V, 929.

power to discredit the company, so as to enable him to absorb the unsold stock & then control the company. I think that he will fail.

We took a ride out to the "Cavalyada," but the horses were out.[35] The foundered one will not be fit to ride for some time.

SAN ANTONIO TEXAS SAT. MAY 14, 1859

I went out this morning & got my watch from the watchmakers, where it has been some time. I hope that now it is in order & will not stop. He showed me what was the matter. He says it is an excellent watch & cheap.

I stopped at Howard & Ogdens.[36] They say on account of the bad roads our things will not be here until 12 days, or about the 19th. One of the firm got a telegraph from Colt, to purchase wagons & oxen, to I suppose sent goods to the mines. There is a prospect of some thing being done.

Gen. Twiggs is better to-day. I went to the offices but it was too late—everybody nearly was gone.

Major Chilton came with his wife & we rode with them to see an old mission about three miles from here on the San Pedro.[37] It is old & very much dilapidated.

SAN ANTONIO, TEXAS SUN. MAY 15, 1859

Rather a pleasant day, though still warm. I wrote to Col. Morris & prepared a letter for Col. Colt, telling him some truths. I will send a copy to Wrightson.

---

[35] A caballeriza is a horse corral or stable.

[36] George Thomas Howard and Duncan Charles Ogden ran a freighting operation between Indianola and San Antonio. At one time during the 1850s, Howard and Ogden were said to have had 800 teams on the road between the coast and the Alamo City. Ogden died in San Antonio on March 10, 1859. His wife, Mary, thirty, was one of the wealthiest widows in San Antonio. San Antonio *Daily Herald*, Mar. 12, 1859; 8th Census, Bexar County; Howard Lackman, "George Thomas Howard: Texas Frontiersman," (Ph.D. diss., University of Texas at Austin, 1954), 304.

[37] Maj. Robert Hall Chilton, an 1837 West Point graduate, was serving as paymaster in San Antonio in 1859. A Virginian, he resigned in April 1861 to become a brigadier general and chief of staff to Gen. Robert E. Lee. In 1864, however, he was released from duty at his own request. Chilton died in February 1879. Warner, *Generals in Gray*, 49.

The mission was probably Nuestra Señora de la Purisima Concepción de Acuña, established on the east bank of the San Antonio River in 1731, a few miles south of San Antonio. Felix D. Almaraz Jr. to the Editor, Dec. 20, 1992, in editor's possession.

S. ANTONIO TEXAS MON. MAY 16, 1859

We sent out this morning to make some purchases. The Gen. is worse & I fear will never recover.

S. ANTONIO TEXAS TUES. MAY 17, 1859

In the afternoon we took a ride. In the evening Dr. & Mrs. Jarvis called. I went out this morning & paid the purchases we made. I then went to the offices & saw Vinton. He will give me all the transportation he can. I drew pay for Apl. $229—from Maj. Cunningham.[38]

It has not been quite so hot as usual.

I got a letter from Mr. Lathrop dated May 1st. All goes on well. He sent me a newspaper & from it I learn the Indians stole eight mules from us. He dont speak very favorably of Wrightson & says he talks of returning home. Donaldson the Collector appears to have discovered some old mines in the mountains east of C. Colorado.[39]

WED. MAY 18, 1859

This is quite a warm day. I was out all the morning. Margaret & I went & did some shopping. After we thought we had everything, still something else is wanted.

Small hopes of the General's recovery.

Lt. Walter Jones of the 1st Infy arrived yesterday from Washington on his way to his post.[40]

I heard from Col. Morris. He has sold most of his furniture & has now decided not to let us have his servants. This is too provoking after offering them & I had hired them. I will at this late day be difficult for us to hire any one.

I got a letter from T. Wrightson, enclosing one from Mr. Poston. Colt has been in N.Y. & nothing done. We must have a stockholders meeting to curb him.

---

[38] Francis A. Cunningham had been promoted to major and made paymaster in 1849. Leaving the army in 1863, Cunningham died in August 1864. Heitman, *Historical Register*, 345.

[39] Kentucky-born John Donaldson, twenty, was collector of customs at Calabasas on the Mexican border south of Tubac where he lived with his Mexican wife, Griselda Gonzales, eighteen. 8th Census, Arizona County, New Mexico Territory.

[40] Walter Jones had been promoted to first lieutenant in the 1st Infantry in 1857. Resigning in May 1861, Jones became a captain in the Confederate Army. Heitman, *Historical Register*, 582.

I am going out to see David Meade & shall see Chas. Anderson.[41] I saw Brucknow & he showed me a letter declining the services of Ohnesinger.

SAN ANTONIO TEXAS FRI. MAY 20, 1859

Yesterday we went out shopping & I then went to the offices. To-day did the same. Gen. Twiggs is much better to-day, but still little hope of his recovery.

Ice is in town to-day. I was invited with some gentlemen to take a Julep at Mr. Howards—H. & Ogden's store.

I walked up to Major Vinton's last evening. We took a short ride yesterday afternoon. I also wrote to Solon. I got a letter from Col. Morris. He wont now hire his servants & has sold most of his furniture. We are trying to find a woman here.

Dr. King is ordered to Utah & Dr. Foard goes to Duncan. Unjust to Dr. King.[42] Very warm.

S. AN. SUN. MAY 22, 1859

Yesterday was a little warmer than usual. The General was much better yesterday though the Doctor dont have much hope. I wrote to Dr. Tripler.

---

[41] Charles Anderson, a Kentucky lawyer, first came to Texas in 1858 and returned the following year with his family to buy a horse ranch near San Antonio. A Unionist, Anderson was arrested and imprisoned in 1861, but escaped to the North where he commanded the 93rd Ohio Infantry during the war. He became governor of Ohio in 1868. Webb, Carroll, and Branda (eds.), *Handbook of Texas*, I: 44; San Antonio *Alamo Express*, Nov. 30, 1860.

[42] From Milledgeville, Georgia, Andrew Jackson Foard, an assistant surgeon since May 1853, arrived in Texas one day after the Heintzelmans. At Camp Verde, Foard and Heintzelman became close friends. During the secessionist crisis in early 1861, however, at which time both men were in Washington, Heintzelman tried repeatedly to persuade Foard to remain loyal to the Union. Heintzelman's journal entries indicate a growing disappointment with Foard. He is "foolish and will regret it," Heintzelman wrote. "I am very much disappointed in his character," he recorded on another occasion. Able to persuade Foard to recall his letter of resignation, Foard nevertheless left on leave for Georgia and Alabama. "He does not come up to the standards of a high toned man," Heintzelman again wrote. After the fall of Fort Sumter, Heintzelman received a letter from the surgeon at which time he wrote only: "I presume he has resigned." Foard has indeed resigned and went on to become a surgeon in the Confederate Army. The two men resumed their antebellum friendship when Foard contacted Heintzelman a few months after the conclusion of the war hoping to rejoin the Federal army. Foard left Georgia for New York in September 1865 but later returned to Milledgeville where he died in 1867. Heitman, *Historical Register*, 426. See also San Antonio *Daily Herald*, May 4, 1859; HJ, Mar. 23, 24, 26, 28, Apr., 15, 1861; Aug. 16, Sept. 26, Nov. 18, Dec. 28, 1865.

The Mex. carts arrived in the morning. Now if the wagon comes we can start. It must be here & we must try & get off Tues. We spent the evening at Dr. Jarvis's. We took a ride in the afternoon.

In the afternoon I got another letter from Wrightson enclosing a letter from Poston with the Resolutions of the Ex. Com. about a loan & Howe's reply. It is an ingenious plan of Colts to swindle all the stockholders.

I have a severe attack of rheumatism in my left big toe.

MONDAY SAN ANTONIO TEXAS MAY 23, 1859

A pleasant breeze to-day. The Gen. is better, but there are still doubts. I cant wear my boots to-day & have had to use the carriage. I have been busy in the final preparations for a start tomorrow. I wrote to Poston & Mr. Howe. We must try & head Colt.

I expect to have plenty of transportation. Warm this evening.

FT. DUNCAN TEXAS SUN. MAY 29, 1859

Monday evening Dr. Jarvis & Capt. McLean called.[43] Next day, Tuesday, the wagons made their appearance. As soon as we got breakfast I saw & loaded the Ambulance & went & got a box with our sheets etc. & a roll of bedding from the other wagons & started them. I left my horses with the Qr M's cavallada. We then loaded up our Ambulance & got off at 10½ A.M.

We rode to Castroville, 26 miles & staid overnight. I bathed my foot & relieved it very much. The house is clean, but table mean. The weather was a little warm, but a good breeze & no dust. We started after breakfast & drove to the Seco, 24 m. where we encamped.[44] Pleasant.

Thursday we drove to Ft. Inge, 28 m. & encamped on the river Leona, just below the post.[45] We intended stopping at the Frio but there was no good shade.[46] I there met the stage & they told me better go on to Inge & that Lt.

---

[43] Eugene Eckel McLean, West Point class of 1842, was serving in San Antonio as an assistant quartermaster. While serving at Fort Yuma, the temperamental McLean had once complained of Heintzelman's favoritism toward Lt. George Stoneman. McLean resigned in April 1861 to join the Confederate Army where he become a quartermaster. Heitman, *Historical Register*, 675. See also HJ, Jan. 30, 1854, May 25, 1855; San Antonio *Daily Herald*, Apr. 30, 1859.

[44] Usually dry as the name indicates, Seco Creek rises in northwestern Medina County and flows southeast past D'Hanis, some forty-five miles into Hondo Creek in northern Frio County. Webb, Carroll, and Branda (eds.), *Handbook of Texas*, II, 588.

[45] The Leona River rises in central Uvalde County and flows southeast some seventy-one miles to empty into the Frio River a few miles north of Dilley in southern Frio County.

[46] The Frio River rises on the southern edge of the Edwards Plateau in northern

Col. Morris & his family were there. They only staid till they got dinner & drove on. We went up in the evening & took breakfast with them next day. They called on us.

We then met more Mexicans with an Indian scalp & a woman prisoner. This was all they saw & the man a Reserve Indian & one engaged in murdering a man on the Frio, about a mile above the road a few days ago.

From Ft. Inge we took an escort of six men. Friday we went 17 miles to Turkey Creek & encamped.[47] Here is the last house on the road to Ft. Duncan.

Sat. left at 6½ & drove to Soladito, 23 m. & stopped & fed.[48] After a rest of 5 hours, at 4 P.M. started & reached here at 8½ P.M.

As soon as we drove into the post we met Capt. Caldwell who kindly invited us into his house & I left Margaret & Mary there & we went & put our things into the comdg. officers qrs.[49] We took tea at Capt. Caldwell's & then went & prepared for the night. Lt. Thomas has had the quarters white washed & scrubbed, making them habitable.

Margaret was quite sick & felt very badly. She is much better & pretty well pleased with the prospect. Our wagons won't be here for two or three days yet & of course we can't do much towards getting settled. We take our meals still at Capt. Caldwell's.

Lt. Washington leaves this evening to go to San Antonio to relieve Capt. Withers the a. adjt. genl. who gets married & goes on four month's leave.[50] I went to the office & had to assume command to issue the necessary orders.

Real County and flows southeast and east some two hundred miles to join the Nueces River near what is today the town of Three Rivers. Webb, Carroll, and Branda (eds.), *Handbook of Texas*, I, 650.

[47] Turkey Creek rises in east-central Kinney County south of Turkey Mountain and flows fifty-four miles through southwestern Uvalde County, past the present-day village of Blewett, to join Comanche Creek in southwestern Zavala County.

[48] Soladito is possibly a tributary of Solado Creek in northwestern Maverick County.

[49] Established on May 27, 1849, on the left bank of the Rio Grande at Eagle Pass to guard the Mexican border, Fort Duncan was just upriver from where the old Camino Real crossed the Rio Grande. Wooster, *Soldiers, Sutlers, and Settlers*, 8–11. Rosella A. Sellers, "The History of Fort Duncan, Eagle Pass, Texas" (M.A. thesis, Sul Ross College, 1960), 15. For Heintzelman being ordered to Fort Duncan, see Special Orders no. 34, May 11, 1859, HP.

[50] Thornton Augustin Washington, an 1849 graduate of West Point, was serving as regimental adjutant of the 1st Infantry. Washington had arrived in San Antonio after a lengthy leave in the east. A native of Virginia, he resigned in 1861 to join the Confederate Army. While Heintzelman was in Galveston in 1867, he received a letter from Washington saying that he was "without a dollar & without property." The

The thermometer is 94°, though it does not feel very warm. Dr. King leaves as soon as the wagons get up. We expect to buy a few of his things & will probably take his servant girl. There is also a black woman to hire, but she has several children.

Wrote to T. Wrightson, Cin.

Ft. Duncan Texas Tues. May 31, 1859

Yesterday the mer. rose to 106° in the shade. We were at work all the forenoon at various matters about the house. At noon the wagons arrived. Almost everything they brought got wet in the Mex. carts in coming from the coast. We opened everything. One of my portfolios is utterly ruined. My new saddle & bridle nearly so & our beautiful illustrated bible got wet. My n. hat & dry goods generally. We will estimate the damage & try & get some pay for it. The box we had to use on the road was wet & everything very badly damaged.

In the forenoon Dr. King had an auction & sold most of his things. They generally sold very low. We bought a walnut dining table before the auction for $12. At auction I bought his poney for $20 & saddle for $10. The poney is thin, has hurt his foot & is 15 years old. He asked me $30.

The band gave us a serenade last night. They play very well.

This morning we have a fine breeze. I had the carpenter here to repair the bureau & little work stand. The former got wet & both are broken. Much of our crockery is broken & the most valuable pieces. It was badly packed.

All the officers & ladies of the post called & Mrs. Colqueen the Sutler's wife.[51]

---

unemployed Washington pleaded for "some situation in which he [could] earn an honest living." Heintzelman confided in his journal that Washington's plight was "a sad confession" but "results of treason." A month later, Washington found employment in Baltimore. He died in July 1894. Heitman, *Historical Register*, 1007; HJ, Mar. 10, Apr. 24, 1867.

[51] English-born Frances Colquohn, forty-eight, was the wife of Ludovic Colquohn (Colquhoun, Coloquhoun), fifty-six, who had represented Bexar in the Senate of the Republic of Texas and who had been taken prisoner by Gen. Adrian Woll in 1842, imprisoned at Mexico City, and later at Perote, before being released in April 1845. By 1859, Colquohn had become the sutler at Fort Duncan. He died between April 1882 and April 1883. Ben E. Pingenot (ed.), *Paso del Aguila: A Chronicle of Frontier Days on the Texas Border as Recorded in the Memoirs of Jesse Sumpter* (Austin: Encino Press, 1969), 98; Thomas W. Cutrer, "Ludovic Colquhoun," in *New Handbook of Texas*, eds. Tyler, et al., I, 231–232; HJ, May 15, 31, 1866; *Alamo Express* (San Antonio), Feb. 8, 1861; 7th Census, Bexar County; 8th Census, Atascosa County.

"This is one of the pleasantest places in Texas."

------◆·●◆·●◆------

FT. DUNCAN TEX. WED. JUNE 1, 1859

We had a fine breeze all day yesterday & not so warm as the day before. In the evening we went to a little dance given by Lt. Thomas & Briggs at their quarters.[1] It passed off pleasantly. This morning Dr. King & his family left. Lt. Briggs went along & Lt. Thomas will start this evening in the stage to visit S. Antonio. Before they left the Doctor received a copy of the order breaking up this post, with many other changes. The impression is that the Head Quarters of the Regt. will go to S. Antonio. The Dept. order has not been received yet. We have commenced packing. I will be well satisfied if we go to S. Antonio as I must confess I do not like this post, although it is called the finest post in Texas.

FORT DUNCAN TEX. TUES. JUNE 2, 1859

Not so warm to-day as it has been. Mer. 95°. We yesterday put the house in some kind of order & it looks much better. I finished my shower bath & tried it this afternoon. It works quite well. Lt. Thomas left in the stage last evening to be gone a fortnight.

Wrote to Mr. Lathrop.

FT. DUNCAN TEX. SAT. JUNE 4, 1859

Yesterday we packed some. In the afternoon we got a couple of mules & took a ride. We made a circuit of 8 or 10 miles & made a call on Mrs. Colqueen. Not a blade of green grass to be seen.

---

[1] Herman Biggs, not Briggs, an 1855 West Point graduate, was in Capt. James Nelson Caldwell's Company A of the 1st Infantry. During the Civil War, Biggs became a brigadier general of volunteers. He died in October 1887. Heitman, *Historical Register*, 218, Post Returns, Camp Verde, AGO, RG 393 (NA).

An express got in at noon with orders for this company & Head Quarters to move to Camp Verde. This is one of the pleasantest places in Texas. There are gardens, grass, vegetables & springs, with a stream of water close to the quarters. The quarters are pretty good, though limited. To-day mer. 96°. Yesterday was not so warm & the pleasantest day we have passed here.

The order breaking up the post has created great excitement amongst the Mexicans on both sides of the river.

This morning the stage came & brought Lts. Thomas & Biggs. The wagons for our move will be in in two or three days. We will leave as soon as they come. We packed some more to-day. We intent to do it quietly. The worst will be the crockery.

I got a paper from Lathrop. The Sta. Rita Co. has commenced smelting. I got a letter from Mr. Howe. Wrightson has gone to see Poston in N.Y. We are trying to head Colt.

Dr. King & his family were overturned on the Leona at Ft. Inge but no one seriously injured.

Major Van Dorn had another fight with Indians near old Ft. Atkinson & out of 100, killed 49 & took 35 prisoners. Capt. E. R. Smith & Lt. Lee 2 Cav. badly wounded. One Sergt. killed & some half dozen men wounded.[2]

Ft. Duncan Texas Sun. June 5, 1859

Mer. today at 98°. We have a fine breeze. This morning at inspection I went & looked at the company quarters. The dirt floor & bunks reminded me much of Yuma. It is not surprising that soldiers at such frontier stations dont reenlist. I also went to the Qr.M. store. It is filled with an accumulation of trash.

Ft. Duncan Tex. Tues. June 7, 1859

Yesterday we had considerable wind. Our wagons which went with Col. Morris returned & this morning we loaded & sent them off with the Band to S. Antonio. Lt. Briggs went with them.

Yesterday afternoon we drove over into Mexico as far as the Escondido. The river is a pretty little stream. The town of Piedras Negras, opposite here is a miserable Mexican town. The Rio Grande is as muddy as can be. On our return we stopped at Major Colqueens & took tea. All the garrison were

---

[2] In a vicious confrontation with Comanches under Buffalo Hump in the Battle of Crooked Creek, about fifteen miles south of Fort Atkinson in Nebraska Territory on May 13, 1859, Capt. Edmund Kirby Smith was wounded in the thigh and Lt. Fitzhugh Lee was shot in the breast. Utley, *Frontiersmen in Blue*, 134–135.

invited, but none of the Caldwells or Lt. Mower's family attended. Mr. & Mrs. Ryan, citizens outside, were there.[3]

To-day windy & Mer. 94°. We are tired waiting for the wagons.

FT. DUNCAN TEXAS JUNE 8, 1859 WED.

Very warm yesterday afternoon. We took a ride with four mules—they work well. After tea went to Caldwells. This morning cool & pleasant. The wagons have gone via Ft. Clark & will not be here under a couple of days.

FT. DUNCAN TEXAS FRI. JUNE 10, 1859

The wagons arrived (9) at 12 to-day. We have nearly finished packing & leave tomorrow. It has been quite warm. Lt. Thomas left in the stage last night for S. Antonio.

CAMP VERDE TEXAS SUN. JUNE 19, 1859

We left Ft. Duncan on Saturday at 2 P.M. & with few regrets.[4] We took a water wagon to the Chacon.[5] We reached there at Sundown & the wagons an hour later.

The next day we stopped at Turkey Creek.

The third day at Ft. Inge. Here we got forage & hard bread. Dr. Brodie & Lt. Hazen went to Capt. Wither's wedding at S. Antonio.[6] Mary fell into the river.

---

[3] This was P. Ryan, forty, an Irish-born merchant, and his wife Alicia, twenty-five. 8th Census, Maverick County.

[4] In response to Special Order no. 39, Heintzelman reported to the adjutant general from Fort Duncan on June 11, 1859: "I have this day abandoned this post." Only an ordnance sergeant and ten men remained at the post to guard the buildings and public property. Heintzelman to Samuel Cooper, June 11, 1859, LR, AGO, RG 94 (NA).

[5] Chacon, a stage stand twenty-five miles northeast of Fort Duncan, was at the crossing of Chacon Creek. Chacon Creek rises in eastern Maverick County and flows into Comanche Creek west of present-day Crystal City in Zavala County. Lipan Apache had attacked a supply train at the crossing in 1853. Pingenot, *Paso del Aguila*, 16.

[6] From South Carolina, Robert Little Brodie had been an assistant surgeon in the army since May 1854. He resigned in May 1861 to become a surgeon in the Confederate Army. Heitman, *Historical Register*, 247. William Babcock "Wild Bill" Hazen, West Point Class of 1855, was a second lieutenant in command of Company F of the 8th Infantry at Fort Inge. Twenty-nine at the time, Hazen was breveted a first lieutenant for gallantry in two engagements with Indians (probably Kickapoo) on the headwaters of the Nueces River on May 20 and again on September 30, 1859. Hazen later commanded a regiment at Shiloh and gained acclaim for his stand with "Hazen's

The fourth day brought us to the Sabinal.

The fifth day we encamped at Verde Creek near the Hondo.[7]

The sixth day we encamped two miles before we got to Bandera.[8] We intended to stop at the cotton woods, but missed them.

The seventh day we got here about 9 A.M. & the wagons about 11 on Friday the 17th.[9]

Lt. Graham of the Arty was absent at S. Antonio at the wedding. We found the quarters dirty & dilapidated. We selected the quarters built by Capt. Palmer & just vacated by Mrs. Simmons (Dr.)[10]

Brigade" at Stone's River. As a major general, he commanded the 15th Corps in Sherman's March to the Sea. After the war, Hazen authored several books on tactics and taught at West Point. He also served with equal distinction in the West from 1866 until his death in January 1887. Smith, *Fort Inge*, 117–118; San Antonio *Daily Herald*, May 31, Oct. 16, 1858; Hazen to Jno. Withers, Dec. 20, 1858, LR, AGO, RG 94 (NA); *Daily True Delta* (New Orleans), Oct. 29, Dec. 16, 1859; Marvin E. Kroeker, "William B. Hazen," *Soldiers West: Military Biographies from the Military Frontier*, ed. Paul Andrew Hutton (Lincoln: University of Nebraska Press, 1987), 193–212; William B. Hazen, *A Narrative of Military Service* (Huntington, W.Va.: Blue Acorn Press, 1933). For Withers, see note 9, May 1859 chapter.

[7] Verde Creek rises in three branches eight miles north of present-day Hondo in Medina County. Intermittent in its upper reaches, it runs southeast for twenty and a half miles to its mouth on Hondo Creek, four miles west of Hondo. Hondo Creek runs southeast for sixty-seven miles through Bandera, Medina, and Frio counties to the Frio River, five miles northeast of what is today Pearsall. Tyler, et al. (eds.), *New Handbook of Texas*, VI, 723; III, 682.

[8] Bandera, the county seat of Bandera County, had been established on the north bank of the Medina River in 1853. Two years later, a group of Polish families came to work in the sawmill there. In 1860 "Bandera City" boasted of a population of 197. Webb, Carroll, and Branda (eds.), *Handbook of Texas*, I, 105; 8th Census, Bandera County.

[9] Camp Verde had been established on July 8, 1856, on the north bank of Verde Creek, north of Bandera Pass in Kerr County. Sometimes called "Little Egypt," Camp Verde was the headquarters for seventy-four camels sent by Secretary of War Jefferson Davis. Albert Sidney Johnston had previously commanded the post. In the heart of the Texas Hill Country, with abundant water, shade, and mild summers, the post was one of the most desirable in Texas, if not the entire trans-Mississippi. J. Marvin Hunter, *Old Camp Verde, the Home of the Camels: A Romantic Story of Jefferson Davis' Plan to Use Camels on the Texas Frontier* (Bandera: Frontier Times, 1936); Post Returns, Camp Verde, AGO, RG 393 (NA).

[10] Innis Newton Palmer was an 1846 graduate of West Point. A captain in the 2d Cavalry, Palmer was in charge of the camels at Camp Verde. Chris Emmett, *Texas Camel Tales* (Austin: Steck-Vaughn, 1969), 64–74, 111.

Along with Lt. Col. Robert E. Lee, Heintzelman had served on the court-martial at Fort Riley in October and November 1855 that found Dr. James Simons guilty

I had two rooms scrubbed out & borrowed bedsteads from the Hospital & we did pretty well. Yesterday we continued our arrangements & begin to feel comfortable. We bought a wild Turkey & have had some beef. Lts. Graham & Biggs got back yesterday. The Band & Lt. Thomas will probably not leave yet until tomorrow, if then. Wagons are scarce.

The train left this morning. I ordered our four wagons to haul our things left at Duncan.

The weather here is delightful compared with Duncan & country green. The last two days we rode through a beautiful country. The Mer. has been 96° but there is a fine breeze & no dust.

We had a wild turkey for dinner, but the flies were so bad we could scarcely eat it. We had our table outside & had to move into the house & shut the door.

We saw several wild Turkeys on the road, but could not get a shot at one. A man brought in two shot near here. I paid 50 cts for a hen. The beef it is said has the black tongue & we are rather afraid to eat it.

Camp Verde Texas Mon. June 20, 1859

Weather pleasant. I went this morning with Lt. Graham & examined all the post. Many things are out of repair but I hope to make every one comfortable. The garden dont look very promising.

Lt. Biggs' wagon is in from S. Antonio. I got a letter from Lt. Shaaff, with bill of charges on a box.

Camp Verde Texas Tues. June 21, 1859

Much warmer to-day than yesterday. We cleaned out the hall, white washed & scrubbed it & to-day dined there. I have at last set to work to write letters & wrote yesterday to Burgess & to-day to Lathrop, Wrightson, Poston & to Lt. Washington sending the latter some accounts to get paid & send to Wrightson to pay Cheever's protested draft.[11] It is now 5 P.M. raining.

Camp Verde Tex. Wed. June 22, 1859

It only rained a few drops. We took a short ride. To-day not quite so warm as yesterday. I wrote to Sister Maria.

---

of leaving his post in the midst of a smallpox epidemic. Dismissed, Simons was reinstated in October 1856 and went on to become a lieutenant colonel of surgery. Simons died in November 1885. Heitman, *Historical Register*, 888; HJ, Oct. 29–31, Nov. 1–10, 1855.

    [11] Benjamin Harrison Cheever was a director of the Sonora Exploring and Mining

CAMP VERDE TEX. THURS. JUNE 23RD

We went out & took a ride to the saw mill below 4 miles, no water & no lumber. At tattoo Dr. Foard & Lt. Thomas arrived & the Band soon after. Gen. Twiggs is much better. There is no other news.

CAMP VERDE TEXAS FRI. JUNE 24, 1859

Our mail got in. I wrote to Capt. McLean & will send him the harness he loaned me by the wagons that brought up the Band.

I also got a printed resolution of the Board of Directors of the 3rd of June calling a stock holder's meeting in Cin. to authorize the sale of stock at less than par & an additional 50 percent to stock holders at $10 per share, one half in 60 days & the other in 4 mos.

CAMP VERDE TEXAS SAT. JUNE 25, 1859

The mail left this morning & the teams that brought up the Band. They took down Mrs. Dr. Simmon's things to S.A. We kept a meat safe & round table.

Lt. Mower left yesterday morning for S. Antonio.

My right foot now has been lame for several days. I put on my boots this afternoon for the first time.

I have spent the most of my time in reading the newspapers, with the first accounts of the war in Europe.[12]

CAMP VERDE TEXAS WED. JUNE 29, 1859

The weather has been pleasant. Yesterday morning we had a little rain early in the forenoon then a very hard one then again later & off & on all night. It is still quite showry this morning. It has been threatening rain for several days. We have not enough for once. I yesterday dug up a few square feet in the yard & sowed some lettuce seed & some tomatoe in a box. If we can get a few plants to grow we will have all the tomatoes we want.

We got the office moved yesterday from my quarters & are trying to put the room in order. We went for lumber & got a few hundred feet, only 450 & that the man had to wait to have sawed.

Company, the Sopori Land and Mining Company, and the Arizona Land and Mining Company. Heintzelman's journals make frequent reference to Cheever. North, *Samuel Peter Heintzelman*, 61.

Burgess is probably an executive or stockholder of the Sonora Exploring and Mining Company.

The children commenced their lessons yesterday. It was hard work. They do better to-day.

We tried our "sewing machine." At first we could not thread the needles, but now I can sew pretty well.

CAMP VERDE TEXAS THURS. JUNE 30, 1859

It rained all day yesterday & in the night 4 3/4 inches of rain fell. We had muster this morning. It was muddy enough. I have sent to Howard & Ogden a list of articles damaged in the transportation from Indianola & also a list of articles we want.

[12] Heintzelman is referring to the War of Piedmont and France against Austria.

❧ July 1859 ❧

"Mer. over 100°."

─•─•─•─

CAMP VERDE TEXAS FRI. JULY 1ST, 1859

It is pleasant & mud drying fast. Lt. Hazen arrived yesterday and our court met this morning. I had all the officers in to lunch or rather cake, wine & whiskey.

The mail got in at 2 P.M. I got another circular from Mr. Poston via Camp Cooper & a letter from Cheever. He makes a lame excuse for not paying his note. He complains of Colt.

I got only a Harper's Weekly. Lt. Biggs had his leave 2 mos. and permission to apply for 6 more.

CAMP VERDE TEXAS SAT. JULY 2, 1859

Our court met to-day & finished the third case. I had the officers to my quarters for a tod[d]y.

We have had the men, white washers & carpenters at work the last two days. The house is very much improved, though it looks badly enough. We cant do anything more until we get the balance of our things from S. Antonio. I sent a wagon after them.

The weather is delightful.

CAMP VERDE TEXAS MON. JULY 4, 1859

We had more rain yesterday & a little to-day. It was too wet for a parade & we have no cannon, so I had the band play at 12½ & invited all the garrison to a lunch. They appeared to enjoy themselves.

CAMP VERDE TEXAS WED. JULY 6, 1859

The wagons returned from Ft. Duncan on the 4th & brought my two boxes of books & a closet. They were principally loaded with things for Capt. Caldwell & his company.

Our court sat yesterday & to-day. We got along slowly.

CAMP VERDE TEXAS THURS. JULY 7, 1859

Very little breeze to-day & of course warm, though the mer. is only 88°. Our court still drags its slow length along. I answered Cheevers letter to-day.

CAMP VERDE TEXAS FRI. JULY 8, 1859

Our mail got in at 2 P.M. I got quite a number of letters, both by the p. office & qr. m. mail. Got two from Lathrop to the 8 June. Things go on well. I wrote to him and postscripts to Cheever & Wrightson. A meeting has been had & stock will be sold at $10. How[e] writes all goes well. Got a letter from him & three from Wrightson. Wrote for two more horse harness—double.

Got a letter from Sister Maria. She has been to Manheim & was in the house & garden. Sent me a leaf from the old apple tree as a forget me not.[1]

The wagon got back from S. Antonio with all our things & Sergt. Candy. He brought me a letter from Dr. Tripler & I got another by the mail.

CAMP VERDE TEXAS SAT. JULY 9, 1859

Mer. 90° & not much wind, so that it has been warm. I unpacked some of our things. The bureau was wet & all in pieces. It can be put together without much damage. Nothing else appears to be damaged.

Our court I am in hopes will get through Monday.

CAMP VERDE TEXAS WED. JULY 13, 1859

We had more rain Sun. Our court got through & adjourned yesterday. We had the mess to dinner yesterday. It went off well. Last evening there was a man brought me a note from Dr. Downs of Cottonwood Springs 8 miles beyond Bandera, that the Indians stole some mules & mares.[2] Lt. Graham & 12 men left this morning in pursuit.

Lt. Hazen left for Ft. Inge this morning. The colored woman & her children we had in the yard left with him. I went with Capt. Caldwell & Lt.

---

[1] The Heintzelman property in Manheim, Lancaster County, Pennsylvania, included an apple and plum orchard. After his graduation from West Point, Heintzelman returned to Manheim and the family home several times and would reminisce in his journal of an earlier, innocent childhood. "The old apple tree still stands and has much grown," he recorded on September 7, 1865. Heigs, "Heintzelman Visits His Hometown," 95, 98, 100; HJ, Mar. 3, 1833; Oct. 25, 1842; Sept. 7, 1865.

[2] Dr. Downs may be the same Dr. Downs who was ordered by Maj. James Duff not to assist wounded German-Texan Unionists following the Nueces Massacre on August 10, 1862. The death of a Dr. W.R. Downs is reported in *The Texas Courier-Record of Medicine* (Dallas), 3 (Aug., 1886), 568; Robert W. Shook, "Battle of the Nueces, August 10, 1862, *SHQ*, 66 (July, 1962), 40.

Thomas to look at the garden & try to divide it. We could not well & agreed to hold it in common. It has wonderfully improved in appearance since the rain. We got squashes & some cucumbers. The whole country has improved in appearance since the rain. We hung up our pictures to-day. I had Mary on the side saddle & poney yesterday.

Camp Verde Texas Fri. July 15, 1859

Yesterday we were at work all day with the sewing machine making curtains. I broke the first needle since we commenced. Towards evening we took a ride. We rode over to Turtle Creek about three miles from here & then rode about three more to the Guadalupe. The country is beautiful.

This morning we had a sprinkle of rain.

Camp Verde Texas Monday July 18, 1859

The detachment after Indians returned on Saturday. There were no Indians. The animals strayed.

The same day Dr. Ganahl & his wife & her mother called. They are quite pleasant people.[3] We had a few drops of rain the night before & heavy rain in the morning.

Yesterday afternoon we walked to the top of the hill across the creek & saw a rattlesnake up there. I tried to kill him but he escaped.

We had a garrison court martial on Saturday tried six men. The Cavalry detachment left to-day to join their company. The weather is warm to-day.

On Saturday we put down our carpets in ours & the children's rooms. They look much better.

Camp Verde Texas Thurs. July 21, 1859

We took Mrs. Mower out riding yesterday. We had a sprinkle of rain. We had from the garden three ears of corn—not a grain yet formed. On Tuesday

---

[3] Dr. Charles de Ganahl, age thirty and a surgeon, is listed on the 1860 census with real estate valued at $4,600 and personal property of $17,200. Ganahl, along with his wife, Virginia Jordan Wright Ganahl, had settled at Zanzenberg or what is today Center Point in 1857. From Savannah, Georgia, Ganahl had named the site after his ancestral home in the Austrian Tyrol. Zanzenberg was the first post office in Kerr County and Ganahl was the first postmaster. A five-year-old daughter, Lizy (Lisa), and New York–born Jenny W., twenty-three, as well as a servant, Scottish-born Fayne Galloway, twenty-three, are also listed on the 1860 census in the Ganahl household. The wealthy Ganahl, who owned twenty-one slaves, was elected from Kerr County to the Secession Convention and became a surgeon in the Confederate Army on the Texas-Mexican Border. Gerald Witt, *The History of Eastern Kerr County* (Austin: Nortex, 1986), 129–131. After the war he refused to sign an amnesty oath and remained in Matamoros for several years. Ganahl later practiced medicine in

a man from Bandera brought a load of Water & Mush melons but sold them enormously high. We bought three little mush m. for 30 cts. He asked 40 cts for a small Water Melon.

Two wagons came up from S. Antonio yesterday to bring us one & seven express mules. One returns to-day.

I enclosed a dollar to Washington for the "Weekly States" & commenced a letter to Dr. Tripler. It is warm to-day. Merc. 96° in the shade, though it dont feel as hot as 87° in Newport.

CAMP VERDE TEXAS FRI. JULY 22, 1859

The paymaster Major Cunningham arrived yesterday afternoon with four wagons. He paid this morning & left in the afternoon to pay at Radziminski etc.[4]

I got my pay for June $245.80. He sent check to T. Wrightson for my pay for May. Lt. Washington can't find my order to join my regt. in Texas. He has only an extract for Buchanan to relieve me. I wrote to Dr. Tripler for it. I am sorry as I thought I had paid Wrightson. I sent Dr. Tripler 60$ to pay Capt. Alden ten dollars & buy some bedsteads & pay the balance to Wrightson.[5] I got two letters enclosing papers from Lathrop. He has had fever & ague, but gets on well with the mines. I got two letters from Poston. He takes his pro rata stock & offers to negotiate for me. Wrightson wants me to sent it to him to negotiate if I cant take it here. I think Poston's offer the best. We had a citizens mail & I got 8 letters in all. I got a long interesting letter from Mr. Howe detailing his visit to N. York. I think that now our work at the mines will go on well. I wrote to Mr. Lathrop & sent by Major Cunningham to Ft. Chadbourn via Camp Colorado & also via S. Antonio to see which will reach its destination first.[6]

Galveston and died in 1883. Jennie continued to manage the ranch and died in 1895. Both are buried in the Center Point Cemetery.

  [4] Named for Lt. Charles Radziminski, a Pole in the 2d Cavalry, who had died of tuberculosis, Camp Radziminski was moved in 1858 to a site on Otter Creek in southwestern Indian Territory by Capt. Earl Van Dorn. Four miles north of present-day Mountain Park, the post was administered as an outpost of Fort Belknap. Utley, *Frontiersmen in Blue*, 130–135.

  [5] A captain in the U.S. Navy, J. Deane Alden was Samuel Colt's private secretary. Heintzelman had met Alden in New York in 1842, California in 1856, Washington in December 1857, and later in 1858 at Hartford, Connecticut, when he toured Colt's arms factory. In June 1858, Alden traveled with Heintzelman to San Francisco. HJ, Sept. 22, 1841; Nov. 15, 1851; Dec. 2, 20, 1857; Jan. 17, June 15, 1858.

  [6] Fort Chadbourne was established in October 1852 on the left bank of Oak Creek about three miles above its junction with the Colorado River, north of present-day Bronte in Coke County. Soldiers at the post were primarily responsible for pro-

Camp Verde Texas Sun. July 24, 1859

We had strong winds all day yesterday. We went to the bathing house & I got Margaret to put on the life preserving jacket & venture into the pond. She is gaining confidence. We then took a ride.

I have been busy most of the day in over hauling & arranging papers. I have concluded to send some of my old stock to Mr. Poston in N.Y. & Mr. Wrightson in Cin. to sell to pay for my pro- rata stock. I sketched letters to both. It is quite warm to-day.

Camp Verde Texas Wed. July 27, 1859

Yesterday we rode to Langs a mile & a half & bought some ducks & got a few ears of corn.[7] He has planted for eight years & this is the first he has got any corn. He wont make half a crop. He gave us some fair wine he made last year from the small grapes that abound here. There will be none here, nor plumbs as the frost in Apl. killed all.

Out sutler Lane arrived yesterday & called. He stutters badly.[8]

I have been busy to-day writing letters.

Camp Verde Texas Thurs. July 28, 1859

I to-day made a sale of 20 shares of Sonora stock to Dr. Foard & 20 to Lt. Thomas. I send on the certificates to be transferred. I also send on 200 shares to Mr. Poston & 200 to Mr. Wrightson to sell to pay for my pro rata. Mr. Thomas gave me a check on N.Y. for $168. I sent to Wrightson & give Dr. Foard a letter to enclose the checks in S. Antonio for the balance of the $800. If in a year this stock is worth in the market $80 they pay me 5$ a share more.

We had the Doctor, Lts. Thomas & Biggs to dinner. It went off well. The Doctor & Biggs leave for S. Antonio tomorrow. The latter may go on a long leave & the Doctor on 7 with permission to apply for 10.

---

tecting the emigrant route from Fort Smith, Arkansas, to El Paso. Frazer, *Forts of the West*; Wooster, *Soldiers, Sutlers, and Settlers*, 135–136.

Camp Colorado had several locations. By 1858 the post had been moved to Jim Ned Creek, twenty miles north of the Colorado River, in Coleman County. Webb, Carroll, and Branda (eds.), *Handbook of Texas*, I: 279; Wooster, *Soldiers, Sutlers, and Settlers*, 135–136.

[7] Lang is probably Ludovig Lange, a master stonemason from Hanover, Germany, who had settled near Camp Verde. 8th Census, Bandera County.

[8] Tennessee-born Samuel Lane, fifty-seven, lived on the Guadalupe River, two miles above Comfort. Lane was killed by Indians near present-day Center Point in the fall of 1860. Ibid. Also, Watking, *Kerr County*, 151.

It has been warm to-day. Mer. over 100°. We had a nice shower of rain in the afternoon.

CAMP VERDE TEXAS FRI. JULY 29, 1859

I was at the young officers & met Mr. Lane the Sutler. He had the imprudence to propose to me to let him sell liquor to the [men] in violation of a recent order. He then said he would open a liquor shop off the lease of the post. Lt. Foard & Lt. Biggs left this morning. I sent all my letters. The mail this afternoon only brought me a letter from Wrightson & Brucknow's pamphlet with Ehrenberg's letter etc.[9] I have not had time to read them yet. They are intended to meet Colt's report. I wrote to Wrightson.

It is quite warm again to-day.

CAMP VERDE TEXAS SUN. JULY 31, 1859

Yesterday we had the first watermelons from the garden. They were not quite ripe. In the afternoon we drove to Dr. Ganahls & did not get back till sometime after dark. They have a pretty situation on the left bank of the Guadalupe. The improvements have just commenced. This morning we had a few drops of rain.

---

[9] Herman Vollrath Ehrenberg, a German mining engineer, had immigrated to Texas in 1834 and was with Ben Milam in the Battle of Bexar in December 1835. Ehrenberg was later at Goliad with James Fannin but was able to escape the massacre. He travelled to Oregon and sailed to the Sandwich Islands and Polynesia but returned to Germany where he wrote *Texas und seine Revolution*. An explorer and cartographer (especially of maps of Sonora and the Gadsden Purchase), Ehrenberg had assisted Heintzelman and Charles Poston in the location and development of Colorado City (present-day Yuma). According to Heintzelman, Ehrenberg also made a sketch of Fort Yuma in June 1854. Ehrenberg, who was never married, was also involved in the formation of the Sonora Exploring and Mining Company and met Heintzelman in San Francisco in June 1858 when Samuel Peter was on his way to Tubac. Ehrenberg, who once proclaimed the Heintzelman Mine the "richest in the world," later assisted in the establishment of the Territory of Arizona. He was appointed agent to the Mohave Indians in 1864 and was killed near Mecca, California, in 1866. Heintzelman learned of Ehrenberg's death at the hands of robbers on October 9, 1866, at Dos Palmas, near present-day Palm Springs, California, from a New Orleans newspaper while he was in Galveston. "He was a true man," Heintzelman recorded at the time. Natalie Ornish, "Herman Ehrenberg," in *New Handbook of Texas*, eds. Tyler, et al., I, 805; Helga Von Schweinitz, "Hermann Ehrenberg, Fighting for Texas," *True West*, 33 (Apr., 1986), 22–26; HJ, July 14, 1854, Sept. 11, 17, Dec. 5, 7, 1857, Dec. 28, 1866; Thrapp, *FB*, I, 435.

❧ August 1859 ❧

". . . one of my horses had kicked Charles."

———◆•◆•◆———

CAMP VERDE TEXAS MON. AUGUST 1, 1859

Quite cloudy this morning & most of the day & a few drops of rain. Margaret was sick last night & most of to-day. She lay in the buffalo robe at the door most of the time.

I opened my books this morning. Some few are a little damaged. I want a few book shelves, but it appears to be impossible to get the carpenter.

CAMP VERDE TEXAS THURS. AUG. 4, 1859

On Sunday I thought of an improvement in the use of pulleys. It is to take a tackle & attach both blocks to the weight, the parts to make a bite & go over another pulley. I have made the pulleys, but not put in the cords to try the matter.

We have had shelves made to put up the books & to-day put them in. It improves the looks of the parlor.

I am getting a little closet made in the Hall to lock up liquors. There is some one about the house [who] cannot be trusted with anything.

I put up my shower bath to-day, but have nothing to cover it. The weather has been threatening rain but it has not come. Our garden wants water. Yesterday I was down with Lt. Thomas & we found a couple of nice mushmelons.

CAMP VERDE TEXAS FRI. AUG. 5, 1859

The wagon got back from San Antonio with my horses. The foundered one looks thin but is much better than I expected. He is not lame. The other is fat. I got quite a number of letters by the mail. Things go on well at the

93

mines. Henry Norton goes to Arivaca.[1] I have a letter from Col. Kennett.[2] Our stock will sell well. I got a letter from Mrs. Norton & from Sister Maria. I got the vol. R.R. Reports. Lt. Washington writes from San Antonio that he thinks hd. qrs might me moved to S.A. A company of cavalry may be sent here. I wrote him we are all satisfied to stay here. I got my pulleys arranged & think that they will work.

Camp Verde Texas Sun. Aug. 7, 1859

I was at work yesterday making a new pulley, a little differently arranged & I think it works better. Some of the sheaves are too small & the line being small gets off. I will change them.

The hogs are in our garden every day & have done a great deal of damage. Several hundred water melons are eaten or destroyed. The weather is warm to-day.

Camp Verde Texas Thurs. Aug. 11, 1859

Margaret has been sick all the week & confined to her bed the last two days. The weather is quite warm & our water is drying up rapidly. The wagon got back yesterday from taking Lt. Graham to Ft. Clark. He brought us a bag of onions from Duncan. They had had no rain there since we left.

Our garden is nearly ruined by the hogs. The melons are gone & the corn destroyed. They are only a few hogs & they belong to a man of the name of Lang who lives a mile & a half below us.

On Monday I took one of the horses & took a short ride. Charles went with me on the poney.

Camp Verde Texas Fri. Aug. 12, 1859

This has been another warm day. The merc. was at 95°. Margaret was quite sick last night. We are unfortunate in her being sick when there is no doctor about.

------

[1] Henry C. Norton, nineteen and a nephew of Margaret Heintzelman, celebrated his birthday on the same day as Charles Stuart Heintzelman. The New York-born Henry is listed on the 1860 census at Arivaca as a clerk for the Sonora Exploring and Mining Company. Henry's brother Charles Stuart Norton, graduated from the U.S. Naval Academy in 1855. HJ, Nov. 26, Dec. 29, 1854; June 20, 1855; Mar. 30, 1856; Apr. 14, 1858; 8th Census, Arizona County, New Mexico Territory.

The Arivaca Mine of the Sonora Exploring and Mining Company was just south of Cerro Colorado.

[2] Henry Gassaway Kennett later served as a lieutenant colonel in the 79th Ohio

I have written several letters. The mail got in & brought me three from Mr. Howe including two from Mr. Poston. Our stock has been transferred on the books of the office at $40 a share for each. Mr. Poston sold his additional stock to Mr. Killbreath of Cin. & Grosvenor & sent in money to buy pro rata.[3] I hope that I shall sell some of mine at a good price. I wrote Mr. Howe & another to Mr. Poston. I this morning wrote to Mr. Howe about that charge of Colts against Major Chapman.

I got a letter from Dr. Summers dated 8 July.[4] Sully's and Davis's companies 2 Infy, go to Kearney.[5] His wife (Dr. S's) expects to be confined in a month.

CAMP VERDE TEXAS AUG. 14, 1859

Yesterday & the day before we took short rides. Margaret feels much better.

This morning Lt. Thomas & I, with Charles rode out to the Methodist camp meeting on Turtle creek about 4 miles. We met several gentlemen from Fredericksburg, pleasant & agreeable. There were scarcely a hundred people on the ground. We heard a little poor preach. There is close by a beautiful cool spring—the coolest water that I have tasted in Texas. The weather continues quite warm. In front of the house it was 102° at 1 P.M.—in the afternoon 96° on both sides. We expected Dr. Foard yesterday, but he did not come.

Infantry during the Civil War. Heintzelman had visited with Kennett in Newport, Kentucky, in January 1859, prior to departing for Texas. HJ, Jan. 29, 1859.

[3] James P. Kilbreath was a trustee of the Sonora Exploring and Mining Company. North, *Samuel Peter Heintzelman*, 217. Horace Chipman Grosvenor, forty and a Cincinnati engraver, had traveled west with Phocion R. Way in 1858 to establish the headquarters and supervise the Sonora Exploring and Mining Company operations in the Santa Rita Mountains. Grosvenor was killed by Apaches on April 25, 1861. 8th Census, Arizona County, New Mexico Territory; William A. Duffen (ed.), "Overland Via 'Jackass Mail' in 1858: The Diary of Phocion R. Way," *Arizona and the West*, 2 (Spring, 1960), 52; HJ, June 17, 1861.

[4] John Edward Summers, thirty-six, a surgeon in the army since 1847, was married to Margaret Heintzelman's younger sister, Caroline, thirty-three. The Summers and the Heintzelmans were frequent visitors in the Stuart home in Buffalo. Both families had lost infant sons who were buried side by side in Buffalo's Forest Lawn Cemetery. In 1851, Summers and Heintzelman were stationed at San Diego, California, at which time Summers married Caroline Stuart. To Heintzelman's delight, Summers, a Virginian, remained in the army in 1861 and became a medical inspector. HJ, Dec. 15, 1851, Nov. 26, 1854, Jan. 18, 1855, Mar. 3, Dec. 11, 1856, Feb. 14, 1858; 7th Census, San Diego County, California.

[5] Alfred Sully, who graduated from West Point in 1841, was adjutant of the 2d

CAMP VERDE TEXAS FRI. AUG. 16, 1859

Yesterday was warm again. We took a long ride. Margaret does not improve as fast as she should. There is great difficulty in finding anything for her to eat. Sunday at tattoo it commenced to rain & continued to rain hard till after midnight. It was needed.

We had a few drops of rain this afternoon. We rode out to the Camp Meeting. On our return I found the Dr. had returned with Capt. & Mrs. McLean & Lt. Blake. They have come up here to spend a week. The heat in San Antonio is excessive.

CAMP VERDE TEXAS FRI. AUG. 19, 1859

On Wed. we were taking a short ride when we met Dr. Howard & Mrs. Ganahl & soon after Dr. G. and Mr. Cameron. The gentlemen are from S. Antonio & spending a little time there. They invited us to attend a fishing party at their house to-day. Margaret is not well enough & we cant go.

I went yesterday with the strangers, Dr. Foard & Thomas to fish at the mouth of Turtle Creek. I caught but one catfish. We had a few drops of rain & more rain the night before.

I sent my horses to Bandera this morning to have shod. I let Charles go along on his poney. Capt. Caldwell has gone down in his ambulance to have his shod. He takes his Children & Mary has gone with him. The weather has been delightful since Sunday. About one P.M. Capt. Caldwell drove up & told us that one of my horses had kicked Charles. We got him out of the ambulance & I sent for the doctor. He examined the leg & pronounced it broken below the knee, a little below the middle—both bones, badly. He set it.

The other day the horse showed that he did not like the poney & tried to kick him. I then repeatedly cautioned him not to ride near the horse.

To-day about 8 miles from here some dogs barked at the poney & he passed near the horse, when he kicked & struck Charles on the leg. Fortunately Capt. Caldwell soon came along & brought him home.

This will lay him up for six weeks or two months.

The mail got in, but brought but few newspapers & not a private letter for me.

Infantry. He was breveted for gallantry at Fair Oaks and Malvern Hill during the Civil War and later in the Indian Wars in the Dakota Territory. Sully died in April 1879. Heitman, *HR*, 936.

Capt. Nelson Henry Davis, West Point class of 1848, had transferred to the 2d Infantry in 1847.

The weather is delightful. I have written eight letters.

CAMP VERDE TEXAS SAT. AUG. 20, 1859

Charles spent a tolerably quite night. This morning the doctor concluded to take off the splints & put his leg into a friction box. He is much easier now, but he was very nervous when it was done.

Dr. Howard is in Garrison & with Mr. Cameron dined at the Mess. The former called with Dr. Foard. Mr. McLean & Mrs. Mower were in & Mrs. Caldwell. It is a little warmer to-day.

A wagon went to S. Antonio this morning. I sent for a few things.

The man with the horses did not get back until after dark.

CAMP VERDE TEXAS SUN. AUG. 21, 1859

Warmer to-day. Charles had a bad head ache most of the afternoon & part of the night. He was very fortunate. His leg is doing well. Margaret is not so well & has kept her bed most of the day.

CAMP VERDE TEXAS TUES. AUG. 23, 1859

Margaret is much better. The Band played some fine dancing music last night & she went over to the other house, but did not dance. She helped them to call off. Capt. & Mrs. McLean & Lt. Blake left his morning in the rain. We had a strong cold wind from the North & a heavy rain. It did not last long.

The Indians some think & others the runaway negroes & Mexicans have been killing & stealing animals the last few days. Cloud who has charge of our Camels is out with a party of citizens.[6]

I went out hunting this afternoon to shoot a few birds. I did not see a quail & the doves were very wild. I wrote to Mahoney at Fort Snelling to pay his six months interest to Mr. Poston.[7]

CAMP VERDE TEXAS THURS. AUG. 25, 1859

Weather pleasant. We took Mrs. Mower out to ride yesterday. Charles leg is doing well. The doctor is not at all well. Some Indians rode through the streets of Bandera the other night. There is a party in pursuit but in such a manner that there is no prospect of their over taking them.

---

[6] Tennessee-born James B. Cloud, age thirty-two and a farmer, along with José Policarpo Rodríguez, had first served as a guide at the post in 1856. 8th Census, Kerr County; Post Returns, Camp Verde, AGO, RG 393 (NA).

[7] Fort Snelling, one of the more picturesque western posts, has been established in 1819 at the confluence of the Minnesota and Mississippi rivers.

CAMP VERDE TEXAS SAT. AUG. 27, 1859

Margaret is not so well. I got a letter yesterday from Dr. Tripler. He sent the order but there is no clause directing me to join my Regiment. I got letters from Poston & Wrightson. Poston sold some of his stock for $21.25. He thinks that I can get $25. Some $20.00 have been paid in to Coleman & things look well. An engine will be sent through Texas. Poston quarreled with Colt & made the blusterer back down. He challenged him. Poston has resigned his Pro-tem Secretaryship & Brown of Boston takes his place till someone can be had.[8]

Wrightson writes that Cheever will pay the $500 & that I had not drawn the money on it. I have thus near $1000 in his hands & the company owes me over $500. This with the $800 I have just sent will go towards paying for my additional stock. I wrote to Sister Maria in answer to her inquiries that she can send in $250 & have the additional stock. I wrote to Wrightson & Poston & Dr. Tripler. My first no. of the "States" has arrived.

CAMP VERDE TEXAS SUN. AUG. 28, 1859

Yesterday afternoon Capt. Caldwell & his family drove out to Dr. Ganahls. Lt. Thomas & I were going in the forenoon, but a mistake prevented. We went in the afternoon & got there at the same time.

Mrs. Ganahl's mother is sick.[9] The doctor told us that most of his horses were missing & supposed that they had strayed. Whilst we were there Judge Scott came & said he had seen their trail & that they were driven off.[10] The supposition is by Indians. A young man out hunting for animals saw 14 Indians & the party followed by Cloud he says was only six. The others must have laid by until the people got careless & let their animals run. Dr. Ganahal turned his out without a herder.

Four of the men who were with Cloud got back to-day. A rain came on & the pursuit was given up.

It threatened rain to-day & we had a few drops.

The wagon from San Antonio got back yesterday. The Doctor got some peaches & sent over eight. I gave mine to the children. The teamster brought me some melons. The children have been filled three times to-day.

---

[8] Charles S. Brown was a trustee of the Sonora Exploring and Mining Company.

[9] North Carolina–born Elisa Thompson, forty-one, is listed on the 1860 census in the Charles Ganahl household near Camp Verde. 8th Census, Kerr County.

[10] Judge Scott is probably Jonathan Scott, fifty-one, a well-to-do Georgia-born farmer, who, with his wife and six children, lived on the Guadalupe River west of Comfort. 8th Census, Kerr County.

Margaret has been sick all day yesterday & to-day. She took neither breakfast or dinner.

Mer. has been 94° to-day.

CAMP VERDE TEXAS MON. AUG. 29, 1859

Warm again to-day—mer. 95°. Charles has been allowed to sit up to-day & to have his bed moved outside. The smaller bone broken in two places, but his leg is doing well.

Margaret is much better to-day.

CAMP VERDE TEXAS TUES. AUG. 30, 1859

Not so warm to-day. We had muster & inspection this morning.

Margaret is better & Charles doing well.

✐ September 1859 ✐

". . . passed through the Bandera Pass."

———•◦••◦•———

CAMP VERDE TEXAS THURS. SEPT 1, 1859

The summer is over & I can scarcely believe it. I have been busy writing letters for the mail.

I wrote to Major Chilton & sent my pay a/cts for Aug. $261.50 & to Capt. E.E. McLean & sent him my transp. a/c for $249.10 & requested them to send the amount to Mr. Poston, N.Y. I also wrote to Poston & Lathrop.

CAMP VERDE TEXAS FRI. SEPT. 2, 1859

Pleasant weather. I have been writing letters. The mail is in as usual. I got but two letters, one from Mr. Lathrop, 2 Aug. & the other from Wrightson 19 Aug. Things are going on slow & well at the mines. T. Wrightson is sick in bed. The drafts have been received. I have written nine letters in all. I wrote to Cheever again about that stock.

I got a letter from Head Quarters. A company of Cavalry will be encamped near here under my direction.

A new post is to be established at the Wishata [Wichita] Mountains of 4 or 5 companies & there is some fear of the Hd. Qrs. going there.[1] The general order is out & I suppose we will know the next mail.

CAMP VERDE TEXAS SAT. SEPT 3, 1859

Mer. 96°, but a good breeze. Margaret & I rode out last evening. She has not ventured for several days, but now feels much better.

The officers who have been north think a large post near the Wishita

---

[1] Heintzelman is referring to Fort Cobb, established on October 1, 1859, by two companies of the 1st Cavalry on the east bank of Pond Creek near the Washita River, north of the Wichita Mountains in the Indian Territory. Named after Secretary of the Treasury Howell Cobb, the post was to guard the newly established reservation for the tribes that had been removed from Texas. Frazer, *Forts of the West,* 119.

Mts. much preferable to here. If the post was built & our things were there I would not dislike the change, but I dont care to move now. It is near the overland mail route & if a post is established there the route will probably be changed.

CAMP VERDE TEXAS SUN. SEPT. 4, 1859

There will [be] 4 cos 1st Infy & 2 Cav. occupy the new post near the Wishita Mts. There is a gentleman here from Camp Cooper.[2] It has been cloudy most of the day & a heavy wind in the afternoon. Rain at 6 P.M. I want to go tomorrow to select that camp but fear the rain will prevent it.

CAMP VERDE TEXAS MON. SEPT. 5, 1859

It rained steadily most of the [day] & two inches of rain fell. I was going this morning to select an encampment for the Cavalry, but the weather was too bad. The wind is in the north & mer. 63°.

CAMP VERDE TEXAS SEPT. 8, 1859 THURS.

It has been cloudy & raining since Sunday night & we have a fire in the children's room. I have not been able to make the selection of a site for the Cav. camp.

Margaret has not been so well since Sunday. I find it impossible to keep her quiet which is essential. There is a prospect of the weather clearing off to-day.

I believe the rain is over. Dr. Ganahl's carriage was in with their children.

We have got to get another servant girl. Ours has done what she was told positively not to do & is no cook. She thought Margaret was sick & would not know it.

CAMP VERDE TEXAS FRI. SEPT. 9, 1859

We had heavy rain again last night & some to-day, but I believe that is now over. This long continued rain will insure grass for the winter.

The mail got in as usual. I got a letter from T. Wrightson. His brother William is at home. I have no doubt, but that he is much relieved in getting away from the mines. I got a letter from Sister Maria. I wrote to T. Wrightson. I yesterday wrote to Howard & Ogden & sent them a list of damages—$36.42½.

---

[2] Established on January 3, 1856, by Col. Albert Sidney Johnston, Camp Cooper was named in honor of the adjutant general of the army, Samuel Cooper, and was located in present-day Throckmorton County on the Clear Fork of the Brazos, about five miles west of the Clear Fork Crossing. Col. Robert E. Lee commanded the post from April 1856 to July 1857. Webb, Carroll, and Branda (eds.), *Handbook of Texas*, I, 279.

McLean will pay my transp. a/c & send on the check to Poston. I have not heard from the paymaster.

Camp Verde Texas Sun. Sept. 11, 1859

Yesterday we had showers & heavy rain, North & South. Dr. Ganahl & his wife were in. The Doctor says that after the 15th of this month we will have a semi-weekly mail to Comfort & Kerrsville. It will be twice as often & nearer than we now have to send to.

We had a few drops of rain to-day, but otherwise it has been warmer & more pleasant. Charles is doing well & Margaret much better. Mr. Lane the sutler leaves here.

Camp Verde Texas Mon. Sept. 12, 1859

We had a few drops of rain this morning, but the promise of a pleasant day.

Mr. Lane called & is going to S. Antonio with our rolls & will pay the men when he returns. I sent by him to try & get us a servant woman.

Lt. Thomas, Mr. C[l]oud & two men went with me to select a site for a camp for the Company of Cavalry that is coming here. We rode near 15 miles. We passed through the Bandera Pass & found two good places, one 5 & the other six miles from here. We tried another place, but there was not sufficient water & is out of the way. I will look on the other side near the Guadalupe. At the entrance of the pass is a small pile of stones [which] marks the site of a great battle between the Comanches & Lipans.[3] It was so long ago that there is even doubt as to what tribes.

Camp Verde Texas Wed. Sept. 14, 1859

Yesterday Lt. Thomas, Cloud & I rode over to Turtle Creek.[4] I took a look at the ground where the Camp Meeting was held. It is a beautiful situation for a camp, though there is not quite so much grass. On our way home we had a heavy shower of rain.

When I got home I found the horse that was foundered, sick with colic. I had him attended to & he is better, but not altogether well yet.

---

[3] Bandera Pass, a gorge some 500 yards long and 125 feet wide, cut through hills that separate the Guadalupe and Medina valleys. Here, in about 1720, a Spanish expedition out of San Antonio de Béxar decisively defeated a large band of Apaches, probably Lipan, in a bloody three-day battle. Allegedly, a second, equally bloody hand-to-hand battle in 1842 between forty Texas Rangers under John Coffee Hays and approximately 100 Comanches was also fought here. Ibid., 1: 105.

[4] In south-central Kerr County, north of Camp Verde, Turkey Creek is a tributary of the Guadalupe River.

I wrote this morning to the general for permission to put the camp on Turtle Creek.

We had a heavy rain again to-day & it is turning cool. Mr. Adams, the Methodist circuit rider was here & preached to-day. Near 20 of the men attended.[5] He dined with us.

I wrote to Marks Odometer Band Co. Hartford Ct. for two sets of Odometers, one for me & the other for Lt. Thomas. I enclose a check on N.Y. for ten dollars.

CAMP VERDE TEXAS THURS. SEPT. 15, 1859

Our mail is in. No letters from Solon—one from Mr. Howe but none from Wrightson. I wrote to Poston & Mr. Rich Hayman at Newport & gave Margaret a check for $60 to send to pay for articles needed. Our bedsteads are at Indianola. Major Chilton writes he has sent my pay to Poston & McLean that he will send my transportation. The steam engines will go in 60 days from Aug. 23 from Bridgeport Ct. I fear I will not make much on my stock.

CAMP VERDE TEXAS MON. SEPT. 19, 1859

We tried to take a ride Sat. but Jackson is so stupid we did not get the mules. We have the two worst servants I have even seen.

Yesterday Margaret took a walk—the first since July. She did not walk over a hundred yards. We sent Jackson on an errand & he did not return till late in the afternoon. The horses were neither fed or watered.

It is cool to-day—a kind of norther.

CAMP VERDE TEXAS TUES. SEPT 20, 1859

Quite cool last night. Mer. down to 59°. Cool to-day. Mr. Lane returned from S. Antonio to-day, with money & pays off the men this afternoon. He brought the mail. I got four letters from Mr. Lathrop, the last dated 22 Aug. He says he gets my letters via Chadbourn, two weeks sooner than by the other route.

I got a letter in answer from Mr. Paine at Niles.[6] My lot there can be sold for $200 & he says as much as it is worth.

---

[5] O. B. Adams, a Methodist minister, was in charge of what was called the "Center Point circuit" that included Camp Verde and Turkey Creek. Hunter, *Old Camp Verde*, 20–21.

[6] Heintzelman had purchased property in Niles, Michigan, a small town a few miles north of South Bend, Indiana. The land was sold in 1867 for $300. HJ, Feb. 21, 1842; Sept. 26, 1866; May 10, 1867; July 10, 1867.

Mr. Jno. Wrightson was murdered by Mexicans near the Tumacacor[i] Mission—supposed for his money.[7] I got a printed notice from W.W. at Cin. & Mr. Lathrop mentions it in his letters. The mines continue to do as well as usual.

We sent by Mr. Lane to S. Antonio for a servant. We can get the Mary we had at Newport. She is married to a soldier in Capt. Kings compy.

Margaret got [a] letter from Mrs. Tripler, Caroline, Mrs. Dr. Shaw.

CAMP VERDE TEXAS WED. SEPT. 21, 1859

Nights cold. This morning Dr. Foard, Lt. Thomas & Mr. Lane started for his cattle Ranche to fish, to be gone two days. I have been busy writing letters. I wrote to W. Wrightson to
Sister Maria & to Mr. Lathrop. We are going to take a ride with mules. One of my horses has been sick is not well enough. Margaret & I went to the garden yesterday. It dont amount to much. There may be a few tomato[e]s.

We will have a semi-monthly mail. Mr. Lane is the postmaster here & has authority to give out a contract from here to Comfort—12 miles, so it dont cost to exceed the receipts.

CAMP VERDE TEXAS THURS. SEPT. 22, 1859

A pleasant day. The Hosp. Stewart lost his child, about 18 mos. old from inflamation of the bowels.

The doctor, Thomas & Lane got home early in the afternoon. No success in fishing.

Margaret & I took a long walk. Her health is improving much.

I wrote to Hooper & to Col. Kennett & sent these letters & those for Solon & Wrightson to Chadbourn[e] to take the overland mail.

The mail reaches Bandera sooner than it does here. Mr. Thomas tells me that Gen. Harney has occupied the disputed Isld. of San Juan in Oregon with 4 com. of troops & the British have sent naval ships of war.[8] I presume that

---

[7] Heintzelman is confused. It was John Ware, a native of Fredericksburg, Virginia, who was stabbed to death by angry Mexicans at Tubac, not John Wrightson. John Wrightson's brother, William, was later killed by Indians in Arizona in 1865. *Weekly Arizonian* (Tubac), June 30, 1859.

[8] In dispute since the Oregon Treaty of 1846, the small but strategically located San Juan Islands, southeast of Vancouver Island, had received extensive coverage in Texas and Louisiana newspapers at the time Heintzelman arrived in Texas. The Treaty of Washington in 1872 gave the islands to the United States. *Daily True Delta* (New Orleans), Oct. 14, 17, Nov. 4, Dec. 3, 14, 1859; New Orleans *Daily Picayune*, Sept. 18, 21, Oct. 25, Nov. 13, Dec. 14, 1859; J. W. Long Jr., "The Origin and Development of

this is the island Mr. S. Campbell, our Commissioner told me [about] last year on our way to California that the British commissioner claimed.

Camp Verde Texas Fri. Sept 23, 1859

Lt. Owen arrived at 11 A.M. with Capt. Bracket[t']s company of Cavalry.[9] I let him encamp near here until the mail comes in. It came & no orders where to locate his company. I did not get a single letter. I wrote to Col. Taylor & to Mr. Poston.

It rained this afternoon.

Camp Verde Texas Sun. Sept 25, 1859

Yesterday we put four mules to my ambulance & went to Comfort. The Doctor rode down in Mr. Lane's buggy & Lt. Thomas & Lt. Owens with me. We arranged about the mails & took a lunch. I looked around for sweet potatoes, but could not find any sufficiently large. I got a few water melons. Mr. Lane went on to his ranche & we drove home. We had several small showers of rain. Comfort is about 14 miles from here & a small german settlement.

Camp Verde Texas Mon. Sept. 26, 1859

Weather pleasant to-day. I will let this company remain here until after the next mail arrives. Took a ride on horseback in the morning to look for a place for a target & in the afternoon Margaret & I in the ambulance, with the horses.

Camp Verde Texas Tues. Sept. 27, 1859

Our mail got in from Comfort yesterday. Only two letters. We sent to Mr. Lane for potatoes & mutton. We had last night a heavy rain, lasted till this morning. I have been trying my pulleys again & have made a drawing & will send on to Mann & Co. of the Scientific American.[10] I want their opinion before I apply for a patent.

---

the San Juan Island Boundary Controversy," *Pacific Northwest Quarterly*, 43 (Fall, 1952), 187–213.
    [9] Second Lt. Wesley Owen, twenty-five and an 1856 West Point graduate, had been assigned to the 2d Cavalry. Albert Gallatin Brackett, a Mexican War veteran, was commissioned a captain in the 2d Cavalry in 1855 and given command of Co. I. Harold B. Simpson, *Cry Comanche: The 2nd U.S. Cavalry in Texas, 1856–1861* (Hillsboro: Hill College Press, 1979), 29–30, 44–45, 80, 100, 122–125, 142–144.
    [10] Heintzelman retained a copy of this letter. Heintzelman to Mann and Co., Sept. 28, 1859, HP.

CAMP VERDE TEXAS WED. SEPT. 28, 1859

It rained hard all night & some this morning. Verde Creek is running again. A small detachment of cavalry with horses for this company arrived to-day from Ft. Mason.[11]

I had a talk with Jackson about the manner in which he does his duties. I will now discharge him so soon as I can get another man. It has dried off beautifully.

CAMP VERDE TEXAS FRI. SEPT. 30, 1859

Yesterday we had rain & pleasant in the afternoon. Margaret & I rode to the Bandera Pass and back. Last night it rained again & this morning. I wrote to Mr. Lathrop & sent it to the Overland mail. The mail is just in—3 P.M. An hour late & the last we will get this way.

This is my birthday. We had a little quiet family dinner. It is hard to get anything. The wagon returned yesterday from Mr. Lane's ranche. He have no potatoes. He sent a few pumpkins & more sheep. We had beans from some vines we planted for shade.

---

[11] Fort Mason had been established on July 6, 1851, by a company of the 2d Dragoons, two miles west of Comanche Creek and eight miles above its confluence with the Llano River in present Mason County. Frazer, *Forts of the West*, 155.

❦ October 1859 ❧

"Our company has lost a few more mules . . . "

❖

CAMP VERDE TEXAS SUN. OCT. 2ND. 1859

Yesterday I dined with the mess. The weather has finally cleared off & is cool and pleasant. Margaret & I rode out towards Turtle Creek.

Lt. Owens left early this morning to establish his camp on Turtle Creek.

I got by the mail another (2 pr. cent) on the Vallecillo stock.[1] Solon heard from Mr. Poston. He cant sell my stock but has it till after the 3rd Oct. when he hopes there will be sales. I also heard from Sister Maria. She sent $250 to secure her additional stock. Mr. & Mrs. Futhey think it a poor speculation.[2] I also heard from T. Wrightson. He is getting well. His wife has a boy. The first out of five children. His brother Wilbur is in N.Y.

I wrote to Mr. Poston & Mr. T. Wrightson.

I had hopes of getting a negro man for a servant, now staying at Dr. Ganahls, but I saw him to-day & he is going to San Antonio. It is useless to try to get along with Jackson. Although I told him never to take a horse without asking, he this morning took the poney to go off & spent a day. The weather

---

[1] Heintzelman had invested in the Vallecillo Mining Company that operated mines near Vallecillo, Nuevo Leon, Mexico. See lengthy journal entry, HJ, Jan. 7, 1860.

[2] Heintzelman's older sister, Juliana, was married to John S. Futhey, a merchant in Wrightsville, Pennsylvania. The family later moved to West Chester, in the picturesque Brandywine Valley, southwest of Philadelphia, where Samuel Peter was a frequent visitor at the three-story brick home of the well-to-do Futheys. In June 1867, while he was in Washington, D.C., Heintzelman received word of his sister's illness and hurried to West Chester only to discover that Juliana had died hours earlier. Heiges, "Heintzelman Visits His Hometown," 106; HJ, July 23, 1842; July 10, 1845; Apr. 6, July 17, 1847; Sept. 12, 1854; May 11, 1855; June 3, 1867.

[3] San Pedro Springs, today in the city of San Antonio, flowed south two miles into the San Antonio River.

is cool & pleasant. "D" company 1st Infy. is in S. Antonio, on its way to Camp Cobb. They are encamped at San Pedro Springs.[3]

Camp Verde Texas Tues. Oct. 4, 1859

Yesterday I suppose Mr. Poston made the payment for my additional stock. Our mail came in but brought no letters for me. I got a Wash. "States" & an American. Our company has lost a few more mules by the Indians. I wrote to Wrightson & Poston.

I hired a Mexican boy for $10 a month & he came to-day. I will discharge Jackson to-day. I think I have a good boy. He dont speak English, but understands. He has been herding for Sergt. Drury.

Margaret is not very well to-day.

Camp Verde Texas Wed. Oct. 5, 1859

I paid off Jackson yesterday & discharged him. He has gone to see about getting a school.

We ride every evening.

Camp Verde Texas Wed. Oct. 7, 1859

Yesterday's mail brought me no letters—only three papers. We took a ride in the afternoon, as usual.

Charles is greatly troubled about getting up. The Doctor was here this morning & will probably fix his leg tomorrow.

I saw the Sec. of War's decision in Major Thomas's case asking for the command of the Wischata expedition. I think that it is correct. I dont think that under that I would ask for the command. I understand that Major Emory wants to go on leave & if he does I could get the command.[4] I think I will write to him & let the time roll on so that spring will be here, before anything is done. Margaret is not very well.

---

[4] William Helmsley Emory, an 1831 graduate of West Point, is perhaps best remembered for his exploration of the Southwest as a topographical engineer and as chief astronomer in the survey of the United States–Mexico boundary. Heintzelman had been introduced to Emory on a Baltimore-to-Washington, D.C. train in 1842. Later in 1849–1850, Emory was a frequent visitor at the Heintzelman home in San Diego. When Heintzelman was ordered to establish Fort Yuma, he called on Emory for information in crossing the desert to the junction of the Colorado and Gila rivers. Still later, Heintzelman gave Emory a map he had made of the lower Colorado River. In 1855, Emory had transferred to the 1st Cavalry. In April 1857, while he was in Washington, Heintzelman visited with Emory in the office of the Boundary Commission. A few months later, Heintzelman saw Emory at Willard's Hotel in

CAMP VERDE TEXAS SAT. OCT. 8, 1859

Jackson went off yesterday morning before daylight in debt to everybody who would trust him & without taking leave of any one. He bought a pistol of one of the men & only paid part. The man has gone after him.

We rode out to Mr. Reeve's & got a half dozen sweet potatoes. The mail came in—the Qr. Mas. & I got a letter from Mr. Lathrop. The works go on well.

This morning the doctor took Charles' leg out of the box & bandaged it. It is doing well.

We rode out to Camp "Ives" on Turtle camp [Creek].[5] Lt. Owens had done a great deal of work & has a beautiful place—much more pleasant than Verde.

The officers have gone to the head of Verde Creek to shoot turkeys.

CAMP VERDE TEXAS MON. OCT. 10, 1859

Yesterday was a beautiful day. We took a long walk in the afternoon. Margaret felt much better after it. She dont sleep well & is quite nervous. To-day is cool. The man that went after Jackson overtook him 15 miles this side [of] S. Antonio & made him give up the pistol. He told him I did not pay him, but still owed him $10. It is strange, if I did that he did not ask for it. The doctor shot two turkeys the evening before last. The other officers did not get anything.

I wrote yesterday to Mr. Poston & the day before to Lathrop.

CAMP VERDE TEXAS WED. OCT. 12, 1859

I wrote to Poston & T. Wrightson. It is cloudy & disagreeable. We rode last evening & ride again this [evening].

Washington and recorded that Emory smelled like a "rum cask." When Heintzelman was in Washington in 1861, Emory gave him a copy of his *Boundary Report*. As a major general, Emory saw action in the Civil War at Hanover Court House, Fisher's Hill, the 1864 Shenandoah Valley Campaign, and Cedar Creek. He commanded the Department of the Platte from 1869 to 1871 and retired as a brigadier general in 1876. Thrapp, *FB*, I, 463; HJ, Sept. 8, Nov. 9, 1842; May 31, June 16, 1849; Mar. 4, 1850; Feb. 6, 1851; Apr. 22, Oct. 27, 1857; Feb. 7, 1861.

[5] A sub-post of Camp Verde, Camp Ives was about four miles north of Camp Verde on Turtle Creek in eastern Kerr County. As Heintzelman indicates, the post was established on October 2, 1859, by seventy-nine men of Company I of the 2d Cavalry commanded by Lt. Wesley Owens. Webb, Carroll, and Branda (eds.), *Handbook of Texas*, I, 282; Post Returns, Camp Verde, AGO, RG 393 (NA).

THURS. OCT. 13, 1859

Beautiful night & pleasant day. I wrote to Sister Maria & to Mr. Lathrop, as our mail comes in at noon to-day.

FRI. OCT. 14, 1859

I got a letter from Matilda at Lexington fair & one from Mahoney. He pays the six mos. interest & keeps the money a year longer. The doctor rebandaged Charles leg again & tomorrow he can use his crutches. We took up the matting & put down the carpet in the parlor.

CAMP VERDE TEXAS SAT. OCT. 15, 1859

Cloudy & a sprinkle of rain this morning. Charles expected to be up this morning, but the Doctor thinks two days.

SUN. OCT. 16, 1859

We took a ride towards Turtle Creek but it commenced raining & we turned back. Some Indians killed a cow three days ago about two miles above the Cav. camp. It rained & is besides too late to go after them. They also killed some horses about ten miles from here towards Kerrsville.

It rained last night but is pleasant to-day. The doctor was in & got Charles in crutches, but he dont make much progress in using them. Friday it was eight weeks since he got his leg broken. He has fretted a great deal & kept his mother sick.

CAMP VERDE TEXAS TUES. OCT. 18, 1859

Yesterday our mail got in & brought me two papers from Mr. Lathrop & two Americans. Things are doing well at the mines. Jarvis has left & Alden is there. The latter is under Lathrops orders.

The "Great Eastern" met with a mishap.[6] An explosion of her boiler, with great damage.

Major Chapman committed suicide at Old Point.[7] Nothing known as to

---

[6] Launched in 1858, the 688-foot *Great Eastern*, a ship designed by Isambard Kingdom Brunel, was far in advance of her day. The ship was designed to carry as many as 4,000 passengers and 6,000 tons of cargo. Driven by a pair of paddle wheels and a horizontal directing engine that powered a propeller, the ship was capable of fifteen knots. Peter Kemp (ed.), *The Oxford Companion to Ships and the Sea* (New York: Oxford University Press, 1976), 353.

[7] Caleb Coker (ed.), *The News from Brownsville: Helen Chapman's Letters from the Texas Military Frontier, 1848–1852* (Austin: Texas State Historical Association, 1992),

the cause. He was subject to fits of depression. It is cool & uncomfortable to-day.

A Mexican a mile & a half from here killed a bear & sent in for a wagon to haul it in. It killed his best dog & weighs dressed about 400 lbs. It is tolerably fat. The doctor sent us five quails—the first we have had.

CAMP VERDE WED. OCT. 19, 1859

A pleasant day—a little warm. We moved into the new Adjutant's Office this morning. It is a Sibley tent on pickets.[8] Three men came & reported Indians. The party who killed a man below Castroville was followed by them till their horses gave out & they came & reported to me. I sent a detachment of 15 men in pursuit. We had roast bear for dinner but with oyster soup, not much of it was eaten. We took a short ride.

A man brought sweet potatoes & turnips. The first for sale at the post.

FRI. OCT. 21, 1859

Yesterday mail brought me no letters or papers. The Doctor loaned me a

---

makes no mention of the death of Bvt. Maj. William Warren Chapman on September 28, 1859, at Fortress Monroe, Old Point Comfort, Virginia. Four days after Chapman's death, Maj. E. S. Sibley wrote: "Within two or three hours after a review by the Secretary of War of troops at Fort Monroe . . . at which Major Chapman attended and took part, he was found by a couple of his brother officers dead in his bedroom, lying across the bed, evidently having committed suicide by cutting his throat, his hand still grasped the razor which rested in his wound. His death was no doubt instantaneous as the left carotid artery had been severed completely." Sibley went on to write that "what led to this unfortunate act is not positively known, but it is conjectured to have been done in a moment of insanity, to which it is stated Major Chapman was liable, having had three or four attacks previously. Mrs. Chapman was not at Fort Monroe at the time, but absent, at New York or in its vicinity." It was Chapman who had introduced Heintzelman to Colt in Washington in December 1857. Chapman, an investor in the Vallecillo Mining Company, had persuaded Heintzelman to exchange stock in the Vallecillo Company for stock in the Sonora Exploration and Mining Company. William W. Chapman should not be confused with Capt. William H. Chapman who served in the army in Texas at the same time. E. S. Sibley to T. F. Chapman, Nov. 4, 1859, LS, Office of the Quartermaster General, RG 92 (NA); HJ, Nov. 30, Dec. 10, 12, 1857.

  [8] The conical Sibley Tent was conceived and patented by Henry H. Sibley, a captain in the 2d Dragoons. Sibley, while stationed in North Texas during the winter of 1854–1855, visited a Comanche village near Fort Belknap and observed the warmth and spaciousness of the Indian tepees. Jerry Thompson, "Henry Hopkins Sibley: Military Inventor on the Texas Frontier," *Military History of Texas and the Southwest*, 10 (No. 4, 1972), 227–248; Jerry Thompson, *Henry Hopkins Sibley: Confederate General of the West*, (Natchitoches: Northwestern State University Press, 1987), 102–107.

"N.O. Pickaun." I see by that that the S.P.R.R. is out of its difficulties & the work going on. I may yet make something out of my stock in it. I had pigeon holes put in a box I use as a desk & keep papers in, makes it much more convenient.

It rained steadily all last night & during the day yesterday. Rain at intervals to-day & rather cool. I yesterday got my bedsteads from Cincinnati. Some of the rollers are lost.

I wrote to Mr. Poston by yesterdays mail & to Lt. Shaaff sending him a draft for express charges.

Sat. Oct. 22, 1859

We put up our new bedstead & it makes much more room in our bed room. It rained all last night & most of to-day but now there is a prospect of a clear off. It is very disagreeable. We have a leg of fine venison. Cost 50 cts.

Camp Verde Texas Sun. Oct. 23, 1859

It cleared off last night & was quite warm this morning. Since the wind came from the N. East it is much cooler.

Mr. Adams the Methodist clergyman came & preached to a small meeting. A friend of his from near Kerrsville came & he made the prayer. They both dined with us. This is his last appearance, as the conference meets in a few days. He invited a collection for missionary purposes. This is the Rio Grande conference.

Tuesday Oct. 25, 1859

It was quite pleasant yesterday & is to-day. The mail yesterday failed. I wrote to Mr. Howe.

This morning I put Margaret on a side saddle & led the horse a mile. She will soon regain her confidence on a horse. She suffers much from Dyspepsia.[9]

Camp Verde Texas. Thus. Oct. 27, 1859

Yesterday I got a poney & put Margaret on & led him & we took a long ride. Yesterday afternoon we asked the Caldwells & took a ride in the Ambulance. This afternoon Miss Helen Lacy will ride with us on horseback.[10] We have a small norther.

---

[9] Gastric indigestion, impaired digestion, or "upset stomach."

[10] "Miss" or "Old Aunt" Lacy was a free woman of color who had been "with the army for years." When her status as a free African American was challenged, Heintzelman and other officers at Camp Verde rallied to her defense. HJ, Aug. 1, 1860.

Our mail came in Thursday. It was delayed because the post master at Comfort lost his keys.

I got a letter from Poston dated Oct. 3rd. W. Wrightson appeared with $15,000 & paid up my pro rata. On what terms I have not heard. Poston made no negotiations. Colt still claims 1,000 shares on the sale I made him & 500 on the pro rata. They have left it to these persons to be selected by Coleman. I should be heard before they decide. Poston says that all the pro rata has been paid in & writes in excellent spirits. The engines were expected to be shipped by the middle of this month. I wrote to Lathrop this morning.

I got a letter about the Odometers—I sent the wrong measure & have sent the correct one now. Solon wrote to Capt. McLean to know when he sent the check for my transportation as it has not yet been received. Cheever is acting the rascall. He still holds 20 shares of my Sonora stock after I returned him his acceptance he gave me for it. Wrote to Mr. Poston. The mail got in late & no letters for us & only one paper.

The scout is back. Lost the trail on account of the rain. The party of Indians is supposed to have been 12. Saw much Indian sign on the Medina.

Camp Verde Texas Fri. Oct. 28, 1859

Still cold & unpleasant. We took up our & the childrens bed room carpets & rearranged the rooms.

Lt. Thomas went yesterday to Camp Ives to stay all night & fish this morning. Rather an unpleasant visit. Mer. 50°. We were preparing for a ride when a cold rain commenced. Last week we had a norther, lasted three days.

Sat. Oct. 29, 1859

Quite cold last night. It is getting more pleasant to-day. The norther is about over.

"I have about 9 companies to rendezvous at old Fort Merrill."

CAMP VERDE TEXAS TUES. NOV. 1ST, 1859

We had muster yesterday. The norther is over & to-day pleasant. Margaret & I took a ride on horseback. She is very timid & nervous. The mail did not get in until late in the afternoon. I wrote to Matilda & M. got a letter from her. She is still in Newport. I got letters from Dr. Tripler. He is planing an Ambulance. I got also a letter from Mr. Lathrop dated 20 Sept. Nothing special. Still at work reducing the old ore.

Polly our new guide came & reported three Indians stole his horse 14 miles from here.[1] I sent 15 men with him in pursuit. He thinks he can over-take them & that there is a large camp on the headwaters of the Concho.

CAMP VERDE. WED. NOV. 2, 1859

I rode out yesterday with Margaret & Miss Lacy as far as the Cav. camp & got back at dark. The weather pleasant. To-day windy & unpleasant. Margaret & I will ride on horseback. The doctor took the splints & bandages off Charles' leg.

FRI. NOV. 5, 1859

We had the uncomm'd officers, sutler's clerk & Lt. Owens & the sutler's clerk at his camp to dinner. All went off pleasantly. The mail came in & brought me a copy of Dr. Triplers address before the Med. Soc. at Newport

---

[1] A legendary figure of the Southwestern frontier, José Policarpo Rodríguez was the son of José Antonio Rodríguez and Encarnacion Sanchez. Born at Zaragoza, Mexico, on January 26, 1829, Rodríguez came with his mother and father to San Antonio in 1841. At age twenty in 1849, he served as a drover and forager for Lt. William H. C. Whiting on an exploring expedition into the Trans-Pecos. Later that same year, Lt. Col. Joseph E. Johnston hired "Polly" as a scout for an expedition to El

on Quaken.[2] A very good address. Also a letter from Mr. Webster of the Vallecillo mine. He wants 2 percent & says the prospects are good. Solon got a note from the post office at San Antonio. A letter for me is there. The mail carrier now stays at the post & goes down for the mail. He took a ride on horseback last evening. An insurrection formented by the Abolitionists has been suppressed at Harpers Ferry.[3] Mason our minister at France is dead.[4]

CAMP VERDE TEXAS SUN. NOV. 6, 1859

We made an arrangement to ride out to Mr. Ruses & take Miss Lacy with us, but her eyes were sore & she could not go.[5] We went on horseback & Lt. Thomas along. We stopped at Camp Ives & Lt. Owens joined us. We staid to dinner & had a pleasant time. It made some variety in this dull place. We found it very warm riding. This morning we had a heavy fog, but now it is quite pleasant.

I see in the New Orleans Pickaune that the S.P.R.R. is through all its difficulties & that the prospect is good for its being worked with vigor. All the debts have been paid or provided for.

I have not felt like writing to-day, but have forced myself to write to T. Wrightson.

Paso del Norte. One of the army's better scouts, Rodriguez settled in 1850 with his wife, Nicolasa, and four children, on Privilege Creek in eastern Bandera County, where he became a Methodist minister. Post Returns indicate that he first signed on as a guide at Camp Verde in August 1856 for $40 a month and rations. "Polly" died at Poteet, Texas, on March 22, 1914, and is buried on the west bank of Privilege Creek, not far from Yglesia Methodista Episcopal Del Sur, which he built of native limestone with his own hands in 1882. His tombstone reads: "By nature strong, fearless, daring by grace an apostle to his people, winning many souls to Christ. He suffered privation, persecution, sorrow, unmoved he went with joy and singing to the end." Today, Polly (sic) Peak and the village of Polly, both in eastern Bandera County, honor his memory. The small chapel and family cemetery continues to be maintained by descendants. José Policarpo Rodríguez, *The Old Guide: Surveyor, Scout, Hunter, Indian Fighter, Ranchman, Preacher* (Dallas, n.d.); Swift, *Three Roads to Chihuahua*, 83, 84, 89; Post Returns, Camp Verde, AGO, RG 393 (NA).

    [2] Quackery or charlatanism.

    [3] A reference to John Brown, a radical abolitionist who led the historic raid on Harper's Ferry, Virginia, on October 16, 1859.

    [4] John Young Mason, congressman from Virginia, jurist, and an expansionist diplomat, was secretary of the navy under John Tyler and was the only cabinet member of the Tyler Administration to be retained by James K. Polk. He died of apoplexy on October 3, 1859. *Dictionary of American Biography* (New York: Charles Scribner's Sons, 1961), VI, 369–370.

    [5] Probably Sidney B. Rees, thirty, a Tennessee-born farmer, who lived near Camp Verde. 8th Census, Kerr County.

The cav. scout returned. The trail got amongst some cattle & they lost all trace of the Indians. They went as far as the Hondo. We took a long walk this afternoon.

I sent off to B.C. Webster of the Valecito S. Mg. Co. $45, my assessment of 2 pr. cent.[6] This they promise to be the last. I also sent $2 to the post master for envelopes & for a letter in S. Antonio Post office. Our mail rider lives at the post, so that the mail closes the night before the day that it arrives.

I have commenced using my copying press again. It does tolerably well.

Camp Verde Tues. Nov. 8, 1859

Yesterday brought the mail. I got a letter from Capt. McLean. Col. R.E. Lee cav. will relieve Gen. Twiggs in command of the Dept. Two companies of arty. from Ft. Clark go to Brownsville. This ends the Arty school.

Ossawatomi Brown of Kansas notoriety took possession of Harpers Ferry & the Arsenal with a small force of Abolitionists. Col. Lee was sent to command the troops sent to subdue them. The Marines soon took the place & ended the affair. It is the most silly affair I ever heard of. It created a great storm in Washington & the neighboring states. There were only 19 whites in all & all but two were killed or wounded. Only one man escaped.[7]

Lt. Owens is summoned as a witness at Camp Lancaster in Lt. Haskell's court.[8] I sent Lt. Mower to relieve him. It is cool & unpleasant. I wrote to Dr. Tripler.

Camp Verde Texas Wed. Nov. 9, 1859

We took a ride on horseback last evening & Miss Lacy rode with us. Lt. Owens left in the morning for S. Antonio.

---

[6] Webster was the New York secretary of the Vallecillo Mining Company. HJ, Apr. 6, 24, 1858.

[7] In his raid on Harper's Ferry, Brown had under his control some eighteen men, five of whom were African American. Although seven of the raiders escaped, two of Brown's sons were killed when U.S. Marines under Col. Robert E. Lee and 1st. Lt. J. E. B. Stuart stormed the engine house which Brown and his men were defending. Brown, along with six others, was later hanged.

[8] Camp Lancaster, established on August 20, 1855, on Live Oak Creek, one-half mile above is junction with the Pecos River, guarded the San Antonio–El Paso road. Today the ruins of the post are a state historical site.

Alexander McDonald Haskell had been commissioned a second lieutenant in the 1st Infantry in 1856. He resigned in May 1861 to become a major in the 6th Texas Volunteers. Marcus J. Wright, *Texas in the War, 1861–1865*, ed. Harold B. Simpson (Hillsboro: Hill College Press, 1865), 19.

The Doctor, Lt. Thomas, & Mr. Newton were in, in the evening & played Eucre.[9]

After tattoo two citizens rode up & brought me a letter from Judge Buckner. A party of Indians killed two men 10 miles north of Quihi & drove off some horses.[10] I sent 15 men in pursuit. Some Citizens are also out. This gentleman told us of an affair Lt. Hazen has had in which he killed four Indians and got shot in the wrist & side badly. He had sent in to Fort Clark for medical aid. The Indians are becoming so bold that it is dangerous to ride out alone.

I wrote to Munn & Co. Sci. Amer. about my pulleys etc., etc. I also wrote to Mr. Lathrop.

I am having my horses shod. It rained a few drops this morning, but now looks pleasant.

Camp Verde Texas Thurs. Nov. 10, 1859

Yesterday at one P.M. an express arrived from San Antonio with orders to send all the available force of I Company 2 cav. in pursuit of 14 Indians seen at Leon Springs 17 miles this side S. Antonio.[11] Lt. Mower started last night at 6½ with 15 men & I sent after him 14 men this morning who were delayed to have their horses shod. The Indians are becoming very bold. I had no guide to send with them, though the guide Lt. Owens took with him will probably meet them.

Margaret and I took a short ride on horseback yesterday. I got my horses shod.

Camp Verde Sat. Nov. 12, 1859

Yesterday was delightful. The mail brought an unimportant order & no letters or papers for me. I saw a S. Antonio paper. It is full of Indian depreda-

---

[9] Euchre was a popular card game played by two, three, or four persons using the thirty-two highest cards in the deck. The game was common at army posts and in eastern social circles, especially the Lathrop and Stuart households in Buffalo. HJ, Feb. 3, Oct. 14, 1842; Mar. 7, 1846; Sept. 27, 1848; Dec. 31, 1854.

[10] Quihi, a small community ten miles northwest of Castroville in Medina County and thirty-five miles west of San Antonio, had been laid out by Henri Castro in 1846. The community was named after the Quichie or Keechie, the white-necked Mexican eagle buzzard. Predominantly German, Quihi was reported by Capt. S. G. French in 1849 to be little more than "a few miserably rude huts." Webb, Carroll, and Branda (eds.), *Handbook of Texas*, II, 424; Report of S. G. French, Dec. 21, 1849, "Reconnaissance of Routes from San Antonio to El Paso," 31st Cong., 1st Sess. (Washington, D.C.: Union Office, 1850), 64.

[11] Leon Springs, some twenty-six miles north of San Antonio, was established as a

tions & murders. Dr. Ganahl & his family called about noon. They are somewhat alarmed about Indians. We took Mrs. Mower & her children out riding
in the afternoon. It was warm & delightful yesterday. In the night the wind
changed & we have a cold norther. Mer. yesterday 82°—this morning 59°.
Capt. Caldwells were in yesterday.

Lt. Mower has returned from his scout. Gen. Twiggs sent Lt. Owens
back & says the court can wait. Lt. Mower reports that at Leon Springs they
reported to him no Indians signs. It will probably turn out a false report.

CAMP VERDE TEXAS SUN. NOV. 13, 1859

Last night an express came from Camp Ives with a note from Mr. Ganahl
that an Indian had been seen near their house. I sent 7, all the cavalry I had
out there. This morning I rode down there with the Doctor, Lt. Thomas &
Mr. Newton. I doubt there ever was an Indian. On our way back we came by
Camp Ives & saw Lt. Mower. On our way home an express met me with
orders to go to Brownsville.[12] That Cortinas was near there with from 600 to
1500 men. I have about 9 companies, Cav. Art. & Infy. to rendezvous at old
Fort Merrill. This company (A) goes also. We expect to leave this evening. I
take with me Lt. Thomas & Hd. Qrs.

Last night mer. was at 25m. The norther still continues.

SAN ANTONIO TEXAS MON. NOV. 14, 1859

We left Verde 6 P.M. & arrived at Staffords 35 miles a little after one A.M.
We stopped, slept & took breakfast at sunrise & reached here at 11¼ A.M. The
general firmly believes the reports. I suppose that I will remain here a couple
of days. Capt. King's company has not yet left. I met all the officers in town of
the general's. I will get my instructions tomorrow. I will be authorized to cross
the river, in case we are in hot pursuit.

It was bitter cold last night. Our barrels were full of ice. It is still cool, but
much more pleasant to-day. The band will be ordered down & Lt. Owens

---

stagecoach stop by a German nobleman, George von Pleue, in 1846. "Reconnaissance
of Routes from San Antonio to El Paso," 49.

[12] Heintzelman retained a copy of orders directing him to Fort Merrill and the Rio
Grande. With Company E of the 2d Cavalry as an escort, he was to proceed to
Brownsville and "return up the Rio Grande via Duncan." He was also to "make a full
inquiry into the present state of affairs at Brownsville." T. A. Washington to
Heintzelman, Nov. 17, 1859; Special Orders no. 100, May 10, 1859; Special Orders no.
103, May 12, 1859; all in HP. For his arrival in San Antonio, see Heintzelman to S.
Cooper, Nov. 14, 1859, LR, AGO, RG 94 (NA). See also New Orleans *Daily Picayune*,
Nov. 29, 1859.

with the cavalry to Verde till we return. I wish Margaret was here with the children, though probably she will be more pleasantly situated where she is.

SAN ANTONIO TEXAS TUES. NOV. 15, 1859

Last evening Dr. Jarvis called & I went with him & made a short visit at his house. I saw Mrs. Jarvis. In the afternoon I called on Mrs. Major Graham. She was very glad to see me & made many inquiries about Margaret. This morning I called at the General's & got my instructions. They are to hunt up Cortinas & his band of Marauders & not to follow them into Mexico, unless in "hot pursuit." If I capture any hand them over to the Civil Authorities.

I have been hunting up Mary DeLaney, the girl lived with us at Newport. She was not in her house.

The weather is delightful.

Ex-Gov. Vidauri is at this house.[13]

P.M. I have my instructions. They are simply so soon as I have sufficient force to pursue Cortinas & his marauders & quit the country. There is a report that Brownsville is taken, but nothing definite.

Capt. Reynolds from Indianola goes with me as a.q.m. I am sorry.

The Sergt. Major & Qr.M. Sergt. are here.

I went with Major Vinton to his house a moment but did not see his wife. I go to tea there this evening. I called to see Mr. Chilton & Mrs. McLean—neither in.

The mail for Verde leaves in the morning. I am writing to Margaret.

SAN ANTONIO TEXAS WED. NOV. 16, 1859

I have been busy all day & have now collected all I meant & attended to everything. I called on Mrs. Lt. Williams & this evening on Mrs. Major Chilton & Capt. McLean.

A letter this evening received by Major Howard from his brother, with Capt. Tobin, without date, says they expect to be in Brownsville in a day or two & that Cortinas is above with 150 or 200 men.[14] So Brownsville can be

---

[13] Santiago Vidaurri, the powerful caudillo of Nuevo León and Coahuila, had been forced from office and was on his way to Washington, D.C. Returning to power, Vidaurri became a nemesis of Benito Juárez and served as minister of finance in Maximilian's Council of State. He was captured and shot without trial in Mexico City on July 8, 1867. Ronnie C. Tyler, *Santiago Vidaurri and the Southern Confederacy* (Austin: Texas State Historical Association, 1973), 139; San Antonio *Daily Herald*, Nov. 10, 16, 18, 1859.

[14] Capt. William G. Tobin, twenty-six, had received a commission from Gov. Hardin Richard Runnels to raise a company of 100 men and proceed to Brownsville without delay. The South Carolina–born Tobin, who was on the trail of Indians near

taken. This letter is postmarked 14th, & the place cant be made out. It is not dated from any place.

I got a barrel of potatoes—irish & lemons & oranges for Margaret & Christmas presents for the children. Capt. Caldwell got in about 9 A.M. & his wagons go back in the morning. We will leave some time tomorrow. I wrote to Margaret & also to Wrightson. Weather pleasant to-day. Called on Gen. Twiggs at his house.

THURS. NOV. 17, 1859

I went & bought a cot & maps & saw with much difficulty my barrel of potatoes & lemons off in the wagon for Verde. I then went to the office & saw Gen. Twiggs. The last days letter has changed the state of affairs. Capt. Caldwell's company & the detachments of cavalry are stopped at S. Antonio. The 20 men from Verde are in town. I go on to old Fort Merril[l] & if things are quiet to Brownsville & then up the Rio Grande to Ft. Duncan. At Merrill I send back the troops there & take Capt. Stoneman's company with me.[15] Lt. Thomas goes all the way & Dr. Foard as far as Merrill.

We had a great deal of trouble but at last—2 P.M. got out of town. I ride in his buggy with Dr. Foard & we have a spring wagon & two road wagons. We take Howe & Norvells & there are three men of Capt. King's company on their way to join him. We came out about 10 or 12 miles & we encamped.

FRIDAY NOV. 18, 1859

We came to the crossing of the Medina, 6 or 8 miles & then took the Laredo road, for 4 or 5 miles, discovered our error & turned back to the river & took the right one & came about 10 miles further. We camped on a pond near the S. Antonio river.

Castroville at the time, recruited sixty men from his headquarter at the Plaza House in San Antonio. Leaving San Antonio on October 16, he recruited more men at San Patricio and reached Brownsville on the evening of November 10, 1859. 8th Census, Bexar County; San Antonio *Daily Herald*, Oct. 18, 27, 1859. During the Cortina War, a letter from Tobin to his wife was published in the *Daily Picayune* (New Orleans), Nov. 26, 1859.

[15] Fort Merrill had been established in March 1850 on the right bank of the Nueces River, at a point where the San Antonio–Corpus Christi Road crossed the river. The ruins of the post are ten miles southeast of present-day George West at the upper end of Lake Corpus Christi. Webb, Carroll, and Branda (eds.), *Handbook of Texas*, I, 629.

An 1846 West Point classmate of George B. McClellan and Thomas J. Jackson, George Stoneman, thirty-five and a veteran of the Mormon Battalion, was a brave and dedicated officer. Heintzelman had grown to trust and respect Stoneman. In 1859, Stoneman was a captain in the 2d Cavalry. He commanded of the 3d Corps of the

Sat. Nov. 19, 1859

We left this morning & have come I suppose 20 miles & are camped at a pool of water, at the road side. It is called 18 & then 25 miles from S. A. to Rocky Creek. I suppose that we are about 5 miles from there. We have no guide & no one that knows the road. Both the doctor & Thomas travelled it once. The road is difficult to keep.

The doctor is supplying us with game. Yesterday he shot a number of ducks, pigeons & culews & this morning ducks, snipe, & ploun.[16] The nights are quite cold, but the days pleasant. The doctor wounded a deer to-day but did not get it.

Sun. Nov. 20, 1859

The doctor wounded two deer to-day, but we got neither. He shot at a sand hill crane & cut out the feathers, but we did not get it.

We stopped last night at the Weedy—a miserable place.[17] No grass & water bad. Last night was cold. The distance to Rocky was at least ten miles & 8 more to Weedy made the animals all tired.

We saw a great many deer along the road. The first part of the day was cloudy & at one time it misted, but the afternoon was hot. We found a wagon stalled at the Wendy & helped the man out.

Sulphur 18 miles from Rocky Mon. Nov. 21, 1859

We reached here at 12 & have a very fair camp. We have here a small town (Oakville) & got some supplies & information.[18] No doubt Brownsville

---

Army of the Potomac at Fredericksburg and was in charge of the Union cavalry at Chancellorsville. Later at the battle for Atlanta in 1864, he directed the Cavalry Corps of the Army of the Ohio and was given the task of using his cavalry to liberate the sick and starving prisoners at Andersonville. At the Battle of Sunshine Church near Atlanta, Major General Stoneman became the highest ranking Union officer to surrender during the Civil War. Stoneman was retired for disability in 1871 and became governor of California in 1882. Stoneman died at Buffalo, New York, in 1894. Hietman, *HR*, 930; Warner, *Generals in Blue*, 481–482.

[16] All are small- to medium-sized wading birds common to South Texas during the winter. Besides the ducks, snipe, and pigeons, the other birds were probably Long Billed Curlews and Mountain Plovers. Roger Tory Peterson, *A Field Guide to Western Birds* (Cambridge, Mass.: Houghton Mifflin Co., 1961) 97, 106, 108.

[17] Weedy Creek rises in western Karnes County and eastern Live Oak County and flows south into the Atascosa River, thirteen miles north of present-day Three Rivers.

[18] Located at a site called Puente Piedra, Oakville (Sulphur or Sulphur Springs) was the county seat of Live Oak County. Webb, Carroll, and Branda (eds.), *Handbook of Texas*, II, 298.

is occupied by Capt. Tobin & his Rangers. Capt. Lee's company of 8 Infy must be now at Merrill. Cortinas is above Brownsville.[19] All the accounts are much exaggerated. I am satisfied that no more troops are needed. The mail for S. Antonio leaves in the morning. I will write to Margaret & to the general. Last night was cold. The doctor rode ahead but did not succeed in shooting a deer. They are scarce. The country is poor & water scarce.

FORT MERRILL TUES. NOV. 22, 1859

The train left Sulphur just as I got up.[20] We got off about the usual time & the Doctor & I arrived on the Nueces at 10½ A.M. As we approached the ford we heard someone calling us to come on. We recognized Cap. King who is encamped about half a mile below on the Ft. Merrill side.[21] The Banks are bad & the water up to the buggy bottom. Our wagons did not get in till near 2 P.M. We are encamped close by King. He received us very hospitably. The day was quite warm, though we had a fog in the morning & a few drops of rain on the road. The road pretty good, distance 15 miles or 108 from S. Antonio.

Capt. King has no more news than we have.

About 4 P.M. we saw troops approaching & were surprised to see Lts. Graham & Ramsey with the two companies of the Arty. Dr. Carsville is along.[22] A little after dark two gentlemen rode up—Capt. Lee & Lt. Reed of the 8th Infy.[23] They could not learn that we were here & encamped at sundown about as far above the fort. We will move down in the morning. They have had a hard march—difficulty about the road. The Arty companies were

---

[19]   This same information was relayed to department headquarters in San Antonio. Heintzelman to Washington, Nov. 22, 1859, Letters Sent Book, Heintzelman Papers (Manuscript Division, Library of Congress; cited hereafter as HLS).

[20]   The San Antonio–Corpus Christi Road crossed Sulphur Creek at Oakville. Sulphur Creek rises in southern Karnes County and flows twenty-eight miles into the Nueces River in southern Live Oak County.

[21]   A New Yorker, Richard King was lured to Brownsville at the age of twenty-one during the Mexican War by a friend, Mifflin Kenedy, to pilot steamboats on the Rio Grande. By 1859, King and Kenedy had established a ranch headquarters on Santa Gertrudis Creek 100 miles north of Brownsville.

[22]   William A. Carswell was an assistant surgeon from South Carolina. He resigned in March 1861 to become a surgeon in the Confederate Army. Heitman, *Historical Register*, 286.

[23]   From Pennsylvania, Capt. Arthur Tracy Lee had transferred to the 8th Infantry and was promoted to captain in 1848. For his brief account of the Cortina War see "Reminiscences of the Regiment," in *Synopsis of the History of the Eighth U.S. Infantry*, ed. Thomas Wilhelm (2 vols.; David's Island, N.Y.: Regimental Headquarters, 8th Infantry, 1871), II, 400–409. Captain Lee even managed a light-hearted poem, "The Rout of the Black Cortina: A Legend of the 'Rio Bravo del Norte,'" about Heintzelman and the Battle of Rio Grande City:

overtaken by the express a little below Laredo. Not a word of Stoneman or Jourdan.[24] Lt. Thomas & the doctor have lost their poneys & one mule we drove & one of the train. I think they will find them in the morning.

Ft. Merrill Wed. Nov. 23, 1859

On the road the Dr. & I slept in one tent. Last night we pitched separate tents. Every night before we went to sleep the Dr. read a chapter of Isabella Arsini. We finished it on the Sulphur. It rained a little last night & is cloudy this morning. The Doctor & Lt. Graham have gone hunting & we have men out after the lost animals.

The Heintzelman, five hundred strong,
Fresh from the land of doodle dandy;
With Texas Rangers, five miles long,
Came sweeping up the Rio Grande.

And gaily rode the Heintzelman,
Not he of fear or death e'er dreaming;
Rode proudly as the Ritter Ban,
With trumpet blast, and banners
    screaming.
Vive Americana!

The Heintzelman his sabre drew,
Drew Captain Ford his old revolver;
Cried King, "Charge on my boys in blue,
And give the devils a dissolver."

The Heintzelman, he swore a swear,
A mighty swear; we'll not repeat it;
But H-r-y when he tears his hair,
And stamps the bunch grass, could not
    bear it.
Maldijos, caramba!

The Heintzelman, he flashed his blade,
The red legs held their brass guns handy;
The Rangers yelled out "Who's afraid?"
As they swept up the Rio Grande.
Vamos, pasearse, hi!

Now ruthless robber, hold thy best,
Or vengeance dire will quick confound
    thee;
No soft arms circle now thy breast,
The Heintzelman is all around thee.
Flash, bang, whiz!

They waver now, and see they fly,
The day is ours, their lines are broken;
But where's the Black Cortina? hi!
Alas! he's gone, and left no token.

Lee, "Reminiscences," II, 406–407. Several excerpts from the poem can be found in Stephen Thomas, *Fort Davis and the Texas Frontier: Paintings by Captain Arthur T. Lee, Eighth U.S. Infantry* (College Station: Texas A&M University Press, 1976), 24–25. Several stanzas have been omitted here.

Edwin W. H. Read had been commissioned a second lieutenant in the 8th Infantry in 1856. Read was in San Antonio when General Twiggs surrendered the Department of Texas. During the Civil War, he was breveted a major for gallantry at Gettysburg. Resigning from the army in 1873, Read died two years later. Heitman, *Historical Register*, 818; *Alamo Express* (San Antonio), Apr. 24, 1861.

[24] Jourdan is Charles Downer Jordan, 1842 West Point graduate and a captain in the 8th Infantry. Heitman, *Historical Register*, 583.

Thoroughly washed & with clean clothes I feel comfortable. We have so far had a tolerably pleasant journey. The road was generally good.

P.M. An express arrived with orders from Gen. Twiggs to breakup the expedition.[25] I had just signed an order assuming command when I changed it & added orders to the troops to join their stations. So soon as Capt. Stoneman arrives we start (the two companies of Arty & Stoneman) for Brownsville. Capts. Lee & King dined with us. King & Dr. Foard start back in the morning. Capt. Lee goes along to take his wife to his post, Camp Lawson, junction of the Frio & Leona. I am sorry that the Doctor cant go with us. Weather quite warm.

FT. MERRILL TEXAS THURS. 24 NOV. 1859

We had a few drops of rain last night & a small shower at 10 A.M. Capt. Jourdan's company 8 Infy got in at 8 & Capt. Stoneman's at 9 A.M. The express left a few minutes before 8. Capt. King with his company, Dr. Foard & Capt. Lee left also this morning, just after the companies arrived.

We have to stay tomorrow for some corn.

Wrote to Cheever & to Mr. Futhey.

FT. MERRILL TEXAS FRI. 25 NOV. 1859

Yesterday was Thanksgiving. We did not have much of a feast. It sprinkled rain again last night & a little in the morning. It then cleared off & has been quite warm. I disliked laying over another day, but felt obliged as we had sent for corn. It did not come, however, but we sent out in the neighborhood & got a small quantity. We also sent to San Patricio to get some corn. We will go down on this side. It adds a day's journey to the road, but we will get along so much better & probably save it in the end. We also issued provisions to Capt. Stoneman's company. The section of the Battery is still behind. I will leave an order for them to return. Two wagons of Capt. Lee's company are also still behind.

I did not have an opportunity to send off my letter so wrote no more. The day after tomorrow we can send from San Patricio. The mail passes up however tomorrow.

CASA BLANCA TEXAS SAT. NOV. 26, 1859

At 7 A.M. we left Ft. Merrill encampment. Capt. Jourdan's company left a

---

[25] With Stoneman's Company E of the 2d Cavalry and Companies L and M of the 1st Artillery, Heintzelman was to continue on to Brownsville. Special Orders no. 113, Dec. 10, 1859; Washington to Heintzelman, Nov. 21, 1859; both in HP; Heintzelman to Washington, Nov. 23, 1859, HLS.

moment before us. Lt. Reed with Capt. Lee's will wait for two wagons & some men they left behind. I sent back an order to the section of Major French's battery to turn them back.

We got here about 12, a distance of about 16 miles, a little over half way to San Patricio.[26] We left the road for a little while. Capt. Stoneman has a guide.

On the hill near here is the ruin of a stone house, built by the Spaniards—a fortified house. It has not been occupied for 40 years. It is one of several along this road.

It has been cloudy, with a strong breeze & quite pleasant. We have the cavalry & two Arty companies

Wrote to Mr. Lathrop.

CAMP NEAR SAN PATRICIO OPPOSITE SIDE NUECES
SUN. NOV. 27, 1859

We got an early start, rode about 12 miles & encamped at 10 A.M. on a lagoon, with indifferent water & good grass. We will have to stop here till 8 or 9 tomorrow for corn. It is near three miles to town. There is a report that Dr. Capt. or Col. Ford will be here to-day from Austin with 500 men.[27] The legislature has passed a law to raise 1000 men.

---

[26] On the north bank of the Nueces River, San Patricio was founded in 1830 by members of the John McMullen and James McGloin colony. Named after the Irish patron saint San Patricio Hibernia, the community grew to become the county seat of San Patricio County. Rachel Bluntzer Hebert, *The Forgotten Colony, San Patricio de Hibernia* (Burnet: Eakin Press, 1981).

[27] By 1859, John Salmon Ford was already a legend on the Southwestern frontier. Born in South Carolina in 1815, Ford came to Texas in 1836, served in the Texas Army, commanded a spy company in the Mexican War, and, along with R.S. Neighbors, explored a large part of the trans-Pecos. Besides practicing medicine, Ford served as a captain in the Rangers on the border in the early 1850s, established a newspaper in Austin, and was elected to the Texas State Senate. In 1859, Ford was in Austin when Governor Runnels persuaded him to raise a company of Rangers and march to Brownsville. Ford later met with Heintzelman in Galveston in 1867. "Gen. Ford, who was with me on the Rio Grande, is here from Brownsville," is all that Heintzelman wrote on the occasion. John Salmon Ford, *Rip Ford's Texas* (Austin: University of Texas Press, 1963), ed. Stephen B. Oates, 260–275; W. J. Hughes, *Rebellious Ranger: Rip Ford and the Old Southwest* (Norman: University of Oklahoma Press, 1964), 160–165; HJ, May 3, 1867.

Typescripts of Ford's unedited memoirs are at the Center for the Study of American History, University of Texas at Austin. Copies of his military papers can be found at the Texas State Archives, Austin. Originals of these papers are in possession of the United Daughters of the Confederacy in Waco, Texas

The weather has been excessively warm. I wrote to Margaret & have sent the letters by Lt. Thomas to town.

We saw quite a number of geese, but since Dr. Foard left we have no hunters. There were plenty of ducks at last nights encampment but the officers shot but one. The men were out & shot a dozen.

The "Casa Blanca" is an old stone house abandoned there 40 years.[28] It is two story & was built by an old Spaniard, one of a family built several such houses along this river. The Indians were friendly when they settled here & they gave them beef, but they began to come too often & when refused they became hostile.

We have a great deal of trouble about corn. We have sent out 6 miles on the other side & will have to wait in the morning for it or loose a day.

Wrote to Dr. Summers. Wrote to Gen. Twiggs.[29]

NEAR CAPT. KING'S RANCHE TUES. NOV. 29, 1859

We did not get our corn until late in the afternoon, when we went 7 miles to Banquete.[30] It was dark when we got there. After we stopped Capt. King & Mr. Richardson, his overseer or superintendent, came in to camp with the notorious Capt. Henry.[31] I did not see them. They brought a paper with the

---

[28]   Casa Blanca was near the mouth of Penitas Creek in what is today the northern part of Jim Wells County. Built about 1800, the fort was erected of hand-cut white caliche blocks. The site was first occupied by Francisco Montemayor, who white-washed the fort. Later Joseph Agustín de la Garza received a large land grant that encompassed the fort. Much of the fortification was destroyed by Indians. Later yet, the U.S. Army established a subpost of Fort Merrill at the site. Nueces County Historical Society (comp.), *The History of Nueces County* (Austin: Jenkins Publishing Co., 1972), 31–32; Agnes G. Grimm, *Llanos Mestenos: Mustang Plains* (Waco: Texian Press, 1968), 20–21; Jack Jackson, *Los Mestenos, Spanish Ranching in Texas, 1721–1821* (College Station: Texas A&M University Press, 1986), 449–450.

[29]   Heintzelman appraised headquarters of the progress of the expedition and that he had come by way of San Patricio to obtain forage. Furthermore, no new information from Brownsville had been received. Heintzelman to Washington, Nov. 28, 1859, HLS.

[30]   Some thirty-seven miles west of Corpus Christi and fourteen miles south of San Patricio, Banquete was the last community of any size on the road to Brownsville.

[31]   Capt. James Richardson, a Mexican War veteran, had been hired by King to act as foreman and to defend the ranch headquarters on the Santa Gertrudis. During the Civil War, Richardson raised a small band of vaqueros, Los Kiñeros, for the Confederacy. He was later dismissed by King and settled in the Beeville area. Bruce Cheeseman, interview, May 8, 1994; Lea, *King Ranch*, I, 117–118, 218–219, 458–459. The "notorious" William Robertson "Big Bill" Henry, forty-three and grandson of

account of 12 cos. ordered to Brownsville from Fort Monroe & Leavenworth. I feel much disgusted, as I fear I will not get home as soon as I expected.

We left this morning & came 25 miles & encamped about 3 miles beyond Capt. King's ranche. He owns 15 leagues of land & foaled last year 1000 colts. He has just sent us two sheep. He runs boats on the Rio Grande. We have one or two sprinkles of rain. It has been cloudy & pleasant. Capt. Rickets compy of Arty is at Brownsville. Cortinas is still on this side.[32]

BALUARE TEXAS[33] WED. NOV. 30, 1859

We had the last half of the road much sand. Before that the roads have generally been good. We have covered immense plains this side of S. Patricio. The day before yesterday we saw quite a number of grouse. To-day we saw only a few deer. At a salt arroyo we saw some ducks & two covies of quails— the first I have seen on the march.

Patrick Henry, had served as a sergeant in the regular army and had fought in the Seminole Wars and Mexican War before becoming a filibuster with Samuel A. Lockridge and William Walker in Nicaragua. Henry, commanding a company from Goliad, had also been with James H. Callahan in the October 1855 invasion of Mexico and the burning of Piedras Negras, Coahuila. In March of the same year, Gen. Persifor F. Smith, commanding the Department of Texas, had severely criticized Henry's company of Rangers for robbing the post office at D'Hanis and pillaging the village. Henry had served as San Antonio city marshall and sheriff of Bexar County from 1856 to 1858. Prior to the Cortina War, Henry had given speeches in Texas highly critical of the U. S. Army. The regulars, Henry said, were known for little more than their "tidy uniforms" and their inability to protect the Texas frontier. To Henry the "dirty shirt Texas Rangers" were far more effective than "the dashing military officers on prancing steeds." To Henry, "government ambulances, filled with champagne and all the luxuries of life, thronged the roads leading to the various military encampments." Ford wrote that Henry "was brave and possessed merit, but had the credit of interfering with his superior officers." Henry, who was wounded in the leg in the fight with Cortina at La Bolsa, was married to Consolación Urrutia in 1850 and the couple had three children. Henry was killed by Capt. W. G. Adams of the Sibley Brigade in a gunbattle on Main Plaza in San Antonio in April 1862. Persifor F. Smith to S. Cooper, Mar. 14, 1855, Letter from the Secretary of War, 46th Cong., 2d Sess., 97–98; Ford, *Rip Ford's Texas*, 267. See also *Tri-Weekly News* (Galveston), Nov. 1, 1859; Elton R. Cude, *The Wild and Free Dukedom of Bexar* (San Antonio: Munguia Printers, 1978), 43–46; *Daily True Delta* (New Orleans), Jan. 17, 1860.

[32] Capt. James Brewster Ricketts, a New Yorker and an 1839 West Point graduate, commanded a company in the 1st Artillery. Ricketts became a brigadier general during the Civil War and died in 1887. Heitman, *Historical Register*, 830.

[33] Balaurte Creek rises in northeastern Jim Hogg County and flows east some twenty-eight miles into the Laguna Salada in eastern Brooks County.

This is a poor place to encamp. It is 13 miles to water. Only enough for the men & 40 miles to the Arroyo Colorado. I think we will start tomorrow at 12 & get a little water & when the moon goes down start out on the long stretch. Our mules are failing.

We have had cloudy weather most of the time & delightful. Came about 25 miles.

❦ December 1859 ❦

"Near 50 miles & a fight is a pretty good business."

BALUARE TEXAS THURS. DEC. 1, 1859

A poor camp. After great delay I got off a party to try & open the wells at Los Mugures.[1] We will leave here at 11 A.M. try & water there, graze & travel in the night. It is 40 miles to the Arroyo Colorado.

Baluarte means a kind of lookout. Here the King of Spain kept a station with a lookout.

About half the way yesterday was deep sand. Until then we had very fair road. From here they say that the sand is heavy as far as the Arroyo Colorado. Our mule teams are failing. We had a strong wind yesterday & it is warm this morning. Wrote to Margaret. This is, I believe the Sta. Rosa Post Office.

LAS ANIMAS[2] FRI. DEC. 2, 1859

We left about 10 A.M. yesterday & came 13 miles to Los Mugures some holes dug for wells. We sent forward some men to dig them out, but they did not give much water & that very bad. We gave each animal part of a pail full & lay down & slept on the ground until about 10 P.M.

We then started & made about 27 miles to some deserted ranches. I thought it was the Arroyo Colorado but was mistaken. We had several showers of rain & got in just at daylight. The water we found was in wells & quite brackish. As we were watering a norther struck us. We made for the mesquite

---

[1] Los Mugures or Mugeres is probably a corruption of Las Mujeres, a mesquital or mott, which is indicated on an 1884 Cameron County map near the San Patricio–Brownsville road in the vicinity of what is today Turcotte in central Kenedy County.

[2] At Rancho Las Animas, in the southern part of present-day Kenedy County, the San Patricio Road forked, one road leading directly south to the Arroyo Colorado and a second angling southwest toward Santa Rita and Santa Rosa.

& encamped. Dr. Carswell rode to the houses & made a fire. We found quite a number of chickens & pigs about the house. I suppose the people left on account of the disturbances. This is the first norther I saw come up. A little before day the air became quite warm. As we were watering a dense fog came down from the north, rolling over & over repeatedly. We had scarcely been enveloped in it before it commenced raining & turning cold.

It rained all day & at night began to freeze. It was a quite uncomfortable day.

Rancho on road Sat. Dec. 3, 1859

We came 21 miles, about half of the way deep sand.

The road the day before was very heavy.

It rained steadily all night & froze. Our tents were stiff as boards & the ground covered with snow & sleet. All the grass & trees coated with ice.

We did not get off until 10 a.m. Before then the rain cleared & the wind went down & it began to thaw. It was bad riding in the wet & slush. All our wagons did not get in till after dark. Some out of corn.

In the morning I started Lt. Ramsey & a man of the cavalry on ahead to go to Brownsville & send out corn for our animals.

2½ miles south of Colorado Arroyo[3] Sun. Dec. 4, 1859

The sun was not out much yesterday & did not dry the roads much. We had very little sun to-day. We started a little before 8 & are encamped about 2½ miles beyond the Arroyo Colorado. We called it 10 miles to the river. We crossed in a ferry boat & was detained near two hours crossing the Cavalry & theirs & our wagons. We left Lt. Thomas there to see the crossing of the two companies of Arty & their wagons. The road is very heavy owing to the heavy rains, so we have not ventured to come any further. It rained much more here. We are out of the sand & in the mesquite & cactus. It is 31 miles from the river to Brownsville. If there is much more such road we cant get in tomorrow. The corn is to be brought out to this camp.

There has no one been along this road for more than a month. Some of Cortinas's men have been almost to the river & there is a report that they killed four Americans in an ambuscade.[4]

---

[3] The Arroyo Colorado, rising in eastern Hidalgo County, flows generally northeast about thirty-seven miles through Cameron County and present-day Harlingen into Willacy County and the Laguna Madre.

[4] On November 18, 1859, Cortina ambushed a party of Texas Rangers under Lt. John Littleton, sheriff of Karnes County, on the edge of the Palo Alto Prairie near the

We stop here to put our arms in order & to march with care. The chapparal is very dense. I fear for Lt. Ramsay & the man with him. They crossed the river at dusk & have the cover of the night. The impression is that there are 300–400 men in Brownsville.

The Arroyo Colorado is 40 or 50 yds. wide with a rope ferry. This is the stream, 12 miles further down, Gen. Taylor met the first Mexicans. It is quite salty. We find water any where on the road side.

We will be three weeks this evening since I left Verde. This is Lt. Thomas's birthday. He was hoping to get into Brownsville by that time. Tomorrow morning will be fifteen years since I married.

FT. BROWN TEXAS TUESDAY DEC. 6, 1859

We had an excellent camp as far as security. We were surrounded by a dense chapparal & cactus on three sides with water & grass in front of our fires.

We left at the usual hour between 7 & 8 & came about 12 miles & stopped to graze & get dinner. Our mules were nearly broken down & as we were led to believe we might be attacked we made frequent stops to close up. The first part of the road was very bad, but afterwards pretty good.

We stopped to graze about the middle of the afternoon & left at dark. We came 16 more miles & with the frequent stops we did not reach the outskirts of the town before 11 P.M. There we were delayed until near one A.M. by the stalling of some of our teams in a large mud hole & in passing the guards & barricades. There were several sentinels. At last we got into the garrison & I called on Capt. Nichols whom I found in bed & we encamped on the parade [ground].[5] As we came in a steamboat arrived from the mouth of the river. We passed some dense chapparal, where we might have been much annoyed & also missed the road several times, though we did not go far astray.

Palo Alto House, north of Brownsville. Captain Tobin had sent Littleton out to escort a company of Rangers into Brownsville that was arriving from Live Oak County. Rangers William McKay, Thomas Grier, and Nicholas R. Milett were killed in the ambush. Another Ranger, John Fox, was wounded and allegedly executed by the *Cortinistas*. The Palo Alto House, owned by Julius Verbaum, included a good cistern, cowpens, stables, and hog shed. Wm. G. Tobin to H. B. Runnels, Nov. 17, 1859, Hardin G. Runnels Papers, Record Group 301 (Texas State Archives, Austin); *American Flag* (Brownsville), Mar. 16, 1859.

[5] From Pennsylvania, William Augustus Nichols, 1838 West Point graduate and a Mexican War veteran, was a captain in the 2d Artillery and was serving at department headquarters as an assistant adjutant. Breveted a major general during the Civil War, Nichols died in April of 1869. Heitman, *Historical Register*, 747, *Alamo Express* (San Antonio), Apr. 24, 1861. For Heintzelman's arrival in Brownsville, see *Daily True Delta* (New Orleans), Dec. 28, 1859.

Where we stopped to graze was on the end of the Palo Alto plain & we crossed the upper end of the Resaca de la Palma. The Palo Alto is a beautiful plain. We saw three large cotton mouthed snakes, one dead & a large Rattlesnake, just killed six feet long & 11 rattles.

We met several Mexicans on the road yesterday & almost the only persons we have seen. We got no definite information. We expected to meet the corn I sent for but no one knew anything. When we got here we learned that Lt. Ramsay had sent some under an escort of 30 Rangers. What road can they have taken? They as well as the people are badly stampeded.

This is quite a good sized town & how they could fear the outlaws is more than I can see. We got nothing definite about Cortinas. He appears to be still above & the Rangers dont care to attack him. Our march in last night quite surprised some people. We were not expected in less than two days.

At 3 A.M. I went to bed, first wrote a letter to Margaret as I hear a mail leaves early & only once in two weeks.

Ft. Brown Wed. Dec. 7, 1859

We take out meals at a very fair Restaurant in town. We went at eight & numbered eight officers. It was quite warm at breakfast, but as we finished a norther struck us & since then it has been quite cold. It rained most of the day yesterday with it. It was so cold & unpleasant that we could not do much. My letter to Margaret has not gone yet. The steamer could not embark on account of the rain. I understand that she will leave tomorrow. A mail also leaves in the morning for Corpus Christi. I must write by it.

We have to send by this boat to Brazos for ammunition for the two howitzers I wish to take along & also for clothing for Capt. Stoneman's company.

Last night the mercury was at 24°. All the men & officers quit their tents & are in quarters. I have a room in Capt. Rickett's quarters. It commenced freezing early in the afternoon. The wind has gone down & it is now much moderated, though I think it will freeze tonight. I had a pail of water within a yard of my fireplace & the fire did not go out all night. I made it up in the morning before daylight & when I got up there were crystals of ice on it & the wet sponge on the mantle piece was frozen.

Capt. Stoneman & I were out to-day looking for a map of the country & finally found one. We also got some reliable information about Cortina's position. I think I will now find no difficulty in turning it. He has some 300 or 350 men, about 100 cavalry & some badly armed. There is no certainty that he still occupies his old position.

I met Capt. Tobin of the vols. He appears to be a clever man. Judge Davis

& Judge Powell [Powers] called this afternoon.[6] The former says he will find me a spy to visit this camp. The two men sent from San Antonio I can hear nothing of, except that one called on Capt. Ricketts for pistol cartridges.

Wrote my report & to Margaret.[7]

FT. BROWN TEXAS THURS. DEC. 8, 1859

Not so cold last night & pleasant to-day. They have not had ice, or frost for some years before at this place. There is a report this morning that Cortinas had moved 10 miles up the river & six back. May be true or not. After breakfast I rode over to Matamoros with Lt. Boggs of the Ordnance. We took a long walk through town. It is much like most Mexican towns. There is a pretty little square ornamented by Major Chapman, when the town was in our possession. The Cathedral is not a striking building & is pretty within.[8] I wanted to buy a few little things & searched the town, with very partial success. We met an American from this side [who] showed us around. We got horses at one P.M. & found the steamer waiting for Lt. Boggs, who goes to Brazos for ammunition & clothing. I will be here till next week.

---

[6] Edmund Jackson Davis, a Florida-born attorney, was judge of the 12th Judicial District, which included the counties of Cameron, Hidalgo, Starr, Zapata, Webb, and Kinney. Davis had served as district attorney for South Texas and had been elected to the Laredo Town Council at the time he was acting as customs inspector at Laredo. In November 1859, he had accompanied Tobin's Rangers to Brownsville. Davis later recruited Texans for the Union and became a general in the Federal Army before becoming governor of Texas in 1870. Davis died in Austin in 1883. Jerry Thompson, *Warm Weather and Bad Whiskey: The 1886 Laredo Election Riot* (El Paso: Texas Western Press, 1991), 14–16; Ronald Norman Gray, "Edmund J. Davis: Radical Republican and Reconstruction Governor of Texas," (Ph.D. diss., Texas Tech University, 1976), 1–8; *Daily Picayune* (New Orleans), Nov. 26, 1859.

From Portland, Maine, Stephen Powers had served as a first lieutenant in the 10th Infantry before helping to develop Brownsville, where he became chief justice of Cameron County and mayor of the town. One of the few slave owners on the border, Powers rose to become a powerful political figure in South Texas. Milo Kearney and Anthony Knopp, *Boom and Bust: The Historical Cycles of Matamoros and Brownsville* (Austin: Eakin Press, 1991), 65–69; Slave Census (8th), Cameron County. For a photograph of Powers, see Ruby A. Wooldridge and Robert B. Vezzetti, *Brownsville: A Pictorial History* (Norfolk: Donning Co., 1982), 64.

[7] Heintzelman complained that he could obtain "little reliable information as to the position, force or object of Cortinas." He did enclose a field return for General Twiggs that showed the total strength of his small army. Heintzelman to Washington, Dec. 7, 1859, HLS.

[8] Damaged by several hurricanes, Catedral de Nuestra Señora del Refugio on Quinta Avenue between Morelos and Gonzales Streets in Matamoros had been built about 1825. Coker (ed.), *News From Brownsville*, 3–47.

Capt. Ricketts is not well to-day. I suppose [he] has taken a cold. The norther appears to be over.

FT. BROWN TEXAS FRI. DEC. 9, 1859

It is mild, cloudy & looks like rain. A norther is prognosticated. A Mexican was caught last evening on the outskirts & on his way to the guard, attempting to escape, was shot & killed. No one appears to recognize him. He probably did not know any better than to attempt escape.

Capt Ricketts is a little better this morning.

I called with Lt. Ramsay to return Judge Davis & Major Powells [Powers] call. We saw the former. He is trying to send a spy to Cortinas camp, but has not found one.

Most of the officers dine in Matamoros with Mr. Mahoney, a wealthy Irishman there, who always knows the officers. When I was over there yesterday I stopped at his business place, but he was over here. He & a Mr. Clark also an Irishman dined with us yesterday.[9] They are both amusing. The latter became too intimate with a wealthy Mexicans wife & he had influence to keep him a year on the chain gang. The Mexican dying he got released & married the widow. They have now quarrelled & separated.

This reminds me of what I heard since we arrived here. Lt. Chapin of the 7th, who got a divorce from his wife under peculiarly atrocious circumstances & married one of the Mim Pauls, has discovered an intimacy between her and one of the officers of his regiment.[10] Everybody says he is served right.

A norther is springing up—so every body says.

7 P.M. The wind is north & it is cooler, but blows very moderately. A.M. Champion who lives above here some 20 miles & has been robbed, came down on the other side.[11] He reports that Cortina's men have been scattered

---

[9] Maine-born William Clark, fifty-five, had been in charge of the Kenedy and King warehouses and repair shops at the mouth of the Rio Grande at what was known as Clarksville. After Heintzelman left Brownsville in 1860, Clark served as vice consul in Matamoros. Kearney and Knopp, *Boom and Bust*, 72; 8th Census, Cameron County; J. Galvan to Heintzelman, June 24, 1860, HP.

[10] Gurden Chapin, an 1851 West Point graduate, was serving as regimental adjutant of the 7th Infantry. Dismissed in August 1861, Chapin was reinstated and served ably as adjutant in the Union Army in New Mexico Territory. Chapin retired from the army in 1869 and died in August of 1875. Heitman, *Historical Register*, 295.

[11] An illiterate Alberto M. Campione came to Brownsville from northern Italy in 1850 and changed his name to Albert Champion. Forty-three in 1859, Champion, his Mexican wife, Estefana, and their three children resided at Point Isabel. Champion's brother Peter, sixty-four and a mail contractor on the Brownsville-Brazos Santiago line who owned the Galveston Ranch upriver from Brownsville, later filed claims with

some distance up the river, but have returned. That if the Rangers had made a serious attack the other day they would have broken up the nest.

He also expresses the opinion, in which I coincide, that Cortinas & his men view this in the light of [a] pronunciamiento on the other side & think that they can make terms at any moment. Cortinas has told them that a Commissioner from Washington has arrived to treat.

This is dull business lying here waiting. There is nothing doing in town. Dr. Carswell, Lt. Sullivan & myself were at dinner.[12] The rest dined in Matamoros. Capt. Ricketts is quite sick & Dr. Holden messes in his quarters.[13]

FT. BROWN TEXAS SAT. DEC. 10, 1859

A dull cloudy day, but more mild.

Dr. Carswell & I walked to old Ft. Brown about 600 yds. below this. There is but one house within the works. Trees & bushes are growing all around & the parapets are now much dilapidated. It is much more extensive that I supposed.

Lts. Thomas & Graham got back from Matamoros after 10 A.M. Capt. Stoneman is still there & Lt. Ramsey with him.

There is no doubt from what they hear that Cortinas has concentrated his men at the old place above. He sent higher up to steal cattle.

I have been occupied arranging my papers. Capt. Ricketts is still quite sick.

As we went to breakfast this morning we saw on the post office door that the mail leaves at 8 A.M. for N. Orleans. Too late to write.

6½ P.M. Capt. Stoneman & Lt. Ramsay got home. A Mexican Colonel gives a small party & all the officers are invited. As my invitation came second hand I wont go & if it had come more direct I could not have gone. Some of the young officers I suppose will go. I saw Mr. Mahoney in the garrison at retreat. He belongs to a wealthy house in Matamoros sells some $3,000,000 in a year it is said.

Heintzelman asserting he lost property amounting to some $16,678 during the Cortina War. Losses included household goods, farming tools, horses, mules, and "220 chickens and 6 turkeys." Another brother, Nicholas, also lived in Point Isabel. 8th Census, Cameron County. See also Peter Champion Claim, Jan. 25, 1860, "Texas Frontier Troubles," 44th Cong., 1st Sess., no. 343, 21–22. Cited hereafter as TFT.

[12] From Ohio, 2d Lt. Thomas Crook Sullivan, 1856 West Point Graduate, was in command of Company C of the 1st Artillery. Field Return of Troops in the Brownsville Expedition, Dec. 14, 1859, HP.

[13] Levi H. Holden, a Rhode Island native, had served as an assistant surgeon since 1840. Heitman, *Historical Register*, 537.

I have been all over this little town of Brownsville. They are finishing a large Catholic church. Have a fine Market house.[14] There are many miserable houses in the outskirts. There is also a Convent. The weather is getting cooler & looks unsettled.

FT. BROWN TEXAS SUN. DEC. 11TH, 1859

The day before yesterday Capt. Stoneman rode out with Capt. Tobin to the Ranger camp, a mile & a half from town. There are three companies in all numbering near 150 men. Capt. S. gave them a drill & showed them a few things they wanted to know. After he got through he left for home & some 100 of them started out for Cortinas's camp. They went till they met the picketts & then after being fired upon, turned & came home. It is reported that one man had his gun shot out of his hand & another with a bullet through his hat.

There has been no mail from San Antonio in five weeks. To-day is four weeks since I left home. I have not heard a word.

It is still cloudy & wind north, though not very cold. Capt. Ricketts is better, though still quite sick. Some of Cortinas's men have been across the Arroyo Colorado robbing ranches. The general supposition is that Cortinas will not oppose the U.S. troops. I dont intend to go out until I am ready. I will have about 150 regular troops & nearly as many volunteers, with two pieces of Artillery.

At dinner to-day Capt. Tobin gave me a memorandum of the forces of Cortinas, obtained by his guide. He makes it 620 men. He deals in round numbers. The steamboat will probably be up tonight or in the morning.

The air is still & warmer & I fear another norther.

FORT BROWN TEXAS MON. DEC. 12, 1859

The weather cleared off last night & we have had a beautiful day. About 4 A.M. we were awakened by the firing of canon in Matamoros. A salute in honor of our Lady of Guadalupe—her saint day. They are having fireworks & processions tonight. Lt. Thomas, Ramsay & Graham are over to see it.

The steamer got up before day & landed our canon ammunition. There is none suitable for small arms. Lts. Boggs & Langdon came up.[15]

---

[14] The Brownsville Market House had been finished in 1852. For a sketch of the structure, see *Frank Leslie's Illustrated Newspaper* (New York), Feb. 20, 1864.

[15] Georgia-born William Robertson Boggs was an 1853 West Point graduate and a first lieutenant in the Ordnance Department. Boggs resigned in February 1861 and eventually become a brigadier general in the Confederate Army. Heitman, *Historical Register*, 228.

I had quite a number of gentlemen at my quarters this morning. Judge Davis brought me a sketch of Cortinas' position. He makes out 260 men.[16]

Lt. Graham's ox cart with company property broke down a mile the other side of the Arroyo Colorado. The Mexican driver left & one soldier came in. The other staid & was found murdered by Cortinas's men.[17] Two parties of 40 men each have been seen across the Colorado. He was not shot, but stabbed & it is supposed when asleep. The property in the wagon does not appear to have been touched.

The young officers have been rather negligent of their duties. They got a hint this morning from Capt. Stoneman. I have had them busy making preparations. I expect that we will start tomorrow night after the moon rises, so as to reach his camp by daylight.

Capt. Stoneman & I went & called on Gen. Carvahall.[18] We got Mr. Mahoney to go with him. He received us very politely & speaks English well. He was educated in Kentucky. We were pleased with our visit. He is not tall & a little stout. He leaves in a few days for Victoria—as to take the field in favor of the Liberal Government. He told us a treaty had been ratified between our governments & appeared to be delighted with it. He wore a black silk cap. We were introduced to the Gefe Politico, an old Mexican. Mr. Mahoney took us back to his house & then drove us to the ferry.

New York–born Loomis Lyman Langdon, twenty-nine and an 1854 West Point graduate, was a second lieutenant in the 1st Artillery. Langdon was on his way down-river from Fort McIntoch to Fort Brown when the Cortina War erupted. Crossing to the south bank, he safely reached Brownsville where citizens of the town persuaded him to write a letter to President James Buchanan pleading for help. Langdon to Buchanan, October 18, 1859, *DSF*, 35; 8th Census, Cameron County.

[16] Three rough pencil-sketches of Cortina's fortifications above Brownsville are in the Heintzelman Papers. As indicated in the journal, the sketches were completed with the assistance of Judge Edmund J. Davis.

[17] The soldier killed on the Arroyo Colorado on December 15, 1859, was named Featherston. Heintzelman, List of Persons Killed by Cortinas on the Rio Grande, Mar. 1, 1860, "Troubles on Texas Frontier," 36th cong., 1st sess., no. 81, 75. Hereafter referred to as TTF.

[18] Born in San Antonio and educated in Kentucky, José María Jesús Carbajal was the son-in-law of Martin de León. Carbajal was active along the Rio Grande in the Federalist cause in 1839–1840, commanded a division in the Mexican Army in 1847, and led filibusters in a bloody attack on Matamoros during the Merchant's War in 1851–1852. Carbajal later became governor of Tamaulipas in September 1864 and again in March 1866, both times succeeding Cortina. He died at Soto la Marina, Tamaulipas, in 1874. Jerry D. Thompson, *Juan Cortina and the Texas-Mexican Frontier, 1859–1877* (El Paso: Texas Western Press, 1994), 12; Herbert Davenport, "General José María Jesús Carbajal, *SHQ*, 55 (Apr., 1952), 475–483.

There is almost a mutiny in the Ranger camp. I dont understand what about Capt. Tobin dont appear to have much influence with them. There are three companies, Tobin's 90 men, Hamptons 27, & Tomlinson 35 or 152 in all. Of them he counts on 125 for duty. There will also be some 35 or 40 citizens—I suppose that I will start with about 300 men.

There was a gentleman at Gen. Carvahall's from up the river, near Edinburg 65 miles.[19] He insisted that Cortinas has 600 men & then fell to 400. The General dont think that he was over 200 & says he is satisfied that he has as good opportunities for knowing as any one, as his people go to their camp to sell cigaritos etc. I think that he is right. He says also that he dont pay his men & that they live on the beef they steal on our side.

FT. BROWN TUES. DEC. 13, 1859

It is a month to-day since I left Verde. All our arrangements are made for an attack on Cortinas's camp. We leave at one A.M. I expect to attack him at daylight. Everything has been done to insure success & the result has to be left in the hands of providence. We all have to take the chances of our profession.

A mail rider came in last night who was stopped beyond the Arroyo Colorado. He met Cortinas & 100 men at a rancho (Viejo) six miles from town & avoided them & sneaked in through the bushes.[20] He was told that they were out to intercept some American troops expected. I also heard that it was to intercept a party I might send out to look after an ox wagon with company property, the other side the Colorado where that soldier was murdered. I cannot get the Rangers to do anything effective in the way of scouting.

I have just finished three letters, to T. Wrightson, Dr. Tripler & to Margaret to leave here. I dont know when they can be forwarded.

The weather was cloudy & cool this evening, but is now more pleasant.

FT. BROWN TEXAS FRI. DEC. 16, 1859

We were called Wednesday morning early enough but contrary to my orders, some chests etc. were taken & we had to get more wagons & other delays so that we did not get in march till 2 A.M. I sent a messenger to the Ranger camp & Capt. Tobin with his three companies about 125 men met us a mile or two from town.

We had a good moon & continued our march steadily until we came to a Ranche near where the fortifications were. I halted and went as near as

---

[19] Edinburg, a small community on the Rio Grande at what is today Hidalgo, was the county seat of Hidalgo County in 1859. See note 47, this chapter.

[20] Eight miles northwest of Brownsville, Rancho Viejo had been the headquarters of the vast Espíritu Santo Grant of José Salvador de la Garza.

proper with a small party & then tried to have the ground reconnoitered. With much delay I got a small party of Rangers, but they did not wish to move till day light. At last Judge Davis who had volunteered to accompany me, volunteered to go with the reconnaisance. They went within about 60 yards & came back & reported nothing to be seen but a dog & the works abandoned. I then ordered the advance. The Rangers were not quite confident & held back, until I rode ahead & being joined by several officers we rode into the works & found them deserted. A few minutes work with axes passed the wagons & guns around & we marched on.

A parapet ten feet thick with two embrasures nearly crossed the road & a few yards further on, another was commenced to face the other way. The position was badly selected & could be easily turned. The remains of fires showed that it had been occupied for days by a considerable party of men. The chapparal was dense but by no means impenetrable. If our guns had passed around their left the shot would have easily passed through the chapparal.

We passed on some two miles or more. I all the time trying to keep out the Rangers in advance & on the flanks, with but poor success. As we approached Vicente Guerra's where 100 men with a four pdr. were reported stationed we entered a dense chapparal of Ebony in what is here called "La Ebonal."[21] Here I dismounted most of the Rangers with orders to flank through the bushes. With the guns & wagons we passed slowly up the road. We soon left them behind.

We had not gone far before we saw in a distance a Mexican waving a flag & then a four pound ball came down the road. I immediately had our guns unlimbered & returned the fire. The men although often drilled at the guns had never used ammunition & were very green. The friction tubes kept missing & the fuses were too long for the distance & no sights on the guns. With all these disadvantages Lt. Sullivan worked the guns steadily & in the most gallant manner.

Lt. Boggs of the Ordnance who volunteered to accompany us was actively employed cutting shorter the shells & at last got nearly the distance. The smoke & dust obstructed the view & Lt. Sullivan sent a man up a tree. He

---

[21] The fortifications at El Ebonal were just downriver from Ranncho del Carmen, a complex of buildings and jacales that made up the ranch of Cortina's mother, Estefana Goseascochea de Cortina.

Vicente Guerra is listed on the 1850 Cameron County census as a farmer, fifty-five, with a wife, Rafaela, thirty, and three children. 7th Census, Cameron County. See also sketches of Cortina's fortifications in the Heintzelman Papers.

In his report to General Twiggs, Heintzelman identifies "El Ebonel" as the ranch owned by Guerra. Heintzelman to Washington, Dec. 16, 1859, HLS.

watched the shots & finally they withdrew their gun. It was admirably served & in the most gallant manner.

Nearly every ball came square down the road, filled with men & our wagons. A spent ball struck a man on the thigh slightly injuring him. Another struck a mule on the ammunition wagon, went through him & into the ammunition. It immediately commenced smoking. I could not conceive what could be on fire. The men through [threw] out the things over the fire & soon found the ball had struck the friction tubes.

As soon as we discovered the enemy, I put out into the dense chapparal on our left Lt. Ramsay with his company to make their way up to opposite the gun & take it. I also urged the Rangers up the other side. From some misunderstanding neither made any progress. Both reported the chapparal too dense to penetrate. Whilst they were out the enemy attacked both flanks, trying to come in on our guns, but were easily repulsed. One of Lt. Ramsay's men was hit by a spent ball.

The Mexicans must have fired some grape or canister as one took of Judge Davis' saddle pommel.

We stopped hear two hours at this place & found some 20 shells. Finding no one had gone forward, I at last prevailed on some of the Rangers to [go] up one side of the road & our train & the cavalry followed.

A short distance above where the gun was first planted was their camp—Vicente Guerra's. We soon routed them out of the houses & pursued them up the road. Four miles or two further we came to Jesus Leon's ranche & just beyond they made another stand at the houses.[22] The Rangers supported by the foot, soon routed them again. A few fled to the river & crossed. The balance with their gun went up the road. Here the Rangers had an admirable opportunity for capturing the gun, but within 40 yards stopped & dismounted—the gun with two horses & two mules soon ran off.

At Vicente Guerras was their camp, said to contain 100 men & the 4 pdr. Here we captured some arms & they left their provisions.

It was 8½ A.M. when we met the gun with the first men. It was now near one P.M. & men & animals were tired. I permitted a short halt to water & lunch. We had come about 12 or 13 miles. At this point one of the volunteers was mortally wounded. Whilst we stopped another man's gun went off accidentally & shattered his left arm above the elbow. This delayed us & then Major Ford, on his way to Brownsville heard our firing, rode on to

---

[22] Jesús León's ranch was on the main Brownsville–Rio Grande City road about two miles upriver from the ranch of Sabas Cavazos, which in turn was two miles beyond Rancho del Carmen.

Brownsville & took the road up. He rode nearly 40 miles with his 50 men & joined us. I delayed an hour longer to rest his horses.

The pursuit was then resumed. We soon saw where the gun took a road leading out on the prairie towards San Jose.[23] As it had commenced to rain we continued on a mile or two & encamped about 15 miles from town.

We encamped on a rather low muddy place but with grass. It rained considerably during the night & continued until we started about 8 A.M. We were delayed over an hour for the Rangers.

As we were drawn out we heard more Mexican bugles. I sent out two scouts, but only two small trails could be discovered. A norther commenced & soon cleared away & in course of time the clouds & we had a very pleasant day. The roads for two miles were quite muddy & not very good all day.

We thought we might find Cortinas united with all his forces on our way back, but we met no one.

At the last point we met the Mexicans, a private in Tobin's compy was mortally wounded—he died in one of our wagons yesterday & they are this moment burying him.[24] The shells, some of them burst near the Ranchos & killed three men we saw. At the last point where the Ranger was killed we found three more dead bodies.

The time this Ranger was killed Capt. Tobin might have captured the gun, but he ordered the men to dismount when within 40 yds of the gun & it discharged.

We have no doubt nearly dispersed the force opposed to us & should have taken the gun. I am mistified at the little we have done with near 300 men. It is very mistifying to us, but no doubt it has had a depressing effect on the enemy. We would undoubtedly have done better without the Rangers.

I have been trying to write this all the morning but have met with continued interruptions.

When we were at dinner yesterday Mr. Ma[r]tinez, a Mexican general with another gentleman came in & we had some wine.[25]

---

[23] According to Heintzelman, Cortina's San José Ranch was back in the chaparral from Rancho del Carmen, not far from the river. In his memoirs, Ford misplaces the ranch near Los Fresnos.

[24] The Ranger killed on December 14, 1859, was David Herman of San Antonio. Heintzelman, List of Persons Killed by Cortinas, TTF, 75. Capt. A. C. Hill of the Ranger Spy Company reached Austin on December 17, 1859, with news of the battle. "The enemy in the midst of our fire, marched up to near the lines . . . bold and fearless, crying out 'Gringoes! Viva Cortina!'" Captain Hill said eight *Cortinistas* were found dead on the battlefield. The exact number of dead, however, was difficult to determine since several bodies were blown to pieces by the artillery. Dallas *Herald*, Jan. 4, 1860.

[25] The general was probably Pedro Martinez.

I came home after & at 7 P.M. went to bed. I did not sleep as well as I did the night before in camp. Howe fired up my india rubber & I slept quite dry.

This morning I have turned over a new leaf. I have ordered a guard & off. day—also an inspection this evening. These young officers are very negligent as to their duties. They would rather go to Matamoros to balls.

Capt. Tobin & Major Ford do not get along well together. There is to be some election for major & Tobin thinks he can be elected & Ford wont order the election. I lent them the drum & fife to bury this man killed.

Major Ford thinks that he can be elected & expect some more men. He is ready to go with me. He has gone to see Gen. Carvahall whom he knows & who has sent for him.

I hope all means that Ford will be elected the Major. He is by all odds the better man. He controls his men & Tobin is controlled by his. I would rather have Ford with 50 than Tobin with all his men.

We had a heavy fog last night but now it is warm & pleasant. Capt. Ricketts typhoid fever is a little better. Capt. Dawson arrived here with or just before Capt. Ford. He will take command of his company.

Dr. Holden handed me back my letters. Judge Davis leaves this evening for the Nueces.

I have been busy all day trying to write my report & a letter to Margaret & have just accomplished it by 9 O'Clock. I have had a constant succession of visitors. Judge Davis was going at 7 this evening, but now will not leave before 7 or 8 tomorrow. He goes to the mouth of the other side & then by the sea shore.

I sent the letter I wrote to Margaret by the sea mail & the other by land. There is a report that Cortinas did rob a ranche belonging to an American between here & the mouth of the river. It is also said that he will take the guns at the Brazos. I think that when he hears of the defeat of his Lieutenant he will turn back.

Lt. Thomas was in Matamoros & saw Gen. Carvahall. The General told him that Zamora the Sup. Judge of Hidalgo County commanded the forces & that he is now a prisoner in Matamoros to be tried for a previous offence.[26] He

[26] Prior to the Cortina War, Teodoro Zamora had served as county commissioner and chief justice of Hidalgo County. Zamora had attempted to resign as chief justice in 1859 but the commissioners had rejected his resignation. Second in command to Cortina, he was indicted for horse stealing by the fall 1860 term of the Hidalgo County grand jury. Minutes of the Commissioners Court of Hidalgo County (1852–1878), reel no. 1017256, and District Court Minutes (1853–1886), Hidalgo County Office of the District Clerk, reel no. 1017257, both in Rio Grande Valley Historical Collection (University of Texas Pan American Library, Edinburg).

abandoned his men & fled across the river. He had over 100 men. We captured a number of papers but they were principally receipts for stores & money. I have established a regular guard & off. Day. These young men I dont think like it much. The off. Day came to me to visit in town, but I told him I did not allow such things in a regular garrison when I commanded.

The weather to-day has been pleasant since the fog cleared off.

As we went up to Jesus Lopes' rancho the men found a barrel of beer. In smoking them out the house caught fire & it & another were burned. I had the fence torn down & water thrown on & thus saved the rest.

On our way down the Rangers set fire to a number of houses. I saved some, but the most were burned. On Cortinas's rancho there was a heavy fence [that] made an excellent cover for the enemy. I had that burned down but strictly forbade burning anything without my express order. This is setting a very bad example to Cortinas & the Rangers were burning all—friends & foes.[27]

My hand is stiff with writing, so I may as well stop & go to bed.

I am going to dine with Mr. Mahoney.

FT. BROWN TEXAS SAT. DEC. 17, 1859

A beautiful day. The steamer left this morning & took my first letter to Margaret with those for Dr. Tripler & Mr. Wrightson. Another letter for Margaret went by Judge Davis to the Nueces. One I wrote this morning to Mr. Futhey will go in the next steamer.

As I was going to breakfast I was stopped in the street & told of the important news from Point Isabel. Cortina's men are in the vicinity threatening to burn it. I saw the letter. There is no doubt some truth in the reports but I presume much exaggerated. There is difficulty amongst the Rangers about the command, but I at last got it arranged. Capt. Tobin with 60 men to go to Point Isabel & route them. Major Ford to Los Fresnos with 60 men to intercept them & Capt. Stoneman & his compy to Las Norias for the same purpose.[28] Lt. Ramsay is relieved from Capt. Dawson's compy & attached to Stonemans. Tobin leaves at one P.M. Ford at dark & Stoneman in the morning. I published orders with all these things.

---

[27] For Ford's version of those events see: Ford, *Rip Ford's Texas*, 267–269.

[28] Established as early as 1770, Los Fresnos was at the same location as the present-day town of the same name.

Heintzelman is probably not referring to Las Norias, some seventy miles north of Brownsville, in what is today Kenedy County. Orders no. 14, Dec. 17, 1859, Heintzelman Order Book (November 23, 1859 to April 27, 1860), Heintzelman Papers (Mansucript Division, Library of Congress; cited hereafter as HOB).

I have just finished reading the Report of the Grand Jury in the disturbances of the County.[29] It portrays a lamentable state of affairs.

FT. BROWN TEXAS SUN. DEC. 18, 1859

Capt. Tobin left at 2 P.M. & I am told with near 150 men. Major Ford a little after dark & Capt. Stoneman this morning. I went & most of the officers to Matamoros to dinner with Mr. Mahoney. We then met Genls. Carvahall & Allanberry the latter Ex-Gov. of Monterrey. Before dinner I saw several other Mex. officers but dont remember their names. Col. Fitzpatrick, the Amer. Consul dined with us. Lts. Thomas & Ramsey & Graham, with Mr. Gilligan, composed the party. The drinking appeared the most important business, though we had a very fair dinner. There were two many bumers.

They brought up a couple of carriages & we took a ride. We stopped at Gen. Allanberry's quarters & took a glass of their wine.[30] The troops were on parade & the general showed us their arms & the new rifled canon. They have new minie muskets. He has about 700 men & leaves do-day or tomorrow for Victoria. He says he delayed to dine with us yesterday.

They drove us to the ferry & we got home at dusk. Capt. Dawson sent a man with a note to me, we met on the road. It is only a report that Cortinas with his two guns is above 25 miles from here on the Ring[g]old road.

The young officers staid back for a frolic. Lt. Thomas dont half attend to his duties as adjutant. He delays everything. I have not yet a return of the Troops I took up the river. It is not an hours work to make it.

I was going with Capt. Dawson to the Protestant church, but when I went to his quarters I found there the Mexican counsel Mr. [Treviño].[31] We had a long talk about the affairs here. I wrote to the Adjutant General.[32] The

---

[29] Copies of the Grand Jury Report, both in English and Spanish, are in the Sam Houston Papers, (Texas State Archives, Austin).

[30] Before being forced from power by Santiago Vidaurri in 1859, José Silvestre Aramberri briefly served as military governor of Nuevo León for two months. Aramberri went on to actively support Benito Júarez and the Liberals during the period of French intervention. He died at Canelo near Matehuala, San Luis Potosi, in January 1864. Israel Cavazos Garza, *Diccionario Biografíco de Nuevo León* (Monterrey: Universidad Autonoma de Nuevo León, 1984), I, 22–23.

[31] The name was left blank in the journal. Manuel Treviño, the Mexican consul, had helped to persuade Cortina to leave Brownsville after the deadly raid on September 28, 1859. After Heintzelman's arrival on the border, the two men would meet on a number of occasions. Treviño, twenty-three, also owned a large mercantile store in Brownsville.

[32] In his report to the adjutant general, Heintzelman repeated most of the information he had sent General Twiggs two days earlier. Heintzelman to Cooper, Dec. 18, 1859, HLS.

lowest class of Mexicans sympathize with him, but one of the more intelligent. The authorities civil & military have done everything in their power to prevent evil disposed persons from the other side to join him.

I saw Clay Davis to-day.[33] He is in bed with a lame foot. He came down with over 35 men by taking a detour into the country.

I got a letter this afternoon from Tobin. He got at 10 P.M. yesterday to Point Isabel. No signs of Cortinas. He will be back tonight or in the morning. I expect also the others in tomorrow. Every information we get is that Cortinas is going up the river to burn & destroy. We will try & get a party ahead & also follow him up. As soon as my parties come in I will follow him up.

I bought a fine Mexican horse to-day for $70. The officers think that I paid too much for him. I think myself that it is high, but he has some good qualities & suits me. I wanted to feel independent in the way of horseflesh. Lt. Thomas has sold his American horse & I did not care then to ride his poney. He would have had to buy a horse to ride. Glavec[k]e picked him out for me.[34] It has been quite warm to-day.

---

[33] In 1847, Henry Clay Davis had established a residence, Rancho Davis, just below what became Rio Grande City. The day before the Battle of Rio Grande City, the residence was torched by *Cortinistas*. Davis, who came to Texas in 1839, frequently served as a correspondent for several Texas newspapers including the Austin *State Times*. During the Civil War the Georgia-born and Kentucky-reared Davis commanded Company H in Benavides's Regiment, Texas Cavalry. Davis, forty-six, is listed on the 1860 census as a planter, with real estate valued at $30,000 and personal property worth $2,000, along with his Mexican wife, Ylarias Garza, thirty, and their four children. Teresa Viele described Davis as "a true specimen of the Texan, tall and athletic; yet his delicately cut features carefully trimmed moustache, and *air distingué*, bespoke rather the modern carpet knight than the hero and pioneer of the wilderness." An "association with the Mexicans," Viele wrote, "had given him a peculiar style of manner, a mixture of Western frankness and the stateliness of the Spaniard; a low-toned voice, and a deference mixed with assurance." 8th Census, Starr County; Teresa Griffin Viele, *Following the Drum: A Glimpse of Frontier Life* (Lincoln: University of Nebraska Press, 1984), 145–146.

[34] Cortina's personal feud with Adolphus Glavecke, forty, was the spark that ignited the Cortina War. Glavecke had broken off medical studies in Germany to come to Matamoros in 1836, where he married Concepción Ramirez, widow of Casimiro Tijerina, Juan Cortina's first cousin. Six children were born of the union. During the Mexican War Glavecke served as a courier for Gen. Zachary Taylor. After the war he acquiring an 800-acre ranch four miles above Brownsville, was elected the first tax assessor-collector of Cameron County in 1848, a county commissioner in 1854, and a city councilman in 1857. The Brownsville City Council, however, once passed a resolution calling for his removal.

After the war, Cortina and Glavecke evidently became involved in rustling

FT. BROWN TEX. MON. DEC. 19, 1859

I went to bed last night at 8 because I had nothing to do & to get rid of visitors. I had scarcely put out my light before I heard steps in the corridor. I did not answer the knock, but in a little time they returned with the Sergt. of the Guard. It was Capt. George [Stoneman] & another man to tell me that they had made arrangements to sent out a reinforcement & rations to Major Ford, for him to go & head off Cortinas.[35] I convinced him that it was not advisable & they staid a full hour.

This morning we have a norther, though not very cold or strong.

At 11½ Capt. Stoneman returned. He found no signs of hostile parties & could learn none. The only thing he saw was a well dressed Mexican hung up, with his toes touching the ground. As he was not robbed it is difficult to say

---

cattle. In time, Cortina came to resent Glavecke's Rasputin-like influence on his aging mother, María Estefana Goseascochea de Cortina. Moreover, Cortina was leery of Glavecke's political connections to the Brownsville legal establishment, especially the way Glavecke and Cameron County Judge Elisha Basse handled the estate of a deceased aunt, Feliciana Goseascochea de Tijerina. In fact, Antonio Tijerina, son of the deceased, charged Glavecke, who was administrator of the estate, with mismanagement. In 1858, Glavecke had Cortina indicted in a cattle-rustling incident that inflamed a bitter hatred between the two men. Cortina came to refer to Glavecke as "infamous and traitorous," the "author of a thousand misdeeds," an "assassin," and he swore to kill him on sight. Indeed, Glavecke was nearly killed during Cortina's September 28, 1859, raid on Brownsville, when he was spotted by several Cortinistas and chased down Elizabeth Street to Levee Street before Glavecke turned toward 12th Street only to run into a second band of Cortina's men, who were plundering arms and ammunition from the store of Frank Cummings. Glavecke finally made it to Samuel A. Belden's store on Levee Street where, with a double-barreled shotgun, he managed to conceal himself. Thompson, *Juan Cortina*, 11; 7th Census, Cameron County; List of Candidates Qualifying, Sept. 14, 1854, Cameron County, Texas, RG 307 (Texas State Archives); Minutebook I (1850–1859), 123, 346–347, City Secretary's Office, Brownsville; Commissioners Court Minutes (1848–1862), 15, Cameron County Clerk's Office, Brownsville; Indictments by the Spring 1859 District Court of the 12th Judicial District, Sam Houston Papers (Texas State Archives). See also *State of Texas v. Nepomuceno* (sic) *Cortinas*, Cause nos. 388, 389, and 393, Minutebook B, 51, Cameron County Clerk's Office; "Proclamation! Juan Nepomuceno Cortinas to the Inhabitants of the State of Texas, and especially to those of the city of Brownsville, Sept. 30, 1859," *DSF*, 70–71. An original of this proclamation can be found in Mexican Border Papers, LR, AGO, RG 94 (NA).

The family name in most antebellum records is Glaevecke although sometime after the Civil War, the first "e" was dropped and the name is generally given as Glavecke. Tombstone of María Concepcion Glavecke and Refugia Glavecke, Brownsville Cemetery.

[35] Orders no. 5, Dec. 19, 1859, HOB.

who did it—the Mexican found hung is a citizen & stood guard here many a night. He was out looking for some cattle.

Major Ford got in this afternoon. He thinks there was a small party at San Jose rancho, but that now Cortinas is above & has 500 men.

Major Ford starts at 10 tomorrow with all the men now in camp. We at 12 N. & Tobin as soon as possible. It is reported he will stay at Point Isabel for the mail. I send an express to hurry him home. The messenger for Tobin's letter has not come. We are short of forage. I wrote to Margaret.

FORT BROWN TUES. DEC. 20, 1859

Before this time I expected to have been in the field again. The man sent to carry the order to Tobin to join I missed seeing & besides he was drunk. We have no forage & will have to wait & a cold norther set in last night. This morning it was freezing.

Lt. Thomas saw the messenger, but as he was drunk, although he saw me a moment after, he did not mention the man's looking for me. I found a hundred bushels of corn in town & now it is highly probably that plenty can be got in Matamoros. Galvan has gone to see.[36] He was waiting for his corn from Brazos, but with this norther the boat cant get in. She is now due.

Major Ford yesterday reported seeing two men leave a rancho, but did not make a thorough examination. He thinks that Cortinas has with him 500 men. I don't think so. The impression now is (at least with Glavecke) that Cortinas has his foot up the river & is with his cavalry near where these two men were seen yesterday. I have sent Major Ford with 100 men to see, as we cant march & Tobin is not in. Six of his men came in last night & report him at Point Isabel. He must be in to-day. If Ford meets the enemy in force I will join him, if not as soon as we can leave I will go & meet him on the river. I am quite disgusted with Lt. Thomas's inefficiency. I gave him orders the other day, should have insured us a sufficiency of corn. He has kept me al[l] morning attending to his business. He went out to breakfast & of course was away when wanted.

---

[36] While in Brownsville, Heintzelman made friends with Jeremiah Galvan, an immigrant from Cork, Ireland. Galvan, thirty-two, had lost his store on Levee Street in a fire and explosion in 1857, but had recovered to become one of the town's leading merchants. Galvan, who purchased a large tract of land on the Rio Grande from Antonio Canales, provided Heintzelman with much of the information relating to the background of the Cortina War that would go into Heintzelman's lengthy report of March 1, 1860. Galvan, a Unionist, visited with Heintzelman in Washington, D.C., during the Civil War. 8th Census, Cameron County; *Bandera Americana* (Brownsville), Apr. 25, 1860.

Capt. Tobin got in this afternoon. Some of his men or stragglers hung that poor man Capt. Stoneman found. Tobin says he knew nothing about it & that it was done without his orders or knowledge—that it was done by citizens who accompanied him. We told him it was due to himself & his company to find them out & expose them. It will have a very bad effect.

I was at Lt. Graham's quarters when Gen. Allanberry & Mr. Mendes the Surg. Genl. called. They spoke of it. Glaveke came in with the Mex. Jesus Leon, whose ranche is where we had our lunch up the river. He says Cortinas with all his men is at Bastrop [Bastone] 30 miles above.[37] That he has 300 or had before the fight, men, 2/3 of them mounted & well armed but poor ammunition. That they will fight there. I tried from him to get an idea of the country, but it is difficult. We will go up & try to cut him off. I will take the two guns along.

Gen. Carvajal left yesterday. He told me that his force was 700 men. Mendes says he counted them Sunday when they went to church & he did not make 400, that there might be that number with the guards. These gentlemen who called leave tomorrow for Monterrey. This has been a cold unpleasant day. I found Capt. Ricketts setting up.

The steamer Ranchero (a riverboat) came up.[38] With this wind the seaboat cant cross the bar.

I have been writing another letter to Margaret. The post master tells me it will go by the expected steamer to Indianola.

Major Ford with one of his men has just been in. I supposed him off on his scout to San Jose, but he says the guide did not come. The guide Thomas has just returned from an excursion after information & brings substantially what I got this evening from Jesus Leon. In addition he says there are 40 men posted a few miles this side & that they can be cut off. I prefer this, as now I doubt any one being at San Jose rancho. I have agreed to his going & cutting them off & their falling back on us. We will move on slowly. It will take us to the third day to get to Baston.

---

[37] Bastone, on the river near La Bolsa, was owned by William Neale and Nestor Maxan. Neale later filed claims asserting that he lost $33,733 in goods and property which was "burnt, stolen, or destroyed" during the Cortina War. Included were hundreds of animals and fifty orange trees. List of Claims, Jan. 23, 1860, TTF, 48–49.

[38] The 205-ton *Ranchero* was built in 1854 in Freedom, Pennsylvania, for King, Kenedy, and Stillman at a cost of $27,538.18. The sternwheeler, which had been in service on the river since January 18, 1855, was designed especially for use on the Rio Grande. An entry in the "Journal of M. Kenedy & Co." dated October 30, 1861, reads: "$495 . . . for breaking up S.B. Ranchero." Pat Kelly, *River of Lost Dreams: Navigation on the Rio Grande* (Lincoln: University of Nebraska Press, 1986) 107; Bruce Cheeseman to editor, Mar. 22, 31, 1994.

It is getting milder, but I fear it will rain. That would interfere materially with our operations.

FT. BROWN WED. DEC. 21, 1859

Glaveke says it will not rain. It is milder, but cloudy & chilly. We leave at 12 to-day. When I went to breakfast Major Ford had not left, but he said he would soon be off.

Tobin told me this morning that Cortinas arrived at his mothers rancho the other day, just after we had left, with 200 men & made a great to do. I dont believe the story, as he might readily have attacked our rear. I presume that a few men followed us at a distance. It is not preferable that the mail will get in, until after we have left. I will put my letters in the P. Office, to go by the Arizona.

STA. RITA[39] WED. EVE.

There appeared to be no end to difficulties & delays in starting. At last at one P.M. we got off.

Col. Fitzpatrick & several gentlemen called & saw us before we got off.[40] We stopped here at 3 P.M. It is called 7 miles but I dont think it is so far. Major Ford has left & took a road about 2 miles back, to the right. Tobins company will I supposed be along towards night. I would have gone further, but there is a little grass here & wood & water & room to encamp. It is quite mild & I fear it will rain.

CARRISITOS TEXAS[41] THURS. DEC. 22, 1859

I drank strong coffee & could not sleep. Soon after midnight it commenced raining & rained lightly until after we marched. The wind from the

---

[39] Santa Rita, the first county seat of Cameron County, was a cluster of buildings on the river four miles above Brownsville. Much of the community had been burned by the Rangers following Cortina's attack on Captain Littleton's Rangers on the Palo Alto Prairie on November 18, 1859.

[40] Richard Fitzpatrick, the South Carolina–born vice consul in Matamoros, is listed on the 1850 Cameron County census as fifty-eight and a "gentleman." Suffering from rheumatism, Fitzpatrick left the border shortly after the Cortina War, but he later returned to become a commercial agent for the Confederacy in Matamoros. 7th Census, Cameron County; James W. Daddysman, *The Matamoros Trade: Confederate Commerce, Diplomacy and Intrigue* (Cranbury, N.J.: University of Delaware Press, 1984), 60–61, 93; Matamoros Consular Despatches, 1858–1860, Records of the Department of State, RG 59 (NA).

[41] The Carricitos Ranch was located on the river a mile downriver from Las Rucias. In 1790, José Narcisco Cavazos, who had come from Montemorelos, Nuevo

north & cold & disagreeable. We got off about 7 A.M. Tobins rangers ahead. He has ox carts & they have delayed us so that we have come only 13 miles. This is the famous Carrisitos where Capt. Thornton was picked up by Gen. Torrehon during the Mexican War.[42] A little way back Clay Davis joined us. He reports the mail in & letters for the officers, but the P. Master would not give them to him. The steamer brought Col. Lockridge & some men.[43] They were to leave at 12 & join this force. He is to bring our letters. It is still cloudy & disagreeable. Stoneman & the Rangers are on the other side [of] the Laguna we have encamped on. Grass is poor. We are now about 12 miles from the Baston. The report is that Cortinas's forces were in Edinburg the day before yesterday—he back with a portion. It is hard to know what to believe. We should hear of Ford here.

SAN ROSARIO TEX. FRI. DEC. 23, 1859

We passed a very cold night. Soon after I went to sleep a shot was fired by a sentinel. I did not suppose it amounted to much but I concluded it best to get up. A sentinel fired at a rustling in the bushes.

After midnight Major Ford arrived. He got out into the country & to join us had to go a long way back.

León, to Reynosa, was given the San Juan de Carricitos Grant. The small community is today at the intersection of Highway 282 and Farm-to-Market 2520.

[42] On April 24, 1846, two companies of dragoons under Capt. Seth B. Thornton were surprised near La Rosita by 500 cavalry commanded by Gen. Anastasio Torrejon. Sixty-three dragoons were either killed, wounded, or captured. Today a historical marker at the site quotes President James K. Polk's assertion that "American blood has been shed on American soil."

[43] Born in Jefferson County, Alabama, in 1828, Samuel A. Lockridge had gone with his parents at an early age to Yalobusha County, Mississippi. Lockridge came to Texas in 1850 but traveled on the California a year later. A professional filibuster, he recruited and led more than 500 Texans in William Walker's 1856 Nicaraguan adventure. Seriously wounded in the leg, Lockridge returned to New Orleans to convalesce. He studied law and briefly settled at Gonzales, Texas. Previous to embarking for the Rio Grande in 1859, Lockridge was in New Orleans and later in San Antonio promoting a filibustering expedition to Arizona, possibly to invade Sonora. As a major in the Confederate Army of New Mexico, Lockridge died on February 21, 1862, at the Battle of Valverde after promising his men he would "make his wife a shimmy" from the Federal banner waving over Fort Craig. George Wythe Baylor, *Into the Far, Wild Country: True Tales of the Old Southwest*, ed. Jerry Thompson (El Paso: Texas Western Press, 1996), 77, 82; Earl W. Fornell, "Texans and Filibusters in the 1850s, *SHQ*, 59 (Apr., 1956), 417–427; Martin H. Hall, *Sibley's New Mexico Campaign* (Austin: University of Texas Press, 1960), 99–101; San Antonio *Daily Herald*, May 6, 1859, quoting the New Orleans *Bee*, n.d.; *Daily Picayune* (New Orleans), Jan. 7, 1860.

We left a little before 7 A.M. As we approached Neal's house or the Baston we saw houses & fences burned. I was satisfied that we could not find Cortinas there.

Major Ford was ahead. We rode on & found the house standing, but sacked & the fences & jacals burned. It is one of the finest houses I have seen on a ranch in Texas. He must have lived very comfortably.

We stopped at a Laguna there & lunched & watered. We were overtaken by Col. Lockridge & Col. McCourtland of Louisiana worth $200,000.[44] He must be fond of filibustering.

We stopped an hour before we got to the Baston to graze & were an hour there. We got here at 2 P.M. The distance to the Baston is 13 miles & they call it 12 to here, but I dont think it over 9.

An Indian express went up this morning. Cortinas passed two days ago & his forces before. It is said he was in Edinburg several days ago.

We got no letters. Lt. Thomas got a few papers. Capt. Rickett's family arrived on the steamer.

The afternoon is as hot as the morning cold. We are near the banks of the river, but no grass.

ON A LAGUNA 7 MILES FROM EDINBURG SAT. 24 DEC. 1859

Not so cold last night & pleasant to-day. We got off soon after sunrise & came to this Laguna. I don't know how far we have come. We had no guide ahead & I turned off for a ranche (Young's) on the river where they told me I could get water.[45] We got no water & had much difficulty in getting back into the road. We stopped here about 2 P.M. as it is the best place for grass we can find. A moment before we stopped Major Ford rode up & told me that a party of Cortinas's men were around his camp last night & that they left Edinburg this morning. It is difficult to tell from the contradictory reports, what to believe. He dont appear to have burned the town.

Our irregular forces are becoming more tractable. Nicolas, the man I had out as guide our first expedition was at our fire last night & talking a great

---

[44] Possibly George McCausland, who was mortally wounded by a fellow officer in an argument following the First Battle of Bull Run. Carl Moneyhon and Bobby Roberts, *Portraits of Courage: A Photographic History of Louisiana in the Civil War* (Fayetteville: University of Arkansas Press, 1990), 47.

[45] This was the La Blanca Ranch of Salomé Ballí de Young, which was about twenty miles downriver from Edinburg. Salomé Young, the widow of John Young, owned most of the Santa Anita Land Grant. Young, age twenty-nine, later filed claims of $8,220 asserting that she lost over 800 head of cattle in the Cortina War. 8th Census, Cameron County; Salomé Young, List of Claims, n.d., *TTF*, 58.

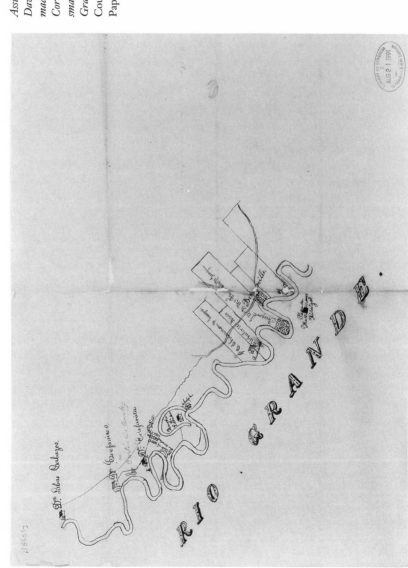

Assisted by Judge Edmund J. Davis, Major Heintzelman made several sketches of Cortina's fortifications and the small ranches on the Rio Grande above Brownsville. Courtesy Heintzelman Papers, Library of Congress.

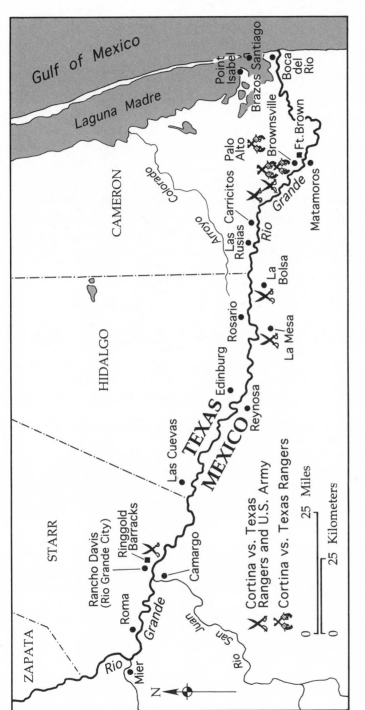

Cortina War, Lower Rio Grande Valley, 1859–1860. Map by John V. Cotter.

deal.[46] He is now full of information, but he never knows at the right time. I would have captured both the guns the other day, if he had given me the information he had. Tobin's guide also knew, but neither would let me know.

One of the Rangers gave me an armadillo we will have for dinner.

8 MILES BEYOND EDINBURG SUN. DEC. 25, 1859

We made an early start this morning & arrived at Edinburg about 6 miles by about 8 O'Clock. The town was deserted. It had been sacked, but not burned. The Customs house was plundered.[47] Cortinas & his forces had passed on. We delayed several hours for the Rangers to get corn. They say he has 380 men & some as high as over 600. I would not have stopped so long, but I was misinformed of the state of affairs. We are encamped on water & as good grass as we have had for several days. The weather has been quite warm. We can scarcely believe that this is Christmas. The armadillo was very good.

LOS CUEVAS TEX.48 MON. DEC. 26, 1859

We had quite a warm pleasant night. It has been rather warm to-day. We have come, they say 18 or so miles. We got here before 12. I heard on the road that Cortinas was at Ringold Barracks & his men drinking & looting.[49] Col.

---

[46] Peter Nickels, forty, had served as sheriff of Hidalgo County in 1850 and had replaced Teodoro Zamora as chief justice in 1859. A South Carolinian by birth, Nickels was also deputy collector and inspector of customs at Edinburg. 7th Census, Cameron County; 8th Census, Hidalgo County.

[47] Chief Justice Nickels claimed that Cortina made off with $800 from his office in Edinburg, $92 from the Hidalgo County Treasurer's office, and $114.50 from the Tax Assessor–Collector. Partly depopulated by the Cortina War, only sixty-seven citizens, excluding a camp of the 2d Cavalry, were in Edinburg in July 1860. 8th Census, Hidalgo County; Commissioner's Court Minutes (1852–1878), Hidalgo County, roll no. 1017256, Rio Grande Valley Historical Collection (University of Texas Pan American Library, Edinburg).

[48] Several Cortina partisans resided at Las Cuevas, a ranch some eighteen miles below Rio Grande City. As a consequence, on January 6, 1860, the ranch was burned, probably by the Rangers. "The presumptions against the Rangers is strong. Capt. Littleton's command was encamped there," Ford later wrote. In June 1861, Confederate forces under Capt. John Donelson hanged a young Cortina partisan at the ranch following the death of two Anglo-Americans at the site. From 1873 to 1875, Las Cuevas became the center of the "Skinning War" between Cortina partisans and the Rangers. Ford to E. Clark, June 14, 1861, LR, AGR (TSA). Walter Prescott Webb, *The Texas Rangers: A Century of Frontier Defense* (Austin: University of Texas Press, 1965), 255–278; Ford to W. C. Thomas, Feb. 22, 1860, HP. An 1875 map of the area can be found in LR, AGO, RG 393 (NA).

[49] Ringgold Barracks was established just below Rio Grande City in October 1848 by a company of the 1st Infantry and named for Capt. Samuel Ringgold of the 3rd

Lockridge stopped & told me of it & wished Major Ford to get ahead of him, at Ford's request. I agreed & intended to leave here at midnight so as to join him. He I found here. The arrangement is perfected & we leave at midnight. It is 18 or 20 miles. If we can hem him in we will end the matter.

Capt. Stoneman & Lt. Graham got into a quarrel here. I put both in arrest.

Los Barreros Tex.[50] Tues. Dec. 27, 1859

We left at midnight. A few (3) miles from town we overtook Major Ford. Cortinas he was satisfied was still in town. We advanced carefully & he went ahead to get above the force. We advanced into town. The advance fired upon a picket. We continued to advance & soon found that he had left the town up the river. We hurried up & the Rangers engaged him. Major Ford had the guns, but was not supported & had to abandon them to defend himself. I sent Capt. Stoneman with his company after a party who fled towards the river. He killed six of them. The rest escaped across the river. We then followed up the road after the tracks of his two guns. He made several stands but finally about 9 miles from town we captured the six pdr. & his ammunition cart. In a mile we got his 4 pdr. The others dispersed, so that not a track could be seen on the road & we abandoned the pursuit & returned to this place about a mile to encamp. There were several Rangers wounded & I dont know how many Mexicans killed—some 20 or more. The Report from Ringold Brks. is that he had 860 men. Amongst them two companies of Mexican troops—of Carvaal. This of course is not true. Another man said he counted them & there were over 400—he counted them several times.

We made a great march & surprised them. They did not know of our advance until we fired on their picket at Ringold Brks. We marched yesterday about 20 miles & this morning 20 more & then 9 in pursuit. Near 50 miles & a fight is a pretty good business. I hope now that the matter is ended. The Rangers went back to town. We must return there tomorrow & then take the road to Duncan.

We got some of Cortinas's returns & orders, with the names of some of his men. An express is in from Roma asking a force. Major Ford is there & will return. I wrote in reply that I had no force to send them.

Artillery, who had died on May 11, 1846, of wounds received at the Battle of Palo Alto. In March 1859, General Twiggs had ordered the post, along with Fort Brown and Fort McIntosh, evacuated. Wooster, *Soldiers, Sutlers, and Settlers*, 8–10, 48, 59.

[50] A ranch halfway between Rio Grande City and Roma. See map in *Reports of the Committee of Investigation sent in 1873 by the Mexican Government to the Frontier of Texas* (New York: Baker and Godwin, 1875).

The men marched 50 miles in 25 hours. The weather last night was quite warm & it still continues so. I presume it will end in a norther.

I had made all the arrangements to leave in the morning from Ringold Brks, to start next day for Duncan, when I got a letter from Roma, that Major Ford was there & that Cortinas with 40 men was on the opposite side of the river ready to burn it. At dusk Major Ford rode in. I have sent Capt. Stoneman up there. Major Ford proposes to take a couple of detachments & enter Mexico & try & cut him off. Cortinas with 20 men crossed the river just above us by swimming. I fear we will be detained several days. He appears to still have power to raise men, though he lost a great many to-day. Lts. Thomas, Graham & Britten started to see if the latter could recognize an officer killed a little above here.[51] On their way they picked up a poor half Indian & Mexican, who was badly burned at the canon. I have him in the Guard House.

Col. Lockridge is here & took supper with us. He went with Ford & was very active.

Camp at Los Barreros Texas. Wed. Dec. 28, 1859

This is Charley's birthday. He is now 14 years old. Last year I also was from home at this time.

A little after breakfast I left for Ringold Brks. Lt. Thomas, Dr. Carswell & one of the men—Col. Lockridge, Col. McCourland & Mr. Britton rode to town. I rode directly to the Barracks. They are occupied by the Rangers. I met Major Ford. Mr. McCluskey who has quarters at the garrison offered us his room to write in.[52] I went there & commenced when Major Hoard, the Dept. Collector called & invited us to his house to dinner & to write without interruption.[53] We accepted his offer & had a pleasant room to write in & a good dinner. His wife was also at the table. They had to flee to Camargo. They plundered the Custom House, but he cant account for their [not] plundering his house, not a thing was disturbed.

I wrote a short report to Dept. Hd. Qrs. & another to the Adjt. Genl.[54] I also wrote a long letter to Judge Iverson, one to Dr. Tripler & another to

---

[51] Not identified.

[52] Irish-born James B. McClusky, thirty-seven, had been the sutler at Ringgold Barracks before the post was abandoned in 1859. 7th Census, Cameron County; Ford, *Rip Ford's Texas*, 270.

[53] Edward R. Hoard, thirty-four and a Virginia-born attorney, had been involved in political affairs along the river ever since he had led support for Carbajal in the 1851–1852 Merchant's War.

[54] These two letters report much of the information in the journal. Heintzelman to Washington, Dec. 27, 1859; Heintzelman to Cooper, Dec. 27, 1859, HLS.

Margaret. I commenced one last night, but left it in my portfolio. It wont make much difference as I can now finish it & send it to Corpus Christi tomorrow by the mail. This mail has never been interrupted.

I made arrangements with Capt. Ford to have an express carry my letters & his Report to Brownsville.[55] I also arranged with him to send out Tobins men to pursue some straggling parties. There was one of 30 men, cavalry plundered a Rancho, the Sauz, 12 miles on the Laredo road.[56]

I will in the morning send Lt. Sullivan with Capt Rickett's company to occupy Ringold Brks. & Dawson & Graham, with L & M companies to return to Fort Brown.[57] Major Ford will send me 15 or 20 men as an escort for Lt. Thomas & I with our wagons to Roma.[58] I hope that there in a few days I can arrange so we can go on.

We did not start home until after dark, but had a young moon to light our way. Young Britten, Pat Nichols & his two Mex. accompanied us. We missed the place to turn off although we put up a paper, but Nichols saw our camp fires & we turned in.

A couple of Rangers who went in this morning & passed near the river amongst some ranches saw some 40 men on the other side. The Mexicans on this side pretended that they were rancheros, but no doubt they were some of Cortinas's men.

A wounded Mexican came into the garrison & died there of his wounds

---

[55] In his report, Ford provided a general outline of the battle and gave a list of the sixteen Rangers who were wounded (including Ford, with contusions from grape shot). Ford concluded his report by saying, "Major Heintzelman has won golden opinions from all for his skill as a commander, and his high-toned bearing as a gentleman and a soldier." Ford to Sam Houston, Dec. 28, 1859, copy in HP. Colonel Seawell telegraphed the news of Heintzelman's victory at Rio Grande City to Washington on Jan. 5, 1860. Seawell to Adjutant General, Jan. 5, 1860, LR, AGO, RG 94 (NA). Governor Houston referred to Heintzelman as "an officer of discretion and valor." Dallas *Herald*, Jan. 18, 25; Feb. 8, 1860.

[56] On the Rio Grande between Roma and Rio Grande City, Rancho de Los Sauses had a population of twelve in 1860. 8th Census, Starr County.

[57] Heintzelman also requested that two supply wagons be sent upriver from Fort Brown. Heintzelman to Commanding Officer, Fort Brown, Dec. 28, 1859, HLS.

[58] Heintzelman received a letter from Noah Cox dated December 27, 1859, urging the retention of Ford's Rangers at Roma. Speaking for a committee of citizens, Cox expressed fears that "some straggling party of Mexicans . . . might attack and plunder our place." Cox urged that "a sufficient force" be sent to Roma as soon as possible. Captain Stoneman arrived in Roma two days later. "I am here with nothing to do or nothing to report," Stoneman wrote, however. Only rumors of Cortina with a hundred or more men having passed upriver had been received. Cox to [Heintzelman], Dec. 27, 1859; Stoneman to [Heintzelman], Dec. 29, 1859, both in HP.

last night. He says that Cortinas was wounded in the leg yesterday. "Quien Sabe." Others say that he kept well in advance—of the retreat.

The Rangers had 15 men wounded, but not one dangerously. It is most extraordinary that no one was killed. Major Ford insists that we killed 50 or 60 & this evening insists even more. A great many were killed in the river.

Major Ford read me his Report.[59] It gave entire satisfaction to the Rangers. Col. Lockridge was with him & no doubt of much service.

The weather was very warm to-day. I wrote in my shirt sleeves & was then too warm.

ROMA TEXAS THURS. DEC. 29, 1859

Weather warm with every prospect of a norther, but cleared off & still warm. Ordered C Compy to Ringgold Brks—L & M to Fort Brown.[60] Sent the guns to Ringgold & small piece & prisoners. The larger piece to Ft. Brown. At 11 A.M. an express arrived from San Antonio ordering more troops & me to remain.

The order is dated 16 Dec. & is issued on the receipt of my letter of 7 Dec. stating that I could learn nothing reliable of Cortinas—that it was said he had 350 men—100 of them cav. & was fortified & that I would carry out the General's instructions.

The section of the Light Battery companies C, D, & F 8th Infy & C 2 Cav. to rendezvous at Laredo, then proceed in company to Ft. Brown.

F 2 Cav. A & I 1st Infy will proceed by way of San Antonio to Ft. Brown—all detached officers & soldiers to join. I am ordered not at present to make the trip up the Rio Grande. If I dont need the cavalry I can send such as I dont need back, but will keep the others with me.

This express came along the coast from the Nueces to Brazos & Fort Brown & then up the Mexican side.

This breaks up all my arrangements. I had just sent off to Ringgold a copy of my report & letter to Margaret to go by today's mail to Corpus Christi & I intended to come here, find out Cortinas movements & in a day or two start again up the Rio Grande. I wrote to Margaret that she might soon expect me home.

---

[59] For Ford's account of the Battle of Rio Grande City, see Ford, *Rip Ford's Texas*, 268–275.

[60] Company C of the 1st Artillery was commanded by 2d Lt. Thomas C. Sullivan, Co. L of the 1st Artillery by 2d Lt. Douglas Ramsay, and Co. M of the 1st Artillery by 2d Lt. William M. Graham. Ramsay was killed while serving under Heintzelman at the Battle of First Bull Run on July 21, 1861. Heintzelman, Returns of the Troops of the Brownsville Expedition, Dec. 14, 1859, HP; Orders no. 7, Dec. 29, 1859, HOB.

The wind blew hard & our camp was very dusty. The escort for me came from Ringgold, but as they had a wagon for corn I sent them on & trusted to ourselves for escort. We left at one P.M. & were here at 4 P.M. The distance is only 5½ miles.

As we came along the road I found that Cortinas abandoned his guns near a turn in the road where we could have cut him off.

Roma is a substantial little town on a high bluff over looking the Rio Grande.[61] I have a vacant room on the banks in the 2nd story with a beautiful view of the opposite shore with the mountains in the distance & the Vallecillo silver mines. I met Mr. Jarvis, a brother of the Dr. who lives at the mines.[62] He left this afternoon to return. It is only 80 miles & a gentleman here has offered to drive me there in his buggy in a day & a half. If I possibly can leave I will visit there. They are getting out an abundance of metal & doing well.

---

[61] Roma can be traced to the Salinas and Saenz families, owners of porciones 71 and 72 in the jurisdiction of Mier. Although Rancho de Los Saenz was abandoned due to Indian raids in the early nineteenth century, a nearby second settlement, Rancho de Buena Vista, survived, and in 1840, the name was changed to Garcias to honor one of the first families of the area. In 1848 the name was changed to Roma. The name came either from a tract of land adjacent to the town called San Roman or possibly from a community across the river, San Pedro de Roma (today Miguel Aleman). See W. H. Chatfield, *Twin Cities of the Border and the Country of the Lower Rio Grande* (New Orleans: E. P. Brandao, 1893. By 1859, Roma, as head of navigation on the Rio Grande, was a thriving distribution center for goods destined for the interior of Mexico. With a population of 562, Roma was also the largest community in Starr County. Mario L. Sanchez, "Roma," in National Register of Historic Places Registration, Editor's files; 8th Census, Starr County.

In 1852, Maj. William H. Emory, chief astronomer for the United States-Mexican Boundary Survey Commission, wrote that "the beautiful town of Roma" was "built upon a high bluff of yellowish sandstone." Emory was at "a loss to know how such fine residences and warehouses, all recently built, could be sustained by its trade." When he ventured into the night to make "observations for the determination of the latitude and longitude," he watched "a long train of mules, heavily laden, directed toward the Mexican side of the river . . . their rich burden of contraband goods, intended for the Mexican market." William H. Emory, "Report of the United States and Mexican Boundary Survey, Made Under the Direction of the Secretary of the Interior," 34th Cong., 1st Sess., no. 135, (Washington: Cornelius Wendell, 1857), 1: 63–64. For an excellent woodcut of Roma, see Ibid., 1: 64.

[62] Samuel Matthias Jarvis, brother of Richard William Hart Jarvis and Dr. Nathan Jarvis, had been with William Walker in Nicaragua where he had been imprisoned for several months. After the Mexican War, Jarvis had gone to Vallecillo to work for the mining company, where he married Inocéncia Flores, raised a large family, and became fluent in Spanish. During Reconstruction, he was appointed mayor of Laredo, chief justice of Webb County, and customs collector. Jarvis died in Laredo in February 1893 at the age of seventy-two. Thompson, *Warm Weather and Bad Whiskey*, 33–38, 124.

They are waiting for a smelter. Capt. Stoneman has forage for his animals & is doing well. Nothing reliable about Cortinas. I heard this evening that he is at Guerrero 45 miles above this, near the Rio Grande with his forces. I am sending a spy to see. This concentration of troops will put an end to all his hopes if he still had any. He has many sympathizers on the other side.

My dear friend Pete Nichols is here & says that he will start tomorrow for S. Antonio. I will probably write by him & send a copy of my Report & a letter to Margaret. She must be much troubled at the sending off that company from Verde. I believe too that the Band is at S. Antonio.

About a week from now the troops will arrive at Ft. Brown & in about 4 or 5 days from Laredo here.

ROMA TEXAS FRI. DEC. 30, 1859

This is a cloudy, cold unpleasant morning. I went to get my breakfast & found Thomas had ordered none cooked. After waiting two hours I got coffee, ham & hard bread. If he had gone to the trouble of sending to me he would have learned whether I wanted any breakfast.

About one O'Clock this morning an express from Capt. Tobin reached me. A man told Mr. McClusky & he believes that Cortinas was at the Baston with 300 men.

I sent the man back this morning with a note to Major Ford that I did not believe the report but that Capt. Dawson was with them last night at Ringgold Brks with the two Arty companies, on his way to Ft. Brown & that he could join him with much force as he saw fit if he believed the report, & follow him up.

This morning I saw a young man I met in Brownsville & who lives there. He came up last night on the other side. He met one of Cortinas's principal officers & some 50 to 60 men in scattered parties, nearly all unarmed & ragged. I am satisfied that fellow cant even again collect any force together. The news of the troops ordered added to his defeat will be a complete damper to his future operations.

It is now ten O'Clock & Lt. Thomas has left here. He has been here a few minutes. This is a pretty time for an Adjutant to appear to commence his morning duties. I am thoroughly disgusted with his inefficiency. He is a fat lazy lout. His own comfort & convenience he considers first & the public service afterwards.

I made another copy of my report last night & will now write to Margaret.

We sent our wagon train to Rio Grande City for hay. Lt. Ramsay went with it. I finished my letters & wanted the express to leave in the morning, but now he has no mule to ride.[63] His mule got lame coming in. My friend Pete Nichols, who was going so early this morning, I doubt whether he does at all, or ever intended.

Mr. Sanders gave me a small specimen of the lead silver ore from the Dolores mine the Vallecillo company works. It is not very rich, but the metal is very abundant. He also showed me a large number of planchets of silver from several mines in the neighborhood. These are some very fine ones. I am very anxious to visit the mines but dislike to leave. I must try to go Sunday evening.

The Laredo mail has failed twice this week—the first time since these disturbances.

ROMA TEXAS SAT. 31 DEC. 1859

Here we are again at the last day of the year. It has been an eventful one to me. I hoped last year at this time that I would be at home this year with my family. I am however even now more pleasantly situated that I was last year.

We have had a cloudy, cold, uncomfortable day, with a keen north wind.

I went up the river a mile & a half with Mr. Sanders to see an old oyster bed. I brought one along near a foot in length & some petrifications of Mesquite & Ebony. They are quite curosities.[64]

I wanted to start for Vallecillo this afternoon, but Saunders has sent his brother up to Guerrero, ostensibly to find out about a party of Cortinas's men, but in reality to buy corn. I will try & leave tomorrow.

Lt. Ramsay got back late this afternoon from Ringgold Brks. He describes a disgraceful state of affairs at that place. The Rangers are shooting all the dogs & killing all the chickens, not only in town but in the neighboring ranches.

Cortinas brother was seen some place below, either at the Baston, or at Tobins co., with 60 men.[65] No one knows where he has gone to. He should have been followed up at once & his force would have disbanded. Capt. Dawson has gone on.

---

[63] Heintzelman to Washington, Dec. 30, 1859, HLS.

[64] Even today, petrified wood remains abundant in the area. For a description of the fossilized oyster bed above Roma, see Emory, *Boundary Survey*, I, 66.

[65] José María Cortina, thirty-eight, was born in Camargo a few years after his more famous brother. He became justice of the peace and tax assessor-collector of Cameron County in 1858, and if Heintzelman is correct, joined his brother sometime after September 1859, although he was at Rancho del Carmen when the census enumerator, J. P. Bane, visited on July 9, 1860. José María later served under his brother as a colonel and a courier to Benito Juárez. He died in Mexico sometime prior to 1875. Commissioner's Court Minutes, Cameron County; 8th Census, Cameron County.

The Rangers are holding an election to-day for Major. Tobin says if he is [not] elected he will resign. If he dont keep better order & do something I will write to the Governor to have the Rangers recalled. They are doing no service & only bringing disgrace upon the country.

That prisoner I had turned over to Lt. Sullivan to deliver to the civil authority, was turned over & hung yesterday. Such things are disgraceful.

After some trouble I got the express off—at 7½ P.M.

I am up unusually late. It is now 10½ O'Clock. We had our supper & I spent the evening in Capt. Stoneman's, Thomas' & Ramsay's quarters discussing military matters.

The weather appears to be moderating.

✖ January 1860 ✖

"The scene of confusion & disorder is shocking."

ROMA TEXAS SUNDAY JANUARY 1ST, 1860

This morning clear & cold. These are the first Christmas & New Year for some time that I have seen no egg-nog. I have not seen an egg in town.

I saw a young man from Mier who reports that Cortinas with about 30 well armed & well mounted men, his body guard, I suppose, demanded permission of the alcalde to march through the Plaza. He told him he could not, that there were other roads to Monterrey, the place he said he wished to go to, besides that through the plaza. This near last night.

Afterwards on his way here, this morning he met a man he knew a few miles this side of Mier who had met 20 or 30 men on the road going towards Camargo.

I immediately sent an express with the news to Major Ford at Rio Grande City.

This afternoon, Juan, Capt. Stoneman's guide returned. He met some armed men before he got to Guerrero on the road to Mier.[1] He saw a man he knew who told him that they were Cortinas's men. He returned & learned that they had entered Mier in small parties. This day he [rode] a circuit & examined the road to Camargo & could not see where any such party had passed. He did not examine the Monterrey road. There is now but little doubt about his whereabouts. He wont trouble us anymore.

At two we dined with Mr. Levy an English Jew.[2] He has a family of 12 children, all at home but three. His oldest daughter married Mecklenberg, a

---

[1] Founded by Vicente Guerra in October 1750, Revilla or Guerrero, as it came to be known, was the most picturesque of José de Escandon's river villages. Just upriver from where the Rio Salado emptied into the larger Rio Grande, much of the ruins of the town are today beneath the waters of Falcon Reservoir.

[2] This was John Levy, a Roma businessman. Only Myer M. Levy, however, nine-

---

very rich man called prince here & who died of yellow fever at this place a year or so ago. They had yellow fever very badly & lost 40 per cent of the population I am told—but dont believe.

A few months ago they had their dwelling house, one of the finest in the country burned down & lost all it contained. They now live in very limited quarters. On account of this war they had no vegetables, but still we had a very satisfactory dinner.

ROMA MONDAY JAN. 2, 1860

Tobin was elected Major of the volunteers. Ford goes home & his company & Herron's.[3] I got a note from Ford & one from Col. Lockridge.[4]

I wanted to start for Vallecillo to-day. I sent off an express last evening to San Antonio & one to-day for Brownsville for the companies A & I & F cav. to march up the river & for supplies.[5] I will now have nothing to do for several days. The weather is cold & unpleasant. Major Ford sent me his Report.

An express has been in with a letter from Major Tobin. He informs me that he is elected & the Governor wants him to co-operate with the U.S. Troops.[6] I wrote I was happy to do so, but that there was nothing to do but send out his whole force in small parties. I also wrote what I was doing with my troops.[7] Lt. Sullivan also wrote about an arrival from Brownsville & rations.[8] Some small parties but unarmed were met on the road. Everything goes to show that they have dispersed.

---

teen and merchant, is listed on the 1860 census. John Levy to State of Texas, n.d., TTF, 25; 8th Census, Starr County.

   [3] Captain Herron commanded a small company of thirty Rangers. Heintzelman, Returns of the Troops of the Brownsville Expedition, HP.

   [4] From Rio Grande City on January 1, 1860, Lockridge wrote Heintzelman of Tobin's election. Ford's defeat, Lockridge maintained, occurred because "he was for establishing some kind of order & discipline and to prevent this indiscriminate robbing and plundering of the Ranches of the Frontier which is a disgrace to the Ranger Service." Lockridge to Heintzelman, Jan. 1, 1860, HP.

   [5] Orders no. 8, Jan. 1, 1860, HOB.

   [6] Tobin also notified Heintzelman that he had sent Captain Littleton on a reconnaissance downriver in the direction of Agua Nuevo. Tobin to Heintzelman, Jan. 2, 1860, HP.

   [7] Heintzelman informed Tobin that Cortina had been at Guerrero and Mier but was last reported to be at a "rancho on the Mexican side of the river, some nine miles above Ringgold." Heintzelman to Tobin, Jan. 2, 1860, HLS.

   [8] Three men, Sullivan said, had arrived at Ringgold Barracks from Brownsville by using the Mexican bank of the river. They had "passed several parties of Cortina's men" and recognized "their horses as belonging to some of the Rangers." The *Cortinistas* were unarmed and were heading downriver. Thos. Sullivan to Sir, Jan. 2, 1860, HP.

Lt. Ramsay returned from Mier. Cortinas encamped the night before last a league & a half from Mier & wanted to pass through the plaza. They would not let him & his men passed in small parties, on their way down the river.

I wrote to Margaret & leave it for the Laredo mail. The day has been mild & pleasant. I am now only waiting for Sanders to start for Vallecillo.

8½ P.M. I got ready to start & waited till after 11 O'Clock before they got back from Ringgold Brks. It was then too late & we have it put off till morning.

There is no doubt but that Cortinas is near Camargo. One of his officers is badly wounded & is some few miles above Rio Grande City. The scene of confusion & disorder is shocking at Rio Grande City. Lt. Sullivan must be having a nice time. Capt. Herron's company left this morning & took the direct road to Sta. Gertrudes, Capt. King's rancho. I believe Major Ford leaves tomorrow.

ROMA SAT. JAN. 7TH, 1860

I got back last night at midnight from the Vallecillo mines. We were to leave on Tuesday at 6 O'Clock, but I got up & were about & saw no signs of starting. We finally got a cup of coffee & got off at 8 A.M. We drove up on this side to the upper ferry & were in Mier, about 8 miles at 10 A.M. We had an old ricketty buggy, very doubtful. Mr. Sanders thought he could get another & did get a very good one, with a top. The delay in getting it & in changing the horses delayed us so that it was 12 before we could leave Mier.

He hired a man who was to act as a kind of an advanced guard, or scout. He never overtook us although his horse was saddled & we stopped to fix the harness & to get a cup of chocolate. I think that some of his friends dissuaded him, thinking it dangerous to escort two Americans & one the "commander" of the American troops that had defeated Cortinas, as it was quite probable that we would meet some of his stragglers. In fact Sanders all the way was looking out for Indians, Robbers, & Cortinas's men.[9]

We drove through a miserable country. There was one stretch of 25 miles [where] there is no house. From Mier to Vallecillo there is one strip of tolerable grass & a few strips where we cross what they call rivers, but the balance of the way is all a most miserable country.

We got to "Villa Nueva" about an hour & a half after dark. We drove into the Plaza ornamented by a single tree & stopped at the Alcalde's house. It con-

---

[9] Heintzelman's escort to Vallecillo was M. Sanders, a German-born, thirty-five-year-old Roma merchant. Sanders is listed on the census with his Mexican wife, Refugia, twenty-five, three infant children, and a housekeeper. 8th Census, Starr County.

sists of one room 30 by 20 feet, with a door kept closed & a little 18 by 12 inches window, or opening in the adobes. There is a kitchen attached, with a recess & chimney, the hearth about three feet from the ground.

We had our coffee along & our bread. We got some tortillas & chili with goat meat for our supper. I slept on a bed & Mr. Sanders on the floor on my Buffalo robe. Next morning we made a late start—8 A.M. We made coffee & sent out & bought a sheet of jerked beef & had it boiled in the coals. In this house men women & children all slept in the same room.

Wed.—4th We drove to the Alamo, on a small stream, a collection of houses & got there at 12 & staid 2 hours & had a sort of dinner & fed.[10] We got to Vallecillo at 6 A.M., 8 leagues.[11] We passed within 4 miles of V., some silver diggins & off the road a couple of miles to the left the now abandoned by us, "Jesus Maria" mine.[12] From "Villa Nueva" we had a servt. of the spy company of Vidauri's army as our escort.

We drove to Valecillo & Mr. Sanders stopped there with the steam engineer of the company. The latter got in to the carriage & drove me up to the Hacienda, half a mile to Major Lowry's.[13] I found him & Capt. Jarvis & Mrs. Lowry's sister at dinner. I was warmly welcomed & sat down to dinner with them. The Major I knew when he was a Lieutenant of Dragoons in Florida.

The moon was so bright that after dinner we walked out & saw all the works. I slept in Major L's office.

THURS. 5TH. After breakfast we went out again & looked at things. We had a misting rain, though not cold. There is nothing to see in the Jesus Maria

---

[10] El Alamo, on a tributary of the Rio Alamo, was a village thirteen miles west of Parras in the state of Nuevo León.

[11] Vallecillo, Nuevo León, on a tributary of the Arroyo Blanco, is sixty-five miles south of Laredo, Texas, and fifteen miles northwest of Sabinas Hidalgo, Nuevo León. The village is today on the Pan American highway. Only a few tailings of the mines remain visible.

[12] Investors in the Jesús María Vallechille Mine included Capt. William W. Chapman and Charles Stillman. For a time, Stillman was president of the mining company which had a capitalization of $4 million with shares of $1,000 each. Chapman, *News From Brownsville*, 284–285; Chauncey Devereux Stillman, *Charles Stillman, 1810–1875* (New York, 1956), 15–16.

[13] Maj. Albert Lowry had served as a quartermaster in the 2d Dragoons during the Mexican War but had resigned in 1849. He was the brother-in-law of Samuel M. Jarvis. Lowry remained at the Vallecillo mines during and after the Civil War and is frequently criticized in Heintzelman's journals for his perceived mismanagement of the mines. Miscellaneous newspaper clipping, Laredo *Times*, n.d. Courtesy of Ruby Lowry, Laredo, Texas.

mine, so I concluded not to visit it, as my time was limited. I did not go down the shaft of the Dolores mine, as it is wet & disagreeable & there was nothing special to see beyond what I have seen in other mines. So I contented myself with looking around & making inquiries.

Major Lowry has been three years Director & wants to leave. I suppose that he will, so soon as he has commenced smelting.

The shaft is 305 feet deep—7 × 9 for 265 feet & then 8 × 12—a drift to the East 220 & to the west 180 feet. The vein is 6 ft thick—the metal from 4 to 24 inches. I saw one mass of metal on the surface said to weigh 2300 pounds estimated. There are tons of the like uncovered & ready to hoist out. They are using an old engine, got out several years ago for the other mine, an excellent one, calculated at 15 horse power. It works a fan for ventilation & pumps & a horse whim (2 animals) drawn up the ore & rubbish. There is another ventilating shaft about 60 yards north, an old shaft a little farther east. This is nearly full of rubbish. We attempted to clear it out but it is bad ground & caved in. This near the rear an[d] the Spaniards abandoned it. Outside the Hacienda, east about a quarter of a mile, is another old shaft said to be 100 varas as deep, nearly full of rubbish. We are cleaning it out & preparing it for use. This Dolores mine near abandoned on account of the foul air.

The ore is galena. The average yield of silver is 60 oz. to the ton. Lead 75 to 80, but yields in the furnace 70 per cent. It contains also 2 oz. of gold.

He works from 40 & 70 men. On the shaft men get $40 the vara & on a drift from 6 to $15. They can drive the shaft 2 vrs. a week.[14] The rock is old Alpine limestone with iron pyrites.

Major L. has the direction of the mines Viejas 25 miles east. They were worked in 1680. It is a basin of carbonate of lead, with silver—usually 50 oz. of silver to the ton—70 prct. lead.

There are a great many old mines around here & some are still worked on a very small scale. Some 25 miles to the S.W. are the "Iguana" mines, one Lloyd when I was in the States was trying to sell. They are believed to be a swindle.

There was much money lost in machinery & labor at Jesus Maria. I saw some of the machinery. It cost $25,000 in Norristown, Pa. & the cost of transportation from Matamoros to the mines was $17,000. From this a slight estimate can be made of its cost. It is now utterly useless. One pump is 14 & the other 20 inches & it threw 2,000 gallons of water per minute. The water ran

---

[14] A vara is a unit of measurement used in Spanish and Portuguese-speaking countries that varies from thirty-two to forty-three inches. A vara in Texas and Mexico was generally equal to thirty-three and one-third inches.

four miles & there emptied into another stream. These pumps worked about three months. Exhausted the reservoirs in the mine, but then lowered the water very slowly. The Dolores, Major L. thinks will now pay. There is a great abundance of metal & the lead alone will pay for extraction. It costs but one dollar to deliver it in carts, a cargo of 300 pounds, at the Roma landing.

The company sent out a smelter at the cost of thousands of dollars & months of time. His labors were a total failure & he has been discharged. Major Lowry doubts whether he ever smelted one pound of lead ore before. Our ores are so de[l]icate that they melt in the candle. The furnace is still standing. He was furnished in New York with all that he required by Major Lowry, with all he required here & every assistance in labor. They have not for another matter, to put up a furnace they have now on the ground. It is a small compact affair & is said can do much. I want to see the Mexican process tried in the mean time. If it is only a little more than pays expenses, it will be a great assistance to the mine.

There are mountains in the distance & the ground immediately around the mine tolerably level. It is a poor miserable country. The water for the animals comes from the shaft, that to drink has to be hauled four miles. The whole country from here to the mines is most miserable & fully equals in worthlessness that which Mr. Bartlett styles "God forsaken" in Arizona.

THURS. 5. We had a little lunch at 12 & I left at one. I was very hospitably entertained. Mrs. Lowry is a sister of Dr. Jarvis of the army.

It rained & misted all day & half the next. We had quite an escort. As we went up Sanders received at the Alamo an express from his brother about corn. He rejoined us there & we had from the mine, the Sergt. of the d[e]scubr[i]dores, the Express from the mines, for the mail & another man.[15] After we left the Alamo, we had four men on horseback. This gave Mr. Sanders confidence, as going up he saw a man in every bush & pointed out many places where people were killed. Zamora with five men passed the Villa Nueva the day we arrived there from Guerrero, on his way around to strike the river below or more probably on their way into the interior.

We reached the Alamo, 8 leagues a little before it became dark.

Before I started I laid aside my uniform & borrowed a hat to wear in place of my cap as I did not care to be recognized as the "Comandante of Los Tropes Americana." It would hardly have been safe to have met a party of Cortinas's men under the circumstances. I passed for one of the proprietors of the Vallecillo mines, who only understood a few words of Spanish.

---

[15] *Descubridores* is used by Heintzelman to refer to scouts.

We slept at the Alamo. There is a small river & quite a settlemen[t], as they can irrigate & raise corn & sugar cane. We stopped at the house of a smart widow with half a dozen or more grown daughters. She is worth 20 to 25,000$ in cattle, etc.

Here is a description of her surroundings. Her principal house is an adobe, 40 feet long, thatched well, with the leaves of the Spanish bayonet. The whole is in one room. At the farther end—it has no window—are a dozen or more little pictures of saints & in the middle a large one of our Lady of Guadalupe, all ornamented with red & yellow rosettes. Under these are two narrow beds on trestles, occupied by the widow & some of her daughters. The room is about 15 feet wide. This leaves a middle space between the beds under our Lady. On the opposite end han[g] also some saints & under them a small recess in which hang a few quite small mugs with gild edges & figures & a few other things. There is here one bed in the end & one on the side & a table between. On the side opposite the door is a sort of a kitchen in which stands the Ojo & a few plates & bowls. Opposite is a platform raised about 6 inches, in which they sit in daytime & which the[y] spread a mattress for two of our guards. There was also a table in the room, covered with a red cloth & a long bench. There was also a very primitive old fashioned spinning wheel. On a cross piece near the wall hung more fine Mexican blankets, one valued at $80. The blankets are made by hand & it sometimes take a year to make one.[16]

When the table was set, they spread a table cloth, not half long enough & a few plates & bowls. We made our own coffee. They killed a kid. Some of the meat was I suppose partly boiled & the water poured off & then cooked a little more. It had that appearance to me. Then we had tortillas, a little chili in one saucer & small earthen saucers or bowls of frijoles. This constituted our supper. Not a spoon, knife or fork. We had three of the native gentlemen sup with us. They used their fingers to turn over & select the meat, each had a saucer of frijoles & when he wanted chili made a spoon of his tortilla & scooped it up. They are all fond of coffee & were glad to get some from us. The widow took her bowl & not waiting for our spoons, put her hand into our sugar bag & helped herself. They all are extravagantly fond of sugar.

They gave Sanders one bed & I the other at the end of the house opposite our Lady. I pulled off my boots & slept in my overcoat. The children had been sleeping in the beds & were removed some ten minutes before. I laid down my head with fear & trembling. The floor was earth & in the middle about a cartload of corn, after which the pigs would come in, whenever the door was unguarded.

---

[16] Well into the twentieth century, this area of Mexico, especially the town of Mier, was known for the quality of its hand-woven blankets.

FRI. 6TH. Before day some were stirring. We made ourselves a cup of coffee & with some dry bread—& we breakfasted. We got off as it grew light. The widow was up & stirring with the first. I almost forgot to mention that I did not venture to look in to the kitchen. Mr. Sanders knows all these people, having lived here some ten years or more & with a Mexican wife. I pretended not to understand a word of Spanish & he went & looked to everything.

It was raining a little when we started & we had several little showers, but not far from noon it cleared off & part of the afternoon was quite warm.

At 12 we stopped two hours to graze our animals & to lunch. Mrs. Lowry put up some coffee, a couple of legs of roast chicken & biscuits for me. Mr. Sanders had a stuffed chicken & some sour bread. Our escort stopped on the way & got a sheet of several pounds of fresh beef.

The distance from the Alamo to Mier is called 24 leagues & it was quite uncertain how far we would go. Mr. Sanders changed his mind about twenty times a day. The roads are very good in dry weather, with the exception of some bad gullies & a few arroyas & crossing of Mexican rivers. We reached Mier at 7 P.M. Sanders talked strongly of getting to Roma. He had left his buggy to be repaired & it was to be ready, but Mexican like, one wheel was taken off & I suppose that not touched. The carriage we had we could not get to carry any farther. Finally it was decided to get saddles & ride the horses & at 9 P.M. we left. We got a cup of chocolate in Mier, with a bit of poor bread.

When the sun set it was clear with not a cloud to be seen & the night was as clear with a moon nearly full. We had some doubt whether we would be able to get the ferryman to put us across, but after very little delay we got across & I was thankful to be once more at home, just at midnight.

I had to leave my carpetbag at Mier to be sent for to-day, but I brought my Buffalo robe & a blanket & a few things in my pockets, as I had sent my mattress & bed to Capt. Stoneman for safe keeping & it would be too late to get them.

Mr. Sanders is a queer man, but good hearted & he done me a great favour. My great annoyance was his changing his mind so continually that I never knew what he was going to do or where we would get to.

We made a great drive yesterday, 24 leagues or 53 miles & 9 from Mier here, make 62 miles. This is the least the distance is estimated. The 8 leagues, 21 m., from the Alamo to Vallecillos makes the whole distance 83 miles. This I think cant be far from the true distance. We drove his two American horses.

To-day is beautiful. The mail from Laredo is in & brings only S. Antonio papers. I have not seen them yet. The mail carrier says that the troops are ordered to halt at Laredo & await orders from S.A. Our express returned from Brownsville. The steamboat was to leave on the 4th—probably nothing of note has occurred since I have been gone.

The widow at the Alamo I forgot to mention, when offered in the morning a drink of Mexican brandy accepted, but the black bottle to her lips & took a mouthful. She then sat down & smoked a cigarrito & spit. How disgusting?

We had Capt. Tomlinson & some of the Rangers up to-day. I had a long talk with him about the excesses of the Rangers. He is opposed to them & I hope will talk with Major Tobin. Three wagons got up with 2,500 rations. Lt. Sullivan, Dr. Carswell & Mr. McClusky also came up. They all left late in the afternoon. The steamer will probably be up on Monday with more rations. Lt. Sullivan has 6 mon. leave.

Our mail got in from Ringgold at dusk. None from Brownsville. There is a N. Orleans Pickaun of the 24 Dec. Congress not organized yet. The news from Brownsville dont close so late as our expedition the first. There is an exaggerated account of our force & all jumbled up.

There is also a synopsis of a treaty with Mexico. It is eventually a protectorate. I dont see how our minister could ask such terms. It provides for the wants of Arizona. Under almost any circumstances we can send troops into Mexico.[17]

It has been quite warm to-day & is a clear beautiful night. I saw two late S. Antonio papers 17th & 24th. Nothing of much interest. I do hope that we will soon get a mail.

Capt. Stoneman thinks from a conversation with Major French that there are at Dept. Hd. Qrs. scant instructions about Mexico.[18] If there are I should have been furnished with them, when I was ordered to this frontier.

---

[17] The McLane-Ocampo Treaty, negotiated between Robert McLane, U.S. minister to Mexico, and Melchor Ocampo, Mexican Foreign Minister, was agreed to in Mexico City in 1859, after lengthy talks. The treaty gave the United States the unrestricted right to use a route across the Isthmus of Tehuantepec for transit and commerce, as well as two similar routes across the northern frontier, one of which ran from Matamoros to Camargo to Mazatlan via Monterrey, Saltillo, and Durango. Furthermore, U.S. forces could be used in Mexico in response to a request from, or with the consent of, the Mexican government. Other provisions of the treaty dealt with religious freedom, exemption from forced loans, compensation, and ratification. Fearing a Yankee protectorate, both Mexican liberals and conservatives came to oppose the treaty and it was eventually rejected by the Mexican government. Sectional and party politics in the United States over the desire for territorial concessions and the fear that internal involvement in Mexico would lead to war also defeated the treaty in the United States in May 1860. Donothon C. Olliff, *Reforma Mexico and the United States: A Search for Alternatives to Annexation, 1854–1861* (University: University of Alabama Press, 1986), 141–47; Edward J. Broussard, "The Origins of the McLane-Ocampo Treaty of 1859," *Americas*, 14 (Winter, 1958), 223–246.

[18] William Henry French, an 1837 West Point graduate, had been breveted a major for gallantry at Contreras and Churubusco during the Mexican War and was serving in the 1st Artillery in 1860. Prior to the Cortina War, French was stationed at

With this treaty I fear very much that I will be kept on this frontier for sometime yet. I may receive instructions to cross the frontier & occupy some of the towns. Stranger things than this have happened. If new Regiments are raised my operations should give me a Colonelcy.

ROMA TEXAS SUN. JAN. 8TH, 1860

We had a beautiful night with a full moon. This morning was a little cloudy, with fog apparently in the distance. It is quite warm & pleasant.

Dr. Dodridge, a merchant of this place whom we met a Mr. Mahoney's arrived last night.[19] Mr. Mahoney drove him up on the other side 60 miles. He brings no news.

We have had a pleasant day, though perhaps a little too warm. Lts. Thomas & Ramsay have gone to Mier to a ball. I spent half the day reading the N.O. Pic. of the 24 Dec. I was far back in the news.[20] The steamer is expected up on Tuesday. Although troops have passed along the road & our three wagons with provisions came up with an escort of six men, people are still afraid.

ROMA TEXAS MON. JAN. 9TH, 1860

The early part of the night was beautiful. A full moon & clear & mild. This morning there was a fog & cloudy. It looks like rain & is quite mild.

There is a report that two companies have arrived at Ft. Brown by sea & that a trading woman, who came up in a day & a half to Ringgold from Brownsville saw Cortinas this side [of] Edinburg, with 35 men & that he is wounded in the hand. Also that he has 60 men on the other side.

Not much truth in all this.

My watch stopped last night & I cant start it this morning. I broke the chrystal several weeks ago, but it is still in.

Those young gentleman were to be back at 12 to-day & were not till sometime after dark. I did not think they would overstay their leave, as I inquired particularly when they would be back. I will bring them up short some of these days. It is still warm & clouding up. Wrote to Mr. Lathrop.

Fort Clark. He became a major general of volunteers during the Civil War and died in May 1881. Heitman, *Historical Register*, 427; *Daily Herald* (San Antonio), Nov. 10, 1859.

[19] Alabama-born Perry Dodridge, twenty-nine, was a Roma merchant. 8th Census, Starr County; Doddridge (sic) and Jacobs to Heintzelman, Jan. 26, 1860, *TTF*, 29.

[20] Although he "was far back in the news," the *Picayune* did print a somewhat detailed account, which Heintzelman surprisingly fails to mention, of the silver taken from the mines of the Sonora Exploring and Mining Company. *Daily Picayune* (New Orleans), Dec. 24, 1859.

Roma Texas Tues. Jan. 10th, 1860

Oh how homesick I am. It is now ten days since our express left & he expected to reach S. Antonio in five days. I dont much expect him under twelve but will look for him after to-day. I have just finished Michelet Lamour. A book written by a ridiculous Frenchman.[21] Much that is good & much that is ridiculous, which only a frenchman could write.

It is half cloudy to-day & warm. We sent a wagon for rations for the men of "I" Company we have with us. Owing to Lt. Thomas's carelessness I suppose their rations are out & Capt. Stoneman has still ten days. Our mess chest was full & he put in the hands of the servants till within a few days & now there is nothing. In the first place the lock was lost or broken & then the hinges.

The wagon got back at noon with the mens rations. A little before 2 P.M. a norther sprung up. It blew hard & dusty & next cold & after dark rain. Lt. Gillam, his wife & two children arrived in the afternoon from Laredo.[22] Lee, Jourdan & Blake are there with three companies 8th Infy.[23] The order is countermanded & they ordered to establish a camp there & cooperate with me.

The order for me is I suppose sent to Ft. Brown. Capt. Caldwell I suppose got the order at S. Antonio & has gone back. I am glad on Margaret's account. It also increases the chances of my getting back to Verde. I dont know when I will get my letters. They have probably been all this time in S. Antonio & may come by the express I am looking for.

It is said that Major McDowell comes to Texas & Withers goes somewhere else.[24]

I wrote to Judge Iverson & a short letter to Margaret. I did not expect the mail back from Ringgold until tomorrow, but it got here tonight & leaves early in the morning. I had only time to write a few lines.

---

[21] It cannot be determined with any certainty what book by the French author Heintzelman is referring to.

[22] This is Alvan Collum Gillem, twenty-nine and an 1851 West Point graduate, who was a first lieutenant in the 1st Artillery. Lieutenant Gillem had evidently preceded Col. Robert E. Lee downriver from Laredo. Heitman, *Historical Register*, 457.

[23] Capt. Arthur T. Lee had written Heintzelman from Laredo on January 6 saying that Companies C, D, and F of the 8th Infantry, along with a section of artillery and twenty-five men of Co. E. of the 2d Cavalry, had arrived at Fort McIntosh. Since orders sending the entire force into the lower valley had been countermanded, only the men of the 2d Cavalry were continuing to Ringgold Barracks. Lee to [Heintzelman], Jan. 6, 1860, HP.

[24] Ohio-born Irvin McDowell, West Point class of 1838 and a brevet captain in the 1st Artillery, is best remembered for commanding the Union Army at First Bull Run.

I got a letter from Kelsey at Rio Grande City.[25] He writes that Cortinas is on the river below with 600 men. The man is crazy.

A gentleman loaned me a short synopsis of the President's message. He wants authority to send troops into Mexico & to establish troops on all the Mexican frontier. The letter proves he already has.

ROMA TEXAS THURS. JAN. 12, 1860

I dont know where I lost a day, but this is the 12th and must be Thursday. Last night was cold & it has been so all day. I heard it spit snow to-day & at bed time it is misting a little. Capt. Jarvis is here & returns in the morning. He dined & supped with us. Mrs. Gillam brought out some fruit cake & made us some mince pies. So we have our Christmas after all. I came to my room after breakfast & read awhile, but it was too cold. I have spent most of the day at Capt. Stoneman's, where we cook & eat. Lt. & Mrs. Gillam stop there.

ROMA TEXAS FRI. JAN. 13TH, 1860

Last night was cold & this morning. The norther is over, the sun is out & it is becoming pleasant.

There is a report to-day that Major Ford & Capt. Littleton have crossed the river to join Carvajal. The companies it is said have disbanded. It if true must be an effort to catch Cortinas. Littletons Company, Tobins I know would not disband, neither would Ford leave now when the state is raising a Regiment of which he no doubt would be colonel.

---

[25] New York–born John P. Kelsey, who had settled at Rio Grande City shortly after the Mexican War, was forty-two and the largest merchant in the community. Only days before, Kelsey told Heintzelman that he had been in Camargo and had been robbed by one of Cortina's men. Obviously exaggerating, as Heintzelman bluntly observes, the *Cortinista* told Kelsey that Cortina was downriver with 600 men. Kelsey was fearful that Cortina would raid Rio Grande City at night and "sack the town" before soldiers could arrive from Ringgold Barracks. "Only days earlier" Cortina's men "had fired twenty shots into the town," Kelsey said, and "no notice whatever was taken . . . of it." Kelsey was also alarmed at the Rangers. "If their late conduct can be taken as a criterion, I have little or no confidence in [our] protection," he wrote. "Our sole safety lies in the discipline of the U.S. Troops," Kelsey continued. Two weeks later, the Yankee merchant wrote José San Roman: "Cortina took from me and damaged otherwise near five thousand worth of Mds." Kelsey promised to "make a claim on Uncle Sam for a pile . . . whether I get it or not." Kelsey would have the opportunity to report on more of Cortina's activities when he became commercial agent in Camargo in 1869. 8th Census, Starr County; Kelsey to Heintzelman, Jan. 11, 1860, HP; Kelsey to San Roman, Jan. 26, 1860, San Roman Papers (CAH); *American Flag* (Brownsville), May 15, 1852; Despatches from United States Consuls in Camargo, 1869–1880, Records of the Department of State, RG 59 (NA).

Gillam, Thomas & Ramsay drove to Rio Grande City. They will be back tomorrow when we will probably know. The Mexicans are collecting soldiers on the other side. I wrote to Mr. Futhey to-day.

ROMA TEXAS SAT. JAN. 14, 1860

The weather has changed. It is warm in the sun, but the air is south thought still cool. This is so for several days after a norther. It was near 3 P.M. when the gentlemen returned. They brought no news but what we heard before. In the morning I heard that Matamoros had pronounced against the Liberals & that Gen. Woll was after Carvajal. It may be true but is doubtful. Neither mail nor express in. For the last day or two my right toe has pained me. It pains me to-day & I fear is getting worse.

The express from S. Antonio got in about 10 P.M. I was still at our mess room. I got in all some 20 letters. Not one from Wrightson. A half dozen from Margaret. She has lost Jesus & the girl wants to leave, otherwise, get on well but lonesome. The letter from Hd. Qrs. is not very satisfactory. Ewell wants to know who was killed & what losses & depredations Cortinas occasioned.[26] It may take a year to learn all this. I fear that I will have to go back to Brownsville.

I have just glanced over my letters.

ROMA TEXAS SUN. JAN. 15, 1860

The night was cold, but the norther is over & the day is pleasant. I did not intent to leave until tomorrow, but every one was anxious to start & we leave at 2 P.M. I have been busy writing letters. I sent my pay a/cts for Nov. & Dec. $429.20 to Major Cunningham. I left off the forage. I also wrote to Margaret & to Major Vinton.

The steamboat started on the 9th & will be up in a day or two.

Ringgold Brks. 10 P.M. We left at 2 P.M. & arrived here at sundown. The cavalry is encamped outside & we are quartered in the comdg. officers quarters. We leave at 7 A.M. tomorrow. I went to see Major Tobin. He talks of moving out & doing something. Reports are here again of 600 men under Cortinas on the river below. We don't believe it. I dont think that there is a man this side [of] the river. We took supper with Lt. & Mrs. Gillam, on some quails he killed on the road. It was quite warm & dusty on the road. We saw Lt. Sullivan & Dr. Carswell.

---

[26] Heintzelman was to "report fully as to the extent of the damage done by Cortinas and his command." Jno. Withers to Heintzelman, Jan. 7, 1860, HP. For depredation claims, see TTF, 15–63.

I wrote to the A.A. Genl. S. Antonio, that I will be through & back in three weeks.[27] Our Express for S.A. leaves in the morn.

Las Cuevas Texas. Mon. Jan. 16, 1860

We were up & had our breakfast soon after daylight, but did not get off until a quarter before 8. Capt. Stoneman left some sick horses & men & company property & delayed us. I took a look around the Garrison. It looks as if it might have been a pleasant post.

It was warm & dusty. We got here at 12½ P.M.—the distance is 18 or 20 miles. From here we made our night march when we surprised Cortinas.

On the road we met a Mexican loading a sore backed horse. We had scarcely stopped at our camp when he rode up & inquired for me. He hurriedly unsaddled his horse, took off the stirrup, leathers & untied various strings. Under the seat he took out a package wrapped in a cloth. It was a letter from San Antonio sent from Brownsville. It is dated the 4th & the one I got at Roma is dated the 7th. This informs me that the Legislature has appointed Col. R.H. Taylor commissioner to investigate the causes of the disturbances on the Rio Grande & to aid him, or rather to furnish him all the legitimate assistance in my power.[28] It is addressed to me as Major, 1st U.S. Infy., Ft. Brown.

There is a letter for Tobin & also one to me from the commissioners to know what risk the frontier will suffer if the Rangers are discharged.[29] The letter is to Tobin I suppose to repair to B'ville to be discharged.

The afternoon has been very windy.

The express came up on the other side & crossed at Edinburg. His brother brought it here. The former was detained by some men on the other side. He says there are some men out at the Salt Lake & also between here & Edinburg. I doubt it. It is possible there are a few stragglers.

----

[27] Heintzelman to Withers, Jan. 15, 1860, HLS.

[28] Robert H. Taylor, thirty-five and a member of the Texas Legislature from Fannin County, was a Sam Houston ally, who, along with Ángel Navarro, a member of the legislature from Bexar County, had been appointed to "inquire into the cause, origin and progress of the disturbances" on the Rio Grande. San Antonio *Daily Herald*, Jan. 5, 20, 1860; Withers to Heintzelman, Jan. 4, 1860, HP; 8th Census, Fannin and Bexar Counties; Orders to Ángel Navarro and Taylor, Jan. 2, 1860, in *The Writings of Sam Houston, 1813–1863*, eds. Amelia W. Williams and Eugene C. Barker (8 vols.; Austin: Jenkins Publishing Co., 1970), VII, 395–394.

[29] Taylor and Navarro appear to have had serious doubts whether Tobin, whom they found "utterly incompetent to command in the field," would report to Brownsville for his men to be discharged. Back in San Antonio, Tobin informed the census enumerator that he was a brigadier general. Navarro and Taylor to Tobin, Jan.

GRASSY CAMP TEXAS TUES. JAN. 17, 1860

Last evening the wind changed to the north & it grew colder at once. It was cool last night & has been all day. We got here 20 miles by 12 M. At a Rancho near the road called the Tobasco near the steamboat mooring. Capt. Ricketts & family & Lt. Langdon & family & Lt. Baird are on board & 10 Rangers as escort. Capt. Dawson has sent 20 men at Point Isabel to guard the Custom House. As safe as Brownsville. Capt. Ricketts saw in all as many as 100 men on the banks on his way up. The water here has dried up but a lagoon is nearby. This is the best camp on the river. We have grass for the animals & a carpet of grass to encamp on. I picked a bunch of verbenas. I noticed yesterday that vegetation has commenced.

ON LAGOON WED. JAN. 18, 1860

The express got back after night & brought me a letter from Tobin.[30] He says he will remain till he hears from me again. I wrote to him from Edinburg, where we stopped half an hour. No one lives there but a Mexican & wife. We met there Dr. Bowie. He is greatly frightened & says he will carry his family home. He says 40 men are below & Cortinas in Matamoros etc., etc.

We had a sprinkle of rain last night but pleasant to-day. It is now quite warm.

I have been busy filing my letters.

ON LAGOON 3 MS. BEYOND SAN ROSARIO THURS. JAN. 19, 1860

The night was cold. We left at the usual hour. At ¼ of 12 we reached San Rosario—we called it 15 miles where we went up but I now think it was 18. We there saw 5 or 6 Mexicans running. I sent 10 men after them under Lt. Ramsay. I did not intend to go, but went & also Lts. Thomas & Gillam. We saw the trail of horse & foot, but lost it in the chaparral. We had some difficulty in finding a road to get back through the chaparral. In looking for one I came on an old camp, may have contained 40 men. We passed a ranch he burned. It must have been a pretty good one. About 3 ms. this side Rosario in a large field, on a lagoon we found our camp. When we went up we made it 15 miles between S. Rosario & last nights camp. I think it is 18 & this 3 ms. beyond makes our march 21 ms. We are now 91½ ms. from Roma.

12, 1860, LR, AGO, RG 94 (NA); Taylor to Sam Houston, Jan. 16, 1860, Houston Papers (TSA); 8th Census, Bexar County; Taylor to Heintzelman, Jan. 12, 1860, HP.

[30] In four lines, Tobin informed Heintzelman that he would remain at Ringgold Barracks "until I hear from you." Heintzelman to Tobin, Jan. 17, 1860, HLS; Tobin to Heintzelman, Jan. 17, 1860, HP; Heintzelman to Tobin, Jan. 18, 1860, HLS.

The afternoon is warm. I gathered a five leaved white flower. A snow drop I suppose. Lt. Gillam shot two geese & sent us one. There is a Ranger along, who was shot in the neck, has given me considerable information.

He got from people in Rio Grande City who counted them, 445 came in in the morning, then 74, then 35 from the town & vicinity & 36 from Camargo & other places in Mex.—in all 590 men. We under estimated the drowned & killed.

We dined at 4½ P.M. & as we finished a Mexican rode up on a mule with the mail from B'ville. He had a letter for Tobin in his shoe. As he went down, he says he was stopped by 25 men, who robbed him of 5$ & his provisions. He reports that 9 ms. this side B'ville, Cortinas is with 150 men. I have no doubt but that the men we chased to-day were robbers they did belong to his forces.

LAGOON 4 MS. BELOW CARRISITO FRI. JAN. 20, 1860

We left at 7 & reached here at 12. I called the distance 10 ms. We came 5 ms. to the Baston (opposite) 4 to Las Ruses, 6 to Carrisito, where Thornton was captured & 4 to this lagoon. We are now about 2 miles from where we encamped the first time we came out of Brownsville, or about 6 miles from town. We have a beautiful grassy camp & delightful weather—last night cold.

Wrote to Henry Howe, Cincinnati. Wrote also to Mr. T. Coleman, N.Y. about the sale of stock to Colt the winter before the last in Washington.

FT. BROWN TEXAS SAT. JAN. 21ST, 1860

We had a very heavy fog, did not lift until after we started. We left at 7 A.M. & were here a little before 11 A.M. The distance, I think is about 16 miles—or in all from Roma 126½ miles. Some of my distances are underrated, as Gen. Smith they say made it 118½ to Ringgold Brrks, & it is 15½ to Roma from there.[31] It was so warm to-day I laid off my coat. Our whole trip we had delightful weather. At the lagoon we staid at last night there were a great many duck & geese—and smaller birds.

A mile & a half from town we met 20 or more Rangers on a scout going up the river. I told them of those Mexicans we saw at San Rosario.

The commissioners have mustered in Ford's company & he is the senior Captain. There are to be one or two more—for a year. Congress not

---

[31] This was Persifor Frazer Smith, a graduate of the College of New Jersey (Princeton) who had been a brigadier general of Louisiana volunteers during the Mexican War and in charge of the Department of Texas from 1851 to 1856. Earlier Smith had commanded the Department of the Pacific at the time Heintzelman established Fort Yuma. Smith had been credited with outlining the frontier defenses of Texas and California. Ill health drained his vigor and faculties and he died in 1858.

organized yet. There has been no pronunciam[i]ento in Matamoros. Carvajal wrote to let two companies of volunteers cross over. They had a town meeting & refused. This is probably the foundation of the report.

I this moment received four official communications from San Antonio. Amount to what I received before.

We went to dinner & there met Col. Lockridge & after Major Ford. They still insist that Cortinas has a considerable force, but on the other side of the river. A pronunciam[i]ento is soon expected in favour of Miarmon. I am satisfied that we will have trouble until we occupy the other side. I was busy writing till eleven O'Clock. I did not make an official report, but wrote a long letter to Vinton. I wrote the Margaret, to Solon, Poston, & C.S. Brown, Sec. S. Ex. & M. Co. I sent Solon's order for transfer of stock.

After tattoo that Ranger scout got in & brought me three prisoners. I told them they had better put them into the hands of the civil authorities, but I would keep them till morning.

Ft. Brown Sun. Jan. 22, 1860

These Mexicans are harmless & were turned out this morning. The scout was not authorized. My letters got off this morning. The boat goes direct to New Orleans.

After breakfast Mr. Navarro, the commissioner called with Col. Dunlap, who has lived on this frontier.[32] Col. Taylor is not well. They dont talk as strong fillibusters as others.

This evening Major Ford & Capt. Littleton called. The latter was over in Matamoros & saw Cortinas in a billiard saloon on the plaza, with some of his officers. He was afterwards seen on the streets at the head of 150 cavalry. They say there are 400 Infantry & 200 Rancheros. They fear an attack from the Rangers & fillibusters. Cortinas it is said holds a captains commission in the Mexican army & is a Mex. citizen.[33] Capt. Stoneman & I dined with Capt. Dawson.

Ft. Brown Texas Mon. Jan. 23rd, 1860

I met Col. Lockridge this morning & he made me a confidant of their plans etc. I now see why they want three companies of Rangers.

---

[32] William W. Dunlop was a Tennessee-born, thirty-five-year-old lawyer. 7th Census, Cameron County.

[33] Cortina had served at the battles of Palo Alto and Resaca de la Palma as a corporal in the *Defensores de la Patria*, a company of the *Guardia Nacional de Tamaulipas*. Largely through the influence of his first cousin, Col. Miguel Tijerina, who commanded the Federal cavalry in Matamoros, Cortina had been able to obtain a captain's commission. Glavecke Affidavit, Jan. 17, 1860, *HRG*, 13; Thompson, *Juan Cortina*, 1–2.

I next went & saw Col. Taylor. Col. Dunlap & Mr. Navarro soon came in. Col. Dunlap just returned from Matamoros where he saw the man yesterday taken for Cortinas. He brought him to town & the person who recognized him, acknowledged that they were mistaken.

I went with Lts. Ramsay & Thomas to Galvans & saw a paragraph he cut from a paper. It is [a] telegraph from Washington that a compy Cav. & one of Infy are sent to the Rio Grande, dated 4 Jan—to quiet disturbances.[34] My report no doubt countermanded the order.

I met Col. Fitzpatrick, our consul in Matamoros. He dined with me.

I gave my watch to a jeweler & he found a piece of glass caught in the second hand. It has been quite a vexation to be without the time.

The weather is quite warm to-day.

I had a visit from Col. Lockridge. He could not find a paper he wished to show me. He gave us a long account of some of his Fillibustering in Nicaragua. I have been looking over the papers. Capts. Stoneman & Dawson & Lt. Gillam called & spent a couple of hours with me. I read a couple of Brownsville Flags.[35] They are full of our campaign. They give great credit to the Rangers & speak well of my arrangements etc. They dont tell what some of the Rangers did not do.

Ft. Brown Tues. Jan. 24, 1860

Still warm and pleasant. I saw the commissioners twice to-day. Col. Taylor is trying to get the Rangers out to cut off a party said to be back in the country killing cattle. I saw Iturria & he tells me there are some back, but that small parties cross & kill cattle.[36] That Cortinas passed up & down on the other side with a few men—that he has been in Matamoros privately. That the authorities have armed the people on the river & are cooperating with Cortinas to have his aid, whether from danger from this side or from the interior. They fear the Rangers & filibusters.

Fresh oysters arrived & we had some.

We start in the morning for Point Isabel.

---

[34] Even through the Civil War, Heintzelman wrote "telegraph" when meaning "telegram."

[35] Heintzelman retained the *American Flag* (Brownsville) issue of Jan. 5, 1860, for his records. See HP.

[36] Of Basque ancestry, Francisco Yturria, twenty-nine, was a leading Brownsville merchant and wealthy landowner who was responsible for establishing the first privately owned bank south of San Antonio. Born in Matamoros on October 4, 1830, Yturria first worked as a clerk for Charles Stillman before becoming a leading cotton broker on the border. As part of the Cameron County establishment, Yturria was one of the few Hispanics to serve on the Brownsville Committee of Safety that had been

FT. BROWN TEXAS THURS. JAN. 26, 1860

Yesterday morning after 8 O'Clock we got off for Point Isabel. Capt. Stoneman, Lt. Thomas & I in Gillam's S. Diego & S. Antonio Stage. He was going along, but Capt. Dawson, who has an idea that his men at night call him names, begged him not to go. The weather was pleasant & we got there a little after 12. We passed near the battlegrounds, but too far South to see them.

At the Point we saw Lt. Graham, who has 20 men to defend it.[37] The gentleman at the Custom House invited us to dinner. Young Butler also lives there with his mother & sisters. At the custom house we saw a number of carts & wagons other goods [to be] taken into Mexico.

We went on board the Cutter & Capt. Harvey sent us down to the Brazos.[38] We called on Mrs. Shannon, Lt. Langdon's mother in law & left a card. We saw some five guns & shot & shell & some Qr.M. stores. There were a few schooners lying there & a brig. outside. It was dusk when we left. We took tea in the Cutter & I slept on board. This morning the Captain went out & caught five red fish & we all breakfasted on them. Lt. Tenneyson of the old Texas navy is also on board. All treated us politely.

We came ashore & went up to see the fresnel light. It is a beautiful lamp. The first I have seen. At 20 min of 11 we left & reached here in four hours. The road is tolerably good & distance 28 miles. There is not the slightest necessity for a guard.

We brought up two fish & I take tea with Mr. Gillam. It has clouded up & threatened a norther, but only gave us a few drops of rain.

The afternoon was quite warm. At sundown it began to grow cooler & the wind came out of the north. Soon after it commenced to rain & continues steadily. I took tea at Lt. Gillams & could not get home for sometime.

FT. BROWN TEXAS FRI. JAN. 27, 1860

The rain continued most of the night & some this morning. Walter, the

---

organized to defend the town against Cortina. After the Civil War, Yturria fled to France but returned to Brownsville in 1867. At the time of his death in 1912, he owned 130,000 acres of land in five South Texas counties. Verna J. McKenna, "Francisco Yturria," in *New Handbook of Texas*, eds. Tyler, et al., VI, 1134–1135.

[37] Point Isabel, population 211 at this time, was one of the few communities in the Lower Rio Grande Valley not seriously affected by the Cortina War. 8th Census, Cameron County. A lighthouse at Point Isabel had been built by the U.S. Treasury Department in 1852. During the Civil War in 1863, Colonel Ford removed the lens to prevent Union forces from using it to guide their ships. The lens was never found, and the lighthouse ceased operations in 1905.

[38] The military warehouses were located on the north end of Brazos Island at Brazos Santiago.

man who pretends to attend to my room, is drunk all the time & did not make a fire this morning. He is always drunk when he can get liquor. It has quit raining & will I suppose be cold tonight. I called on the commissioners & a Mex. prisoner was brought in. He was captured yesterday up the river stealing cattle. He is recognized as one of Cortinas's original men & will no doubt be hung. A ranger scout went up the river & exchanged shots with Cortinas men on the other side. There were quite a number there. I have been busy most of the day with Cummings a lawyer & one of the Committees of safety in making notes of events that passed. Thomas will never get me any information. If I have to stay here I will apply for the Adjutant!

Col. Lockridge showed me a letter dated Victoria 23 Jan. from Carbajal asking them to join him with 700 Riflemen, 1,000 Infantry, 28 pieces of artillery as agreed upon. He also speaks of Col. Duncan of New Orleans. Ford is in the State service & will not go—the letter is addressed to him & Lockridge thinks it advisable to wait.

It is midnight, I took a nap at dusk & have since been reading the Brownsville Flag extras & making notes of events.

Ft. Brown Texas Sat. Jan. 28th, 1860

The weather more pleasant & norther nearly gone. I made some more notes this morning & also saw Cummings again. I then made a short visit to the Commissioners. A Mexican captured near the Arroyo Colorado & guilty, no doubt made his escape from the Rangers. I made a visit to Col. Lockridge. Some letter Carvajal wrote to Gen. Guadalupe Garcia to make a forced loan, or fine of $100,000 on some there in Matamoros, who pronounced the other day & send them to Victoria is to come out in the Matamoros paper. He was to call on Ford for aid if necessary. This letter creates more excitement. Lt. Ramsay saw Gen. Garcia & says he has issued an order for the troops on both sides to pass mutually to put down these robbers. He was coming to see me, but has been too busy. I must try & see him on Monday. I went to Victors for a cup of tea this evening, sat a while & was bored by a drunken doctor.

Ft. Brown Sun. Jan. 29th, 1860

This morning a little before day I had to get up & heard the blowing of bugles & beating of drums in Matamoros. I supposed it a pronunciam[i]ento, but at breakfast could hear nothing of it. I have just learned that the express sent to Juarez has returned & brought the information that he disapproved of Gen. Carvajal's orders about the $100,000 & the arrest of certain citizens he wished sent him under Major Ford. They had great rejoicing.

This has been a beautiful morning. I have had to spend it in writing a report for Dept. Hd. Qrs.[39] I am getting very tired of the way Lt. Thomas does his duties. He only makes a convenience of them. I would apply for Lt. Washington at once but I dont want the Hd. Qrs. changed, as I hope to get off. If I am to be kept here I may as well have the Hd. Qrs. of the Regt. here & my family. I will wait until I hear from Margaret & from Vinton. I wrote to Margaret. Lt. Graham & his detachment got back from Point Isabel to-day. How ridiculous it was for the Collector to apply for them.

FT. BROWN MON. JAN. 30, 1860

In the night it commenced to rain & we have had showers all day. It is also quite warm.

I went this morning & got or rather made copies of two of Cortina's letters in which he says, it is a private quarrel.[40] The Cutter is ordered to carry Gen. Duff Green to Vera Cruz.[41] The ship of war Brooklyn is expected at the

---

[39] Heintzelman to Withers, Jan. 29, 1860, HLS.

[40] Juan Eponuceno (sic) Cortinas to Estevan Powers, Oct. 31, 1859, HP. Cortina maintained that he did not want to attack Brownsville but challenged several personal enemies, especially Adolphus Glavecke and Robert Shears, to "select their battle field" and meet him outside of town. Heintzelman also copied a note from Francis M. Campbell to Stephen Powers, which had been received in Brownsville at the time Campbell was being held as a hostage, possibly in exchange for Tomás Cabrera. Campbell to Powers, n.d., HP. The first letter was printed in the *American Flag* (Brownsville) extra of Oct. 29, 1859.

[41] A political intriguer and champion of the South, Duff Green was born in Kentucky in 1791. In 1823 he purchased the St. Louis *Enquirer* and became a Jacksonian Democrat. Turning against Jackson in support of states' rights, however, Green befriended President John Tyler in 1841 and was made the unofficial agent to Great Britain with orders to secure a commercial treaty. Heintzelman had met Green at the White House in November 1842. In 1848, President Zachary Taylor made Green agent to Mexico.

In 1859, Green was sent by Secretary of State Lewis Cass as a special agent to investigate "atrocities committed by parties of armed Mexicans during insurrections in Texas." Arriving in Galveston from New Orleans in early December, Green talked to several individuals recently arrived by steamer from Brownsville. "What we required on the Rio Grande is a person in command who has no interest in provoking a war with Mexico," Green reported. Passing himself off as a railroad executive, Green reached Austin on December 9, 1859, during the bitterly cold norther that Major Heintzelman recorded in his journal. Learning the Rangers had been defeated a second time, Green was fearful Cortina's success could motivate bands of Indians to unite with the *Cortinistas* and launch a series of raids on the frontier settlements. Gov. Hardin H. Runnels informed Green he would not send more troops to Brownsville unless compelled to do so by the legislature. While in Austin, Green became convinced that affairs on the Rio Grande were greatly exaggerated and, in part, a veiled attempt to secure a greater expenditure of public money.

Brazos, with our minister to Mexico.[42] The mail is expected tonight.

FT. BROWN TUES. JAN. 31ST, 1860

Weather pleasant. No mail yet. Col. Dunlop & Mr. Navarro called this morning. I went with the latter to Matamoros & got Col. Fitzpatrick our Consul to go with us & call on Gen. Guadalupe Garcia.[43] He showed us his

---

Green attended the inauguration of Sam Houston and sent Secretary Cass copies of Governor Houston's proclamation, which was written in both English and Spanish, that advised Cortina and his men to "lay down their arms," yet promising a "redress of grievances of which they complain." On December 31, 1859, Governor Houston shared Ford's report of Cortinas's defeat at Rio Grande City. Although sure that Cortina was no longer a major threat, Green, who was ill, was planning to proceed to Brownsville with Henry Lawrence Kinney, who spoke Spanish, knew Cortina, and would be reporting on the "cause of the disturbances." In early January 1860, Green warned of "a desire on the part of many in this state to involve the U.S. in a war with Mexico" and as evidence, he sent Secretary Cass an extra of the Austin *Intelligencer*. Although an advocate of southern expansion, Green was concerned that "Rangers will pass over the River in pursuit of Cortinas & his band."

When Captain Nichols and William Henry arrived from Brownsville, Green learned through Governor Houston that the wide scale burning of farms and ranches during the Cortina War that was blamed on the *Cortinistas* was actually started by the Rangers when they set fire to Rancho del Carmen "occupied by the mother and wife of Cortinas." In a confidential letter on February 10, 1860, Green asked Cass to urge prudence on President James Buchanan. "All that prevents Gov. Houston from moving on Mexico with a major force is money and a justifiable pretext," Green said. There was little doubt that Houston was interested in a protectorate leading to an eventful occupation of Mexico. "If Houston did move on Mexico," Green went on to say, "he would not only carry Texas & the South . . . 'the Protectorate' would become the controlling issue in the next Presidential Election."

State Senator Edwin Scarborough told Green that Heintzelman was "strongly in favor of . . . taking the city of Matamoros." There is no further correspondence or final report in the records of the Department of State. Duff Green to Lewis Cass, Nov. 29, Dec. 3, 10, 24, 31, 1859; Jan. 8, 9, 10, 1859 [1860], Feb. 4, 10, 1860; all in General Records of the Department of State, Despatches from Special Agents, RG 59 (NA). Proslavery and a secessionists, Green later advised the Confederate government and died in 1875. Richard E. Ellis, "Duff Green," *Encyclopedia of Southern History*, eds. David C. Roller and Robert W. Twyman (Baton Rouge: Louisiana State University Press, 1979), 558; HJ, Nov. 4, 1842.

[42] For the arrival of the sloop-of-war Brooklyn carrying the U.S. minister to Mexico, Robert M. McLane, see San Antonio *Daily Herald*, Feb. 8, 1860; *Daily Picayune* (New Orleans), Sept. 7, 8, 9, 25, Dec. 21, 22, 1859; Jan. 13, 1860; *Daily True Delta* (New Orleans), Dec. 21, 1859.

[43] Gen. Guadalupe García had been an early supporter of the Plan de Ayutla. Commanding the "line of the Rio Bravo," Garcia continued in the liberal cause until he was removed in 1862.

letter from the Governor of Tamaulipas directing him to cooperate with us in putting down Cortinas. The order is from the Sec. of War. He proposes that we should mutually cross the river. I told him that if he took care of his side we would of ours. I dont think that he cares to do much. He will send me a copy. He told us that four years ago Cortinas was a Lt. under his command & that he appropriated the horses given to him for a remount to his private benefit & that he then discharged him. He also says that six months ago (in June) Cortinas wished to raise fifty men & join him & that he declined his services.[44] We called on Mr. Mahoney & saw his partner Mr. Hale. This is the gentleman Dr. Foard wishes me to see. The Rangers are having a parade, what for I dont know. I went out about 8 P.M. to see what news about the mail. The boat was in sight at 10 this morning & must now be in. We will get the mail tomorrow. A warm norther set in at 5 P.M.

---

[44] By 1855, Cortina had risen to become a lieutenant in the *Movil de Matamoros*, a local militia unit. Juan N. Cortina, Compiled Military Service Record, Secretaria de la Defensa (Mexico City, Mexico).

❦ February 1860 ❧

"...the Mexicans have attacked the boat."

———◆•◆•◆———

FT. BROWN FEB. 1ST, 1860 WED.

Cold enough this morning, with prospect of rain. The Rangers had an election yesterday & elected Littleton capt. I believe Ford is capt. of the other company. An express arrived last night from above. The Ranchero is on her way down with 40 men. Major Tobin & Lt. Sullivan are on board. The Rangers are coming by land. They have reports that Cortinas is on the road with a large force. Some Rangers are to start up to-day. Col. Taylor the commissioner told me this morning that Cortinas had left for Victoria.

The mail got in about 2½ P.M. & was distributed at 4½. I got a letter from Margaret dated the 22 Jan. All well & she writes in good spirits. A little troubled by the uncertainty. I also got a letter from Sister Maria at Leavenworth City dated the 30 Dec. She is not pleased. William Haller & his wife are there.[1] Also a letter from Mr. Poston N.Y. Dec. 28th, enclosing a copy of my agreement with Col. Colt. It is substantially as I said.

We have N. Orleans papers to 17 Dec. Congress not organized. No news of importance. The weather still cold & threatening rain.

FT. BROWN TEXAS THURS. FEB. 2, 1860

Weather mild & pleasant. I wrote to Margaret, to Col. Poston & a report to Adj't. Genl.[2] I got a note from the Commissioners asking about retaining Texas Rangers in service. I wrote them that the two companies they had

---

[1] William Haller, eldest son of Elizabeth Heintzelman Haller, was Heintzelman's nephew.

[2] Heintzelman wrote Adjutant General Cooper that on the six-day march from Roma to Brownsville he had "found all the ranches but one on the road this side of Edinburg destroyed and many burned; until we came almost insight of this town." Analysis of the 1860 Census confirms this. Between Brownsville and Edinburg, enumerator J. H. Bane recorded 411 dwellings as "unoccupied." Forty of these were at or near Rancho del Carmen. Beyond Edinburg in Hidalgo County, 699 dwellings were

mustered were enough.[3] They went up the river to-day & Capt. Stoneman leaves tomorrow. I expect to cover the road as far as Edinburg or Rio Grande City.

FT. BROWN FRI. FEB. 3, 1860

It was clear & pleasant this morning, but has clouded up & looks like rain. Capt. Stoneman's compy & Lt. Ramsay left at one P.M. to hunt grass & scout a short distance up the river. I had Col. Lockridge dine with me. He brought me several papers with important information for me. The mail dont go till tomorrow. I wrote to T. Wrightson & sent my pay a/cts for Jan. without the forage to Major Cunningham, to send me a check—Amt. $208.60. I have an invitation to a ball at Matamoros. Thomas & Graham went. Ramsay was much disappointed that he had to go with Capt. Stoneman. There was quite an alarm in Matamoros last night. Some Rangers at the upper ferry fired across the river. Some Mexicans crossed the night before & threw stones at the ferry house. The Indianola is still aground, but hopes to get off tonight.

FT. BROWN TEXAS SAT. FEB. 4, 1860

The Indianola got off the bar uninjured. A man—Pena an Editor in Matamoros, accused of writing Cortinas's proclamations & a Reactionist, was arrested & fined 300$ & 6 mos. imprisonment.[4] He escaped & came here yesterday. The citizens & Rangers were after him to hang or shoot him. Some gentleman found it out & warned him. Mr. Navarro, Ituria & some others got him & he gave them much information about Cortinas.[5] It only confirms what

---

listed as "unoccupied." Heintzelman to Cooper, Feb. 2, 1860, HLS; 8th Census, Cameron and Hidalgo Counties. See also Leroy P. Graf, "The Economic History of the Lower Rio Grande Valley, 1820–1875," (Ph.D. diss., Harvard University, 1942), 390–391.

[3] Ángel Navarro and Robert H. Taylor asked, "Will you please give us your opinion as to what force of Texas Rangers will, for the present, be necessary to be kept in the service for the protection of this frontier?" Heintzelman responded that "the two companies of Rangers now in the service of the State are sufficient." It would be, however, Heintzelman went on to say, "difficult to give complete protection . . . unless the troops are authorized to occupy the opposite side of the river." Navarro and Taylor to Heintzelman, Feb. 2, 1860, HP; Heintzelman to Navarro and Taylor, Feb. 2, 1860, HLS.

[4] For Miguel Peña as author of Cortina's September 30 and probably November 23, 1859, pronunciamientos see: [Richard] Fitzpatrick to Lewis Cass, Jan. 4, 1860, Matamoros Despatches, RG 59 (NA); Thompson, *Juan Cortina*, 14.

[5] Six months before arriving in Brownsville, Ángel Navarro III, thirty-two, had been reelected to the Texas House of Representatives from Bexar County. Third son of José Antonio Navarro and Margarita de la Garza, Ángel had graduated from Harvard

we all believed, of the Mexican sympathy & aid. The authorities on the other side learned what was going on & sent him overtures. He accepted them & went back last night. He made a written statement, but when he found he could go back, he put it into his pocket.

We have had another pleasant day, except too windy. In the morning it was a little cloudy.

11½ P.M. I was in bed reading, when an hour ago an express arrived that the Mexicans have attacked the boat & also fired on Capt. Ford's Rangers wounding one mortally. Fortunately all the Rangers are there (at the Bolsa) or Bastone & Capt. Stoneman who stopped at our old camp, 15 miles from here opened the letters & started at 8 P.M. to meet the boat.[6] The Rangers crossed

---

Law School in 1850. A political ally of Sam Houston, Navarro, along with Juan N. Seguin, was active in the Union League in San Antonio prior to the Civil War. During the war he nevertheless commanded a company of the 8th Texas Infantry, but, unable to cope with the blatant racial discrimination in Texas, fled to Mexico. Navarro later became sheriff of Zapata County and attorney for the City of Laredo before being killed in Laredo in 1876. Thompson, *Warm Weather and Bad Whiskey*, 41–43; *Alamo Express* (San Antonio), Oct. 1, 1860; San Antonio *Daily Herald*, Aug. 12, 1859; 8th Census, Bexar County; Navarro to Vidaurri, Dec. 1, 1863, Correspondencia de Santiago Vidaurri, Archivo General del Estado de Nuevo León (Monterrey, Nuevo León, Mexico).

Arriving in Austin, Navarro wrote Governor Houston that the Cortina War had its origins in a "private feud between Juan Nepomuceno Cortina and sundry individuals of Cameron County." Cortina, a "thief and a murderer," had a murder indictment "standing against him since the year 1850." Moreover, "authorities on the Mexican side of the river are cognizant now and have been all the while of his movements and that his men have been armed by them and he has been furnished ammunition and secured aid and comfort from the beginning." There was little doubt, Navarro asserted, that Cortina was "sustained by Mexican money and arms." The only way "to stop these disturbances is to occupy the right bank of the Rio Bravo," he concluded. Navarro to Houston, Feb. 15, 1860, LR, AGO, RG 94 (NA).

6 Hastily scratching a note from "Old Camp," Stoneman said he would immediately ride for La Bolsa, but would cross only upon receiving orders from Heintzelman or in the event the *Ranchero* was attacked. John Martin, captain of the *Ranchero*, had written Ford that the boat had been fired on from the Mexican shore at La Bolsa and that he expected another attack before reaching Brownsville. "I respectfully request that you will afford me all of the protection in your power," Martin wrote. The *Ranchero*, Martin asserted, was carrying goods worth $200,000.

Heintzelman later learned the Ranger version of the attack. Just as the *Ranchero* was entering La Bolsa, the steamboat was fired on with one shot passing through the United States flag on the masthead. Ford's Rangers, who were about one-half mile downriver, claimed they too were fired on from the south bank and that one of the Rangers, Fountain B. Woodruff, was mortally wounded.

After the attack, Ford wrote Heintzelman that he was preparing to cross into

the river & drove the enemy back. The bells were ringing at Matamoros this evening rather suspiciously. I thought as it was Saturday night it might be that, but I have no doubt they know of this attack & of Ford's crossing.

I got up & went to town & saw Col. Taylor. Mr. Navarro is on the other side. As I was coming home someone came & told me that some men were going to cross & take the boats from the Mexican side. I went at once & per-

---

Mexico to "beat the bushes in the neighborhood." The following morning the Rangers crossed on horseback to the Mexican bank to escort the *Ranchero* downriver. Lt. Loomis L. Langdon, commanding the artillery on the boat, wrote from La Bolsa that at 4 P.M. Ford was crossing. Langdon said that he had been at dinner on the boat when it was reported to him that a shot had passed through the flag. Upon landing, he found Woodruff badly wounded, whereupon he gave orders for the gun on the *Ranchero* to fire into the chaparral along the Mexican bank. Stoneman to [Heintzelman], Feb. 4 (8 p.m.), 1860; Martin to Ford, Feb. 4, 1860; Ford to Heintzelman, Feb. 4, 1860, and Langdon to Heintzelman, Apr.. 28, 1860, HP.

Heintzelman was fearful that the Rangers would retaliate for the attack on the *Ranchero* by plundering the ranches along the river. He was also concerned that Ford would be lured deep into Mexico and ambushed. "It is of utmost importance that you preserve the most rigid discipline amongst your troops & that no injury that can be avoided is done to the inhabitants, or their property. Do not allow yourself to be drawn from the river but confine your operations strictly to the protection of the boat." At the same time Heintzelman wrote Capt. Arthur Lee to move downriver with two companies of the 8th Infantry and to bring the two 24-pounder howitzers from Ringgold Barracks. Heintzelman enclosed his letter to Captain Lee in a note to Stoneman asking that the letter be forwarded by express to Laredo. Heintzelman to Ford, Feb. 4, 1860; Heintzelman to Ford, Feb. 5, 1860; Heintzelman to A. T. Lee, Feb. 4, 1860; Heintzelman to Stoneman, Feb. 4, 1860, HLS. See also Langdon to Heintzelman, Feb. 4, 1860, LR, AGO, RG 94 (NA).

On the afternoon of February 5, Heintzelman wrote Ford that General García had dispatched a force upriver from Matamoros to "return tranquility" to the south bank. Ford was to "immediately recross to the north bank." Heintzelman urged Ford not to confuse García's *Rurales* with the *Cortinistas*. At the same time, Heintzelman wrote Adjutant General Samuel Cooper in New York and Department Headquarters in San Antonio of the attack on the *Ranchero* and the movements of the Rangers in Mexico. Heintzelman to Cooper, Feb. 5, 1860, Heintzelman to Withers, Feb. 5, 1860, HLS. See also Heintzelman to Cooper, Feb. 5, 1860, LR, AGO, RG 94 (NA).

On February 6, Stoneman wrote from Rancho Galveston that the *Rurales* had arrived from Matamoros and that Ford, by using the *Ranchero*, had crossed to the north bank. Both the Rangers and Stoneman's company of the 2d Cavalry had gone into camp at the ranch. The *Ranchero* could be expected in Brownsville the following day, February 7, he said. In an addendum, Stoneman reported that Cortina was "near or with the Rural Guards—and the Guards state that their authority extends simply to the guarding [of] the Steamer but not to the apprehending or molesting [of] Cortina." Stoneman to Heintzelman, Feb. 6, 1860, HP. See also *Daily Picayune* (New Orleans), Feb. 12, 1860.

suaded them to stop. We are in the right & such an act would make the Mexican guard fire & we would then return it.

I will write tonight to Capt. Lee for two of his companies to join us here. I will enclose the letters to Capt. Stoneman & get him to send them along. Haynes the representative from Starr county was hung in effigy in town last night.[7]

---

[7] A native of Virginia, John L. Haynes settled at Rio Grande City after serving as a lieutenant in the Mexican War. Elected county clerk of Starr County, Haynes was also elected to the Texas House of Representatives in 1857 and 1859. One of the few Anglo Texans to sympathize with Juan Cortina and the *Cortinistas*, Haynes rejected the bitter anti-Tejano rhetoric of the state legislature and the Anglo establishment in Brownsville. For his unpopular stand on the Cortina War, Haynes was condemned and ridiculed by several leading Texas newspapers, especially the Austin *State Gazette* and the Galveston *News*. The *American Flag* (Brownsville) went as far as to jokingly boast "Juan Nepomuceno Cortina, the Hero of la Bolsa" for President of the United States and J. L. Haynes for Vice-President. The Brownsville newspaper also wrote of Haynes:

With his honor bright, and with Keen insight
Among his Peers he stood,
His soul in the land, of that greaser band,
Who shed his country's blood.

There's a fraud he cries: with my own good eyes,
I see the record plain;
Let the Gringos bleed. For the wicked deed
They lie among the stain.

Johnny Haynes was right in the bandit's sight,
He loved the story well.
And he drew his knife, for the white man's life,
And pray'd his soul to hell.

The fierce north-wind blew, and the tidings flew,
To rouse the slumbering town;
A greaser came by, with a tear in his eyes,
And beg'd he might come down.

As a follower of Gov. Sam Houston and a Unionist, Haynes fled to Mexico at the beginning of the Civil War and came to command the Union 2d Texas Cavalry. Haynes was married to Angelica Wells, a granddaughter of President Martin Van Buren. Active in Reconstruction politics, he died in Laredo on April 2, 1888. Jerry Thompson, *Vaqueros in Blue and Gray* (Austin: Presidial Press, 1976), 85–87; Jerry Thompson, *Mexican Texans in the Union Army* (El Paso: Texas Western Press, 1986), 13–14: Austin *State Gazette*, Jan. 14, 1860; Galveston *News*, Feb. 23, 1860; "Minority Report to the Honorable M. K. Taylor, Speaker of the House of Representatives," John L. Haynes Papers (CAH).

FORT BROWN TEXAS SUN. FEB. 5TH, 1860

We had a little rain this morning & quite warm. Mr. Navarro left for the Steamer & San Antonio this morning. I left my letters at Col. Taylor's for the Rangers to take up. Mr. Navarro was in Matamoros last night. The express reached there at 9 P.M. & by 11 P.M. some 80 to 100 men had left to join Cortinas. The whole community sympathizes with him. I sent a letter to Gen. Garcia informing him of what has occurred & asking him to co-operate.[8] The bearer to wait for his answer. He will now have to show his hand. 40 men were sent out by the officials.

FORT BROWN TEXAS MON. FEB. 6TH, 1860

The weather has turned colder & it is quite unpleasant. Major Tobin is in town. I understand he says that 25 Mexicans were killed. We have one wounded.

I have just finished a reply to Gen. Garcia & find I have spelled a couple of words wrong. Lt. Thomas is copying it. I answered him in the same style he wrote, but tell him distinctly of the importance of the peace of both countries to put a stop to these outrages. The Ranchero is reported aground.

---

[8] Heintzelman informed García on February 5, 1860, that Ford had crossed the river and, referring to a letter García had previously sent in which he promised assistance, Heintzelman asked for cooperation in apprehending Cortina. In response, Garcia sent Miguel G. Cavazos, Second Alcalde of Matamoros, and Manuel Treviño, Mexican consul, across the river with a letter telling Heintzelman that García, from other sources, was well aware of the Rangers being in Mexico. Besides the *Rurales*, García was dispatching a second force and asked that the Rangers be withdrawn. Heintzelman to García, Feb. 5, 1860, HLS; García to Heintzelman, Feb. 5, 1860, HP. Joaquín Arguilles, commanding García's forces on the river, wrote Heintzelman on February 7 that the Rangers had burned ten jacales at La Bolsa. Furniture and fences, as well as several fields, had also gone up in smoke. In return, Arguilles asked for reparations. Never mentioning reparations, Heintzelman reminded García that Cortina had "armed & equipped" his forces "on the Mexican side of the river . . . for the purpose of crossing to this side, to rob and murder." Heintzelman urged García to use "energetic measures . . . to apprehend this man & to put a stop to these outrages." Three days later, Heintzelman wrote Arguilles, quoting Emmerich de Vattel's *Law of Nations*, in an attempt to somehow justify the destruction at La Bolsa. The major asserted that the *Cortinistas* had occupied the ranch for over a month. Ford, in an eight-page letter, claimed that the dwellings "were burnt by someone not attached to my command and against my express orders." Arguilles to comm[an]d[er] of Fort Brown, Feb. 7, 1860, HP; Heintzelman to Garcia, Feb. 6, 1860, HLS; Heintzelman to Arguilles, Feb. 9, 1860, HLS; Ford to W. C. Thomas, Feb. 8, 1860, HP; Ford *Rip Ford's Texas*, 280–289.

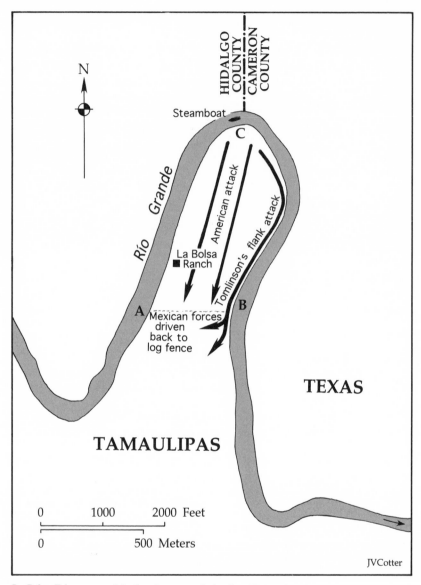

La Bolsa, February 4, 1860, based on a rough sketch in Heintzelman's journal.

Mr. Gillam yesterday sent me a plate of nice jelly. The boat will not get out till this norther is done.

I went to town & handed the letter to the Mex. Counsel, Mr. Trevino. I met Mr. Latham, the collector & made an agreement to call with him tomorrow on the Mex. General. Yesterday I had a long conversation & he told me of the murder of Cross & having lived here for years next to Cortinas & Glavecke, is well acquainted with the misdeeds of both.[9] I am to have a statement from him.

I went to see Col. Taylor & found Major Tobin there just finishing a report to the Governor. Tobin gave me an account of what occurred up the river. They had several skirmishes on the way down & he took 300 head of cattle. On Saturday they first fired on Fords men & wounded one. Then on the boat. The Bolsa is a purse as I have drawn the bend, with Jacales & a fence of ebony logs at a. b. & at c. the steamer was fired upon. The men were landed & enemy driven to a. b. Capt. Tomlinson on our side discovered that the position could be turned by following under the bank beyond c b & the Mexicans were driven with great loss, abandoning some 40 saddled horses, 80 arms & sharps rifle cartridges. He says it was a harder fight than that at Rio Grande City.

The American flag has published an extra dated Feb. 5th headed Startling news!! Steamer Ranchero attacked!! The Rio Grande crossed by Rangers!!! Battle fought on Mexican Soil!!! & then gives a flaming account. Numbers of these ridiculous & mischievous extras go to the States in the Steamer. I presume we will have another with Tobins account.

Weather disagreeable to-day.

I went out for a cup of tea & took this last letter. It is another communication to Gen. Garcia about co-operating with me against Cortinas. I could not get it fully translated. As I entered Victors, Galvan took me to a table where Major Tobin, Col. Latham, the collector, & Lt. Thomas were drinking

---

[9] On April 21, 1846, Col. Trueman Cross, chief quartermaster for Gen. Zachary Taylor, was killed near Rancho del Carmen by "Mexican Bandits" allegedly led by Ramón Falcón. Prior to the Mexican War, Heintzelman had been a guest in the Cross home in Washington, D.C. Heintzelman had received the news of Cross's death while he was at Buffalo, New York. Cross, whose body was found lanced and stripped was said to have been on his way to visit a lady friend. In 1859, Cortina alleged that Adolphus Glavecke had somehow been involved in the crime. Thompson, *Juan Cortina*, 11–12, 16; Fayette Copeland, *Kendall of the Picayune* (Norman: University of Oklahoma Press, 1943), 149–150; K. Jack Bauer, *The Mexican War, 1846–1848* (New York: Macmillan Publishing Co., 1974), 36, 46; HJ, July 7, Sept. 12, 14, Oct. 11, Nov. 5, 1842; Jan. 15, 1843; May 4, 11, 13, 1846.

wine & some Rangers at another table.[10] I had to sit down with them. Tobin was discussing the reports. He says that the Mexicans ran so soon as they the regular troops cross[ed] the ridge with the white top wagons. At the time Col. McCourland told Lt. Thomas that we came just at the right time that the Rangers had just about made up their minds to run.

I got a letter from Capt. Stoneman. The Matamoros troops have arrived & Ford has recrossed. My letters have been sent up to Capt. Lee.

FORT BROWN TEXAS TUES. FEB. 7, 1860

The collector, Mr. Latham, Lt. Thomas & I went to Matamoros to call on Gen. Garcia. He had just left for Reynosa with 100 men & two guns. We took a carriage & overtook him a couple of miles up the road. He stopped & we had a few minutes conversation, but could not discuss matters as we wished. We returned & called on Col. Fitzpatrick & on Mr. Hale.[11] I am sure that we saw some of Cortinas's men in town. I got a Spanish pamphlet on the Carvajal correspondence with Ford & the fillibusters.[12]

The Ranchero got down this afternoon. Ford met the Mexican forces & had an understanding with them, when he recrossed. They killed some 7 or 8 men & took 8 horses & a few arms. I am to have a full report. All the Rangers are here. Lt. Langdon & his wife & Lt. Sullivan are here. Mrs. L. was at Mrs. Gillams & I called upon her. Sullivan & I took tea at Lt. Gillam's.

We hoisted our flag to-day for the first time since the reoccupation of this post. It shows well & has a moral effect.

I have just heard that the Sunday's mail for the Steamer was lost in the Bay & one man was drowned by the upsetting of the boat. Wrote to Judge Iverson & enclosed the Mexican pamphlet & American Flag extra.

FORT BROWN WED. FEB. 8TH, 1860

The night was cold. I wrote a letter this morning before I went to break-

---

[10] Connecticut-born Francis W. Latham, forty-two, was collector of customs at Brazos Santiago. His letter of September 18, 1859, was the first news received at department headquarters in San Antonio of Cortina's Brownsville raid. Latham to Twiggs, Sept. 28, 1859, *DSF*, 32; San Antonio *Daily Herald*, Oct. 6, 1859.

[11] William G. Hale, a New Hampshire–born Harvard graduate, who was practicing law in Galveston, sent, in the wake of Cortinas's September 28, 1859 raid on Brownsville, copies of the *American Flag*, as well as telegrams and letters, to Secretary of War John B. Floyd pleading "the necessity of immediate aid" for Brownsville. Hale moved to New Orleans in 1873 and died there three years later. *DSF*, 43–44.

[12] Not in the Heintzelman papers.

fast & put it into the office. I then learned that the mail boat capsized in Brazos bay, drowned the man & lost the Sunday's mail. Further enquiry said all the mail that went down before. I went to work, wrote a letter to Vinton, made out another set of pay a/cts & sent them to Major Cunningham & copied my letters to Dept. & Gen. Head Quarters. The post master told me that the mail would go tomorrow at 7, but after 12 Lt. Thomas came & said it would close at one. I took my letters & when I got there found it a mistake. This evening we learn the boat capsized & no mail was lost & I suppose no man drowned. The whole town was busy all day duplicating letters.

I got a letter from the military commandant. It was not signed when first delivered. I sent it back. It is a declaration about the burning of some houses & the crossing the river. Mr. Clark translated it for me. I will get Fords report & answer it tomorrow.

Tobin's volunteers will be mustered out tomorrow. Capt. Ford told me that there was talk of their going towards Reynosa & Camargo to sack these places & return into Texas. The collector this evening told me that they intended to cross a short distance above town & make a dash at Matamoros to try to plunder it. He also says that Ford & Littleton intended to cross the river above here & join Carvajal at Victoria & then take & hold Tampico. That Duncan will be here with funds [on the] next boat to join them. I dont believe these tales.

I gave an order to-day for Ford & Littleton to march up the river tomorrow & not to cross the river, rather to confine their operations to this side.[13]

Lt. Ramsay with some Dragoons brought in a prisoner taken near Las Ruses. The mail carrier was captured near there by Cortinas & some nine men. He took the mail cut it open & rifled it & threatened to han[g] the man. They took & kept him at La Bolsa until the fight on Saturday when in the confusion he escaped. They talked freely of capturing the boat. Cortinas has frequent visitors from Matamoros & the neighboring towns & got letters. He had from 50 to 150 men. Ford told me to-day that a Mexican from the other side told him that they lost over 50 men killed & wounded.

FORT BROWN THURS. FEB. 9TH, 1860

Lt. Ramsay started for camp this morning. I have been waiting all day for Ford's report. He brought it in & I read it, but I want to copy. I got an extract. I commenced writing an answer, but have to wait for the reports. Clark did not translate the Mexican letter exactly right. I got the translator of the

---

13 Orders no. 10, Feb. 8, 1860, HOB.

Custom house to do it.[14] It now states more distinctly the cause of grievance & our crossing the river.

Weather warm & pleasant.

It is now ten O'Clock. I have been employed all the evening writing an answer to the Mexican authorities & I am pretty well satisfied with it.

FORT BROWN FRI. FEB. 10TH, 1860

Warm to-day, but very windy. Night clear & beautiful. I have been busy all day & finally got off my answer to the Mexican authorities. It will make them squirm. I dont think they believed we knew so much of their duplicity. I did not mince matters, but accused them directly of harboring & aiding Cortinas. I sent a copy of it & a report to Dept. Hd. Qrs.[15] I also gave Ford a copy for the Gov. I wrote to Margaret. My fingers are stiff from writing so much to-day. Tobin & the Rangers from above were mustered out to-day. I gave the order yesterday, but Fords & Littleton's companies wont get off before tomorrow.

FORT BROWN TEXAS SAT. FEB. 11TH, 1860

The Rangers, I believe started up the river to-day; but I dont know at what hour. Most of those discharged have left town. It begins to look quiet again. I gave my letters to Ford to send by his express. I spent all the forenoon arranging my papers. Jno. Clark went to Matamoros. He reports that something like a pronunciam[i]ento was had at Victoria in favour of Carvajal, against the action of the Matamoros people I suppose. There is also a report that some of Cortinas's men have started on the Monterrey road to join the Centralists. I heard yesterday that Cortinas was going on the road. His dilu[t]ed followers must see that there is no hope for him or them, on this frontier. It has been very warm to-day; but this afternoon the wind came from the East & at tattoo there is a mist. I thought at one time that we would have a norther.

FT. BROWN TEXAS FEB. 12, 1860

A beautiful day it turned out to be, though we had a sprinkle of rain in the morning. The Rangers did start, but both their Captains did not leave until to-day. I stopped at several places & did not get back to the garrison until eleven & then it was too late for church. So I went to work & filed all my letters.

---

[14] Heintzelman to Arguilles, Feb. 9, 1860, HLS.
[15] Heintzelman to Withers, Feb. 10, 1863, HLS.

I went out to Galvans at dinner time & dined with him at Miller's hotel.[16]
I sat down to the best dinner I have seen since I left S. Antonio. I would go
there, but he has too many all sorts of people there. I suppose it is a cheaper
house & is not considered the fashionable one.

Lt. Graham was officer of the Day. Lt. Thomas & Lt. Sullivan went to
Matamoros early in the morning. After sundown Clark & I rode over & took
a short walk in town. He knows everybody. I saw several handsome ladies &
he pointed out his two step daughters—young ladies, out riding in a carriage.
He & their mother have separated. They are good looking & bowed to him as
they passed.

We went to Mr. Hales & there met all the other gentlemen. Whilst there
nine companies of the National Guards paraded, in all about 300 men, or perhaps a few more. They are in citizens closes [sic] & without arms. We came
home at dusk.

When I got to my room I found it full of smoke. The man, although it
was so warm that I slept with the window open & lay most of the night in the
bed clothes, had started a large fire. A stick rolled off beyond the hearth & had
burned a hole its length & breadth through the floor & it was still burning.

Ft. Brown Texas Mon. Feb. 13th, 1860

It is three months to-day since I left Verde on this campaign. I did not
expect to be absent over a few weeks & now it is doubtful whether I will return
to Verde at all.

About a week ago I gave Lt. Thomas some letters to copy & this morning
when I went to see how far he had progressed he has not touched them. I took
them & intended to try & get a man from one of these companies, but I did
not find Capt. Dawson in. So I sat to work & before dinner I had all copied
that I gave him. They filled 14 pages in the folio post letter book. I am now at
work to copy all the others that have accumulated since. I wish I had
Washington here. This procrastination dont suit me. I frequently write letters, that should be orders in the order book, because I cant find him or he is
too dilatory.

---

[16] The Miller Hotel, originally called the Cameron Hotel, had been constructed in
1848 by Henry Miller, a German immigrant from Hanover. The two-story frame building with wide verandas contained a restaurant, barroom, and limited lodging for men
only. It stood on the corner of Elizabeth and 13th streets, only a block from the
Matamoros ferry. Thirty-nine years-old in 1859, Miller was said to have been a bitter
enemy of Cortina. A. A. Champion, "The Miller Hotel in the Antebellum Period," *More
Studies in Brownsville History*, ed. Milo Kearny (Brownsville: Pan American University at
Brownsville, 1989), 163–167; *La Bandera Americana* (Brownsville), Apr. 26, 1860.

It has been very warm & very windy to-day & in town quite dusty. Dr. Holden & I this morning took a walk around the Lagoon to windward to us.[17] The water is green & begins to smell. I fear that it will make this place sickly, though everybody says it is not. There has been yellow fever & cholera, but no [o]ther sickness.

I wrote till eleven & I have finished copying all my letters & reports. I have 32 pages. Thomas & Graham have gone to visit a lady in Matamoros. She only speaks Spanish & they not a word of it.

FT. BROWN TEX. TUES. FEB. 14, 1860

Quite warm all day & not so much wind as yesterday. I have done nothing but read some old newspapers to-day. I had a long visit from Col. Lockridge this evening. He has traveled a good deal for a man of 28 years.

A drunken fellow in town killed his drunken wife last night or yesterday. They quarrelled for years. He is arrested, but there is no jail. There is a suspicion that some of Cortinas's men were in town last night.

FT. BROWN TEXAS WED. FEB. 15, 1860

Warmer than yesterday. Powers predicted a norther but it did not come.

There is a report at last that the Liberals have gained a battle, but it appears to have been on a small scale.

Gen. Garcia has returned. I hear he says that he saw nothing of Cortinas. Others say that he was certainly in Cortinas camp. Capt. Stoneman is in for provisions & says that Cortinas is a few miles from "La Bolsa" near a ranche called "La Mesa," with 67 men. He also says that he had 67 but that the account given to Ford's is exaggerated & this is I presume below the number. Some of the officers have set out to disbelieve everything the Rangers do. Lt. Gillam is one of them.

I called with Capt. Dawson on the Mex. Consul, Mr. Trevino. He has three sisters, the youngest speaks Spanish.[18] The two Miss Smiths were there. We had play & sing on the piano. Quite a number of gentlemen were there. This is the first visit I have made in Brownsville.

Tobin & Lockridge had a quarrel last evening about the latter's report of Rio Grande fight.[19]

---

[17] Levi H. Holden had been an assistant surgeon in the army since 1840. Heitman, *Historical Register*, 537.

[18] Heintzelman probably meant to say the youngest Treviño daughter spoke English.

[19] Lockridge's account of the Battle of Rio Grande City appeared in the January 22, 1859, issue of the New Orleans *Daily Picayune*. Although generally praising the Rangers, Lockridge wrote, however, that after the initial attack the Rangers had

FT. BROWN TEXAS THURS. FEB. 16, 1860

There is no order from S. Antonio. Capt. Stoneman has a letter. Sewell wont give any more orders till he hears from Washington.[20]

The mail from Corpus in this evening, no letters. Congress is organized—Pennington Speaker & Fordrey clerk. I suppose this steamer mail will bring orders. It has been warm & cloudy & several sprinkles of rain. There is a very severe letter in the papers reflecting on Mahoney for advising the people here to give up Cabrera one of Cortinas' captains on the 28 Sept.[21] His friends deny it, but I am satisfied that it is true.

FT. BROWN TEXAS FRI. FEB. 17, 1860

Capt. Stoneman left this afternoon to join his company. Very windy & dusty all day. [Spent] all day at the newspapers. Rain since tattoo.

FT. BROWN TEXAS SAT. FEB. 18, 1860

A norther to-day. Mild in the morning, then more wind & now getting quite cool. Some men are down from Capt. Ford for provisions. The Rancheros are crossing to plant. Few of Cortinas's men have been seen. He is still near the Mesa, about six miles back from "La Bolsa" with from 40 to 60 men & has small parties along the river. The Mex. authorities pretend not to know where he is. I took tea at Mrs. Gillams.

FT. BROWN TEXAS SUN. FEB. 19, 1860

The norther is over & this is a beautiful day. I went with most of the officers to the Catholic church.[22] It is a fine building but unfinished. They have

---

become "dismounted and were acting as skirmishers, which prevented a second charge, to take the cannon, and by the time they were remounted and in order, the enemy had stolen a retreat of about a mile."

[20] Washington Seawell, Virginia-born and from the West Point class of 1825, had temporarily replaced General Twiggs in command of the Department of Texas. A lieutenant colonel in the 8th Infantry, Seawell was promoted to colonel in October 1860, and transferred to the 6th Infantry. He retired in February 1861 and died in 1888. Heitman, *Historical Register*, 872.

[21] Tomás Cabrera, Cortina's second in command during his raid on Brownsville, was lynched by Tobin's Rangers and citizens of Brownsville in Market Square on the night of November 11, 1859. Ford to W. C. Thomas, Feb. 22, 1860, HP.

[22] Constructed by the Oblate Fathers of Mary Immaculate, Immaculate Concepción Church was one of the town's most imposing structures. With Fr. Pierre Yves Keralum as the architect, the Gothic revival structure, at 12th and East Jefferson had heavily buttressed walls, an eighty-eight feet tall bell tower, and was said to have been constructed with 250,000 bricks. Bay, *Historic Brownsville*, 49–50

an organ & indifferent singing. I wrote a letter to Margaret, goes in tomorrow's mail for Corpus. As I went to get a cup of tea near tattoo I found the Arizona had arrived, with a mail. I only got one letter & that from New York. The endorsement Gen. Scott made on my report of the 27 Dec. He calls it a brilliant affair & that I had distinguished myself, as I had done often many years before & asks a Brevet as some compensation for the outrage done me by the War Dept., when Casey a junior & inferior Capt. of the same regt. was made Lt. Col.[23] This reflects too hard on the War Dept to benefit me much. Besides they want to abolish all Bvts.

I took a walk this afternoon with Lt. & Mrs. Gillam. I may get letters yet as the mail is still back. The Corpus mail is in & I should have letters one way or the other from Margaret. Col. Harvey Brown is here on a tour of inspection of the Arty.[24] He has been to Ft. Clark & came by way of San Antonio. He brings no news. He met Col. Lee at Indianola, on his way up.[25] He did not appear to have any instructions about this frontier. They appear to be at a loss [as] what to do at Washington. There appears to be a large fillibuster movement on foot to land at Tampico & at Vera Cruz. Some 5,000 men in 17 States are ready. The Indianola was to leave to-day for Tampico.

Lt. Ramsay came in yesterday afternoon.

----

[23] Lt. Col. Henry Lee Scott, writing from army headquarters in New York, copied a portion of Lt. Gen. Winfield Scott's endorsement of Heintzelman's report of December 27, 1859: "This is the report of a brilliant affair in which Major Heintzelman distinguished himself as he has done often many years before. I beg to ask a brevet for him—in small part to compensate for the outrage done him by the War Department, which took Casey, a junior and inferior captain, from the same regiment [2d Infantry] March 3, 1855, and made him [Casey] Lieutenant Colonel of the 9th Infantry." While he was in Washington, D.C., in early 1861, Heintzelman tried in vain to obtain a brevet as lieutenant colonel. H. L. Scott to Dear Sir, Feb. 1, 1860, HP.

[24] From New Jersey, Harvey Brown, an 1818 West Point graduate and a major in the 2d Artillery, had been breveted a lieutenant colonel for gallantry at the Battle of Contreras during the Mexican War. Heitman, *Historical Register*, 251.

[25] Lee had returned to Texas in February 1860 after an extended leave of some twenty-eight months at his home in Arlington, Virginia. Lee replaced Lt. Col. Washington Seawell of the 8th Infantry, who had temporarily replaced General Twiggs, as commander of the Department of Texas. Ordered to the border, Lee left San Antonio on March 15. Joined by Capt. Albert Brackett with Co. I of the 2d Cavalry, Lee reached Fort Duncan where Lt. Nathan Eagle with Co. H of the 2d Cavalry joined the march. Riding downriver, Lee arrived at Fort McIntosh late on the evening of March 25. "I have come," Lee said, "with full power to put down the outlaws and will do it if it takes all the soldiers on the frontier." Outside of Laredo, the party was hit by a cold norther with sleet and snow and two of Lee's men died of exposure. Jerry Thompson, "When Robert E. Lee Came to Laredo," *Laredo: A Pictorial History* (Norfolk: Donning Co., 1986), 152. See also Carl Coke Rister, *Robert E. Lee in Texas* (Norman: University of Oklahoma Press, 1946), 106–110.

FT. BROWN TEXAS MON. FEB. 20, 1860

Cloudy & windy. I stopped at the post office & got letters. The Texas mail was found in a newspaper bag. I have three from Margaret—8, 11, & 25 Jan. one from Dr. Tripler & a circular from San Francisco about a petition to Sec. of War to buy clocks for Military Posts. Gorden C.C. Qr. M. Gen. sends me Sec. of W's Report.[26] Major Brown inspected this morning & the troops fired the 12 pdrs. The mail from Ringgold is in. Major McClure the paymaster will be here to pay to the end of this month.[27]

FT. BROWN TEXAS TUES. FEB. 21, 1860

We had a high wind & squalls of rain last night. I did not hear it. This morning the wind was north & the air delightful. It was vocal with the songs of birds.

I went this morning to see the troops fire at a target. The firing at 200 yds was pretty good. The locks of the rifle musket are not so good as the old ones & the Maynard primer missed often & sometimes the caps.

Lt. Sullivan went in the boat to the mouth of the river at 12 to-day, to take the boat to N. Orleans. He has six months leave to try a professorship in a college in Mississippi. Major Tobin & Allen Howard left on their way to S. Antonio.[28] Lt. Thomas went down with them & Lt. Graham to inspect old Qr.M. stores. I wrote a long letter to Margaret this evening. The weather has been quite warm & wind changed to South.

FT. BROWN TEXAS WED. FEB. 22ND, 1860

Col. Brown & Lt. Ramsay left this morning for up the river. I sent the P.O. mail with them. It has been warm to-day, but the wind is now north & cooler. I wrote to Mr. Lathrop, Sergt. Kasntinger & the Adjt., 3rd Arty, S. Francisco. Col. Taylor the commissioner & Capt. Littleton left this afternoon & took letters down.

There has been considerable uneasiness in town most of the day about

---

[26] Possibly W. H. Gorden, forty-one, Virginia-born and living in San Antonio at the time. 8th Census, Bexar County.

[27] Daniel McClure, West Point class of 1849, had resigned from the army in November 1850, but had returned to active duty in 1858 to become a paymaster. McClure remained a paymaster during the Civil War and died in 1900. Heitman, *Historical Register*, 657.

[28] Olien Howard, one of Tobin's Rangers, wrote two letters to the San Antonio *Daily Herald* on Nov. 18, 22, 1859. The civilian contractor for the Rangers was a C. Howard. *Daily Picayune* (New Orleans), Jan. 2, 1860.

troops going up the river from Matamoros & the report that Ford had crossed the river. Some went about one this morning & more since. I fear he has crossed & without sufficient cause & without sufficient force. There is a report also that the troops went out to arrest Cortinas.

I saw mulberries turning red, last Sunday.

FT. BROWN TEXAS THURS. FEB. 23, 1860

We have a cold norther. Sun warm but cold tonight. The news from Matamoros is that the troops went after Cortinas. The Corpus mail brought letters. Margaret's is Feb. 2, has the rheumatism & is discouraged & writes in very bad spirits. The trouble is I don't see how I can remedy it. I got a long letter from Major Cunningham. Has no money, but will soon have & send it. Writes flattingly about what I have done.

I got an order—G. 2 Cav. to escort the paymaster here & report to me & D. 8 Infy to Ringgold & report to me. The Steamer Ranchero got up, but not Thomas or Graham.

FORT BROWN TEXAS FRI. FEB. 24, 1860

It has been cold and unpleasant all day. I sat down & wrote to Margaret. The balance of the day I read newspapers. I have found a fire comfortable.

FT. BROWN TEXAS SAT. FEB. 25TH, 1860

Much pleasanter to-day, though still cool. Wind North & then East. Lt. Gillam went to the Brazos to relieve Lt. Langdon, when the latter will join his company at this Post. Mr. Galvan rode down with him. The Doctor & I took a ride after dinner. Capt. Ford is in. He & Col. Lockridge called this evening. The report now is that Cortinas has gone to Camargo. He has evidently left the Mesa. On the 21st Ford gave his men permission to fire off their guns & the next day was warm & some went into the river & crossed. This he thinks brought the Mexican troops up. It is also supposed that the authorities have orders to send him away, to prevent trouble on this frontier. My letter in reply to the complaint of our crossing has been sent to Tampico & Vera Cruz. The Mex. are coming over and planting.

One of Capt. Stoneman's Sergts is there. The Capt. has moved out to San Jose Rancho.

This has been a long tiresome day to me. I concluded not to go to the ball. The steamer has not left last night.

FT. BROWN TEX. SUN. FEB. 26, 1860

Warm & pleasant to-day. I went to the Presbyterian Church, with Mr.

Gillam & heard Mr. Chamberlin.[29] He is a good man, but not much of a preacher. He is a missionary and gets but $500. The Doctor & I took a ride this afternoon. My horse has been idle so long that he is disposed to be [sluggish]. The Corpus mail is in, but I have no letters. I wrote two pages more to Margaret. The steamer did not get out until yesterday.

Ft. Brown Texas Mon. Feb. 27, 1860

As I went to bed the steamboat Grampus was heard puffing.[30] Thomas & Graham came up in her & Galvan. They lay at the mouth of the river three days & were at the Brazos only a few hours. Not the most agreeable visit in a norther.

We have a few days later news by a sch. from N. Orleans, Miramon is on his way to besiege Vera Cruz.[31] He left on the 8th (Mexico) & his advance was at [the[National Bridge. Great excitement at Vera Cruz. This will reject or delay the ratification of the Treaty.

A few drops of rain this morning.

A beautiful day. About 12 M. Capt. Lee arrived with his company & Capt. Jourdans—about 100 men. I got some letters. Three from Lt. Washington—about the Band & Regt. & speculations as to the Hd. Qrs. He sent me a letter from Capt. Plummer at Ft. Cobb. He is delighted with the post. Lt. Thomas heard from him also. He is to be married, but dont say to whom.

I met Mr. Gillam & the two Miss Smiths & we took a walk below the garrison to a couple of grave yards.

Capt. Jarvis is here from Vallecillos. I got from Webster in N.Y., the Sec., my certificate of stock.

Lts. Read & Harts are with these companies.

---

[29] Vermont-born Hiram Chamberlain, sixty-three, had come with his third wife, Ana Adelia Griswold, to Brownsville where he organized the Presbyterian Church in 1850. Henrietta Maria Morse, a daughter by his first marriage, married Richard King. Bruce S. Cheeseman (ed.), *My Dear Henrietta: Hiram Chamberlain's Letters to His Daughter, 1846–1866* (Kingsville: King Ranch, 1993), 13–52; Lea, *King Ranch*, I, 63.

[30] The *Grampus*, a 221-ton steamboat built in Freedom, Pennsylvania, and owned by Kenedy and King, had run on the river since 1850. Kelley, *River of Lost Dreams*, 511–512.

[31] Miguel Miramon was an army general who led Conservative forces in the War of the Reform. Since the spring of 1859, Miramon had tried repeatedly to dislodge Liberal forces from Vera Cruz. Later in 1860, Miramon purchased two warships at Havana to supplement a planned land attack on Vera Cruz. Olliff, *Reforma Mexico and the United States*, 147; *Daily Picayune* (New Orleans), Mar. 20, 1860.

FT. BROWN TEXAS TUES. FEB 28, 1860

Beautiful day. In town windy & dusty. I saw Mr. Mohoney. He was over here. Lt. Thomas & the young officers have gone to Matamoros. I had some business for Lt. Thomas.

FORT BROWN TUES. FEB. 28, 1860

This is Mary's birthday. She is getting to be a big girl.[32] 12 years old. I have the luck always to be from home at birthdays. We have had a beautiful day. I went to breakfast & waited half an hour & then breakfasted alone. Mr. Mahoney was in town. I had a long talk with him about Mexican affairs. He is getting tired of the present condition of affairs. The Liberal party has squeezed him pretty hard for assistance.

I also had a talk with Capt. Jarvis & his mother, out from New York, on his way to the mines. When the troops arrived yesterday they stopped opposite the ferry to see where to encamp. The Mex. on the other side thought that we were going to cross & sent an express to Matamoros. They had a report too that 3,000 regular troops had landed at Vera Cruz. They are beginning to get uneasy. Those young gentlemen only staid a couple of hours in Matamoros. I had a visit from the music teacher in Matamoros. I forgot his name.

FORT BROWN TEXAS WED. FEB 29, 1860

This morning was cloudy & a norther. It only lasted an hour or two & then changed & became warm. Lts. Gillam, Langdon, his wife & her aunt

---

[32] Mary was born on February 27, 1848, while her father was encamped near Mexico City. At an early age, perhaps from birth, Mary had developed a serious problem with one of her legs and walked with a noticeable limp. Heintzelman's journals are full of his concern for his daughter's health. Although Mary had endured one operation in 1848, it was while the family was at Newport Barracks, Kentucky, in 1858, prior to Heintzelman's departure for Arizona, that it was decided that Mary, age ten, must have a more complicated operation. Heintzelman vividly recalls the ordeal that followed. Mary, upon seeing the army surgeon Dr. Charles S. Tripler approach, had secluded herself in horror. The surgeons began the operation before Mary was completely under the chloroform, at which time she began to scream. Finally able to continue, Tripler reported finding an "orifice" and began scraping the bone. Later as the influence of the chloroform lessened, Mary began to scream again in pain. "She abused the doctors," Heintzelman wrote, thinking "they were going to hurt her." A year later, Mary was still using crutches. After the Civil War, she remained with her parents in Washington, D.C., where she wrote letters to magazines and newspapers defending her father's Civil War record. She died in Washington, D.C., on March 24, 1927. North, *Samuel Peter Heintzelman*, 190; HJ, Oct. 1, 1848; Feb. 28, 1851; Feb. 27, 1854; Jan. 12, June 16, 1855; Feb. 28, 1856; May 10, 27, 28, 1858.

Mrs. Shannon got up last night from the Brazos. The steamer Ranchero started up the river at 12 to-day. At 10 A.M. I mustered & inspected the two Infantry companies.

I wrote to Dept. Hd. Qrs. that the Cortinas war is over.[33] I also wrote to Margaret & to Lt. Washington.

There is a report in Matamoros, said to have been brought from Vera Cruz, that 3,000 American troops have landed there & that the ayumentio [ayuntamiento] of Matamoros would have a meeting to decide what to do. Some of the officers wished me to cross over & occupy Matamoros.

---

[33] After the fight at La Bolsa, Heintzelman wrote that Cortina had retired to La Mesa Ranch where he remained for three weeks, after which he was reported to be in Camargo. Heintzelman went on to say, however, that more recent information had been received that Cortina was at the Reyotaño Ranch a few leagues above Matamoros and that he was possibly planning a raid into Texas. Heintzelman to Withers, Feb. 29, 1860, LS, HP. On March 7, Heintzelman sent a copy of the letter to Army Headquarters in New York. Heintzelman to Cooper, Mar. 7, 1860, HLS.

❦ March 1860 ❧

"Cortinas was no doubt at the rancho & made his escape."

FORT BROWN TEXAS THURS. MARCH 1ST, 1860

Cloudy this morning but warm. There is now a report that a general at the city of Mexico has pronounced against Miramon in favour of Marques.[1] There is another report that there was a pronunciam[i]ento prepared in the castle of San Juan in favour of Miramon. It was discovered & a number shot.

Major Brown got back this afternoon.

I have been busy writing all day & have 22 pages written. I thought at first that I would give a full history, but I think I will merely glance at the battles as the Rangers call them.

Major Brown says that everybody he saw up the river thinks the war over. One of Cortinas's officers is lying at Reynosa mortally wounded. The doctor told him that he did not think that he could live.

FORT BROWN TEXAS FRI. MARCH 2ND, 1860

Cloudy & windy but warm. The Corpus mail brought me no letters. I have been at work all day on my report.

FORT BROWN TEXAS SAT. MARCH 3RD, 1860

Windy & warm, but pleasant. I have been at work on my report. Col. Lockridge called this afternoon & I read what I have written. I want to be sure of the facts.

I read the Progressista of to-day, published in Matamoros.[2] They claim

---

[1] Leonardo Marquez was another general who commanded Conservative forces in the War of the Reforma.

[2] *El Progresista* was known for its style and for its articles by leading Mexican scholars, including the poet and lecturer Laura Aguirre. Kearney and Knopp, *Boom and Bust*, 96,

great credit for having dispersed Cortinas & think it due to the perseverance with which they have pursued him.

FORT BROWN TEXAS SUN. MARCH 4TH

This is a beautiful day. The birds are all around chattering & singing. I have been occupied all the forenoon with my report & have just finished the first draft. I have 25 foolcaps pages.

FT. BROWN TEXAS MON. MARCH 6 [5], 1860

Cloudy & a drizzle this morning, but it did not amount to much. The balance of the day quite pleasant. The Infantry commenced drilling & the Arty fired the 12 pdrs. with blank cartridges. There is a report this evening that some of Ford's men killed two of a party of armed Mexicans they met on this side. There is a report in the papers that 3,000 Americans have taken possession of Sonora & that Fauntleroy is ordered to occupy Chihuahua.[3] I saw in the Intelligencer that Gen. Johnson is to be ordered on the 1st of Apl. to leave C.F. Smith in Utah, with 1 company Light Arty, 3 of Dragoons & 6 cos of Infy. He is to come to New Mexico & Texas with two regts, to protect the Rio Grande Frontier. It appears now to be the impression that the Treaty will pass. The Laredo mail is in. No steam boat yet. Lt. Thomas has been in & tells me that Lt. Washington will not be married until the 21st of this month. He will apply for orders to go to Verde & take back the band. This has been a nice arrangement.

FT. BROWN TEXAS TUES. MARCH 6, 1860

A very windy dusty day. I looked over my report again & made a few verbal alterations & think I will let it rest a while. In the afternoon I went to Matamoros with Mr. Galvan.

FT. BROWN TEXAS WED. MARCH 7, 1860

The steamer got in yesterday & the mail last night. I got no letter from Margaret, but one from each of the Wrightsons. The one from William with a full account of what he did about my stock. His brother sent me a circular about the new organization contemplate[d] & a postscript that our company has been sold out & that he will write me more fully on the subject. This I dont understand, as the company dont owe a dollar.

---

[3] Thomas Turner Fauntleroy, a colonel in the 1st Dragoons, became a brigadier general in the Confederate Army and died in September 1883. For Fauntleroy's reorganization and command of the Department of New Mexico, see Robert W. Frazer, *Forts and Supplies: The Role of the Army in the Economy of the Southwest, 1846–1861* (Albuquerque: University of New Mexico Press, 1983), 147–162.

The news from Washington is warlike. Forbes Britton, Gov. Houston's Brig. Genl has arrived in Washington & orders have been sent to Col. Lee to cross into Mexico after Cortinas if necessary.[4] My letter of the 29th Feb. makes it not necessary. It is also said that troops have been ordered to Chihuahua from Fort Bliss.

The company of cavalry Lt. Kimmel & the paymaster Major McClure arrived here about noon.[5] The latter handed me a letter from Margaret. As I finished my letter to her I recollected that this boat does not put in at Indianola. But the Corpus mail leaves in the morning. Some of the officers & Clark were at Matamoros this afternoon. The newspaper reports & arrival of this cavalry has created great alarm across the river. Col. Fitzpatrick spent the afternoon with me. Warm & windy to-day.

FT. BROWN TEXAS THURS. MARCH 8TH, 1860

Quite warm to-day. The paymaster paid & left this afternoon for the steam boat. Dr. Holden [&] Col. Brown left also & later Col. Lockridge. Dr. Holden's father is 80 years old & very ill & he got a leave. I dont know who attends for him.

------

[4] After the Mexican War, Forbes N. Britton, a graduate of West Point, class of 1834, who had served as a captain in the 7th Infantry before resigning from the army in 1850, established a freight line from Corpus Christi to Brownsville. He became a wealthy Nueces County merchant and land owner and in 1857 was elected to the state senate from South Texas. In early 1860, Governor Houston sent Britton to Washington to request more troops and money for the Texas Frontier. Britton died in Austin on February 14, 1861, while attending a legislative session. Britton's daughter, Elizabeth, was married to E.J. Davis. Gray, "Edmund J. Davis," 15; Tyler, et al. (eds.), *New Handbook of Texas*, I, 744; Heitman, *Historical Register*, 246. See also footnote 10, this chapter.

Governor Houston wrote Secretary of War John B. Floyd on April 14, 1860, complaining that the regular army was "useless [in] rendering protection to Texas." Only the Texas Rangers were "acquainted with Indian habits and also their mode of warfare. They are woodsmen and marksmen." The Rangers "know where to find the haunts of the Savage and how to trail and make successful pursuit after them," the governor asserted. Houston tried to dispel the idea, which was widely accepted in Washington, that Texas had territorial designs on Mexico and that he would use the Cortina War as a pretext for an invasion. "I have never yet stooped so far as to substitute a pretext for manly action," the governor continued. Quoting Heintzelman as saying that most of Cortina's forces were from Mexico, Houston nevertheless hoped that "the dictates of humanity will rise above all party or personal considerations." Houston to Floyd, Apr. 14, 1860, LR, AGO, RG 94 (NA).

[5] This was Manning Marius Kimmel, a Missourian and 1857 West Point graduate, who was a second lieutenant in the 2d Cavalry. Maj. Daniel McClure, West Point class of 1849, was a paymaster, as Heintzelman indicates. Heitman, *Historical Register*, 598, 657.

I drew my pay for Feb. leaving out the forage $201.40 & this evenings mail brought me Major Cunningham's check for last month $208.60. I also got quite a number of letters that had been accumulating. Margaret's on the 12 & 19 Feb. She dont write in very good spirits. One thing I am glad of—she has her old girl—Mary. That is a treasure to her. Lizzy was getting to be rather worthless. I got a number of letters dated some in last year. Dr. Summers, Jan. 10th, W. Wrightson, Jan. 5, Sister Maria Leavenworth City Mo. 27, '59. Col. Jas. Taylor, Nov. 20 '59. Dr. Tripler, Dec. 9, E.W. Eddy, Dec. 26 & Hooper Nov. 31 [30?]. The latter enclosed two bills for taxes in S. Diego.[6] This is a pretty good mail. Some of them it would have been worth while to have got sooner. I have an order for Col. Lee dated 20 Feb. assuming command of the Dept. & putting the Hd. Qrs. of the 8th Infy at San Antonio. Capt. Lee has letters from his wife. Lee says that the government wished to avoid war, that six companies were expected to be ordered to the Rio Grande frontier.

Fort Brown Fri. March 9th, 1860

It blew very hard last night, but it has not been cold to-day & I suppose tomorrow the norther will be over. It is doubtful whether the steamer got out & I have been trying all day to find out. I am trying to get a man to go to the Brazos with a letter. I wrote to Dept. Hd. Qrs. & one for Margaret.[7] Mr. Trevino the Mexican Consul called & I had a long talk with him. He insists that Cortinas has not recently been in Matamoros—that they would arrest him & that he's not at the Quijan said to [be] 30 miles back from here on the San Fernando road.[8] He told me that the Liberals have been defeated again in the interior. That Miramon was ready to commence the siege of Vera Cruz on the 24th or 25th.

---

[6] As a captain in command of two companies of the 2d Infantry at San Diego in 1850–1851, Heintzelman, along with Dr. John Summers, had purchased property in the town near the beach.

[7] Heintzelman reported that Lt. M. M. Kimmel, along with sixty-three men, had arrived in Brownsville on March 7. Although Kimmel's horses were broken down, the company had been ordered on a reconnaissance upriver. At the same time, Captain Jourdan's company of the 8th Infantry had been sent to Ringgold Barracks. Heintzelman further reported that one man had been killed on the river above Brownsville but his death had not been traced to the *Cortinistas*. Although Cortina had collected a small force at the Quijano Ranch, south of Matamoros, Heintzelman expected "no further disturbances from him on this side of the river." Heintzelman to Withers, Mar. 8, 1860, HLS.

[8] The village of Quijano, near the Gulf of Mexico, was twenty-eight miles south of Matamoros. Martin Reyes Vayssade, et al. (comps.), *Cartografía Histórica de Tamaulipas* (Ciudad Victoria: Instituto Tamaulipeco de Cultura, 1990), 200–201.

I saw Mr. Dougherty the Rep. from this district.[9] I had a long talk with him about affairs here. He appears to think that Houston is trying to make political capital. I saw Judge Davis this evening. He came over in the boat with his wife, a daughter of Forbes Britton.[10] The boat is stuck in the river less than a mile below. Lt. Robinson & his family & a number of persons are on board.[11]

Lt. Thomas got the man & I suppose that he went. But I believe he was hired, instead of one of our men. I learned last night that all the citizen teamsters have been discharged by Lt. Gillam. He might have consulted me first. If ever I start up in such another expedition I will have things arranged very differently.

FT. BROWN TEXAS SAT. MARCH 10, 1860

There has been the usual coolness since the norther. The steamer had not left & the express was in time. The Grampus got in this afternoon. I saw Lt. Robinson. He & his wife are staying at Gillams. I spent most of the day at Galvans & read Linder-Laucets. I saw an account of a case similar to Mary's & it ended in similar treatment. The patient got entirely well.[12]

I have felt badly yesterday & to-day. Not sick, not low spirited, but as if something unpleasant would happen at home. I issued the order to-day for Capt. Jourdan's company to go to Ringgold Brks. & Lt. Kimmel up the

---

[9] A soldier turned lawyer, Edward Dougherty had come to Brownsville from County Cavan, Ireland, where he became district attorney. In August 1859, he had been elected state representative from Cameron and Hidalgo counties. Dougherty was active in rallying forces against Cortina and accused Governor Houston of a lack of will power in dealing with the *Cortinistas*. A secessionist, Dougherty became district judge at the end of the Civil War but was removed by the Radical Republicans in 1870. At one time, Dougherty owned the Brownsville *Cosmopolitan*. Kearney and Knopp, *Boom and Bust*, 73, 112, 179; San Antonio *Daily Herald*, Aug. 19, 1859.

[10] See footnote 4, this chapter. Edmund J. Davis, a Presbyterian, had married Ann Elizabeth Britton, a devout Catholic and the daughter of Forbes Britton, at Corpus Christi in April 1858. After the death of her husband in February 1883, Ann married A.J. Smith and moved to St. Landry Parish, Louisiana. After Smith's death in June of 1891, she moved to Washington, D.C., where she died in poverty in May 1925. Gray, "Edmund J. Davis," 14–15, 428–439.

[11] Virginia-born James Watts Robinson, thirty-two and a 1852 West Point graduate, was a first lieutenant in the 1st Artillery.

[12] See footnote 32, February 1860 chapter. The year before the Heintzelmans arrived in Texas, Mary had undergone surgery for the removal of a tumor on her leg. Mary Lathrop Heintzelman died on March 24, 1927, after donating her father's journals, diaries, and papers to the Library of Congress. North, *Samuel Peter Heintzelman*, 9, 71, 113, 117, 190; HJ, Sept. 1, Oct. 30, Nov. 4, 1858.

road—to leave on Monday. The men have had a fine time since they were paid off.

Major Ford I heard was hurt by his horse stepping into a hole & falling on him.[13] He is hurt in the chest. Capt. Stoneman went back to his camp yesterday. He came in the day before.

Fort Brown Texas Sun. March 11, 1860

This has been a pleasant day. I visited Mr. Galvan to come & hear me read my report, as he had given me most of the items. I was writing to Col. Jas. Taylor, when he came.[14] He thinks that it is all right. I then went out & went to town with him. We then heard that a Mexican had brought the news that 600 men had landed at the Brazos. The mail came in & dont confirm it. I went over to Matamoros at 5 p.m. with Mr. Galvan with some of the officers. We saw about 300 of the National Guard out, without uniforms or arms. Many ladies were out in their carriages.

The Corpus mail brought me a circular from N. York about a new organization of our company & a letter from Margaret dated 27 Feb. She is quite dispirited about the delay in giving orders. Dr. Foard is not very well & Lt. Washington & the Band is not going to Verde. I wrote to Margaret this evening.

Ft. Brown Texas Mon. March 12, 1860

A pleasant day. I have had a last look at my report & went & read it to Mr. Cummings who has lived here the last ten years & who gave me his letter book to take notes from. I made one or two corrections & it is now ready to copy when Lt. Thomas gets some statistics ready. I expected to get off these troops to-day, but they have so much preparation. I suppose it will not be until tomorrow. Capt. Lee & Jourdan have been together most of the time since the Mexican War & dont like to be separated.

Mr. Mahoney & Lt. Langdon called. I walked to town & staid till after tea. On my return home I went & spent part of the evening at Lt. Langdon's. I then met Lt. & Mrs. Gillam & Judge Davis & his wife. She is a daughter of Forbes Britton's & no handsomer than her father.

---

[13] Ford was drilling the Rangers and had ordered a mounted charge in the direction of a chaparral thicket, when his horse fell on top of him, crushing his chest. "For more than a month the captain 'spit blood,'" Ford wrote. Ford, *Rip Ford's Texas*, 291.

[14] This is probably Joseph Pannel Taylor, a Kentuckian and a veteran of the War of 1812, who was a lieutenant colonel and assistant commissary general. Taylor became a brigadier general in the Union Army but died in 1864. Heitman, *Historical Register*, 948.

Mahoney told us that they are much alarmed in Matamoros. They heard the report, ever-exaggerated that troops had landed.

FORT BROWN TEXAS TUES. MARCH 13, 1860

Heavy fog & cool in the morning. Weather pleasant & a wind N.W. Capt. Jourdan's compy got off about breakfast, Lt. Kimmel's cav. an hour or two later. Capt. Stoneman is in & has returned.

I read my report to Capt. Lee & to Judge Davis. The judge says it is all right. I then read it to Capt. Stoneman. He says cut it down. That is my opinion. The amount of claims present is $336,826.21. Some of these are grossly exaggerated, but then there are but few Mexicans who have put in theirs. There is a note from the Brazos that a large ship is in the offing with Am. colors flying—supposed to have troops on board.

I got a letter from Powers our fool Mayor about the soldiers wearing their revolvers. He dont see other people.

I got a note from Gen. Garcia.[15] Cortinas was Sunday at La Mesa with about 40 men & started up the river with 8. He has sent after him & I suppose gives me this information, after what I said to Mr. Trevino the counsel.

Capt. Lee & Lt. Thomas are complaining of fever & some of them have chills. Mr. McCluskey has had an attack.

Fort Brown Texas Wed. March 14, 1860

A pleasant day. I answered Gen. Garcia's note, merely saying that I would be on the alert.[16] I sent up three notes to Stoneman, Kimmel & Ford to put them on their guard.[17] Stoneman sent back a note, that he thought that Cortinas was collecting a force to attack the boat, that he would go to Los Ruses & if necessary concentrate all the troops & cross over to protect the boat, asking my approval.[18] I approved of it & gave him instructions & told him not to be drawn from the river, only to strike a sudden blow & that I

---

[15] García wrote that he had received information that the "Banditti Cortinas" had been at the Mesa Ranch with forty men on March 11, 1860, but had left upriver with an escort of only eight men. García promised to send a force in pursuit of Cortina and asked for "united measures in the matter." García to Commissioned General of the Government, Mar. 13, 1860, HP.

[16] In a brief note, Heintzelman thanked García for his letter of March 13, 1860: "I am happy that you are taking steps to apprehend him," Heintzelman concluded. Heintzelman to García, Mar. 4, 1860, HLS.

[17] These notes are not in Heintzelman's Letters Sent Book.

[18] Hearing that Cortina was "uniting his forces to attack the Steamer on her way down," Stoneman was prepared to "cross the river and protect her." Stoneman to Heintzelman, Mar. 14, 1860, HP.

would make a demonstration on Matamoros to prevent their sending reinforcements. I have been busy all day reducing my report. Capt. Lee &
Thomas are still complaining. I wrote to Margaret. That large ship is not yet
in. I called at retreat on Lt. & Mrs. Robinson. She appears to be a pleasant
woman. They met Matilda at Major Burbank's at Newport Brks.

Fort Brown Texas Thurs. March 15, 1860

I this morning issued an order directing that four of these heavy guns be
prepared with mules & ammunition for service & that the[y] put 40 rounds of
ammunition in their boxes & sent word to Capt. Dawson that I wished the
mules put on at 4 p.m. to see that all was right.[19] I saw no preparations made &
after 4 I sent Lt. Thomas to see him. He told him flatly that he would not
obey the order. I then sent to place him in arrest—that he would not obey. He
had seen no order giving me the command, or something to that effect. I then
sent Lt. Thomas with the original orders for the expedition & some others.
He would not look at them. I next issued an order putting him in arrest & Lt.
Gillam in command of the post. That he would not look at. I then went with
Lt. Thomas & he would not take the order. I told him what it was & he wished
to enter into a discussion. I declined & laid down the order & left. The man is
crazy. He says he will give up the command only on the orders that put him
here. He forgets that he went up the river on my order & returned & occupies
this post by my order. The Corpus mail is in & only brings me one letter—
from Poston in N.Y. dated 12 Feb. He speaks of the organization in N.Y. as
the only one that could be made & the best. He sent me some proxies to sign,
but it is too late for the election.

About 100 men left Matamoros yesterday about 11 a.m. for up the river.
It has been warm to-day.

I have finished rewriting my report. I only shortened it three pages &
part of that is fallacious, as it is much more closely written. I like it much better however.

Fort Brown Texas Fri. March 16, 1860

This morning after I returned from breakfast Lt. Gillam came in. After
talking of everything he at length touched on Capt. Dawson. He dont dispute
my authority to order him into the field, but still thinks that I have no authority to order him to prepare. He thinks I have no right to interfere in his post
& that the authority that sent him here can only order him away & much
more stuff of the same sort. I reminded him that I ordered him here & that I

---

[19] Orders nos. 13, 14, and 15, Mar. 15, 1860, HOB.

had studiously avoided interfering in the post, but only because I did not expect to stay here anytime & did not want the trouble. I told Gillam that all I wanted was to have the battery prepared. He went & saw Dawson & he soon sent word that he would comply with my orders. I then sent Lt. Thomas & released him & he came to explain. He said it was a misunderstanding & that Capt. Lee had said so much about the command of the Post. There was nothing to misunderstand & as I consider him half crazy I did inquire into the misunderstanding. He went to work at the guns & had even more trouble than I anticipated. Lt. Gillam with his company got two guns ready & drove them around the parade. Capt. Dawson did not succeed with him. It will take several days to make the mules work well.

I heard this evening that Pena has joined Cortinas & that they were not far above here collecting a reactionist force to take Matamoros. About 60 men went out yesterday & about half cavalry. They have joined this party. They are in much alarm in Matamoros & are arriving. I heard this morning a report that Cortinas had said, or sent in word that he would have the city at 9 A.M.

I have been most of the day copying letters to accompany my report. A norther set in about 10 P.M. yesterday & I have a fire to-day.

FORT BROWN TEXAS SAT. MARCH 17, 1860

The norther gone & a beautiful day. I have finished copying letters. The report to-day is that Cortinas is with the reactionists & that there will soon be a proclamation, or a pronunciamento.

Late this afternoon Mr. Trevino called & told me that there was a report that the Rangers had crossed & that Cortinas was not at the Mesa. That orders had been sent to Vargas who commands the troops that left a day or two since to cooperate with Ford. At dusk Mr. Trevino came back & read me a letter to him from Gen. Garcia, that Ford had crossed & that his men had come in contact with Vargas' men at the Mesa & before the mistake was discovered one man was slightly wounded & a girl badly.[20] I wish I could get instructions, so as to dispense with the Rangers. Everything is going on well & I fear that they will spoil it.

FT. BROWN TEXAS SUN. MARCH 18, 1860

I went to bed at tattoo but read till near 11. At ½ past the express arrived & sure enough all the troops had crossed the day before & had attacked Cortinas at the Mesa. They intended to surround it on foot, but met a

---

[20] For Ford's account of the skirmish at La Mesa, see Ford, *Rip Ford's Texas*, 291–295. See also Ford to Heintzelman, Mar. 18, 1860, HP.

sentinel & then a picket & had to make a charge, which was done on three sides. Some shots were exchanged, when they discovered that the men were the National Guards from Matamoros. One Mex. solider was wounded & a Mexican woman, she mortally. She was trying to close a door from which an officer was firing at the cavalry, as they passed. Whilst at Breakfast near the ranch, Vargas with about 150 men, foot & mounted came up & asked a conference.[21] He was told our men were after Cortinas & he said he was & came to cooperate with our troops. Cortinas was no doubt at the rancho & made his escape. Our troops remained on the other side to wait for the boat.

I sent an order up to attack Cortinas if they could learn certainly of his being in the vicinity & if not return to this side & protect the boat—if necessary to cross again.[22] Lt. Gillams compy left at 1½ P.M. with two 24 pdr howitzers to cover the crossing. It took them six hours to get ready, although Dawson said they were always ready. I went & read the letter to the Mex. counsel. Stoneman also wrote me a private letter & asked for a gun. Some women & a boy say that Cortinas was in the rancho that night & a man said he was there the day before. I have no doubt but that the authorities are sincere, but I dont believe that the troops are at all reliable. The express returned in the morning.

Lt. Thomas & I dined at Millers with Galvan. We got a nice dinner. After I went with Galvan to Judge Garland's.[23] His eldest daughter was to be baptized. They had already left for the Convent, so we followed. Her mother we found at the house & neither she nor the father were at the Convent. Her sister was there.

Soon after we got there the ceremony commenced. We went into the school room, where an altar was & all the other preparations. There was about a dozen men & they sang, a part of the ceremony. Miss Mary Garland was dressed in white with a wreath of orange blossoms, like a bride. She is a

---

[21] Ford identified Vargas as a colonel. Ford, *Rip Ford's Texas*, 294.

[22] "Should you have certain information of Cortinas being in the vicinity, you will attack him, but if not you will recross to the American side of the river." Heintzelman to Stoneman, Mar. 17, 1860, HLS.

[23] Rice Garland, a sixty-two-year-old Virginia-born attorney, had served in the U.S. Congress from Louisiana where he was on the Louisiana Supreme Court from 1840 to 1846. In 1848, Helen Chapman referred to Garland as "a gentleman of great learning, high standing and talents, who committed a forgery in Louisiana." Garland lived in Matamoros "with his mistress as his wife," Chapman reported. According to the 1860 Census, Garland and his "wife," Lucinda, had two daughters, V. E., nineteen, and A. M., sixteen. While in Galveston in 1866, Heintzelman learned from one of the daughters that her father had died in 1861. Coker, *News from Brownsville*, 93, 343; 8th Census, Cameron County; HJ, Mar. 26, 1866; Apr. 11, 1867.

tall graceful girl & tolerably good looking. The ceremony lasted near an hour. After it was over we were invited into the parlor & had cake & claret. Then they showed us their garden—mostly vegetable, but sadly in want of rain. They then took us upstairs & showed us the sleeping rooms. There are two large rooms with iron cots & looked neat. The mattress were not the softest. They also showed us the chapel. The sisters & padre were quite pleasant & sociable, laughing & joking, with each other & their friends.

We got back about dusk. The Corpus mail was in & I got one letter from S. Antonio & only about wagons—no instructions. I also got a letter from Sister Juliana & one from Margaret dated 4th. Marg. enclosing one from Mary, quite an improvement in her writing. I sat down & answered Margarets letter & wrote to Dept. Hd. Qrs. sending Stoneman's report & my reply.[24]

The day has been exceeding warm & close.[25] Before I got through it turned to the north, the wind & is sensibly cooler.

Ft. Brown Texas Mon. March 19, 1860

Capt. Lee, Thomas & I breakfasted with the Langdons. The weather is quite cool & pleasant out this morning.

I did some writing & then went to town. Thomas is not done yet with my writing. Much to my surprise this evening the mail arrived. The steamer was still outside. The reports were that a Light Battery is in New Orleans & would have come but the steamer was full. The Galveston asked $6,000 & the Qr. M. would not give it. They will come in the next. Also that there are 500 new recruits. The first I dont believe & the second is only partly true. There is also a report that Col. Lee left S. Antonio on the 15th for here. This I also doubt. I got a letter from there dated 10th about Capt. Rickett's compy. Based on the Gen. order for it to go to Old Point on the 1st of April. No letter from Margaret.

I have a letter from Col. Lockridge. He thinks the President wants war, but dont want to give orders to begin it.

There is an order in the papers disposing of the troops that leave Utah. It is very long, the 3rd Infy to Texas & our cos. to Ft. Clark & 5 to Ringgold Brks. There is also a letter from the Sec. of War about the Rio Grande troubles, to the President. He dont give me a word of credit for what I have done.

I got a letter from Col. Lockridge with a bundle of papers. He went over

---

[24] Stoneman to Heintzelman, Mar. 1860, HP; Heintzelman to Lee, Mar. 18, 1860, *TTF*, 79–80. See also Heintzelman to Stoneman, Mar. 19, 1860; Heintzelman to Withers, Mar. 18, 1860; Stoneman and Ford to C. W. Thomas, Mar. 18, 1860, all in *TTF*, 80–86.

[25] Heintzelman uses "close" to mean humid, stagnant, or oppressive.

with Col. Brown & considers him an old fogy. I got a letter this afternoon from Capt. Stoneman.[26] The steamboat is this side of Los Ruses & the troops have gone up the river to visit some ranches, that Cortinas frequents & tomorrow expect to be back to where they crossed. I wrote to him.

FT. BROWN TEXAS TUES. MARCH 20, 1860

A pleasant day. The steamer Ranchero got in this morning. I had several visitors. Dr. Graff of Cin., who lives at San Fernando Mex., Judge Davis & Mr. Cummings. They occupied most of the morning. I have wrote to Poston & to Dr. Tripler. I have had Thomas at work & he has finished copying my Report & will have all the papers ready tonight.

Mr. Phelps, Mr. Galvan's partner, got ashore last evening & brought us all this news. I cut out of a N.O. paper the Sec. of Wars letter to the President, with more accounts of the Rio Grande affairs for the Senate.[27] My name is hardly mentioned, although he uses [it] in much of his report, the very words I did in my reports.

This morning the steamer was not in sight. She however got in afterwards & stuck in the bar till she threw over several hundred sacks of corn. The passengers did not get in until tattoo. There is a newspaper mail but not distributed tonight.

Mrs. Capt. Ricketts & his daughter came down in the Ranchero & are staying in Lt. Graham's quarters. He is up with Lt. Gillam. I called & saw them this evening at retreat. Mrs. Ricketts told me how provoked she was at me because I ordered her husband's company to Ringgold. She lays it all to Dawson. She had the promise from Lt. Col. Thomas & Major Townsend that the capts compy would on the 1st Apl. start for Old Point.

FORT BROWN TEXAS WED. MARCH 21ST, 1860

Quite dusty to-day. I finished my Report & got it into the mail today. It is quite a relief. I have written to Lockridge, Vinton, & to Margaret. I got another letter from Gen. Garcia.[28] He complains that a man was shot &

---

26 Stoneman to Heintzelman, Mar. 19, 1860, HP.

27 John B. Floyd to James Buchanan, Mar. 5, 1860, *HRG*, 1–4.

28 In a restrained tone, García complained that the Rangers had attacked twenty-seven men of the Matamoros National Guard at La Mesa Ranch. García had also received news that on March 20, 1860, at the Maguey Ranch, also in Mexico, the Rangers had killed a man. García did not understand how officials on the Texas side could be "blind to the injustices of these acts." García was hopeful that Heintzelman would "be so kind as to take measures so as to prevent the likes from happening again." García to General of Brigade, Mar. 21, 1860, HP.

desires me to prevent such things, but dont say a word about withdrawing our troops. They should & I hope did cross the river to-day. I want them on this side, as I know that they will be guilty of all kinds of outrages.

I went to town to get Clark to read the letter to me & whilst there Capt. Littleton rode in with 32 recruits he collected on the Nueces.[29] He reports, I understand, that Col. Lee is on his way with 600 men. I still dont believe it.

Col. Fitzpatrick was over here this afternoon. How very bitter he is against the Mexicans. I should have an express this evening that our troops have returned to this side.

I wrote to Judge Iverson.

Ft. Brown Texas Thurs. March 22, 1860

Quite windy & dusty all day. Mr. Dewitt who is sutler at Ft. Quitman came down with Capt. Lee, left this morning for San Antonio. I sent out an express to Capt. Stoneman with orders for the troops to cross to our side & to send Lt. Gillam & his comp. & guns back.[30] I also answered Gen. Garcia's note.[31] I saw the Mex. Counsel & he told me that he had a letter from the Mex. Minister in Washington & that he saw the Sec. of War & of State & was told that Col. Lee a prudent discreet officer was ordered to this frontier. I am glad they have found out that I am not discreet & hope that now I will be permitted to return to my post. The Corpus mail came in this afternoon & brought me a letter from Lt. Washington. Col. Lee was to leave on the 16th & to bring with him the company of Cavalry from Verde & one from the Hondo. Capt. Lee got a letter from his wife that he would come via Laredo. I suppose that he will be here about the first of April. I hope that he will let me go home. Washington wrote me that he is married & will remain in S.A. till I return. I wrote to him & to Margaret. Mr. Galvan sent down an express to the boat. I got a letter also from Mr. Wrightson. There is a good deal of dissatisfaction

---

[29] Capt. John Littleton, with Co. A of the Rangers, was in the fight at Rio Grande City when he had his gun shot out of his hands. It was Littleton who had previously been ambushed by Cortina on the Palo Alto Prairie. He had also been at La Bolsa. Littleton had supported Tobin in the election for major of the Rangers, but had fallen out with Tobin and had led his men back to Brownsville. Littleton later commanded a company of Confederates in South Texas during the Civil War.

[30] Heintzelman to Stoneman, Mar. 22, 1860, HLS.

[31] Heintzelman had received a complaint from García "of the putting to death of some men by our troops at or near the Maguey rancho." Heintzelman asked Stoneman to "make a full report of the occurrences." In a short note, Heintzelman assured García that he was inquiring into what had happened at the Maguey on March 19. Heintzelman to Stoneman, Mar. 22, 1860; Heintzelman to García, Mar. 22, 1860, both in HLS.

with Mr. Lathrop. He made Mr. Brown his proxy & sold some of Wither's stock to Alden for Colt at $15 a share. I see that he wont stay out there much longer as our director. I am beginning to loose faith in the gentleman.

FORT BROWN TEXAS FRI. MARCH 23, 1860

This has been a warm day & tolerably dusty. Lt. Gillam & the guns got back about ten A.M. He has not been near me to report. If I am kept here in command I will turn over a new leaf with some gentlemen here. I understand that he reported to Capt. Dawson. He has one of his crazy fits in him. He asked Mrs. Ricketts if she did not hear the soldiers about the quarters abusing him etc.

Capt. Ford is down & called. Capt. Stoneman has much to report, but let Ford make a verbal one. They recrossed the day before yesterday.

I went out this morning & called at Dr. Jarvis & at Mr. Chamberlins & Judge Davis's. I spent most of the day reading. I also called on Lt. Robinson, who is sick in bed—a remittent fever. I met Dr. Trotsin to-day. He says he has but two sick soldiers, but that there is considerable fever in town. Mr. Mahoney was over to bid us good by. He leaves for Monterrey in the morning.

FT. BROWN TEXAS SAT. MARCH 24, 1860

Warm & calm this morning, but a little more breeze later in the day. We rode out to Resaca de la Palma in the forenoon. Lt. Thomas, in Capt. Lee's ambulance with Mrs. Ricketts & Mrs. Langdon, Lt. Reed in a buggy with Mrs. Ricketts & Capt. Lee and myself on horses. It is about 2½ miles from town & on a road a little above the one we take to Point Isabel. The ground is considerably changed in the way of chapparal. I cant see however where Gen. Arista disposed of so many men. He had about 8,000 at Palo Alto & at least 5,000 at Resaca.[32] The gully or resaca is not over 60 yds. wide with a pond of water on each side of the road. We had pointed out to us the groves where the Americans were buried on one side & the Mexicans on the other side of the road. Capt. Lee also showed us where he buried one of his men & got a tooth from the skeleton & gave to Mrs. Ricketts. We staid an hour & the ladies gathered some flowers.

I got Capt. Stoneman's report & also one from Capt. Ford.[33] I understood

---

[32] Gen. Mariano Arísta commanded the Mexican forces at Palo Alto on May 8, 1846, and at Resaca de la Palma the next day. Arísta became secretary of war in 1848 and president of Mexico from 1851 to 1853, before being banished from the country in 1855.

[33] Stoneman to Heintzelman, Mar. 23, 1860 (two letters); Ford to Heintzelman, Mar. 24, 1860, HP.

him that the former would not make one & asked him to do so. I have a letter
that the Governor wishes to know whether I consider the services of the State
troops any longer necessary on this frontier. I will refer him to Col. Lee for an
answer.

The troops visited a rancho 42 miles on the Monterrey road from
Matamoros. They marched 100 miles in two days. The excursion or incursion
ha[s] had an excellent effect.

At the Bolsa they captured a captain of the Indians who was a captain of
Cortinas & killed him.[34] Cortinas has fled to a rancho 80 or 90 miles back.
They dont think that he will again attempt to collect a force near the Rio
Grande.

FT. BROWN TEXAS SUN. MARCH 25, 1860

It has been warm to-day & when I got up looked like a norther. About
one P.M. it rained two or three showers & commenced again after tattoo &
now I fear it will continue. I wrote a report to Dept. Hd. Qrs. & then went
with Mr. Galvan to the Catholic church.

There is a story in town most people believe a hoax, that our fleet captured part of Admiral Morin's squadron, which sailed out of Havana under
Spanish [colors] & was to [raise] Mexican colors.

I took a nap in the afternoon & at dusk went to the Post Office. I have
orders to meet Col. Lee at Ringgold & to take Capt. Lee's compy there, to be
part of the garrison.[35] I hope this will be so for on my way home. I wrote to
Washington also a report.[36] I got a letter from Margaret dated 11th with a
neck handkerchief & answered it. Capt. Lee is delighted with the prospect of
being stationed at Ringgold. I admire that Post about as much as I did
Duncan. He got a letter from S. Antonio. Col. May died of apoplexy.[37] I
believe that he is the third of his family [that] has died within a short time that
way.

I will do most of my packing tonight.

---

[34] Several Tampacuas Indians had joined Cortina. Thompson, *Juan Cortina*, 100.

[35] With Capt. Arthur Lee's Company C of the 8th Infantry, Heintzelman was to
meet Col. Robert E. Lee at Ringgold Barracks. Withers to Heintzelman, Mar. 13,
1860, HP.

[36] Heintzelman to Cooper, Mar. 25, 1860, HLS.

[37] The only Colonel May in the army at this time was Charles Augustus May, a
brevet lieutenant colonel and a hero of the Battle of Palo Alto, who died in December
1864. Heintzelman is probably referring to 1st Lt. Julian May who died on November
22, 1859, of apoplexy. Heitman, *Historical Register*, 698–699.

FORT BROWN MON. MARCH 26, 1860

I went to bed at midnight. It rained all night & blew a regular wet norther. When I got up & soon saw it would be folly to start before it was over. It rained hard & blew all day & grew colder. Thomas did not come home & I had to send for him. He brought an invitation for me to dine with Mr. Hale & to meet Col. Fitzpatrick, the counsel. I concluded to go & then call on Gen. Garcia. Lt. Thomas & Mr. Galvan & I dined with Mr. Hale & then met the counsel.

Mr. Thomas was not ready, so we went over first & made our call on the General. He was very courteous & read us a few lines of a dispatch he was writing to the Governor stating that our troops had acted with good accord & that no outrages had been committed, that the man they had killed was one of Cortinas's corporals & a noted horse thief & his death a good riddance.

Whilst we were at dinner Lt. Langdon came in. We sat till dark & there were no carriages. He got Mr. Hale to send us home in his. We left Lt. Thomas there. It was very wet & muddy from the carriage to the river. Mr. G. fell twice out of the skiff & I caught him.

FORT BROWN TEXAS TUES. MARCH 27, 1860

The rain appears to be over, but it must be very bad on the road. I think that we had better wait until tomorrow.

Everybody advised us to wait until tomorrow, as the road is very bad. I sent an invitation to Matamoros for Col. Fitzpatrick & Mr. Hale to dine with me & invited Mr. Galvan & Mr. Phelps. The latter's health is not very good & he declined. We had a very quiet dinner.

I heard to-day that the mail that left here for Laredo was taken by some robbers above Edinburg. The mail coming down was met on the road on foot.

I called at Langdons, Robinsons & Gillams & should have called at the Mexican counsels.

It is sprinkling rain again. I hope that it wont last.

BARRANCA TEXAS WED. MARCH 28, 1860

It only sprinkled a little last night. To-day has been pleasant & we started at 12:40 P.M. I called & bid some persons good bye. We did not find the roads at all muddy. We got into camp a little after 4 P.M. We have come about 18 miles—about two miles beyond our old camp at the Rito Ebonal.

The grass is already green & the trees in bloom. Plenty of verbinas.[38]

---

[38] Prairie verbinas, called *alfombria morado* by natives, was a purple wildflower

Camp 3 miles short of San Rosario Thurs. March 29, 1860

We have come about 18 miles & are encamped at our old camps when we went down. The Rangers are two miles behind us & Stoneman about half a mile beyond us. We went off the road & stopped an hour with Lt. Kimmel at his camp about 12 miles from here. I ordered him forward as far as between Edinburg & Ringgold. The weather is delightful & the roads dry.

Camp on Lagoon 6 mls from Edinburg Fri. March 30, 1860

We have come 24 miles to-day. I was quite tired. We were about five hours on the road. The road was better—not so much cut up by carts as yesterday.

Last evening at dusk Capt. Stoneman came to camp & staid till quite late. He told me about their trip into Mexico. I had reason to be uneasy when they were there. Ford wanted them to march down to near Matamoros, or in fact to there.

At dusk Mr. McCluskey & Mr. Moses drove up & have travelled with us to-day.[39] We have a nice camp within a few hundred yards of where we encamped before going & coming. We have no dust & a delightful breeze. Light clouds, but I had my hair cut a few days ago & my ears are very much burned. We will get to Ringgold Monday.

Lagoon Tortuga March 31, 1860. Sat.

We came 19 miles to-day. We met Capt. Rickett's compy about 3 miles from where we encamped. He had Lt. Beard with him. We stopped about an hour. He informed us that the report of the naval engagement was true. They had it at Ringgold from Galveston.

We stopped a little while at Edinburg. We then saw Capt. Smith keeping a store. He has the two daughters I met at Lt. Gillams & at the Mex. Counsels. They told us that Zamora was on the Mexican side not far from Reynosa.

---

common to the area. Blooming in early spring, verbinas were anywhere from six to sixteen inches tall and grew in dense colonies with the lower branches of the plant sprawling on the ground. Campbell and Lynn Loughmiller, *Texas Wildflowers: A Field Guide* (Austin: University of Texas Press, 1984), 236.

[39] New York–born Joseph Moses, forty, was another Roma merchant. Heintzelman later met Moses by accident on a New York street in April 1861. 8th Census, Starr County; HJ, Apr. 13, 1861.

❧ April 1860 ❧

"Col. Lee...wanted them to catch Cortinas soon."

———————

CAMP 2 MILES BEYOND LOS CUEVAS SUN. APL. 1, 1860

We came about 18 miles to-day. It was very foggy in the morning & had been exceedingly hot all day. We have not a very good camp. It is close & the breeze is kept off by the trees.

We left two men behind to bring up the mail. They got in about 2 P.M. No mail from Corpus. I have a letter from the Post Master.[1] The news from Tampico is that the report we heard of the naval engagement is true. We will have the particulars in the Flag.

RINGGOLD BRKS. MON. APL. 2, 1860

I left at 20 min. before 7 & arrived here at 20 past 10. The ride was pretty warm. I found Col. Lee here. He arrived here on the 31st March. He had a storm of snow & ice, when we had our rain storm. He had all sorts of reports of Cortinas at Ft. Duncan & Laredo & has ordered troops there.

I dined with him & after dinner he showed me his instructions. They are, if the Mexican authorities do not break up Cortinas & his bands for him to cross & do it. He will write to the Governor of Tamaulipas & ask him to put a stop to it. I fear that it will be sometime before I get home. I was partly prepared for the disappointment.

I am going to write to Stoneman to stop below Edinburg. Lt. Kimmel will stop about ten miles this side Edinburg.

It is warm & windy, but with this wind, but little dust. Mr. Phelps & Mr. Moses leave in the morning for Roma. We have all been sitting in front of

---

[1] F. F. Fenn told Heintzelman that the mail from Rio Grande City had been taken "almost [in] sight of Edinburg" by the *Cortinistas*. Fenn to Heintzelman, Mar. 30, 1860, HP.

Col. Lee's Quarters talking. I see no prospect of my getting away from this frontier for some time.

RINGGOLD BRKS. TEX. TUES. APL. 3RD, 1860

The morning was cool & pleasant. Lt. Thomas took Col. Lee's letter to Camargo, but the Alcalde told him that the Gov. was at Tampico or Tula & by the mail might not get his letter in six weeks.[2] We then sent a copy to Mr. Trevino the Mex. Consul to have forwarded to its destination.[3] We sent down a train for provisions & the letter went with it. I think that we will start down for Brownsville again in a few days.

The Cavalry Col. Lee brought down have come from the Saus to within six miles & Lts. Owens & Harrison came in & they & Col. Lee dined with us. Seeing Owens so recently from Verde makes me think more about going home. It is quite warm & reminds me of Duncan, but it is not dusty, at least in my quarters. I wrote to Margaret.

RINGGOLD BRKS TEXAS WED. APL. 4, 1860

The two cavalry companies (Capts. Brackett & Evans) got here soon after breakfast & encamped near the hospital. Capt. Bracketts will be posted about ten miles above Edinburg; Capt. Evans' under Lt. Eagle about as far below Edinburg & next Lt. Kimmel & then Capt. Stoneman.[4] The Rangers will be

---

[2] In his letter to Ándres Treviño, governor of Tamaulipas, Lee said that he had been instructed by the secretary of war to notify Mexican officials on the Rio Grande that the "bands of banditti" must be broken up and that Mexican authorities would be "held responsible for the faithful performance of this plain duty." Lee to Treviño, Apr. 2, 1860, TTF, 85. Before leaving San Antonio for Laredo on March 15, 1860, Lee received information that Cortina had moved upriver and was preparing to attack Fort Duncan. Consequently, Lee marched for Eagle Pass where he arrived five days later to find "this Section of Country . . . quiet." Lee left for Laredo the next morning. Lee to Cooper, Mar. 20, 1860, LR, AGO, RG 94 (NA). Lee's letters from "Troubles on the Texas Frontier" and a number of other sources are reprinted in John H. Jenkins (ed.), *Robert E. Lee on the Rio Grande, The Correspondence of Robert E. Lee on the Texas Border, 1860* (Austin: Jenkins Publishing Co., 1988).

[3] Emphasizing the importance of Colonel Lee's communication, Heintzelman went on to tell Manuel Treviño that Cortina had left for Burgos, three days' march from the Rio Grande, and that "it is not believed that he will again venture to concentrate a force in the vicinity of the Rio Grande." Heintzelman to Treviño, Apr. 3, 1860, HLS.

[4] In command of Co. H of the 2d Cavalry, 2d Lt. Robert Nelson Eagle had joined Colonel Lee at Fort Duncan. Eagle had previously recruited many of the men of Co. E of the regiment at St. Louis, Missouri, in 1855. Heintzelman had met Eagle in Washington in November 1857. Simpson, *Cry Comanche*, 14, 27; HJ, Apr. 13, 1861.

dispersed with. We will probably leave here on Friday for Brownsville. The troops will have orders to cross over into Mexico whenever they hear of Cortinas or any of his men. Col. Lee was saying to some of the officers that he wanted them to catch Cortinas soon, & then they might go back to their stations & I too. If I stay till Cortinas is caught it will be sometime before I leave this frontier but if only till the troubles are over I could leave now. I observe that the Colonel is very punctilious in Military matters. Capt. Brackett went to Capt. Lee to know where to put his company before he came to report. Although Owens took out a message for him to come in & encamp here.

In the evening the mail came in with the mail from Laredo. I got a letter from Lt. Washington about the recruiting service. Lts. Williams & Thomas are the first on the roster & both wish to go. The former is in San Antonio & will join his company if I will detail him. Lt. Craig of the 8th Infy, joins his company (Jourdan's) here with recruits.[5]

The weather is warm & was quite dusty. I cant see how anyone can like this post in Texas.

RINGGOLD BRKS TEX. THURS. APL. 5, 1860

The early morning cool & pleasant, but since warm. It was warm last night. After tattoo last evening I went to Capt. Langdons with the officers about the Post. We were told that he would sing. He is said to know more songs than any officer of the army.

We have been busy making arrangements to station the cavalry & supply them with corn. I think that we will leave tomorrow. The Corpus mail got in & brought the news that those Spanish Mexican vessels were taken at Anton Lizardo etc. Capt. Lee has just come in & states that an express at Matamoros states that Vera Cruz has fallen & that Miramon has given them seventeen days to come under his jurisdiction. This letter came in an express sent by Capt. Dawson with our letters, but principally to bring on an application for a leave for him.

I got a letter from Margaret. All are well, but provoked at the Secretary's letter to Gov. Houston, that he would send an officer of discretion etc. to regulate matters on the Rio Grande—after I had settled them. Major Vinton also sent me an open letter addressed to Lt. Thomas complaining of his not sending all of the papers required, or not in time & of making transfers of funds. I think that Vinton is rather unreasonable & entirely too hard on Thomas. I sent an instruction to Lt. Washington to detail Lts. Williams & Thomas for

---

[5] William Craig was an 1853 West Point graduate and a second lieutenant in the 8th Infantry. Craig became a quartermaster during the Civil War and died in May 1886. Heitman, *Historical Register*, 334.

the recruiting service. Williams has to be relieved from commissary duty first.

Mr. Phelps & Mr. Dodridge rode in after dark from Roma. We sent Howe up to let the former know that we were going to start in the morning. In the New Orleans papers is an account of the poisoning of a dinner party, by a negro boy putting arsenic in some Charlotte Rose. His wife & son were amongst the number & were scarcely out of danger. A child, not his, had died.

Las Cuevas Tex. Fri. Apl. 6, 1860

After many arrangements we got off at 11:20 & arrive here at 3:20 P.M. The road was very dusty & the ride very hot. I rode with Col. Lee in his ambulance. About half way we met an express with Capt. Ford's report of his operations in Mexico. He heard of Zamora & crossed at Tobosa.[6] Surrounded Old Reynosa & then the new & demanded Cortinas's men. They, the authorities, paraded some men & told them to look, but they did not recognize any one. They had a correspondence & have sent to Matamoros for instructions & our Rangers withdrew to our side (Edinburg) to wait. What an outrage on a friendly Government!

Capt. Stoneman & Lt. Kimmel are about three miles above Edinburg.

---

[6] Ford had received information from Sixto Dominguez, fifty-one-year-old sheriff of Hidalgo County and part owner of the Rosario Ranch, that seventeen *Cortinistas*, including Teodoro Zamora, Cortina's second in command, were at Old Reynosa, upriver from Edinburg. Using the Tabasco ford, some thirty miles downriver from Rio Grande City and south of present-day La Joya, Ford crossed under the cover of darkness with eighty Rangers and surrounded the town. One detachment of Rangers, however, failed to deploy on time, Ford said, and most of the *Cortinistas* were able to escape. After purchasing supplies and attending a fandango, the next morning Ford marched eleven miles downriver along the Mexican bank to New Reynosa, opposite Edinburg. Fearing an attack, Ford had arranged with Captain Stoneman to station two companies of regulars in a bend of the river near Edinburg as reinforcements. Fearful that the Rangers had come to rob the town, 400 heavily armed citizens and local militia, commanded by Juan Treviño and his brother Manuel, angrily greeted the Rangers. After tense negotiations on the town plaza, in which Ford demanded that ten *Cortinistas* and fourteen other men he accused of aiding Cortina be arrested, the town *ayuntamiento* agreed that all "outlaws and refugees from justice" in Texas should be "delivered to justice," but delayed, saying any such demand would have to be approved by Gen. Guadalupe García in Matamoros. Two *Cortinistas*, the *ayuntamiento* said, had already been arrested and sent to Matamoros. Furthermore, they would give Ford's list to Juan Benavides, the local military commander. Retreating into Texas, Ford remained convinced of the "complicity of the authorities of Mexico in the Cortina affair." Moreover, he was certain that several of Cortina's men were serving in the Mexican National Guard. Ford, *Rip Ford's Texas*, 299–305; Ford to Heintzelman, Apr. 5, 1860, HP; and Ford to the Authorities, Civil and Military, of Reynosa, n.d., HP.

The steam mail was with these first men—the rangers, sent up by Galvan. I got two or three slips from Col. Lockridge & a letter from Dr. Woosoncraft to write him a memoir on the Colorado desert, as he wished to get a grant of land from the Government.[7] No letters from home. Col. Lee is at a loss what to do & wants my opinion.

CAMP 2½ MILES ABOVE EDINBURG SAT. APL. 7, 1860

It was quite warm last night when we first went to bed, but soon became comfortable. We had revile earlier than I used to here it & were on the road a quarter before six. The Colonel insisted on my riding in his carriage with him to discuss matters & decide what had better be done under present circumstances. He is determined to trust to my experience & judgement, although the Sec. of War has sent him here as an officer of prudence & discretion.

We got to the Tortugas, 18 or 20 miles, before one, but there was so little grass that after a long consultation we continued on to this place, a canebrake not quite three miles from town.

Here Kimmel was encamped, but this morning heard firing & went in a hurry & left his wagons to follow. He found that it is a Mexican Fiesta & they took advantage of it to fire into Col. Ford's camp & they returned it, wounding one or two Mexicans. There was also some firing in Edinburg. Col. Ford had a conversation with the authorities & a correspondence since & both parites are satisfied. We may be as none of our people are hurt. Capt. Stoneman & Lt. Kimmel with their companies are encamped about six miles below Edinburg. The Col. was in trouble about this firing & asked me what to do. I did not think that it amounted to much. He finally sent Lt. Thomas with

---

[7] Oliver Meredith Wozencraft, an Ohio-born physician, was Indian agent in Southern California and was with Heintzelman in the fight with Cahuilla Indians at Los Coyotes on December 21, 1851. Wozencraft, along with Col. John B. Magruder, had visited with Heintzelman in Washington in April 1857, at which time Wozencraft was campaigning to become superintendent "of one of the wagon roads to the Pacific." Magruder had penned a letter to the Secretary of the Interior recommending Wozencraft, which Heintzelman agreed to sign. Wozencraft devoted his time to expansionist politics and the construction of a transcontinental railroad. He also became convinced that water from the Colorado River could be used to irrigate the Imperial Valley in Southern California—an idea that was not considered realistic at the time. In April 1869, after Wozencraft had returned from a two-year trip to South America, Heintzelman conversed with the adventurer-physician in Washington. He "still talks of his plan for irrigating the Colorado desert," Heintzelman recorded. William B. Secrest, "Wozencraft," *Real West*, 24 (Oct.–Dec., 1981), 6–13, 56, 36–40, 54; Thrapp, *Frontier Biography*, III, 1599–1600; HJ, Dec. 31, 1851; Jan. 8, 1852; Apr. 15, 1857; Apr. 6, 1869.

a couple of men & a note to Edinburg to see. He met Col. Ford & returned with him. I tried to keep out of the way, but the Colonel would not let me & had me talk with Ford & get all the facts & decided that we though best to be done. Ford took dinner with me & then rode back to his camp, near town. After retreat Col. Lee drew me out in a walk & we had another talk as to what had better be done. We have concluded to let the Troops remain where they are & ride to town in the morning. Have a correspondence with the authorities & if things can be arranged go in to Stonemans camp.

The riding was pleasant this morning, but warm after we got to camp in the canebrake. There is plenty of cane.

I will try again to ride my horse.

Wrote to Capt. Lee at Ringgold telling him what has occurred here & asking him to send me that letter of the Sec. of War to Gen. Houston, that I saw in a San Antonio paper.

CAMP 6 MILES BELOW EDINBURG SUN. APL. 8, 1860

We sent a note to Capt. Stoneman to meet us at Edinburg & left at 7 A.M., the Colonel, Capt. Brackett & Lt. Thomas with our wagons. It was less than three miles & we soon got to town. The boats were all on the Mexican side, no ferry man & no guard near to river—not a soul to be seen. Capt. Brackett sent a man up the river waving a white flag, but no one came. Capt. Smith said the ferry man had gone to breakfast & after awhile he came. We invited him over & he & the officers communicate with the authorities & they brought over the boat. Capt. Brackett, with Mr. Phelps as interpreter & two men crossed. In the mean time Capt. Stoneman & Lt. Kimmel, with some 20 men—came in. The wind & dust were terrible. In this we waited over five hours when three members of the ayuntiamiento came over with a written reply. We got one of Ford's men to read it to us & I dont think that it was a full answer to our demand.[8] They however in the long conversation promised all that we asked & even offered to send that man Jantes, who was badly wounded at Rio Grande City & is now dying of consumption by express at that time.[9] This was of course declined. They told us that their women could not go to the river for water & even with their children

---

[8] Francisco Zepeda, alcalde of New Reynosa, told Lee in person that "all good Mexicans" wanted the "most pleasant relations with a friendly people." Zepeda complained, however, of Ford's incursion into the town on April 4 and how Mexican customs officials, as well as the men and women of the town, were unable to go to the river for water, since they had repeatedly been fired on from the north bank. Zepeda to Lee, Apr. 8, 1860, *TTF*, 86–87.

[9] Ignacio Jantes is mentioned in Ford's April 5, 1860, letter to Heintzelman.

suffering from the want of it. Many of the families too had fled to the chapparal, as Mr. Phelps saw.

When the Capt. got over he found the troops under arms & the streets barricaded & every thing prepared to resist an attack. Troops were expected from Camargo & from Matamoros.

The conference at last ended & we went to Capt. Stoneman's & Lt. Kimmel's camp about six miles from town. We had sent our wagons on before & our tents were pitched. It is the most beautiful spot for a camp I have been at in Texas. We all took dinner with Capt. Stoneman. I wrote to Capt. Lee.[10]

Soon after we got into camp an express arrived from Ringgold with a letter from Gen. Garcia, that went up the day before from Matamoros, for Col. Lee complaining of this attack upon Reynosa.[11] The Rangers evidently intend to make war if they can.

BLANCO TEXAS MON. APL. 9, 1860

We invited all the officers & had dinner at Capt. Stoneman's camp & left at 3½ P.M. The translation was brought down of the letter of the Reynosa authorities & found satisfactory & an answer returned. We came about 14 miles to this place & encamped. I rode in the carriage with Col. Lee.

CARRISITO TEXAS TUES. APL. 10, 1860

We got off pretty early & got here about 12½ P.M. after stopping half an hour at Capt. Ford's camp, near the Bolsa.[12] He took us to the river & showed us the place & described the operations. We also drove by the Bastone. We met the wagon master Edgar with a train of provisions & another train from Ft. Brown with provisions. I got a letter from the Mex. consul saying that the letter I sent him had gone on & also one from Col. Lockridge with a large bundle of newspapers. The distance travelled to-day, to make up our distances should be 30. The weather has not been uncomfortably warm, nor was it at all dusty. We ought to be in Brownsville by 10 A.M. to-morrow.

FT. BROWN TEXAS WED. APL. 11, 1860

We were up & had breakfast before it was light. We left at 5 A.M. & were here at 8 A.M, at least 20 miles. We found Major Hunt in command.[13] Col. Lee

---

[10] There are no letters in Heintzelman's Letters Sent Book from April 3 to April 28, 1860.

[11] This letter is not in the Heintzelman papers or *TTF*.

[12] For Lee and Heintzelman's arrival in Brownsville, see Lee to Cooper, Apr. 11, 1860, LR, AGO, RG 94 (NA).

[13] Henry Jackson Hunt, a 1839 West Point graduate and a captain in the 2d

took Capt. Stoneman's old quarters & I am back in mine. Lt. Jones is in front of me & Lt. Burns in rear. I called & saw Mrs. Gilliam & then Mrs. Langdon & Mrs. Shannon. I also called to see Mrs. Robinson, but she was engaged. I dined with Mr. Galvan at Miller's. I dont think that I will go to Victors, though I believe that the other officers are there.[14]

I got a letter from Dr. Simmons dated 18 March. Col. May was there at Ft. Kearney. I also got some slips from Col. Lockridge. No letters from Margaret. I hope to get one by tomorrow's mail.

I find that my reports have killed the Governor's plans. I thought that I would be in time for him. He has published a kind of a proclamation. He has also sent a sort of commission & addressed Col. Lee to know whether the Texas troops will be any longer wanted. I told him no & I suppose that will be the reply. The Col. has since been in & has replied. He was looking for me to show his letter, but I was at dinner.

I wrote to Margaret, as the mail for the steamer leave[s] tomorrow.

Fort Brown Texas Thurs. Apl. 12, 1860

I wrote to Col. Lockridge & sent the letter by Mr. Phelps who left at 12 to-day, to take the steamer for New Orleans.

Col. Lee yesterday wrote to the commissioner that the Texas troops could not be mustered into U.S. service & that they were no longer wanted. They are ordered to Goliad to await orders. They expect to be mustered out. It is a great disappointment to them.

There are a great many strangers in town. Some came by water & others by land. They are said to belong to the order of Knights of the Golden Circle, whose objects seem to be the invasion of Mexico as aid of the Liberal Government.[15] It is said that there will soon be 2000 of them here. I dont see

---

Artillery, had been breveted a major for gallantry at the Battle of Chapultepec. Hunt became a brigadier general of volunteers and was praised for his conduct at Gettysburg and later during Grant's 1864–1865 Virginia Campaign, especially the Battle of Petersburg. Hunt died in February 1889. Heitman, *Historical Register*, 556.

[14] Victor's Restaurant was owned and operated by Victor Hasslaeur, a forty-two-year-old French immigrant. The restaurant boasted of a menu of "green peas, mushrooms, truffles, French sausage, Swiss and French cheese, American, Havana, and French Jellies, etc. Fine Claret, white Champagne and Sherry Wines, etc." 8th Census, Cameron County; *American Flag* (Brownsville), Jan. 6, Dec. 19, 1858; Mar. 16, 1859.

[15] The Knights of the Golden Circle was a secret, ardent, states' rights, pro-Southern organization. It appealed to those who feared the spread of Roman Catholicism and the influx of foreigners. It also brought together, especially in Brownsville, many men who sought adventure, fame, and fortune. With the creation of a slave empire in Mexico and the Caribbean as a major objective, the Knights were

how they can do anything, without the sanction of our Government. The Corpus mail brought me a letter from Margaret dated 25 March. I am afraid that Mr. Lathrop is not doing exactly right at the mines. I have not heard from him for some time & have had my doubts about him.

FT. BROWN TEXAS FRI. MARCH [APRIL] 13, 1860

It rained a little above here, but none with us. It has however been warm all day. Mr. Clark went with me to Matamoros. I went to see Gen. Garcia & delivered to him a communication from Col. Lee in reply to his & informing him what Lee came for. Gen. Garcia told me that Cortinas was seen 45 leagues back from here with his family—wife & two children & two men going west—to Burgos it was supposed.[16] I saw Mr. Hale. Col. Fitzpatrick was sick & I did not see him.

I got a bucket of blackbeans & gave some to Mrs. Gillam. I am going to tea at her house. I wish I could send some to Verde, though I suppose there will be some there this season.

There is a good deal of talk about the K.G.Cs. The town is filling with them. They have straggled into Matamoros already & behaving badly. They will give us trouble.

FT. BROWN SAT. APL. 14, 1860

Yesterday made five months since I left Verde. I took tea with Mrs. Gillam & Col. Lee & Lt. Thomas were there. We had some conversation about it & I gather that he will leave me here. I yesterday got the Secretary's letter to Gov. Houston. He says "An officer of great discretion & ability has been dispatched to take command of the department of Texas" etc. It is not so strong as I supposed. Col. Lee & I went & called on Langdons. Her sister Miss Moffatt is there & we met Judge & Mrs. Davis. Mr. Phelps got down too late for the steamer. My letter to Margaret went in the mail. He had one for Col. Lockridge.

Col. Lee got an answer from Matamoros. It dont amount to anything

---

particularly active in Texas, with San Antonio having two "castles." Roy Sylvan Dunn, "The KGC in Texas, 1860–1861," *SHQ*, 70 (Apr., 1967), 543–569; C. A. Bridges, The Knights of the Golden Circle: A Filibustering Fantasy," SHQ, 44 (Jan., 1941), 287–302; Ollinger Crenshaw, "The Knights of the Golden Circle: The Career of George Bickley," *American Historical Review*, 47 (Oct., 1941), 23–50; Galveston *Weekly News*, Feb. 16, 1861.

[16] José de Escandon's old colonial town of Burgos, Tamaulipas, is located on the coastal plain between the low-lying Sierra de Pamoranes and Sierra de San Carlos, seventy miles southwest of Matamoros.

special. I gave it to Lt. Thomas to have translated. Thomas & Graham were all day in Matamoros. Tomorrow will be the middle of the month & I have not yet the field return. I will jog the gentlemans memory tomorrow. I will not regret at all his leaving my staff. If he remains he would have to turn over a new leaf.

Victors Hossless the restaura[teurs'] daughter was married this evening in Matamoros to a young Spaniard who is a clerk in St. Roman's store, the largest in town.[17] They were married in Matamoros, because they cant be here, as she has a streak of black down her back & it is against the law in this state. The groom's friends are much provoked at the marriage. She is said by all to be a nice girl. We are all invited to the house this evening to a dance & supper. Col. Lee & I do not go. Several of the officers are going. It has been raining up the river & the river has risen three or four inches.

I went to Col. Lee & we made several calls in town.

FT. BROWN TEXAS SUN. APL. 15, 1860

I went to the early breakfast at Millers Hotel & then saw the Light Artillery, one section inspection. The horses are very fine. I went with Col. Lee to the Presbyterian Church & heard Mr. Chamberlain preach. We then made a call at Mr. Dyes.[18]

The Colonel's man is drunk again & the Colonel has gone to Victors to eat his meals. I went by Major Hunts invitation & dined there. We had a most miserable dinner.

This forenoon the Ranchero got up with the recruits, over 100 men for these three companies. Lt. Tipton brought them.[19] Lt. Platt of the Light Arty

---

[17] Thirty-eight-year-old José San Roman, a quiet self-made bachelor with merchandise in excess of $200,000, was the wealthiest man in South Texas. At the age of sixteen, San Roman left Bilbao, Spain, for New Orleans, where he spent ten years before making his way to Matamoros. Here he opened a mercantile house and in 1850 expanded to Brownsville with a store on East Elizabeth Street. Despite a low profile, San Roman exerted a powerful hand in Matamoros and Brownsville politics. His business records at the Center for the Study of American History are extensive. Robert Mario Salmon, "Don José San Roman as Brownsville Capitalist, 1822–1877," paper delivered at the Annual Meeting of the Texas State Historical Association, Apr., 1986.

[18] This is probably George Dye, who had been mayor of Brownsville since the smallpox epidemic of 1858. Dye was a founder of the Brownsville Lyceum for the advancement of literature and science. Kearney and Knopp, *Boom and Bust*, 90, 97; Bay, *Historic Brownsville*, 126.

[19] John Tipton, an 1856 West Point graduate, had recently been promoted to first lieutenant in the 3d Artillery. Tipton died in May 1861. Heitman, *Historical Register*, 963.

Compy also got up with the balance of the horses for this compy.[20] Lts. Harrison & Hertz got in with the prisoners to be tried. We will have a court tomorrow.

Weather has been warm & windy.

The wedding last night was a great affair. All the "elite" of Matamoros were there. It lasted till 4 A.M.—the dancing & drinking. There was plenty of the latter. The Corpus mail brought me no letters. I wrote to Margaret. I have got rid of being on this court.

FT. BROWN TEXAS MON. APL. 16, 1860

The steamer is in but no letters for me. The editor of the Brownsville Flag showed me a communication from the Sec. of War to the House about the disturbances on this frontier. Col. Brown's letter to Gen. Scott is the staple of it & he asserts several things which are not true. Why dont they take my reports? In time they will find that they are the only reliable ones.

The Court Martial met this morning & I am not on, much to my gratification. Capt. Smith of the Arizona is up & Mr. Phelps. The boat will leave Thursday. There is a report that Miramon has thrown up the Government in Mexico.[21] I spent the evening at the Mexican Consuls & he tells me that Miramon borrowed money on the faith of the Custom House bonds & that now his defeat before Vera Cruz will prevent his paying them or borrowing more. He cant keep his Army together.

The weather has been warm to-day & is so this evening.

FT. BROWN TEXAS TUES. APL. 17, 1860

This has been a warmer day than usual. I wrote to T. Wrightson & to Margaret & sent off the field returns for last month. I also wrote to Capt. S. Williams for an army register.[22] I got a letter from Capt. Stoneman.[23] All is quiet. There is a report that 50 men passed up beyond Laredo, supposed to be Cortinas men. It is not believed. I took tea at Lt. Gillams. There are 253 men in the garrison belonging to the three compys here.

---

[20]   Edward Russell Platt, thirty and a West Point graduate of the class of 1849, was a first lieutenant in the 2d Artillery. Platt saw action at First Bull Run and Fredericksburg during the Civil War and died in June of 1884. The 1860 Cameron County census lists Platt's birthplace as "unknown." Ibid., 794. See also 8th census, Cameron County.

[21]   Heintzelman uses "throw up" to mean abandonment or to give up.

[22]   From Maine, Seth Williams, West Point class of 1842, was a brevet captain in the 1st Artillery. A decorated Civil War veteran, Williams died in March 1866. Heitman, *Historical Register*, 1042.

[23]   Stoneman to Heintzelman, Apr. 16, 1860, HP.

FT. BROWN TEXAS WED. APL. 18, 1860

Another warm day. The passengers left this morning at 10 O'Clock for the Brazos to take the steamer. Lt. Tipton, Mr. Phelps, Mr. Moses, Victor etc. Col. Lee, Major Hunt & I breakfasted with Lt. Langdon. I asked him last night for a report of occurrences at the Bolsa & I to-day answered Major Ford's letter about the affair at Rio Grande City.[24] The Rangers will all be down [with] Dr. Jourdan & Major Tobin.

I borrowed Brook's History of the War with Mexico & am reading it.[25]

To-day in trying to hoist the top [of the flagstaff] to take out the chuck & lower it, it was raised too high & fell over, but fortunately hurting no one & not breaking. It has been repaired, the havelyards move[d] & the flag was flying again.

The Brownsville Flag today gives it to Col. Brown for his foolish letter to Gen. Scott. He deserves it all.

FORT BROWN TEXAS THURS. APL. 19, 1860

It blew very hard last night & continued all day. The steamer is not yet unloaded & has of course not left. Lts. Kimmel & Owens came in this afternoon. Col. Lee dont like their coming. There is a report that Cortinas has crossed above with 400 men—Mexicans, Indians, & Negroes. There are even some who believe it. The Corpus mail brought me a letter from Margaret dated Apl. 5. She has had an attack of fever. The children are well. I also got a

---

[24] This particular letter is not in Heintzelman's Letters Sent Book. Powhatan Jordan had accused Ford, probably in a San Antonio newspaper, of disobeying Heintzelman's orders during the Battle of Rio Grande City. Ford to Heintzelman, Apr. 18, 1860, HP.

[25] Paso de Ovejos is on the road between Vera Cruz and the National Bridge before Jalapa. Heintzelman, having left Vera Cruz on September 11, 1847, with six companies of the 2d Infantry, many of them recruits, had gone into camp at the pass and posted sentinels when he was attacked by guerrillas. The enemy, Brooks wrote, "poured a destructive fire into the camp which disconcerted the raw troops." Heintzelman described the attack in his journal. At 2 p.m., just as he had retired to his tent for the evening, the camp was fired into from a graveyard on a nearby hill. Heintzelman ran out of his tent only to injure his foot on an exposed tent peg. One recruit was killed in the attack. In another chapter, Brooks detailed the American attack on Humantla, halfway between Perote and Puebla. Here, Heintzelman, with six companies, was ordered to attack Gen. Santa Anna's forces. Prior to Heintzelman's attack, Brook discussed in some detail the demise of Capt. Samuel H. Walker, whose death by a sniper caused American forces to plunder the town. Nathan Covington Brooks, *A Complete History of the Mexican War, 1846–1848* (Chicago: Rio Grande Press, 1965), 455; Bauer, *Mexican War*, 330; HJ, Sept. 14, Oct. 10, 11, 1847; Apr. 27, 1860.

letter from T. Wrightson. Cheever is a swindler. He wont return my stock & says I guaranteed his stock at $50 a share & it has not been so. He guaranteed some he purchased me to give him to sell to his friends at $50 a share & without my authority & I afterwards accepted it. I got a number of printed orders from Army Hd. Qrs.

Ft. Brown Fri. Apl. 20, 1860

Warm to-day, but not so windy. Mer. was 86°. I had a long visit from Judge Davis. He wants to write an article for the papers & I gave him items. We, Col. Lee & I, had a visit from the custom house officers about special protection on the river. There is a report that the Liberals have again been defeated near San Luis Potosi.

The Mexicans are putting out extra sentinels to watch for the K.G.Cs The latter had a meeting last night here in town. Judge Davis thinks that their expedition will be abandoned for the present. It is said these have 500, landed at Corpus Christi. The general information here is that the thing will be postponed.

Fort Brown Sat. Apl. 21, 1860

The colonel is full of reports about Cortinas. The report now is that he is half a days march opposite Las Ruses with 300 men. I dont believe it. There is also a report that 500 K.G.Cs have landed at Corpus & that they have Arty. I wrote to T. Wrightson & to Bartlett, about Cheever. In the afternoon I went with Galvan & Clark to the funeral of La Sra. Da. Ursula Garcia de Martinez, who died yesterday. She was a sister of Gen. Garcia & Clark married another sister, but dont live with her. We did not go to the house but followed the procession to the church & then to the grave. There was a long ceremony at the church. The grave yard has some five tombs. I met several Mexican gentlemen I knew. The weather was warm yesterday. We stopped in at Mr. Hales. We met Judge Garland's bros. wife & daughter there & saw them home. The girls are very well behaved.

Ft. Brown Texas Sun. Apl. 22, 1860

Major Hunt had four of his guns out at inspection. We had a number of Rangers & citizens there to see the inspection. The guns are two 12 & 2—6 pdr—the Louis Napoleon pattern. They are quite light. We also took a look through the Quarters. The citizens were struck with the order & regularity. There are no doubt the finest horses ever seen in Texas, in one company.

After the inspection I commenced a letter to Margaret. I went with Col. Lee & Robinson to the Methodist Church. There was none in the

Presbyterian & all nearly attended. The room was quite full & nearly all ladies. I had no idea that there were so many in town. When I arrived here not one was to be seen on the streets. I was quite surprised to see Mr. Adams our Verde clergyman in the pulpit. He did not preach but was an assistant. After service I stopped to speak to him. I came home & finished my letter, then went to Galvan's & there found all the officers nearly amusing each other with juggling & other tricks. At three Mr. Galvan & I crossed to Matamoros to dine with Mr. Hale. We just escaped a heavy storm of dust & wind & then rain & thunder & lightning. It rained pretty hard for near half an hour. It was much needed & will make the corn crop. In some of the gardens I saw corn over six feet high.

Col. Fitzpatrick is suffering from rheumatism & was not at dinner. After dinner Mr. Hale & I took a drive about town. It is quite a considerable town & crowded with people. Since it was made a free city it has much improved. We then called on Mrs. Garrate a lady I met here & saw one of the Miss Garlands there. We were going to the Theater, but Mr. Hale thought it best for us to wait until the next Sunday. As he is the best judge of what had best be done, we concluded to wait. This rain will make beautiful weather.

Ft. Brown Texas Mon. Apl. 23, 1860

This has been quite a warm day. In the afternoon a fine breeze sprung up & made it more pleasant. Last nights mail only brought me a couple of Mining Magazines & a statement on the arbitration case with Colt—our side. I dont see on what he hinges his claim. I went in the afternoon with Col. Lee & we called on Judge Bigelow & Mr. Galvan & on Mr. & Mrs. Viscayan—or Victor's daughter. As we were on our way home we met Mrs. Gillam & the Langdon's & went home with the latter & staid to tea.

I saw Mr. Trevino about reports Cortinas being on the river again. I did not believe it, but Col. Lee's uneasy. I met a man this evening from above & am now more than ever convinced that the reports are untrue. The Rangers circulate them to keep up the disturbances on the frontier.

I here had a long conversation with Col. Lee & think that I will get away from here in a few days.

The District Court commenced its sessions to-day, only one juror present.

Ft. Brown Texas Tues. Apl. 24, 1860

I met Col. Lee this morning to see the order he had prepared preparatory to leaving. He wished my opinion. He proposed leaving on Thursday & Thomas & I to go along & to return by land. He is a little uneasy about these reports, but I dont believe them. I met Col. Fitzpatrick at Galvans. The steamer is in & the mail arrived this afternoon. I got a paper from Lockridge.[26] He has had a difficulty with Gen. Walker & backed him out. I got a letter from Lt. Washington, but no others. I called with Langdon & saw the Miss Smiths. I called at Judge Davis's this evening.

FORT BROWN TEXAS WED. APL. 25, 1860

Quite warm this morning, but about norm, wind north & a shower rain. Much cooler now.

---

[26] From the St. Charles Hotel in New Orleans on March 15, 1860, Lockridge wrote a "private" letter telling Heintzelman that he had telegraphed friends in Washington, inquiring into what course the government "would pursue as to the Rio Grande affairs, etc." Lockridge's sources had answered in "strong terms" that the "Buchanan Cabinet intended taking the most energetic steps to chastise Cortina and [his] sympathizers if they had to pursue him into Mexico." Recruits from as far away as the East Coast and Utah were to be sent to the Rio Grande. "This portends some grand movement but I fear Old Buch wants the nerve to do any thing," Lockridge wrote. "Companies are forming in all the counties in Texas and all the Southern States to aid Texas if the general government fails to demand Cortina and his Mexican friends," Lockridge went on to say.

Two weeks later from the St. Charles Hotel, Lockridge told Heintzelman that he had read "with much pleasure and was rejoiced to find your forces had again paid Cortina a visit upon Mexican soil. I hope they have had sufficient cause to remain upon the west side." Lockridge assured Heintzelman that volunteers were "ready to sail if required to your aid" and that the recruits were "drilling and preparing."

Two weeks later, Lockridge was still at the St. Charles and wrote Heintzelman in reply to a letter Lockridge had received from the major. Lockridge praised Heintzelman for having been "bold and vigorous" and having "performed wonders" on the Rio Grande, even if the "fossil government" in Washington was not fully appreciative. Lockridge admitted in a "private" section of the letter that he had been duped by the Knights of the Golden Circle into believing that President Buchanan and his entire cabinet supported the Knights "heart and soul and that they had plenty of money arms & munitions of war to carry out their intentions and proposed plans." Assured that New Orleans steamship companies would "transport men and material to Mexico and that an agreement had been reached with the Juárez government allowing such an army into Mexico," Lockridge had investigated further only to realize the whole scheme to be a hoax. An individual identified only as "g" had become suspicious and asked for proof. Lockridge then realized the entire plan was one big "humbug" and that he would "have nothing to do with any expedition . . . I don't know what g shall do. g may go down to the frontier as soon as g [is] through with Walker who is, g regrets to say, showing the white feather." "I have spent a great portion of my life filibustering and about forty thousand dollars," Lockridge concluded. Lockridge to Heintzelman, Mar. 15, 1860; Lockridge to Heintzelman, Apr. 1, 1860; Lockridge to Heintzelman, Apr. 12, 1860, all in HP.

I went yesterday to see about having a ster[e]oscape made & Mr. Rand tried one & several photographs.[27] I went again this morning & had more undertaken. He has not finished them so I cant say how he has succeeded. Some ice came up to-day & we had an iced cobbler. I saw Col. Lee this morning & I believe that he has determined to wait a few days longer. I would not be surprised if we did not leave before Monday. The mail leaves for the boat in the morning & I must write. At dinner we had cucumbers. I will miss the vegetables. The Court Martial adjourned to-day & the corn is up, so that all the officers who dont belong to the Post will leave tomorrow—I suppose. I see that Col. McKnight, the Texas commissioner, is back. I suppose that the Rangers will now leave.

After tea I called & made a short visit at the Mexican Consul's & then came home & wrote to Margaret & Lt. Washington—that we would probably leave here on Monday at fastest. We have had thunder & lightning & it is now raining.

FORT BROWN TEXAS THURS. APL. 26, 1860

It rained all night & all day. A train of wagons which came down with Lt. Owens loaded with corn & left to-day. He & Lt. Kimmel left in the afternoon. Judge Davis called & showed me an article he has written to the Galveston Civilian in reply to Gen. Scott's letter found in Col. Brown's report. It is more full than the article in the Flag.

FT. BROWN TEXAS FRI. APL. 27, 1860

The Rangers moved from up the river to Rancho Viejo 7 miles from here on the way to the Nueces. I suppose that we may now consider them on their way from this frontier.

It has not rained any to-day & has turned quite cool since late in the afternoon. I had fire all day yesterday & this morning. I took tea with Major Hunt. I spent the evening at Judge Davis's.

Lt. Hartz & Harrison left this morning. The mail brought me the order detailing Lts. Reynolds & Thomas for the Recruiting Service. Thomas wants to leave on this boat. He has to go to Verde to settle his accounts. The steamer is not gone. I finished reading Brook's War with Mexico. It is full of errors where I know. I dont know where he got his account of my affairs at the Paso de los Ovejos, as I made no report.[28]

---

[27] C. A. Rand was a thirty-two-year-old "artist" from Maine. 8th Census, Cameron County. David Haynes, *Catching Shadows: A Directory of 19th-Century Texas Photographers* (Austin: Texas State Historical Association, 1993), 90.

[28] See footnote 25, this chapter.

FORT BROWN TEX. SAT. APL. 28, 1860

Quite cold last night. Warm to-day, but cool again towards night. The river commenced rising early in the morning & has risen about four feet. I have been to Mr. Rand's the Stere[o]scopes & he has some excellent ones of me. I left him coloring one. I am told it is excellent.

I went with Mr. Clark over to Matamoros late in the afternoon. We tried to find a silversmith & there is but one in the town & he has nothing. We got home before dark. I wrote a note to Capt. Stoneman & sent it up by one of his Sergts. We heard in Matamoros that Cortinas is near San Luis Potosi with 900 men, but the person only saw 60. I have no doubt he has left this river. The steamer has not left yet. Wrote to Dr. Summers.

FORT BROWN TEXAS MON. APL. 30, 1860

Yesterday was quite a pleasant day. I went with Col. Lee to Mr. Chamberlin's church. Before church Mr. Trevino came in the garrison & I went with him to see Col. Lee. He handed him a letter from his brother the Gov. of Tamaulipas. He says it is a diplomatic affair & he has sent it to the Supreme Government. But that he has already given orders to apprehend or disperse these men. The Counsel told us that 16 of them are now in prison in Matamoros.

In the evening I went to Matamoros to the Theater. Capt. Stoneman got in, in the morning. He, Lts. Graham, & Thomas & Mr. Galvan went. The Theater is a poor affair. We had to walk back to the ferry. The road is not dusty & a bright moon. The strong man of the company is a deserter from Capt. Brackett's compy, deserted at Edinburg.

I got a letter from Margaret last night & answered it before I went to bed. I wrote to her that we would no doubt leave on Wednesday & to meet me in S. Antonio.

I saw Col. Lee this morning & he has settled to leave Wednesday morning. The steamer is not out yet, but my letter went by land. The Rangers I believe leave tomorrow. There was muster in the garrison this morning.

I had my ster[e]oscope taken last week. I got it this morning & some views. It looks very well.

I went with Col. Lee this afternoon & we called at Mr. Trevino's the Counsel, Mr. Dyer, Mr. Chamberlin's the Presbyterian clergyman, & Judge Bigelows.[29] We stopped at Galvans & there met Col. Fitzpatrick & Mr.

---

[29] Israel Bonaparte Bigelow, a forty-seven-year-old Connecticut lawyer and a beef contractor during the Mexican War, had been elected the first chief justice of Cameron

Gilligan. They told us of some changes in Matamoros, against Carbajal, though still Liberal. I did not exactly understand the merits of the case. The steamer mail got in a little after dusk. I got a roll of papers & a long letter from Col. Lockridge. I like his sentiments. He gave me also some interesting items about the K.G.Cs. & Gen. Walker.

The Charleston convention has done nothing yet & scarcely will. Our river is falling still, though slowly.

The members of the Dramatic compy arrived. I suppose that they will open this week. I got from Langdon a report of the attack on the Ranchero on the 4th of Feb. I give it to Col. Ford to take a copy & will send a copy to Gen. Scott, for Col. Brown's edification.

County in 1848 and the first mayor of Brownsville in 1850, only to be ousted six months later. In November 1863, when anarchy threatened the town following the Confederate evacuation, Bigelow was forced to call on Cortina, who had seized power in Matamoros, to help restore order. Cortina calmly refused. Thompson, *Juan Cortina*, 30; 8th Census, Cameron County.

❦ May 1860 ❧

"I felt that I had done something for the town."

———•·✦·•———

FORT BROWN TEXAS TUES. MAY 1ST, 1860

Warm but pleasant day. Went to Matamoros & saw Col. Fitzpatrick & Mr. Hale & took leave of them. Next went to see Gen. Garcia. He told me he had just received a letter from Reynosa, that Cortinas was on the river again & he had sent for Mr. Trevino the Counsel. He handed me the letter & the consul came in. Cortinas was said to be at the Gancho rancho, near the river & about 40 miles above. He had been seen with ten armed men going into a "labor."[1] Gen. Garcia's plan was to press 20 horses, buy 10 & take 15 of the Matamoros home guards & he want[s] 50 of our men. I told him his plan would not do. Every one would know before they left town. That we had plenty of men up the river & all we wanted from them was a guide & letters to the authorities. He said he would write & also send an officer at 3 P.M. to our side.

I came home with the Consul & we saw Col. Lee & I told [him] my plan. He sent for Capt. Stoneman & gave him the necessary orders. He is to cross tomorrow night with parts of his & Kimmel's company & send an order to Capt. Brackett to cross at Reynosa with part of his & Eagle's company to join him. He left with two Mexican officers about 4 P.M.

Lt. & Mrs. Gillam, Miss Smith, Col. Lee & myself took tea at Lt. Langdons. I then came home & wrote to Margaret. We dont go tomorrow.

FORT BROWN TEXAS WED. MAY 2, 1860

Pleasant morning. The mail dont close till tomorrow. I got the order yesterday stationing the troops on this frontier & relieving me of the Brownsville Expedition. Capt. Dawson has his leave, 2 mos. & apply for six. He goes down

---

[1] A "labor" is a cultivated field.

to-day. I believe Lt. Thomas wants to go & I have consented. I would try to go too in the boat, but I have written to Margaret to meet me in S. Antonio. Lt. Thomas is going in the morning. I have just written a letter to send by the land mail, to make the matter sure, as the steamer may be delayed—to Margaret.

I went this evening with Col. Lee & called at Capt. Smith's. We then took tea with Mrs. Gillam.

I have written an order relinquishing the command of the Brownsville Expedition.

Ft. Brown Thurs. May 3, 1860

Weather not too warm to-day. Had a few drops of rain in the morning. I went & started one letter to Margaret, by the Corpus mail & the other by the steamer. The mail this evening brought me no letters from home. I got a letter from T. Wrightson & one from Mr. Allen about Sta. Rita S.M. stock asking me to pay up my subscription on 476 shares of stock, by dividend on my Sonora stock.[2] This is rather a strange dividend. I always understood that the shares were unassessable. Mr. Wrightson offered to advance the money. I have no idea of how much & wrote to him to inform me.

This is Mr. Gillams—birthday & we all were there to a supper. Mr. Thomas was there a little while & then left to go to the Brazos to meet the boat. We have no news from above yet, but I hope it will be here by morning. I am heartily tired of waiting & will insist on going in a day or two. Mr. Galvan went down with Lt. Thomas.

Lt. Platt was thrown as he was mounting his horse & put his left shoulder out of place.

Fort Brown Texas Fri. May 4, 1860

Not so warm to-day. I got up this morning quite sick. The supper did not agree with me. I am now nearly over it. Capt. Littleton's compy Rangers left Wednesday & Capt. Ford's to-day.

Mr. Galvan went with Lt. Thomas last night. He & Lt. Langdon got back at 1 p.m. Lt. T. just managed to get on board the steamer. He will be in San Antonio Sunday evening. I called at Judge Davis's this evening.

I am invited to a ball in Matamoros tomorrow. The people up the river are complaining already, because the Rangers here left. A fellow at San Rosario, says they are crossing cattle near his place & fired on one of his men.

---

[2] This was Thomas H. C. Allen, a member of the board of directors of the company. North, *Samuel Peter Heintzelman*, 39.

FORT BROWN SAT. MAY 5, 1860

Very windy & dusty this morning. This has been a long day to me & not a word from Stoneman. I have no idea of where we will go. I saw Mr. Trevino & he told me that he saw a gentleman from Reynosa, who left two days ago. He heard of Cortinas at various places with from 16 to 40 men. I presume that Capt. Stoneman has no reliable information of where he is & wont cross.

All the officers were invited to a ball in Matamoros for tonight. I did not go. I stopped at Mrs. Gillams to tea & went with her & her husband to the theater this evening. I did not care to go, having seen enough of Matamoros. It did very well for a small town & the people were well behaved. It is cool & pleasant this evening.

FT. BROWN SUN. MAY 6, 1860

Major Hunt, Lts. Robinson & Burns, with Mr. Clark, went to the ball. They got home about one A.M. The latter was locked out & slept in the garrison. They had a very pleasant ball. There were a great many ladies.

This morning I went with Major Hunt & Mr. Graham all through the inspection of the Light Battery. After inspection a while Major Hunt & I started for the Catholic Church & got in about five minutes before it closed. He took dinner with me. This evenings mail brought me no letters. I fear Margaret has quit writing, expecting me home. The Corpus mail goes out in the morning. I have written to Margaret & enclose one to Mary. I tried to persuade the Colonel to start tomorrow, but he dont want to go now until we hear from above. I told him there is nothing to hear or we would. Tuesday will be a week, when Graham must be back. Lt. Thomas must be in S. Antonio tonight & in two more in Verde. But I suppose that all his hurry was to get away from here. He wont surprise me if he stays a week in S.A. I went with Col. Lee & called upon Capt. King & his wife. She is a daughter of parson Chamberlin. Capt. King had a boat on the river during the war & owns boats here now.

All the officers here then know him.

It has been windy & dusty to-day.

The supper the other night at Lt. Gillams made me quite sick & I am not entirely over it yet. Lt. Platt is out of bed again, but it will be sometime before he is quite well.

LOS INDIOS RANCHO MON. MAY 7, 1860

Capt. Stoneman & Lt. Graham got back at day light. As I went to breakfast I met them. Cortinas had been at the Gancho rancho, but was gone when they got up. He came down the river to a rancho 7 miles from Matamoros & drove off some of his stock & has gone back beyond Burgos.

I immediately went to see Col. Lee. He could not decide to leave, so I told him I would go & left at 2½ P.M. I was particularly anxious to go as some of the citizens of B'ville at the eleventh hour, were preparing a party [for] Major Ford. As I felt that I had done something for the town & no one had recognized it I did not care to remain though I very much esteem Major Ford. There was also a devotion party for Mr. Chamberlin. Capt. Stoneman was to see Gen. Garcia & I suppose Col. Lee will leave in the morning as well as Major Ford. But as my wagons were loaded & I was ready I determined to start alone, but told them they could easily overtake me the next day, or the day after.

Lt. Langdon insisted on my taking a glass of Champagne with him & Mrs. Langdon put me up a nice lunch. As to the citizens of Brownsville, I dont feel under the slightest obligation to the town, although every one said they were so sorry I was leaving & how much I had done for them. It is now over five months since I entered their barricaded streets.

Our wagons had about an hour start & drove so fast that I did not overtake them until we got to where we encamped. At Rancho Viejo they took the lower road & after going some distance found from some Mexicans that they were wrong & struck off through the prairie for a middle road. I kept Howe & Williams back to start with me. If we had been fifteen minutes later we would have missed the wagons & I suppose [would] have had to encamp out, without anything but looking across the prairie we saw the wagons & overtaking the Mexicans learned what was wrong. We will have difficulty in getting back to the right road. It was sundown when we overtook them. We rode fast, have [sic] the time [at] a gallop & were 3½ hours on the road. It must be 18 or 20 miles. A man asks 3$ to put us on the right road.

Rancho San Aguitas[3] Tues. May 8, 1860

Anniversary of battle of Palo Alto & yesterday we crossed Palo Alto prairie.

We started at 5½ A.M. I would not give the $3.00 but rather go back as far as Rancho Viejo, as he says there is no road, but one we can scarcely find across the prairie. He says it is 4 & then that it is 8 leagues.

We did not go far when we struck a road turning in the proper direction

---

[3] Rancho San Aguitas was on the Brownsville-San Patricio Road just north of Laguna Larga and south of the Arroyo Colorado, on the northeast outskirts of what is today the city of Harlingen.

& I determined to venture. We soon came to some Ranches, but the reports were not very encouraging. At the third rancho we met a more intelligent man, who had lived in Brownsville. He said he would go with us part of the way. We travelled one hour before we met him & then with him an hour & a half. He could not go any farther, but got us a boy who would guide us across. I paid the two $2.50 & much more cheerfully than I would have paid the first men. This man that guided us so cheerfully said pay him what I pleased & the boy insisted on 75 cts. for his services. The road most of the way wound through prairies & occasionally amongst mesquite & cactus. We drove pretty fast & our mules were very tired. We struck the main road at Los Fresnos. We rode two hours more to this rancho & the man says it is two leagues from the river. I dont think that it is but little over one. It was cloudy cool & pleasant on the prairie but warm & dusty on the main road. I stopped here, as our animals are tired & there is grass. I paid 37½ cts for well water. I expect the Col. & Major Ford here.

Camp near Las Animas[4] Wed. May 9th, 1860

Anniversary of battle of Resaca de la Palma. Col. Lee & Major Ford did not come up. They may have taken the wrong road. They wont overtake me now.

We started at 5½ A.M. & found it 4 miles to the river. We were detained 40 min. ferrying. The weather has been delightful. We had a fine cool breeze nearly in our faces & cloudy most of the day. The rain has been abundant along the road & no dust. The corn everywhere looks well & the grass. Everything looks fresh & green. I think that we are within a mile of Los Animas & if so we have come 34 miles. We got here about ½ past 2 P.M. I would have stopped sooner, but tomorrow we have 27 miles to do & the weather & most of the road to-day have been very fine. We have to make long drives to make up for our two short ones, or at least on our direction. Our load lightens every day. I think that we will have considerable sand tomorrow. We came in a good deal of doubt to-day. About 10 miles from here our road leaves the main road & it is ahead imperceptible. The only trace I could discover was the trace of our wagons when we passed here last fall. We are encamped near [a] Mott with some water & good grass & a very fine pleasant breeze.

Las Muguin Thurs. May 10, 1860

Last night was cold & dew heavy. We left at 5¼ A.M. We encamped about a mile from Los Animas. We had some trouble to find the road after passing

---

[4] See footnote 2, December 1859 chapter.

the rancho. We met two Americans, who are travelling with one horse & have lost him. One was out looking for him. They are bound for the Rio Grande, evidently to join the K.G.C.'s. I put a damper on his prospects.

One of the men this moment reported the arrival of Col. Lee. It is now 7½ P.M. & his first wagon has got in. The others are two miles back. He has come about 36 miles to-day. He left Tuesday but took the wrong road at Rancho Viejo, following us & the Texas Commissioner. He soon found his mistake & struck my trail & got the same boy to guide him in to Los Fresnos. Major Ford is still behind & stopped at Taylor's well to make coffee. He will be in soon.

The road to-day has been very heavy. We got a little poor water & enough for our mules at Taylor's wells, 15 miles this side of Las Animas. There are several salt ponds & this side a few spots with fresh water. At one we watered our horses. After that I pushed on & got here [at] Los Mujers at 2 P.M. & our wagons, the mules very tired at 3½. When we passed here last fall we opened these wells, but they were brackish. The water now is excellent. We found enough to water our animals. The grass is poor.

The Commissioner is some where back on the road. He took the wrong one at Rancho Viejo. We have all been unfortunate in our start. I suppose it can all be laid to my teamsters taking the wrong road. We had a few gnats this forenoon & it was quite warm until near noon when a strong breeze sprung up.

After I had my supper sometime Major Ford arrived. He had had his supper & I furnished him blankets, coffee, & bread.

SALVADOR CAVASOS RANCHO[5] FRI. MAY 11, 1860

Our men overslept themselves & we did not get off quite so early. I rode in his ambulance with Col. Lee. We travelled 13 miles to the wells near Sta. Rosa & watered. We then drove in & arrived here at 2 P.M. The whole distance is 30 miles. Water is very scarce & scarcely any grass here. There is one well here with tolerably fair drinking water, but that for our animals is quite salt[y] & scarce enough of that for them. What a country to live in. Two women I saw here belie the miserable country. The[y] cant well be fatter. This Cavasos

---

[5] Sabas Cavazos, age fifty-one and a half-brother to Cortina, was a member of the Brownsville political establishment and one of the few Tejanos to serve on petit and grand juries in Cameron County in the antebellum era. Cavazos refused to join Cortina in 1859 and even befriended and assisted Ford and the Rangers. Ford would later allege that Cavazos, one of the wealthiest men in Cameron County, gave Porfirio Diaz $50,000 in 1876 to have Cortina removed from the border. Ford, *Rip Ford's Texas*, 281, 412; 1850 and 1860 Agricultural Census, Cameron County.

is a half brother of Cortinas.[6] I saved some of his property on the river from being burned.

The road to-day for the first 13 miles, to what I was told is called Bulverte, is very sandy. This side is much better. They call it two leagues to San[ta] Gertrud[i]s rancho but "Quien sabe." We have had a fine breeze to-day & I did not suffer from heat. At San Gertrudes we will try to take a shorter road to the Casas Blancas. If so we there part with Major Ford.

BANQUETE TEXAS SAT. MAY 12, 1860

We were up quite early this morning. Before I got up I heard that some of our mules were missing. We at last found them two miles from camp. We got [a] trace of them & I left with Col. Lee in his ambulance. We drove 7 miles to Capt. King's ranche San Gertrudes. Here we stopped intending to take the road by Casa Blanca, but learned that it is rough & may only save half a dozen miles. Col. Lee very reluctantly gave it up. We stopped on the road & watered. Water is very scarce & bad. Most of the usual places are dry.

We reached here at 2½ P.M. 23 miles from King's rancho, or 29 miles for the days march. King's rancho is on a rise & is quite a comfortable place. The road to-day has been fine & a very strong breeze from the S. East. The water here is so muddy it is not fit to drink.

I dined with Col. Lee & Major Ford. I put up a tent for the latter & furnished him with bedding. The Rangers are encamped about 5 miles down this creek. They go on to San Patricio in the morning. The Commissioner is still missing. I suppose when he found himself on the wrong road that he turned back to Brownsville, or across the way we went. This would put him at least a day behind us.

GROVERS RANCHO LEFT BANK NUECES SUN. MAY 13, 1860

It is six months to-day since I left Verde. We left Banquete at 5½ A.M. rode 8 miles to the Nueces & waited till 8 A.M. then crossed by fording, passed through San Patricio & arrived at this ranche at 12 P.M. & the wagons at 2 P.M. distance 26 miles. The road on the other side very good & pretty good on this. Some sand, but plenty of grass. Have a fine camp. I rode with Col. Lee in the ambulance. We part with Major Ford at our camp at the Banquete. He waited for his company & goes on to Goliad. A fine breeze & cloudy. River only knee deep to horses.

---

[6] Heintzelman may have confused Sabas Cavazos with Juan Nepomuceno Cavazos, who with 539,000 acres, was the largest landowner in Cameron County.

One mile of Sulphur Mon. May 14, 1860

A rain shower at day light. All the forenoon cloudy & warm. Left at 5¼ A.M. & arrived here at 10 A.M., the wagons at 12½ P.M. We make it about 9 mls. to opposite Fort Merrill & 12 to here—22. Road pretty good. We are encamped on a fine pond.

Camp one mile beyond Rockey Tue. May 15, 1860

We started at 5¼ A.M. The ambulance reached the Weedy at 8 A.M. We estimate the distance at 15 miles. We found a little water & stopped 3/4 of an hour. At the Rockey which we reached in three hours & call 15 miles, the water is gone & none drinkable in less than 4 miles. We drove a mile to a pond but the water is so bad our animals will scarce touch it & the grass is very poor. We preferred this to going off our road four miles. It is now 20 miles to water & that on the San Antonio river. By the road I went I am now 55 miles from S. Antonio but by crossing the river at Grays ferry 8 miles can be saved.[7] We might drive in tomorrow, but I suppose the Colonel wont. We can get in the next day by 9 or 10 A.M. easily. I will be greatly disappointed if Margaret is not in San Antonio.

It has been cloudy all day & a good breeze most of the time.

Gray's ferry on S. Antonio river Wed. May 16, 1860

We had a few drops of rain last evening & some thunder in the night. We made an early start—5 A.M. Stopped & watered this side Calavares rancho 18 miles, on the San Antonio river.[8] We then drove on & arrived here at 11 A.M., 10 miles further in all about 28 miles. The banks are steep, but the ford good. We have had but little breeze & the afternoon is quite warm. I went into the river & took a bath.

Before we crossed the Arroyo Colorado, I saw two deer yesterday. This morning we saw near a hundred. We are now about 18 miles from S. Antonio & will be in by 9 A.M, I hope.

San Antonio Texas Thurs. May 17, 1860

I am awaken this morning by hearing the men getting ready for breakfast & having them say that it was 3 A.M. They soon called me & we had breakfast by candle light & were off before sunrise. We reached here about 20 min after

---

[7] The ferry was probably owned by James Gray, a local landowner for whom Graytown was named.

[8] The Calaveras Ranch, probably a corruption of calvillo, was on the north bank of the San Antonio River in northwestern Wilson County.

7 A.M. I was disappointed not to find Margaret here, but the officers told me that they expected Lt. Thomas here to-day & that she would be along.

I went up to the office & saw Capt. Withers & several of the officers. Capt. & Mrs. McLean are still here. Lt. Blake, Capt. Reynolds & Capt. & Mrs. Lee, but to leave to-day. I went & called upon Mrs. Lee. I met the Captain afterwards.

I had gone to dinner when Capt. McLean came & told me that Dr. Foard & Lt. Thomas had just arrived with Margaret & the children. I at once went & met them in their room. Margaret & the children all look very well.

Last night we had a Ladie's [sic] supper party at the Menger House. We were all invited. Margaret commenced dressing but was too tired & did not go. I went & she went to the door & looked on. The party was well attended & the ladies looked well. They had a supper & it did not break up until 3 A.M. I went to bed at 2 P.M.

Dr. & Mrs. Abadie are here. Capt. King etc. etc. The afternoon & evening were warm.

The stage came in soon after I got here & brought Ehrenberg from N. York on his way to Arizona. I got at the Qr. M. letters from Solon.

San Antonio Texas Fri. May 18, 1860

This has been a warm day. I went to the offices & saw the officers. I also met a number at the Hotel & so passed all the forenoon. I am going to dinner at Major Howard's tomorrow. I met Major Vinton in his office & we took tea at his house. We saw Mr. Walker of the Rifles there.[9] We had quite a number of calls later in the afternoon.

San Antonio Sat. May 19, 1860

I dont feel at all well to-day. Margaret was quite unwell last night. Lt. Blake left in the forenoon, expecting to overtake Capt. Lee & his wife. I called at the offices after writing my reports to Hd. Qrs. & also sent a reply to Col. Brown's letter to Gen. Scott. I rode with the Doctor (Foard) & Margaret to the dentists & left them there. In the afternoon I dined at Major Howard's with Major Vinton, Capt. McLean, & Major Colqueen. Mrs. Howard was at the table. Had a very fine dinner & sat three hours. I got two letters from Solon, one from Mr. Howe, Wrightson, Col. Kennet[t] & also one from Margaret dated Apl. 27 which all had been to Brownsville & back to Verde. Warm & dusty. The children of the schools had a picnic at the head spring of

---

⁹ This is probably John George Walker, a captain in the Mounted Rifles who later became a Confederate major general. Warner, *Generals in Gray*, 319–320.

S. Antonio river. Mary drove out with Capt. King & Lt. Thomas. Charles has been sick all day.

San Antonio Sun. May 20, 1860

A fine breeze all day, but warm. I dont feel at all well & have not been out of the house, in fact lying down most of the day. I have not answered all my letters.

San Antonio Wed. May 23, 1860

I read my letters & find that Mapes has been turned out & now says that he has almost paid me the principal in interest & as I understand him, wishes me to forgive him the principal. He speaks of difficulties in collecting it. Nothing but bad luck. I wont agree to any compromise of that kind.

The weather here is very warm, dusty & uncomfortable. I have forgotten what I did Monday. Yesterday we drove out & did more shopping & then went & made a few calls. I had my odometer put on the carriage. It cost considerable labour to put it on. When we were out the wheel stuck fast as we started to return, but it began to revolve & at a black smith shop we loosed the screw, I had it completed this morning. Last evening we called on Major & Mrs. Chilton.

I intended starting in the morning, but Margaret feels so badly at the prospect of going back to Verde, that we will stay a day or two longer.

We were out this morning making some purchases & getting ready to start.

San Antonio Thurs. May 24, 1860

To-day Margaret went & had a Photograph taken but it is not good. Dr. Foard had his also taken but it is not good & neither is taken.

I settled at last with Lt. Thomas & paid for our messing last winter $138 & some cents. I also signed a number of papers. He & Capt. & Mrs. McLean left about 10 A.M. They waited over an hour for him. We are all ready to start. Col. Lee called, & Major & Mrs. Chilton, last evening.

Birney [Boerne] Texas[10] Fri. May 25, 1860

We had the Ambulance & 6 wagons at the Hotel at 8 A.M. but Margaret wanted to buy a riding hat & some few things & drove to town & I wanted to

---

[10] County seat of Kendall County, Boerne had been established in 1849 as Tosculum. When the site was abandoned in 1851, a new townsite was laid out two miles away and named for Ludwig Boerne, a German poet and historian. Unfortunately, the 1860 Blanco County census, including much of what is today Kendall County, was lost. Webb, Carroll, and Branda (eds.), *Handbook of Texas*, I, 181.

go to the offices so we did not get off until near 11 A.M. I went & saw Col. Lee & had a talk with him about withdrawing some of the troops from the Rio Grande. He is very secret about all he does, or proposes to do. The Indians are very troublesome on the road to El Passo.[11]

The ice got in & I had some ice drinks before I left. My bill at the Hotel was much less than I expected. I sent one of the wagons to town to collect some of our purchases. I could hardly find room as Lt. Thomas had so many of his things to carry to Verde. I yesterday hired William, his old servant.

We had a very hot ride & got here (Staffords) at 3 P.M. I started on horse back, but out of town let Charles ride my horse. I rode part of the time in the Ambulance & part in the Doctor's buggy. We stopped at the Leon Springs, 18 miles & had lunch. We there overtook Lt. & Ms. Washington.

The gentlemen all went & took a bath in the Cibola at this place.[12] We got lager at Leon Springs & some very fine here. The accommodations are not very good at this place.

Our wagons are badly packed & the Doctor's cigar boxes are mashed & a box of tea all broken & contents scattered on the road.

CAMP VERDE SAT. MAY 26, 1860

We had breakfast & left at 6:10 A.M. The weather is not near so hot as yesterday. We came about 20 miles, stopped & lunched. We got some lager at Comfort.[13] We got here at 2:15 P.M. All the officers & ladies called immediately & Capt. Caldwell waited dinner for us.

Although not near so hot as yesterday when we got here the thermometer stood at 96° & not much breeze.

Our things were badly abused in the wagons & the market basket I bought with the vegetables were left behind at the Menger Hotel. I had all the baggage out on the pavement & pointed out to the men, but they let some one carry this back into the Hotel.

---

[11] This is probably a reference to a clash on May 7, 1860, between a party of Comanche or possibly Kiowa and a detachment of troops at Leon Holes, west of Fort Stockton. Wayne Austerman, *Sharps Rifles and Spanish Mules: The San Antonio–El Paso Mail* (College Station: Texas A&M University Press, 1985), 157.

[12] Cibola Creek rises in eastern Kendall County and flows southeast to form a portion of the Bexar-Comal, Bexar-Guadalupe, and Guadalupe-Wilson County boundaries, before emptying into the San Antonio River.

[13] Comfort, about twenty miles northwest of Boerne, had been established in 1854 by Ernst Altgelt. The predominantly German-American village had a population of ninety-two in 1860. 8th Census, Kendall County.

Camp Verde Texas Sun. May 27, 1860

We had the Band play yesterday afternoon. All the officers & ladies were over till tattoo. Lt. & Mrs. Washington take their meals with us. Margaret felt quite sick in the afternoon, but got up to tea. She is much better to-day.

Camp Verde Texas Mond. May 28, 1860

Yesterday was very hot—mer. 98(. Margaret got up to breakfast & was about most of the forenoon. She then lay down & dosed & slept & ended in a kind of a stupor. About 5 p.m. I went & called Mrs. Caldwell. She advised me to call the Doctor. It was difficult to rouse her & we sat with her till midnight. She slept pretty well.

This morning she dressed herself, but had to lie down. She has had something of a chill & a fever. She has kept her bed all day & is better this afternoon.

Mary our girl is also sick. Whenever Margaret gets sick it appears our girl does too. Mrs. Washington's girl is sick too. My wagons went back to San Antonio. I wrote to Mr. Menger about the market basket & vegetables our men left for me.

Lt. Washington has commenced his kitchen. They take their meals at out house. The mer. today has been 101(. The wind is hot. I cant write letters in this heat.

Camp Verde Texas Wed. May 30, 1860

Yesterday it was not so warm by ten degrees & the wind cooler. I had the Doctor & Mr. Newton to dinner. Margaret would not keep quiet & in the afternoon had a fever & was delirious. I broke my nose glasses & sent them to Hines & also wrote to Mr. Galvan.

To-day Margaret is much better. Our mail is in. I have a letter from Howe & from Wrightson. The former sends a statement of the yield of the Heintzelman mine. The latter is in answer to mine about Sta. Rita stock. The claim is on the 80 shares I subscribed for to oblige Wrightson. They decided that those who did not pay up should be released if they would relinquish their dividend stock. I dont like the proceeding.

Mary & Marian Caldwell have gone out riding with Mr. Newton.

Camp Verde Thurs. May 31, 1860

The weather is not so hot. I had monthly inspection this morning. In the afternoon I walked with the Doctor to the garden. It is very dry but looks well. The worms & bugs have done a great deal of damage. In the afternoon

Mr. Ramsay got back, with the news that the Alamo was burned. That portion across the street from the main building, with old wagons, wheels, hay & materials. The loss to the government 30 or 40 thousand dollars. Mr. Edgar also came with him—for the camels. They take 20.

They also brought a letter from Capt. King to the Doctor, that Lt. Col. Geo. Morris is in San Antonio on his way to join. What a nuisance! He will be here in a few days. It provoked all but the Caldwells! They dont dislike him.

❧ June 1860 ❧

"Quite an affair...in the garrison today."

———•◦•◦•———

CAMP VERDE FRI. JUNE 1ST, 1860

I got my basket & vegetables, that were kept back at the Hotel in S.A. The 20 camels left this morning. I had arranged for Lt. Washington to relieve Lt. Mower as a. a. gen. & a. c. s. as he wished to transfer from the Adjutancy to R. Qr. M. but this morning he wishes to wait until the end of the month. It is too much work to make out quarterly papers for part of a quarter. I am not at all pleased with his industry. He told me this morning that he had some regimental papers that he got in S. Antonio & amongst them a report from Lt. Col. Morris that he would join. This he did not open in San Antonio. Had he done so I would have had an opportunity to have had a talk with Col. Lee & would have known somewhat, what to do. It is unpardonable negligence.

CAMP VERDE SAT. JUNE 2, 1860

A fine breeze & more pleasant. I appointed Sergt. Candy Sergt. Major & Sergt. Cloud Qr. M. Sergt. I would have wait for Lt. Col. Morris, but the Adjt. urged me to make the appointments.

I wrote to Burgess about the old claim I left in his hands last year & also to Sister Maria. I have been trying to put things in order about the house.

Dr. Foard & Mr. Newton have gone fishing.

CAMP VERDE TEXAS SUN. JUNE 3RD, 1860

They got but few fish. Sent us a trout & we had it for supper. To-day Mer. 90° & warm, though a pretty good breeze.

I wrote to Sister Juliana & also prepared a letter to Mahoney & one to Wrightson about the Sta Rita stock.

CAMP VERDE TEXAS MON. JUNE 4, 1860

Mer. 98° to-day—warm & uncomfortable. Mr. Hunter our corn contractor was in garrison to-day. I sent to Hines the Jeweller in S. Antonio, the first piece of silver from the Heintzelman mine, given me by Mr. Poston, to have a pair of goblets made for Dr. Foard.

Mary & Marian rode out on horseback with Mr. Newton & Margaret in the buggy with Dr. Foard. The latter drives one of my carriage horses.

CAMP VERDE TEXAS TUES. JUNE 5, 1860

I finished my letters to Mahoney & Wrightson on business & wrote to Poston. It was very hot in the forenoon—mer. 100°. Soon after dinner a violent storm with rain & hail came up. The hail stones were half an inch in diameter & cut off the leaves of the oak trees. Some branches the wind blew down. Much damage must have been done to vegetation, gardens & corn. The heavy rain was much needed.

We had plenty of ice to make cool water & Margaret is making ice cream. Mary shoveled up a tub of ice.

CAMP VERDE WED. JUNE 6, 1860

The morning pleasant. In the afternoon a heavy storm of rain, wind & a little hail. The gully behind our quarters was full of water.

The mail brought letters from Dr. Tripler & Mr. Bartlett & Solon. The excuse Cheever made is only a get off. Mr. Bartlett values the Sonora stock highly & I suppose has no idea of asking the guarantee. I got two letters from Margaret, one dated 12 Dec. went first to Ft. Duncan.

The order for a court martial & to change the Hd. Qrs. 1st Infy to Chadbourne, where Lt. Col. Morris is ordered to command. The Adjutant is very much disgusted. There is a report also that he wants to appoint Lt. Mower R. Qr. M. It would be just like him. If he does I will ask him to resign when I get command of the Regt. again.

CAMP VERDE TEXAS THURS. JUNE 7, 1860

Cloudy & pleasantly cool this morning. Margaret is suffering & suffered all night with a neurolgic head ache. Our girl in the kitchen has a chill also.

The kitchen walls to Lt. Washington's quarters were nearly up & fell down last night. It is what is called Pisa work.[1]

Our servant girl, I believe wishes to leave us. It is a constant annoyance. I dont see what she can do.

CAMP VERDE TEXAS FRI. JUNE 8, 1860

The morning was cool & pleasant, but warm in the afternoon. Our court

---

[1] Probably a humorous reference to the Leaning Tower of Pisa.

met & tried one case & adjourned. Tomorrow we meet & finish. I sent my watch to S.A. for a crystal. The ten men escort (part) for the Top[ographical] party & Camels left this afternoon. Lancy, Mary's husband went along. He was very indignant because he was detailed & his wife said she would leave. When she talked to Margaret, she changed her tune.

I had Lt. Shaaff & all the officers but Lt. Mower to dinner. He & Capt. Caldwell have quarreled. We had a nice dinner & they were well pleased.

The mail got in at ten A.M. I have another assessment of $90 to pay to the Vallecillo min. co. I also got a long letter from Chas. S. Brown our Sonora Sec.

Camp Verde Tex. Sat. June 9, 1860

It rained a little last night & a few showers to-day, now clear & pleasant. We had another case to-day. A man slept on post last night. We tried him & adjourned. Our servant girl has been bitter since her husband left.

Camp Verde Texas Sun. June 10, 1860

We all went to Dr. Foards after tattoo & had a clam [supper] till near midnight. It was pleasant. To-day is clear & warm. Lt. Shaaff left this morning. A carriage with a gentleman & three ladies stopped at our door, on their way to Bandera to settle.

Camp Verde Mon. June 11, 1860

The Doctor, Margaret & I rode in our ambulance to Dr. Ganahls & saw Mrs. Thompson, his mother in law. The Dr. is sick in New Orleans & Mrs. G. has joined him. We went & saw the enclosure & grave where his son is buried. Mrs. T. has made it a flower bed. We got back at 2 P.M. The day was delightful. It has been warm this afternoon. Margaret has suffered all day with neurolgia & took a little chloroform—inhaled, but principally outward application.

Camp Verde Texas Tues. June 12, 1860

I wrote to Mr. Webster & sent him $90, my last assessment for the Vallecillo silver mine. I hope & have no doubt but that this is the last. I also gave Margaret a check for $50 to get a tablet for our baby Henry—to send to Matilda.[2]

Quite an affair occurred in the garrison to-day. Mrs. Mower pushed both

---

[2] After weeks of illness, Henry Summers Heintzelman, who was born on August 25, 1857, at Newport Barracks, Kentucky, died of whooping cough in Buffalo, New York, on February 11, 1858. The infant was buried in Forest Lawn Cemetery where Heintzelman would be laid to rest twenty-two years later. Matilda was Margaret

Miss Helen & Mrs. Caldwell, on the stoop, because they were in the way.[3] He is intolerable to every one in the garrison & she is in a fair way of becoming so. Mer. over 90° to-day put pleasant.

Camp Verde Texas Wed. June 13, 1860

Not quite so warm to-day. The mail brought me no letters. Margaret got one from Matilda.

Margaret has had neurolgia in her head.[4] I gave her chloroform to bathe in, but she would inhale it. The Doctor did the same the other day.

Camp Verde Texas June 14, 1860 Thurs.

We had a dance at the Doctor's again last evening & staid till midnight. Pleasant. Margaret did not sleep well after. The mail is in, but I got nothing. Lt. Col. Morris is on his way & will stop as he passes. We go on a fishing party tomorrow. Mer. 93° & warm.

Camp Verde Tex. Fri. June 15, 1860

Storm of wind & rain last night. We all but the Mowers left at 6½ A.M. on a fishing excursion to Mason Creek, about 8 miles S.W. from here.[5] We took Cloud as guide & 8 men for a scout. About 4 miles from here we passed through an oak grove well stripped by the second storm we had. It was there more distinctive than the heavy hail storm we had the day before. The oaks were stripped of their branches or broken off. I saw one tree broken close to the ground & fell at least six feet from the stump. A large track the leaves were all off the trees & on the wind ward side the trees were speckled by the hail storm.

The carriages followed the road, but I rode with Capt. Caldwell & the men on a trail. We had three Ambulances, mine, Capt. Caldwell's & Lt. Washington's. Dr. Foard & Mr. Newton caught the most fish. I only fished a few minutes & caught one catfish. Mr. Newton brought in 42 fish—the Doctor not quite so many, but mostly trout & much finer. We had a nice dinner, spent a pleasant day. It was very hot & until late. We got up the horses but the ladies were not ready to start. We left the escort & Cloud & I rode home. It was after sundown & the carriages got in soon after.

Heintzelman's younger sister. HJ, Aug. 25, 26, 29, Sept. 9, 1857; Jan. 9, 24, 27, 30, Feb. 8, 12, 1858.

  [3] A stoop is a small porch.

  [4] Neuralgia is generally defined as a form of nervous disorder.

  [5] Mason Creek was twelve miles southeast of Camp Verde in southeastern Kerr and northeastern Bandera counties. The creek empties into the Medina River at Bandera.

There was some misunderstanding about the starting & some dissatisfaction. [They] learned on the way that Caldwell's company was ordered to Fort Cobb & it created quite an excitement as with it they coupled 14 wagons. Sergt. Drury who had been on a fishing excursion, came in soon after & had seen the wagons told me they were for the Band & that Lt. Col. Morris was on the way up, but had been out in the storm the night before.

Camp Verde Tex. Sat. June 16, 1860

This has been a warm day. Mer. 98°. The wagons 10 for the Band & staff & 2 with provisions have arrived. Lt. Col. Morris is still back. He is feeble & sick & can scarcely travel. The wagon master dont think that he will get beyond here. He did not have his tent pitched when the storm came up.

There is a new excitement. The Sec. of War has ordered the Hd. Qrs. to the 8th Infy to San Antonio & Capt. Jourdans compy. Capt King's will have to leave & it is said that Capt. King will come to this Post, Caldwell [to] go some where else & I to Fort Cobb. I doubt either of us being moved before fall. But everything is uncertain. I think I will write to Capt. Withers & let him know for Col. Lee's information that I dont care to move before fall if at all. If they will give me sufficient transportation I will be satisfied to go to Cobb. The allowance sent for the Hd. Qrs. & Band is quite liberal. Lt. Washington hired a Mexican cart & has sent his furniture, in part of it ahead with the two married men of the Band. I told him it was premature.

Camp Verde Texas Sun. June 17, 1860

Mer. has been 101½° to-day. Before 10 a.m. Lt. Col. Morris arrived & stopped near the Sutler's store & sent for Dr. Foard. A few minutes later the Dr. drove him to his quarters. It was inspection morning & our guard was just mounting. As soon as it was over I called & took Lt. Washington to call on him. He looks tolerably well. He did not pitch his tent the other night & got wet & has the gout. He says that he will stay here until he gets well. The doctor is very much disgusted with him, but I am glad not to have him. If he staid with us a week he would make Margaret sick with his vulgar habits.

From what he says I dont doubt but that I will be ordered to another Post ere long. I will reduce my baggage as rapidly as possible. I would rather be at Fort Cobb but dont care to move & at this season particularly.

I wrote to Mr. Lathrop at Tubac & also finished my letter to Capt. G.W. Cullum, U.S. Eng. for the cadet register—my services.[6]

We have been here one year to-day & already there are rumors of a move.

---

[6] In a three-page letter, Heintzelman briefly outlines his service in the antebellum

I have been absent over six months. If I dont get promotion & a good post, if the mines do well I will resign.

CAMP VERDE TEXAS MON. JUNE 18, 1860

Warm to-day. Mer. 101½° though the wind has not been so hot as when we had the mercury the same. Col. Morris is better & talks of leaving in a few days.

I have been inspecting some damaged property—under the new orders. I also called on Col. Morris & had a talk about Regimental affairs. I presume that he will appoint Lt. Cone Adjutant & make Washington R. Qr. M.[7]

The Doctor & Margaret rode out in the buggy to Dr. Ganahl's. Mrs. Thompson sent in about a sick negro. They lost one not very long ago & another is taken in the same way.[8] Dr. Ganahls family have been unfortunate for the last year.

He lost his son, is now in N.O. sick, lost a valuable negro, then had a horse killed & then two mules strayed & now another very sick & one past hope with consumption.

CAMP VERDE TEXAS WED. JUNE 20, 1860

I wrote several letters yesterday—to Lathrop, Chas. S. Brown & Capt. Stoneman. Margaret & I rode out to Bandera Pass. In the evening we heard the last dance, as the Band has left to-day. It was at the mess room & broke up at one A.M.

The wagons are loaded & the Band has left. Lt. & Mrs. Washington are staying with us till they leave. Col. Morris has the gout in his hand very badly, but I suppose will leave in the morning. The mail came, but no private letters for me. Margaret got a short one from Lathrop & one from Mrs. Sloan & Mrs. Chilton.

---

army despite "having lost most of [my] papers." The major recalled his limited duty in the Seminole and Creek wars, having been on a board to investigate the claims of the Florida Militia, as well as combat at Paso de la Oveja, Humantla, and Atlixco during the Mexican War, a fight with the Cahuilla Indians at Coyote Canyon in Southern California, and the establishment of Fort Yuma. Heintzelman to G. W. Cullum, June 4, 1860, HP.

[7] Aurelius Franklin Cone, a Georgian from the West Point class of 1857, was a second lieutenant in the 1st Infantry. First Lt. Edwin D. Phillips, not Cone, replaced 1st Lt. T. A. Washington as adjutant of the regiment on August 1, 1860. Heitman, *Historical Register*, 81, 320.

[8] In 1861, Dr. Charles Ganahl owned twenty-one slaves valued at $12,000. Watkins, *Kerr County*, 34.

CAMP VERDE TEXAS THURS. JUNE 21, 1860

At 8 A.M. Lt. & Mrs. Washington left & Lt. Col. Morris one hour later. The latters gout is better. I fear he will be laid up on the road.

I went & had my ambulance fixed by changing the Odometer to the other side. The Doctor, Margaret & I rode out towards Turtle Creek. The Verde Pass is 2¼ miles from here. The garrison looks very quiet since the band & head Qrs. have left.

CAMP VERDE TEXAS FRI. JUNE 22, 1860

Warm to-day. Mer. 93°. The mail brought me no letters. Lt. Mower has moved into Lt. Washington's quarters. We had green corn, the first time this year & the grains just beginning to form.

CAMP VERDE TEX. SAT. JUNE 23, 1860

We went out 8 miles up the country to cut a bee tree found by Polly our guide. The Doctor, Mrs. Chilton, Charles & two soldiers. We found the tree & got three tin pints full of honey. We saw a deer & a turkey & the Doctor shot a black quail. We were two hours going & two returning. We got home at 2 P.M. & the mercury was at 99°. We had a breeze & the ride was not very hot. The hills or dividing ridges is very rocky.

CAMP VERDE TEXAS JUNE 24, 1860

Mer. is about 90° again, though it dont feel as hot as usual. I wrote to W. Wrightson & inquired about a school to send Charles to. I also inquired what S.P.R.R. stock is worth & so soon as it will bring anything I will sell it. I also wrote to Mr. Paine in Niles to sell my lot there for what it will bring. I mean to get rid of all my outside speculations & turn all that I can into money.

CAMP VERDE MON. JUNE 25, 1860

Margaret was quite drowsy this morning & about noon fell asleep in her chair. I got her to lie down & she lay over three hours. I could only wake her after bathing her hands & face in cool water. It appears to be owing to over nervous excitement.

Our subsistence carts got back from San Antonio. They bring the report that Gen. Jesup died on the 10th.[9] Who will succeed him? Col. Thomas is I believe in the office in charge.

---

[9] Thomas Sidney Jesup, a captain in the War of 1812, became a brigadier general in 1818 and a major general in 1828. Jesup served for many years as Quartermaster

CAMP VERDE TEXAS TUES. JUNE 26, 1860

Much cooler & more pleasant than it has been since my return home. Dr. Foard & Charles rode to the Medina to fish, to be gone till tomorrow.

We have had several showers of rain this afternoon. I wrote to Mr. Howe, Cin.

CAMP VERDE, WED. JUNE 27, 1860

We had heavy rain last evening, will make corn & melons in this neighborhood. The Doctor & Charles will have had a nice time fishing. It rained harder in the direction they went.

Gen. Jesup died on the 9th of June. Gen. A.S. Johnson is spoken of as Qr. M. Genl.[10] I got a letter from Mr. Lathrop. Col. Talcott has arrived out & is in want of money.[11] It was quite cool last night & is cool & pleasant to-day.

I opened my white & red Cal. wine. The red is not clear. They have not turned sour & I shall bottle so soon as they are settled.

CAMP VERDE TEXAS THURS. JUNE 28, 1860

Not uncomfortably warm to-day. Margaret, Miss Helen Lacy & Mrs. Newton, Dr. Foard & I took a ride on horseback. We rode down the Verde about four & a half miles.

CAMP VERDE TEXAS FRI. JUNE 29, 1860

The mail is in & not a letter or paper for us. We got some very fine corn—roasting ears. The first for to eat this season. We have our rooms turned topsy turvy for white washing & house cleaning. Mer. is 94° to-day, but a pleasant breeze.

General of the United States and died on June 10, 1860. Heitman, *Historical Register*, 573.

[10] Heintzelman is mistaken. See journal entry of July 8, 1860. It was Lt. Col. Joseph Eggleston Johnston, not Col. Albert Sidney Johnston, who replaced Jesup as Quartermaster General of the Army on June 28, 1860. Charles P. Roland, *Albert Sidney Johnston: Soldier of Three Republics* (Austin: University of Texas Press, 1964), 240–241.

[11] Andrew Talcott, a Colt associate, was an agent for the Sonora Exploring and Mining Company. North, *Samuel Peter Heintzelman*, 173.

☙ July 1860 ❧

"Our mail is in, but not much news."

———◆◆◆◆———

CAMP VERDE TEXAS. SUN. JULY 1ST, 1860

On Friday Mrs. Ganahl, her mother Mrs. Thompson & the latters brother Mr. Martin called. Dr. Ganahl got home from N. Orleans a day or two before where he has been sick.

This morning Dr. Foard, Mr. Newton & I rode out there & a rain came up & we staid to dinner. The Doctor looks tolerably well, but still uses his crutches. Yesterday we rode out to Turtle Creek & find it five miles. Pleasant breeze to-day.

CAMP VERDE TEXAS TUES. JULY 3, 1860

On Monday Margaret & I with Mrs. Newton & Miss Helen Lacy rode on horse back. In the morning Dr. Foard & Charles rode out to the Medina to fish.

We left 10' before 7 A.M. & rode in the ambulance. We took a party of men. Capt. Caldwell's & our ambulance went. We staid out at the river till 10' of 7 P.M. & drove in in two hours—12½ miles. The day was generally cloudy & cool. Polly our guide shot a buck & the Doctor caught a number of fish. I did not put my hook into the water. The road is pretty good & I measured it with the Odometer on my wheel.

CAMP VERDE TEXAS WED. JULY 4, 1860

One of the men was a short distance above where we stopped & saw two men on poneys he took for Indians. I sent out [a patrol] but we could not trail them.

Our mail is in, but not much news. Capt. Caldwell has just called to say that Col. Plympton is dead. This promotes Waite & Rains & Ketchum.[1] Capt.

---

[1] Col. Joseph Plympton of the 1st Infantry died on June 5, 1860, the same day Carlos Adolphus Waite was promoted to colonel, Gabriel Jones Rains to lieutenant

& Mrs. Caldwell, Miss Lacy, Margaret & I dined with Dr. Foard & Mr. Newton. At 12 I had the officers in my quarters for a glass of wine. We all went to see the men's dinner table. Capt. Caldwell's compy had a fine dinner.

CAMP VERDE TEXAS FRI. JULY 6, 1860

Yesterday we had ours & the children's bed rooms white washed & cleaned & put down the matting in the Parlor. We got through white washing & house cleaning. Margaret was not very well, having been up too late on the 4th, to the dance at the Doctors. It was one A.M. when we got home & abed. To-day she is quite well. I sent the Doctor & Capt. Caldwell each a bottle of red & white California wine. We took a short ride late in the afternoon in the Doctor's buggy. Margaret is much better to-day. She & the Doctor have gone out to ride in the buggy. The night we returned from our fishing excursion the Doctor saw a comet. It was quite plain last night. We had the Mer. at 100° to-day. I am badly bitten by red bugs from my fishing excursion.

CAMP VERDE SAT. JULY 7, 1860

Dr. Foard, Margaret & I rode out to Dr. Ganahl's this morning. They were out plumbing, but returned in a few minutes. We got home a little after one P.M. The Mercury was at 103°—the hottest day we have had at Verde. I measured the distance & it is 7 $\frac{1}{16}$ miles to Dr. Ganahl's. The Paymaster will be up in the morning.

CAMP VERDE TEXAS SUN. JULY 8, 1860

By breakfast time the Paymaster arrived. He pays to-day. Lt. Col. Jos. E. Johns[t]on has been appointed Qr. M. Genl. & confirmed. He was a good topog. & has done nothing since. It is an outrage on the officers of the Qr. M. Dept. He is a relative of the Sec. of War & his wife a daughter of McLean the Minister of Mexico.

I drew my pay for May & June & all my back forage I could think of. The amount is $608.80.

Mercury was at 100° Major Cunningham left this afternoon to join his escort & wagons at the crossing of the Guadalupe, 7 miles from here.

I got $400 of my pay in a check to send to T. Wrightson to help pay for my Sta. Rita stock. I would have sent more but I will want some money to send Charles to school before long. Dr. Foard thinks that he will get away from here in six weeks or two months & will take Charles along.

---

colonel, and William Scott Ketchum to major. Heitman, *Historical Register*, 595, 813, 993.

CAMP VERDE TEXAS MON. JULY 9, 1860

Mer. 98° & hot wind. I wrote to Lathrop & to T. Wrightson including the latters $400 in part payment of my Sta. Rita Stock. Dr. Foard has gone with Polly on a fishing expedition, to be gone a day or two. He expects soon to get orders out of the country. Margaret is busy getting Charles ready to go with him. I wrote to T. Wrightson asking him to hurry his brothers reply to my inquiries about a school.

CAMP VERDE TEXAS TUES. JULY 10, 1860

Mer. 98½°, with fine breeze. The children dined with Mr. Newton. I wrote to Mr. Lathrop & to Mr. Futhey to the latters enquiring for a school for Charles.

Margaret & I took a ride on horseback down the creek yesterday & will take another this afternoon as soon as it gets cooler.

CAMP VERDE TEXAS WED. JULY 11, 1860

Warm again to-day. Our mail brought a letter from Ehrenburg. He speaks favorably of our mines, but the barrels are not running & our machinery is not there. I also got a letter from Poston. We owe $75,000 & all is doubt & uncertainty. I wrote to Ehrenburg & also to Poston & sent him E's letter. I begin to doubt Brown's faithfulness to the company. He has transferred 1000 shares to Jarvis for Colt. It is supposed that Colt advanced the money to buy it. I have advised Poston to go & see the Wrightsons & act with them. Coleman has resigned the Presidency of the compy & will have nothing more to do with it.[2] I fear that Colt will at last get the control of the compy.

Dr. Foard got back last evening. He brought some fish & Polly the guide with him shot a deer after dusk near the lime kiln a short distance below. I took a long ride with Margaret on horseback last evening & passed them not half an hour before. She & the Doctor rode out in the buggy this afternoon.

On their way home a lug broke & the horse started to run, but the Doctor stopped him & they returned safe.

CAMP VERDE TEXAS THURS. JULY 12, 1860

Mer. 102° to-day. I wrote to Mr. Dawson, St. Pauls & said I would only accept my previous offer, made to Mahoney, as he no doubt saw the letter. I also wrote to Dr. Summers & advised him to look to his money loaned out there.

---

[2] William Tell Coleman was a California and New York shipping and commission merchant. North, *Samuel Peter Heintzelman*, 73, 171.

The Doctor, Margaret & I take a ride in the Ambulance to gather a few plumbs. We had a green water melon from the garden yesterday & a half ripe one to-day.

Camp Verde Texas Fri. July 13, 1860

Mrs. Ganahl gave us a couple of cocoa mi[n]ts & we had the Doctor & Mr. Newton to dinner. I gave them the California sparkling wine. The Doctor thinks that he will learn to like it. It has been quite hot. We took a ride in the afternoon, up the creek. I am all covered with hives or something else. The mail brought me the 11th vol. P.R.R. reports.

Camp Verde Texas Sat. July 14, 1860

On the front step in the shade Mer. 106°—on the back only 92°. It is much hotter than last summer. This has been decidedly the hottest day we have had. Mer. was 107° in front of the house & then 97° on the back step. It was hot till late in the afternoon. It then blew, thundered, lightened & rained. The air is now much cooler.

The Doctor cleaned Margaret's sewing machine. Charles went out with some of the men hunting & brought home but one quail. He shot it on the wing. He saw some deer & a number of turkies.

The Capt. went out in his ambulance & Mr. Newton & Miss Helen on horseback, but the storms drove them in. The Doctor & Margaret were going to ride in the buggy but the weather looked too threatening. The other day when they were run away the wheel struck a tree & knocked off the outer band. It was a narrow escape.

Camp Verde Texas Sun. July 15, 1860

I wrote to Col. Kennett & Mr. Lathrop. It has been warm to-day—Mer. 104°, but a pleasant breeze. Polly gave us a mushmelon—the first this season.

After dark the Doctor came & said they had one of the negroes from the men's dance would play half an hour or more. We all had to go & dance for half an hour or more. After we all went & the ladies staid an hour & a half looking on to a dance of the soldiers & camp women in the mess room. I dont know how long they would have staid had it not commenced to rain. How fortunate it is that some people have heels to amuse themselves.

Camp Verde Texas Mon. July 16, 1860

Mer. has been 101°, but it has not felt half so warm as yesterday. Charles & Mr. Newton were out all the forenoon hunting. Charles shot three doves & Mr. Newton some young turkies.

The doctor finished cleaning & oiling the sewing machine. It now works better than ever.

Mr. Hemphill the Texas Senator sent me a copy of the documents published about the Cortinas war.[3] I got it a few days after I got here, but did not read it till to-day. There are a great many ridiculous statements. Col. Harvey Brown made the most uncalled for.

Capt. Caldwell & his family rode out & gathered plumbs. Mary rode with them & brought some honey that were collected. Margaret & I rode to Turtle Creek to Camp Ives. It is deserted & looks forlorn. We got a drink of cool water.

CAMP VERDE TEXAS WED. JULY 18, 1860

Not so warm to-day as usual. Our mail is in. Mahoney accepts my offer & I wrote to him & also to Capt. Dana at St. Pauls sending him the Mortgage & Mortgage note to complete the release on the payment of $1,000 & sent it to me at this place.[4] I also heard from Mr. Lathrop. He complains of our Director & I fear there will be trouble before the machinery is in operation. I also heard from the Wrightsons. They also fear trouble about our Sonora company. I wrote to Wrightson, Lathrop & to Brown. I have answered up all the business [that] came to-day. Margaret & I take a ride in the buggy.

Got cards for the wedding of Lt. Biggs & Miss Amea King at West Chester Pa.

CAMP VERDE TEXAS FRI. JULY 20, 1860

Yesterday we were up at reveille & left at 10' before 7 A.M. in the Ambulance for Mason's Creek to spend the day at Dr. Ganahls hay camp. The Doctor, Margaret, Mary, & I rode in our Ambulance & Charles staid at home. Mr. Norton rode with Capt. Caldwells family & the Capt. took an escort. Dr. Ganahl has selected a miserable camp the grass I consider poor. He has a mower & rake & a press for the hay. We staid till near night & were home by dusk. My odometer makes the distance 9½ miles. We had dinner & passed a pleasant day. The doctor & then Newton caught fish enough for dinner.

---

[3] A South Carolinian, John Hemphill had come to Texas in 1838 where he became Chief Justice of the Texas Supreme Court and later U.S. senator, succeeding Sam Houston. A secessionist, Hemphill died in Richmond, Virginia, in January 1862. Webb, Carroll, and Branda (eds.), *Handbook of Texas*, I, 795.

[4] Dana is probably Napoleon Jackson Tecumseh Dana, 1842 West Point graduate, who was breveted a captain for gallantry at Cerro Gordo during the Mexican War, but who had resigned in March 1855. Dana came to Texas as a major general of volunteers with the Union Rio Grande Expedition in late 1863. Heitman, *Historical Register*, 352.

This morning's mail brought orders relieving Dr. Foard & ordering Dr. Byrne, a new appointment here.[5] I also got a very satisfactory letter from Mr. Webster N.Y. with receipt for $90 assessment I sent him. Our Vallecillo furnace works successfully.

Capt. King's compy 1st Infy is ordered to Ft. Chadbourne. Quite a change from S. Antonio & he is no doubt much disgusted. The order of Lt. Col. Gov. Morris assuming command of the Regt. Capt. Caldwell has received but they forgot to send me a copy.

Capt. Caldwell & Mr. Newton asked Charles to ride with them after plumbs & then went off without him, much to his disgust. The doctor & Margaret took a ride in the buggy.

CAMP VERDE TEXAS SUN. JULY 22, 1860

Mr. Lane, Mr. Smith, Dr. Foard, & Mr. Newton dined with us. Mer. 106°. Mr. Lane says that Capt. Evans's compy cav. will come here when they leave the Rio Grande. We will then move I suppose. What a nuisance to move so frequently. They called again in the evening, the Dr. & Mr. Smith & took a cup of tea with us.

CAMP VERDE TEXAS MON. JULY 23, 1860

Another quite warm day. Mer. at 5 P.M. at 95°. I wrote to Hooper, about our S. Diego lots & to T. Wrightson & sent him a copy of my agreement with Cheever & what he wrote me he did. He owes me about $1,300 if he dont return the stock he agreed to.

CAMP VERDE TEXAS WED. JULY 25, 1860

Warm again yesterday. I wrote to Major Ketchum. In the evening rode with Margaret on horseback. Our mail today brought me a letter from Dr. Tripler. I also got notice of Flinn a cavalry man who left here a few days ago for S. Antonio.[6] He was on his way back & killed about five miles from town. Warm to-day.

---

[5] From Maryland, Charles Christopher Byrne had been appointed assistant surgeon on June 23, 1860. A Civil War veteran, Byrne retired from the army in 1901.

[6] The area west and northwest of San Antonio, especially the small settlements along the Lower Military Road, was hit hard by a series of Indian raids in 1859 and 1860. Thirty-five citizens of Bandera petitioned President James Buchanan for protection against raiding Comanches. William Ballantyne, et al., to the President, n.d., with G. F. Towle to A. J. Hamilton, Jan. 16, 1860, LR, AGO, RG 94 (NA).

CAMP VERDE TEXAS THURS. JULY 26, 1860

Warmer than ever to-day. Mer. 107° at 3 P.M. I got my watch this morn-ing by the return of Sergt. Drury. Yesterday Margaret, Mary & I rode after plumbs, but only got a few poor ones. Margaret & the Doctor took a ride in the buggy. Margaret was quite sick last night with pain like neurolgia through her chest. She is much better to-day.

CAMP VERDE TEXAS FRI. JULY 27, 1860

Mail brought letters from Capt. Stoneman & Matilda Stuart.[7] The Capt. writes all quiet & has been since before I left. Margaret & I rode on horseback.

CAMP VERDE TEXAS SAT. JULY 28, 1860

Charles went with Polly the guide to his ranche.[8] I have to send a man to S. Antonio about flour on Lt. Mowers account. We have only three days on hand & dont know when we will get any.

Mer. 107° to-day & now 6 P.M. 94°.

Dr. Foard & Margaret ride in the buggy.

CAMP VERDE TEXAS SUN. JULY 29, 1860

Polly & Charles got back after 11 P.M. They met a she bear & cubs. Polly killed her & got the two cubs. He brought one in alive & Charles strangled the other & brought him in. Mer. at 6 P.M. is 94° but a pleasant breeze.

---

[7] Much of the news that Stoneman reported from the border probably did not surprise Heintzelman. "Everything along the Rio Grande is perfectly quiet and has been so since the departure of the Rangers," Stoneman said. There had been some "horse stealing, now and then carried on by returning Rangers and K.G.C.s in con-junction with Cortinistas on the other side. The latter do the stealing and the former the disposing," Stoneman continued. Stoneman had heard rumors that five American horse thieves "had been caught on the other side, bound to a tree, skinned alive, and then stabbed to death."

Although the *American Flag* (Brownsville) was asserting that the Rio Grande frontier was in turmoil, Stoneman had inquired of "every property holder" on the north bank and all had said that "not an animal had to their knowledge been taken across the river into Mexico since the 1st of May." Moreover, Cortina had not "been heard from for a long time—and no one appears to know where he is or what he is doing. Some of his men have gone into partnership with some ex-rangers and are car-rying on their favorite occupation—and with no small success," Stoneman concluded. Stoneman to Heintzelman, July 8, 1860, HP.

[8] In 1858, José Policarpo Rodríguez had established a ranch on Privilege Creek in eastern Bandera County. See footnote 1, November 1859 chapter.

◈ August 1860 ◈

"...misting rain when we started."

CAMP VERDE TEXAS WED. AUG. 1ST, 1860

Our warm weather still continues. On Monday a sheriff called with a warrant for Old Aunt Lakey, a negro who has been with the Army for years, but is free. Yesterday Capt. Caldwell, Mr. Newton & some men went to attend the case at Comfort. I also drove down in the Ambulance. The case is put off till next November. She chose Capt. Caldwell for master. Whilst we were there Dr. Ganahl rode up from his hay camp. We rode with him to his house & stopped there till sundown & saw the ladies. They all go back to their camp to-day. We there found many Mustang grapes.[1] They are a poor grape in my estimation. We also drove near two miles out of town after Melons & got a few poor ones. There are none in town. The men took the seine along for fish on Verde Creek, but only caught a few.

At Comfort we met H. Mayers a merchant of San Antonio.[2] He is there with his family & is pleased with the place. S. Antonio is quite hot & dusty.

I measured the distance to Comfort 15 miles & by Dr. Ganahls to this place 16 miles.

We got part of our mail. I got letters from T. Wrightson & Mr. Howe. They gave a most gloomy account of our Sonora compy affairs. I got a letter this morning from Capt. McLean. My transportation a/c when I came to

---

[1] Common to the Texas Hill Country, the Mustang Grape (*vitis candicans Engelm*), a high-climbing vine of forty feet or more, produced small black or red berries, one-half to seven-eighths inches in diameter, that matured in summer. Robert A. Vines, *Trees, Shrubs, and Woody Vines of the Southwest* (Austin: University of Texas Press, 1960), 715–716.

[2] H. Mayer, forty-two and a merchant in San Antonio, is listed on the census as having real estate valued at $10,000 and personal property worth $15,000. 8th Census, Bexar County; *Northern Standard*) (Clarksville), Sept. 4, 1858.

Texas is suspended for the order sending me here is overpaid. I will never get out of the clutches of the Auditors. I wrote to T. Wrightson, Coleman, Poston. We run great risk of losing everything by someones rascality.

Camp Verde Texas Thurs. Aug. 2, 1860

The doctor, Margaret & I rode on horseback up the creek yesterday afternoon. In going out of the bed of the Verde she let a limb of a tree pull her off her horse. She rubbed her elbow & got a bruise on her chest, but was not much hurt. She is too car[e]less in riding in not looking where the horse goes. She rode in the buggy this afternoon.

The Mer. at 5½ p.m. is 96° but a good breeze.

I wrote to Henry Howe as our mail dont close till tonight. Mary is a little unwell to-day. I am having a new tongue put on the carriage. The old one was too short.

Camp Verde Texas Fri. Aug. 3, 1860

Mer. 96° but pleasant breeze. This afternoon I got a note from Dr. Ganahl that his horses had stampeded the night before last & Indian signs had been seen near Kerrsville. I sent out a scout of 10 men. Margaret & I took a long ride in the buggy.

Camp Verde Texas Sun. Aug. 5, 1860

Dr. Foard, Margaret & I rode in the Ambulance to Dr. Ganahl's—no Indians—horses found. The weather not so hot. This morning Polly got back from S.A. Dr. Byrne arrived on the 3rd. The three co's of the 3rd Infy arrived at Fort Clark. Gen. Twiggs wants to get back to Texas so he writes to Capt. Withers. Capt. Carpenter's compy 1st Infy goes to Camp Cooper.[3] Weather pleasant.

Camp Verde Texas Mon Aug. 6, 1860

The weather is moderating. Mer. at 5½ p.m. is only 91°. Margaret is getting Charles ready to go with Dr. Foard to go to school with Stuart Tripler at Gambier. Capt. Caldwell has gone up the creek fishing with the sein[e]. He on Sat. caught a great many fish below. Margaret & the Doctor have gone in the buggy below. We have Texas flour from Uvalde for this month. It makes bad black bread.

---

[3] Stephen Decatur Carpenter, West Point class of 1840, became a major in 1862 but was killed at the Battle of Stone's River on December 31, 1862. Heitman, *Historical Register*, 285.

CAMP VERDE TEXAS AUG. 7, 1860

It was cloudy this morning & turned into rain. We have had a fine rain & it will probably continue. I wrote to Matilda Stuart & Dr. Tripler & Mr. Lathrop. I wrote that probably Charles would go to Gambier.[4] Dr. Foard expected Dr. Byrne to-day, but he did not come. Margaret has been getting Charles ready.

CAMP VERDE TEXAS THUS. AUG. 9, 1860

Yesterday forenoon rain, but we rode out on horseback in the afternoon. It rained again last night & 6½ inches of rain have fallen since it commenced.

Our mail yesterday brought me a letter from Mr. Wrightson, with a circular for the Groton seminary in Connecticut. He recommends it highly, but I think we had better send him to Gambier. W.W. has gone to New York to meet Poston & Brown & try to arrange Sonora affairs. Our debt is $60,000 & they last year spent $80,000 in costs. He says that if the management is given to the West he will put us again on our legs.

I got a letter from Sister Juliana. They are going to Cape May to see the "Great Eastern."

CAMP VERDE TEXAS FRI. AUG. 10, 1860

Our mail has not come to-day. The Verde was quite high & carried off the log we crossed to the Sutlers. The Guadalupe was high, but could readily be crossed to-day. I met Charles & William & they only found it a foot higher than usual. It rained a few drops this forenoon, but is now clear. Our weather has moderated very much & it is much cooler.

Dr. Foard, Margaret & I rode on horseback up the creek. The doctor took his gun & killed two quails & a rabbit. The little water courses have water in them & grass is already springing up making the country look pleasant. The water looks clear & cool.

CAMP VERDE TEXAS SUN. AUG. 12, 1860

Yesterday was pleasant. In the afternoon we intended to ride, but could not get up the ponies.

To-day was quite pleasant. Towards evening Dr. Byrne arrived & reported. He came with Major Van Dorn as far as the Guadalupe.[5] I am much

---

[4] Fifty miles east of Columbus in central Ohio, Kenyon College was founded in 1824 by the Episcopal Church as Ohio's first private college. Gambier was just east of Mount Vernon, near where Heintzelman's sister Elizabeth had settled.

[5] Mississippi-born Earl Van Dorn, thirty-nine, had recently been promoted to

pleased with his appearance. Dr. Foard will not leave for several days. I will go as far as S.A. with him & Charles to school in Ohio.

Margaret and I took a walk.

Dr. Byrne brought a box from Hines the Jeweller with the goblets I ordered to present to Dr. Foard.[6] I like them very much.

CAMP VERDE MON. AUG. 13, 1860

A delightful day. The mail we should have had last week got here this morning. I got a letter from Mr. Poston. A stock holders meeting will be held in Cinn. on the 15th this month. I got a letter from Mr. Poston dated 28 July. The freighters demanded pay & not receiving it order sale of machinery etc. to pay charges, but we learn a wagon upset & broke the balance wheel so they must replace it & in the meantime we can raise the money to pay & I should think demand damages. Mr. Poston still writes hopefully.

I wrote to Mr. Poston & to W. Wrightson.

Dr. Ganahl was here & has gone on to his hay camp. Mary has gone riding with Mr. Newton & Marian on horseback & Margaret & the Doctor in the buggy.

CAMP VERDE TUES. AUG. 14, 1860

We had Dr. Foard, Dr. Byrne & Mr. Newton to dinner. After dinner Margaret & I rode on horseback, with the two doctors, & Polly hunting up the creek. We only got two quails. The weather pleasant. The wagon [that] brought Dr. Byrne returned to S.A. I wrote to Dr. Tripler that Charles would start this week for school—Gambier.

CAMP VERDE THURS. AUG. 16, 1860

Yesterday I got a letter from T. Wrightson. He is despondent about

---

major in the 2d Cavalry. Van Dorn had gained a national reputation for his exploits against the Comanches in Texas. Van Dorn's thirty-one-year-old wife, Caroline, along with their two children, Olivia, eight, and Earl, five, were also at the post. Van Dorn resigned from the army in January 1861 to join the Confederate Army. As a major general commanding the Confederate trans-Mississippi Department, he lost the Battle of Pea Ridge. He also lost the Battle of Corinth and faced a court of inquiry. Exonerated, he was given a cavalry command and performed well at Holly Spring during Gen. Ulysses S. Grant's Vicksburg Campaign. A womanizer, Van Dorn was murdered by an irate husband in May 1863. 8th Census, Mason County. Robert G. Hartze, *Van Dorn: The Life and Times of a Confederate General* (Nashville: Vanderbilt University Press, 1967), 74, 307–327.

6 Charles Hine, "jeweler and watchmaker," ran a shop on Commerce Street. San Antonio *Daily Herald*, Dec. 17, 1859.

Sonora Co. The stockholder's meeting took place yesterday. I wrote to him.

Dr. Foard, Margaret & I rode out in our Ambulance & dined at Dr. Ganahl's. We had a pleasant dinner & left at sundown.

CAMP VERDE TEXAS SAT. AUG. 18, 1860

Yesterday morning Mr. Sherbourne from Dr. Ganahls called, staid to dinner & all the afternoon. Margaret was not well & quite sick all night.

Dr. Foard has gone to Lane's ranche. Dr. Byrne, Newton & Charles went hunting & fishing. The Doctor was relieved yesterday by Dr. Byrne.

The hunters & fishers did not get back till dark. They did not catch many fish or kill much game.

C.V. SUN. AUG. 19, 1860

Looks like for rain this morning. Margaret well again. I wrote to Capt. Stoneman. Dr. Foard got back this afternoon. He brought from Comfort a letter for Margaret from Matilda with a circular from a school near Boston. He goes to Gambier. Lt. Washington has taken his wife to San Antonio. Dont like Ft. Chadbourne. Lt. Phillips Adjt.[7]

CAMP VERDE MON. AUG. 20, 1860

Weather delightful. Dr. Foard leaves Wednesday. I will take him & Charles to San Antonio. I will drive four mules & have been making arrangements. We will leave so soon as the mail gets in.

I took a ride with Mary on horseback & Margaret & the Doctor rode in the buggy with Polly's poneys.

We all went to Capt. Caldwell's & had cake & wine—Franks 6th birthday.

CAMP VERDE TUES. AUG. 21, 1860

I enclosed a check for $8.52 the balance due Mr. Hayman. We had a little rain last night & threatening to-day. We are going out to Dr. Ganahls with Dr. Foard & in the evening we invite the garrison in.

CAMP VERDE TEXAS WED. AUG. 22, 1860

We had all the garrison in last night. We went to Dr. Ganahl's & got home at dusk. The Caldwell's & Mowers not speaking made it awkward & they all staid late. Margaret did not feel well & could not sleep.

The mail got in & brought no letter from Dr. Summers & from Mr. Futhey.

---

[7] First Lt. Edward D. Phillips, 1852 West Point graduate, was made adjutant of the 1st Infantry on August 1, 1860. Heitman, *Historical Register*, 83, 789.

BOERNE BLANCO COUNTY TEXAS WED. AUG. 22, 1860

The mail got in & we read our letters & started at a quarter of ten A.M. The wagon started sooner & went by Dr. Ganahl's for some trunks. We reached here at 3 P.M. The distance of 32½ miles. We had a few drops of rain as we started, but it was cloudy & pleasant riding. Dr. Foard, Charles & I were in my Ambulance & we had four mules. The wagon got in a couple of hours later.

SAN ANTONIO TEXAS THURS. AUG. 23, 1860

It commenced raining a little before daylight & rained hard for over an hour. We did not start till it was over 7:25 A.M. The road was bad til this side Leon Springs. We got here at one P.M. & the wagon after 4 P.M. The distance is 47¾ miles or from Verde here 62¾.

We got dressed & went out & at[t]ended to some business. I then went with some officers & heard the 8th Inf. Band. I there met Capt. & Mrs. Reynolds & Mrs. Ash & Dr. & Mrs. Abadie. Dr. Foard & I called on Major & Mrs. Graham this evening. I met Capts. Whiting, Clets, Bowman & Truitt & Blair & King & Major Cunningham.[8] It was too late to call at Hd. Qrs.

SAN ANTONIO TEXAS FRI. AUG. 24, 1860

I went to the office & reported.[9] I saw Col. Lee, Capt. Withers, Major Vinton, the three paymasters, etc. I then went out & made some purchases. It rained a heavy shower in the afternoon. I wrote to Dr. Tripler.

After the shower Charles & I went out & I finished nearly all my shopping. Towards evening Capt. Withers & Mr. Dwyer called & after tea Col. Lee & then Major Macklin. I was preparing to go to Major Vintons, but it was now too late. The Doctor goes tomorrow evening.

SAN ANTONIO TEXAS SAT. AUG. 25, 1860

Rain last night & all to-day & still continues. I went & draw of Major Cunningham my pay for July & Aug. $523.60. I had the Ambulance up & Dr. Foard & I called around town. Col. Lee detained me first in the office an hour

---

[8] William Henry Chase Whiting, a Mississippian who graduate first in the West Point class of 1845, was a captain in the topographical engineers. Whiting had led an exploring expedition into the trans-Pecos in 1849. Henry Boynton Clitz, West Point class of 1845, was a captain in the 3d Infantry. Andrew W. Bowman, West Point class of 1841, was also a captain in the 3d Infantry. Truitt cannot be identified with certainty. For Blair, see footnote 10; for King, footnote 17; and for Cunningham, footnote 30, all in the May 1859 chapter. Heitman, *Historical Register*, 234, 310, 1030.

[9] For Heintzelman's arrival at the Menger Hotel in San Antonio, see *Alamo Express* (San Antonio), Aug. 25, 1860.

about Capt. Caldwell's claim for pay for bunks made for his compy & for which he paid from his company fund. I dont think that it will be allowed.

We called at Capt. Wither's, Capt. Reynold's, Col. Sewell's & Dr. Abadie's & at Mrs. Washingtons's but was sick. After we returned we got dinner & at 5 P.M. the stage came & the Doctor & Charles left in it for Indianola. Charles went off in good spirits.

After they left I called on Cols. Lee & Backus & on Major & Mrs. Macklin.[10]

I saw Mr. Smyth who was at Verde a few weeks ago & he sends Margaret a basket of peaches.[11] I would have gone to Vinton's but it got too late & rains too hard.

I wrote to Wrightson & to Dr. Tripler & enclosed a check for $180 & gave to Charles & also $80 to Dr. Foard to pay his expenses.

I have made all my arrangements & shall leave at 7½ A.M. tomorrow. I saw Major Graham but his wife was not dressed. Since the Doctor & Charles have left it appears quite lonesome. I have made arrangements for a peck of peaches & a lunch for the road.

San Geronimo Texas Sun. Aug. 26, 1860

It was misting rain when we started. I directed the wagon to be at the Hotel at 7 A.M., but it was late & did not get out of town till nine O'Clock. I sent for peaches but I did not get them until near 9 & then very poor ones. I left at a quarter before 9 in a drizzle.

After we had been on the road out of town I saw what looked like the wagon on the road. The drizzle turned into a heavy rain at intervals. The first part of the road was very heavy & in the last the mountain a little rough, but not by any means a bad road. We got to this creek at 4:45 P.M. & I made the distance 26 miles.

Camp Verde Texas Mon. Aug. 27, 1860

It rained very hard all night. I slept in the carriage. The wagon did not come up & we could not get anything for our mules. The men got sup & breakfast at a house close by & slept in the rain. We waited till 8:45 A.M. & the wagon not coming we went on. There is one rough mountain to descend, but by no means a bad one. We found the road badly washed in one place & had to go around. It did not rain on us, but the road was in many places very

---

[10] Electus Backus, West Point class of 1824, was a lieutenant colonel in the 3d Infantry. Heitman, *Historical Register*, 86, 179.

[11] This may have been Payton Smythe, thirty-six and a well-to-do Bexar County farmer.

muddy. We got here at 6 P.M. & as the odometer did not register I estimate the distance 22 miles or 58 in all. I think this the preferable road, & particularly in wet weather. I dont think that I could have reached here in two days by Boerne. It rained here very hard to-day & the ground is covered with water near here. The Verde was so high that it reached in the side of the carriage. We could just cross. It was been raining here since. 11¾ inches rain have fallen. Margaret did not go out to Dr. Ganahls, as she expected.

CAMP VERDE TEXAS TUES. AUG. 28, 1860

About 10½ P.M. a discharged Sergt. who was with the wagon came in & reported the wagon upset at 3 P.M. yesterday from the breaking of a frame string & that one of the soldiers & Capt. Bracketts cold. woman had their shoulders out of place & Mrs. McNulty badly bruised. I sent out a wagon & my Ambulance got in at 2 P.M. & the wagon at 6 P.M. It upset about 18 miles from here. They only came 15 miles on Sun. The roads were so heavy & the wagon also. It did not rain yesterday & the sun was out a little.

CAMP VERDE TEXAS WED. AUG. 29, 1860

It rained again last night & is dull & unpleasant to-day, with a drizzle. Lt. Mowers kitchen is partly down again.

We have no mail—on account of high water.

CAMP VERDE TEXAS AUG. 30, 1860

It was cloudy this morning, but I believe the rain is over. We rode out on horseback yesterday & found it very wet. I brought home from S. Antonio some peaches & find them quite a luxury. We have some pigin grapes.[12]

CAMP VERDE FRI. AUG. 31, 1860

Had muster this morning. Weather pleasant. Pollicarp & the Doctor went out yesterday hunting & killed a deer & found a bee tree. No mail yet from S.A. One from Sisterdale got in.[13] Everybody went out riding. Margaret & I in the buggy, but it was so wet & muddy we did not go far. The hills are [composed of] layers of limestone & the water ooses from them.

---

[12] From a high-climbing vine, the Pigeon or Summer Grape (*vitix aestivalis Michx*) produces a dark blue to black fruit from one-fifth to one-half inch in diameter, usually in September and October. Resistant to cold and drought, the Pigeon Grape was common in the Texas Hill County. Vines, *Trees, Shrubs, and Woody Vines of the Southwest*, 713, 718.

[13] A predominantly German community, Sisterdale was located about fifteen miles north of Boerne in Kendall County. The community originated in 1847, when Nicholas Zink built a log cabin in the valley of Sister Creek. Webb, Carroll, and Branda (eds.), *Handbook of Texas*, II, 616.

❧ September 1860 ❧

"Our first norther commenced last night."

CAMP VERDE TEXAS SUN. SEPT. 2, 1860

Yesterday afternoon a man from near Kerrsville reported three of his horses stolen by Indians & a calf killed—arrows in it. I sent the guide & ten men in pursuit. I also had reported some trails in the direction of Bandera.

Margaret & I took a ride on horseback yesterday & a walk with the Caldwells this afternoon.

MON. SEPT. 3, 1960

Wrote to Mr. & Mrs. Futhey & to Lt. Gillam & sent the latter a pamphlet of directions for sewing machines. In the afternoon Margaret & I rode on horseback. Our scout has not returned. I presume they have found an Indian trail. The camels & party that went from here returned yesterday. They made no discovery.

TUES. SEPT. 4, 1860

Wrote to Major S. Macklin about the short route to this place from S. Antonio.

Two men came in from the scout with broken down horses, having left the party yesterday 50 miles from here on the trail of three Indians. Some citizens are along with our party.

WED. SEPT. 5, 1860

Our mail got in to-day & late & the first mail from S.A. in two weeks. I got from Capt. Dana $980 in a draft on New York, which closed by business with Mahoney. I had to pay $20 for a draft or sustain an entire loss of $270. I am glad it is no worse.

I have sent it to T. Wrightson to first pay up the Sta. Rita & help the Sonora. I have letters from him & H. Howe with copies of Stockholders meeting. The prospect is that something will be done to relieve us from our embarrassments. There is a letter from Mr. Ehrenberg to Poston giving a most gloomy account of our affairs at the mines. Poor Brucknow has been murdered with two other Mexicans at the St. Louis Mines 35 miles from Ft. Buchanan.[1] It is a sad fate. I also got a letter from Col. Emory in reply to one I wrote him at Ft. Cobb near a year ago. Also wedding cards, Lt. Graham to Miss Ricketts. A letter from Matilda Stuart & a circular for a school. Plenty of newspapers. Wrightson writes that Cheever had paid up the $500 acceptance, but it comes minus $48 expenses. W. also sent me a long letter detailing the attempt at swindling of the New Yorkers with our company.

Camp Verde Texas Thurs. Sept. 6, 1860

Weather beautiful. I have been busy all the morning writing letters on our Sonora affairs. I have written to Mr. Howe Cin. Ehrenberg at the mines & Schuchard. I feel quite encouraged at our prospects again. Wrote to Mr. Lathrop, Arivaca.

Fri. Sept. 7, 1860

A few drops of rain. We rode out yesterday in the buggy—very muddy in places. To-day rode on horseback. I sent my letter by Cloud's carts to S. Antonio & am in hopes that those for Cincinnati will arrive before the meeting of Sonora Ex. & M. Co. on the 17 Sept.

Camp Verde Texas Sat. Sept 8, 1860

Back of our quarters is a small ravine. At night about 10 O'Clock the water commenced running & stops about 10 or 11 next day.

Margaret got a letter yesterday from Charles. They were five days in getting to Indianola & delayed a day & a half at Yorktown by the high waters. He lost his pocket book, in the stage—with $2.50.

Sun. Sept. 9, 1860

A few drops of rain yesterday & a shower last night. The scout was out of provisions yesterday & should be home.

---

[1] Brunchow, along with J. C. Mapes, a chemist, and James Williams, a machinist, was murdered at the San Pedro Silver Mine near what became Tombstone by Mexican employees on July 23, 1860. North, *Samuel Peter Heintzelman*, 196; 8th Census, Arizona County, New Mexico Territory.

MON. SEPT. 10, 1860

The mosquitoes were very bad last night. We put up our bar this morning. Nothing from our scout yet. Their provisions were out on Saturday. One of my American horses has had a nail in his hoof & is quite lame & my Mexican [horse] is also lame. The blk smith was drunk when he shod him.

TUES. SEPT. 11, 1860

Wrote to Dr. Summers. The scout got back this afternoon. Went as far as the headwaters of the San Saba & were near the Indians, but could not overtake them. One horse gave out & had to be abandoned.

I started with Margaret & the Doctor to take a ride but my horse is lame & I turned back.

WED. SEPT. 12, 1860

Weather cloudy last night & this morning. We are going in the morning on a bee hunting expedition.

To-day's mail brought me a printed letter from Mr. Killbreath, offering me my pro rata of the Bonds. I wrote to W. Wrightson that I had sent all my spare cash to his brother to invest as he would his own. I also got a long letter from Mr. Lathrop. It is gloomy enough. He has been to Sonora & is pleased with his trip. He thinks that Col. Talcott does not understand business.

I wrote to Lathrop & Wrightson.

CAMP VERDE TEXAS THURS. SEPT. 13, 1860

As we were mounting to go out to cut the bee tree Major Macklin drove up. We went, but in less than [an] hour it commenced a heavy rain. Margaret & Miss Helen got quite wet—the first time in their lives with rain. We got near the place but in the rain & cloudy weather. Pollicarp lost the direction & we could not find the tree. We turned & got back soon after eleven. I dont think the distance over six miles.

I drew my pay for this month—$157.

I dont think that Margaret feels any inconveniences from the rain. It has continued.

SUN. SEPT. 16, 1860

On Friday morning the pay master left. He took tea with us & he & his son spent the evening here. It was raining when he left & also yesterday. In the afternoon we rode on horseback. I shot a rattle snake on the hills & got his rattle—six rattlers.

It is clear & pleasant to-day.

Camp Verde Texas Mon. Sept. 17, 1860

Last night was the coldest we have had this summer. We had this morning a heavy dew. The day has been pleasant. Miss Lacy & Dr. Byrne rode with us on horseback.

Wed. Sept. 19, 1860

I wrote a letter yesterday to Matilda. Margaret & I took a short ride in the evening.

The mail to-day brought letters from Charles. He had started from Baton Rouge. I also got a letter from Dr. Tripler. He has put Stuart to another school & there will be a vacation for October. I am sorry as Charles has not studied much since I came from the Rio Grande & I fear not much whilst I was there.

I got a long letter from Ehrenberg. He thinks that Col. Talcott is no business man. I fear that he is right about it. I wrote to Poston & Wrightson & Ehrenberg. I got a letter from Galvan.[2] No news. I got the order for Bracketts compy to Camp Ives & Evans to Camp Cooper.

Thurs. Sept. 20, 1860

Our first norther commenced last night. Mer. this morning at 61° & at no time to-day over 74°, Margaret & I took a ride towards Turtle Creek. The road is quite steep beyond the Pass of Verde.

The soldiers had a dance at the Hospital last evening. Some one tried to steal money out of one of the camp women's trunk & broke it open.

Camp Verde Texas Sat. Sept. 22, 1860

We—Margaret & I & Dr. Byrne, Mr. Newton, Pollycarp & Miss Lacy rode out in the hills about six miles & cut a bee tree & spent the day. We brought home two pails of honey & spent a very pleasant day. All were pretty tired.

---

[2] This particular letter is not in the Heintzelman Papers. Three months earlier on June 24, 1860, however, Galvan had written Heintzelman from Brownsville. Although the border was relatively quiet, troops were on patrol for *Cortinistas* and the Knights of the Golden Circle, Galvan said, who were stealing horses in Mexico. Although Cortina had not been heard from, he was rumored to be a short distance from the border and three of his men had been caught on the north bank. They had managed, however, to bribe a temporary jailer while the regular jailer was at a fandango and had escaped into Mexico. Galvan to Heintzelman, June 24, 1860, HP.

The soldiers had a dance last evening at the Hospital for Sergt. Drury, the Ord. Sergt. who goes to Ft. Duncan next week. The weather quite pleasant though a little cool. It is pleasant to-day.

WED. SEPT. 26, 1860

We took a walk Saturday afternoon. On Monday I wrote to Galvan & to Lt. Washington. We then took a ride on horseback.

Yesterday after dinner Margaret & I rode on horseback to Dr. Ganahl's. He has been sick since he returned from S. Antonio. He got from Major Howard the Doctors (Foards) & Charles daguerrotypes, or rather Photographs. They are good.

This morning mail brought me three letters from Mr. Lathrop dated Aug. 31st & Sept. 5 & 6th. He is very much disgusted with Col. Talcott & says he will not do for us. I also got a letter from Major Lowry at the Dolores Mine Vallecillo Mexico. His furance does well. I wrote to Solon & to T. Wrightson. We had rain last night & shower or two to-day.

CAMP VERDE TEXAS THURS. 27 SEPT. 1860

We had a few drops rain this morning. Dr. Byrne by last mail heard of the death of his uncle, Dr. Byrne at Fort Moultrie. He went yesterday after his horse got lost & did not get home until 11 P.M.

The mail this morning brought me a letter from Dr. Foard. He has 4 mos. leave & is on his way to Milledgeville. I also got a letter from Schuchard.

Sun. Sept. 29, 1860

The captain & all his family, Mary & Mr. Newton rode down the creek to fish. Margaret & I rode out on horseback & joined them. They caught some fine fish & Mr. Newton sent us a large one. We had it for breakfast.

We had a review this morning preparing for Col. Mansfield, the Insp. Genl.[3]

---

[3] If Colonel Mansfield inspected Camp Verde, his report is not in LR, AGO, RG 94 (NA). Mansfield, in a spring wagon drawn by four mules and an escort of eleven men, left San Antonio on October 4, 1860, to inspect Fort Inge on October 7 and 8. Traveling to the upper Nueces, he inspected Camp Wood on October 11 and 12, but continued west on the Lower Military Road to Fort Davis, which he inspected on October 28 and 29. Continuing west, he inspected Fort Quitman on November 5 and returned east to inspect Fort Stockton on Novemer 29 and 30, before riding south to the Rio Grande to Fort Duncan, Fort McIntosh, Ringgold Barracks, and Fort Brown. "In consequence of indisposition," but in reality because of the growing secessionists crisis, Mansfield departed San Antonio on January 23, 1861, and arrived in

This is my birthday. I am now 55 years of age.

Washington on February 1. In command of the Union 12th Corps, he was killed at the Battle of Antietam.

Mansfield had inspected Fort Yuma on June 5 and 6, 1854, while Heintzelman was in command of the post. The Inspector General had also inspected Newport Barracks on April 6, 1856, while Heintzelman was stationed at the post. The two had also served on court martial duty at Fort Leavenworth in 1855. Mansfield to Cooper, Nov. 1, Dec. 1, 31, 1860; Feb. 2, 1861; Mansfield to Lorenzo Thomas, Oct. 9, 13, Nov. 7, 17, 21, 26, Dec. 6, 13, 19, 1860; Jan. 11, 14, 17, Feb. 22, Apr. 20, 1861; all in LR, AGO, RG 94 (NA); HJ, June 5, 6, 1854; Sept. 24, 1855, Apr. 6, 1856.

❧ October 1860 ☙

"Drove to the Guadalupe to gather pecans."

———◆•✦•◆———

Mon. Oct. 1st 1860

A dull day for me & as little happy as any one I ever spent in my recollection. Some matters I had doubts about begin to turn up into certainties. The past year had what should have given much satisfaction, but it was obtained at too great a cost. My birthday was forgotten & I although I was at every moment present, never mentioned It.

Last night I went to bed at the usual hour, but did not sleep until after one A.M.

I wrote a couple of letters this morning—one to Dr. Forad & one to Mr. Schuchard. I have not felt like doing more. I am waiting to see how facts will develop themselves, when I will decide what I will do.

Dr. Byrne & Mr. Pollycarpio spent the evening on our stoop. To-day has been quite warm. I have been trying to read.

Camp Verde Wed. Oct. 3, 1860

Yesterday afternoon we rode in the ambulance. Margaret, Mary & I & the Caldwells in theirs & Mr. Newton to Turtle Creek to fish. We fished in the Guadalupe. We went in the afternoon & did not get home till night.

I wrote to Mr. Wrightson yesterday.

I had a serious, or rather have, misunderstanding with Margaret about some letters. It is cool this morning. I feel I have done right, whatever consequences may follow.

To-day's mail brought Margaret letters from Caroline & from Charles. I also got one from the latter & his account of expenses to Newport. His letter is well written & the account well kept.

I also got a letter from Mr. Poston. The meeting came off satisfactorily & we have a Cin. Board of Directors. No Bonds have been sold yet.

I am sorry to hear that John D. Lark is involved & may involve T.

Wrightson. I also got the printed proceedings to Stoneman. I have also a short note from Mr. Lathrop. He expects to leave soon for home.

It looks like rain. I sold my 4 mule harness to Pollycarpo Carpi for $50 payable on 30 Nov. I am determined now to sell off everything that I can & get ready for leave. I think I will sometime this month write to Col. Lee & tell him I want to leave & give some good reasons. That I want to know so as to have time to make my arrangements.

I wrote to Mr. Lathrop & enclosed it to Capt. Reynolds in San Antonio. I also answered Charles letter. It appears odd to be writing to a son. This is I believe the first I ever received from him, except one or two in his mother's letters. I thought I would be at a loss to fill up a sheet, but there was no difficulty. He writes an excellent letter.

CAMP VERDE TEXAS OCT. 4, 1860

All hands rode out to Mason's creek to fish. We left the Caldwells there & Margaret & I, Mary & Dr. Byrne & two of Caldwell's children rode to Polly's rancho to get melons. We had as many as we could eat & I brought the carriage full. He has a nice place about three miles from Mason Creek. He made some corn but it was full of weeds.

The men fished with the seine but there was too much grass & they only caught two. Mr. Newton caught a string & we had a good dinner. On the surface everybody enjoyed themselves, but I know there was one whose heart was almost broke. We got home at dark.

C.V. THURS. OCT. 5, 1860

I wrote to Dr. J. Simmons about some furniture of his left at the post, as I see he takes the late Dr. Byrne's place at Ft. Moultrie.[1]

I did not put my letter to Mr. Lathrop in the office last night as I proposed changing it. I read it over this morning & let it go as first written. It is indefinite enough.

The Dr. Ganahl's were in to-day & made us a visit. In a few days he goes to Uvalde & will leave their little girl Lisa to stay with us. They made quite a long visit.

I learned from them as well as from Mr. Newton a little before that a triweekly stage will come to Comfort. I sat down & wrote to Mr. Lathrop to take it to Comfort & I will come after him. I think I will ride down to Comfort tomorrow & see how the mails will run. This will be a great convenience to

---

[1] James Simons, a South Carolinian, had been a surgeon in the army since 1839. Heitman, *Historical Register*, 388. See footnote 10, June 1859 chapter.

us. I also heard that Lt. Col. Morris had gone on 4 mos. sick leave. I fear this will prevent my going until late in December.

Sat. Oct. 6, 1860

Dr. Byrne, Mr. Newton & I rode on horseback to Comfort to inquire about the mails. We are to have a stage tri-weekly from S.A. to Comfort & Fredericksburg. It will probably commence in a few days. We met Mr. Smyth of S.A. on his way up here & returned together. We stopped on the road & had lunch. I was very tired when I got home.

Camp Verde Mon. Oct. 8, 1860

Mr. Smyth took breakfast with us & left to return to Boerne before dinner yesterday. He came to me about the corn contract he has for this Post & Mason.

Mrs. Ganahl sent in her little girl & Jane her maid to stay here till they return from Uvalde. She wrote for Polly the guide & I reluctantly let him go. We can ill spare him. He will be gone over a week.

It is close & cloudy this morning.

Margaret & I are all right once again I hope.

Tues. Oct. 9, 1860

Quite warm yesterday. We rode on horseback in the afternoon. In the evening the wind came from the north & this morning it is much cooler.

Polly the guide left yesterday morning to join Dr. Ganahls. Wrote to Mr. Poston.

Wed. Oct. 10, 1860

Cloudy & cool. Our warm weather is no doubt over. The Caldwells went out yesterday afternoon for Pecans. They never said a word to any one. When the herd came in we rode out in our Ambulance. It was so late we got but few. It is too early—they are only beginning to ripen.

Thurs. Oct. 11, 1860

The mail came in & brought me a long letter from Mr. Hooper. He is in San Francisco & has a house. He sent me his bill for Taxes paid. It is over $80 for Dr. Summers & mine. He dont separate them.

Our Comfort stage is I believe a favour. We arranged to go to Bandera & try to make some arrangements there.

CAMP VERDE TEXAS FRI. OCT. 12, 1860

We started for Bandera on horseback, but it was cold & drizzling rain commenced. We went half a mile & turned back. It quit rain, but is cloudy & cool.

I have a violent pain since yesterday through my left shoulder & chest, made me turn back.

FRI. OCT. 12, 1860

I am a day ahead. The mail got in to-day & I got a long letter from Col. Kennett. Our Sonora co's affairs promise well again. Mr. Killbreath has gone to N.Y. to raise money & Mr. Poston is to go to Arizona & buy a portable steam engine & start the works.

The weather is quite cool. Woolen clothing in demand.

SAT. OCT. 13, 1860

Still cool. Lt. Harrison & wife arrived from Duncan with horses for Capt. Evans compy & our wagons.[2] We got no potatoes. Capt. Evans & his company will be here in a few days. Lt. H. has to go to Ft. Brown—the G. Court Martial had when I was there reassembled. Lt. Thomas has also to attend & Lt. Burson, one from N.Y. & the other Burton.

Lt. H. & his wife stay with us.

SUN. OCT. 14, 1860

Mr. Sherbourne came in from Dr. Ganahl's & spent the day. The weather has been cool & fires necessary. I believe that Lt. & Mrs. Harrison will leave tomorrow. He wants a wagon to take his baggage to San Antonio.

CAMP VERDE TEXAS MON. OCT. 15, 1860

Mer. 41° this morning, but clear & pleasant. Lt. & Mrs. Harrison left here this forenoon for S. Antonio. I had to let them take a wagon for their baggage. They went the short road. They had scarcely been gone before Dr. Ganahl drove up & Lisa & her governess Eunice. He left his family at the crossing of the creek waiting for him. After camping out, they did not care to come into camp. We are now again alone. Lt. & Mrs. Harrison are quite pleasant. She is a daughter of Mr. Leeper, the Indian Agent at Cooper.[3]

---

[2] James E. Harrison was a second lieutenant in the 2d Cavalry. Capt. Nathan George Evans had served in the 2d Cavalry since 1855. Heitman, *Historical Register*, 410, 505.

[3] On March 14, 1857, Matthew Leeper had been appointed to succeed the con-

THURS. OCT. 18, 1860

The mail in yesterday & brought Margaret a letter from Charles. He saw the Prince of Wales in Cincinnati. I got a letter from Mr. W. Wrightson enclosing one I wrote to Mr. Lathrop & misdirected. He also sent me a very good map of the Arizona Mines made by Mr. Grosvenor. It dont make our mines as prominent as it might. He also sent me a copy of the last proceedings & of a letter he wrote to Mr. Poston. I will answer it today. It is still cool. Mr. Lathrop writes that he expects to leave on the 10 Oct. Mr. W. writes hopefully about raising the money & that Mr. Poston will go out.

FRI. OCT. 19, 1860

Lt. Mower left this morning on 6 days leave for S. Antonio. He & Capt. Caldwell had some words about a remark the former made about a carrion as he called it, hung on his door.

Capt. Brackett arrived this forenoon & his & Capt. Evan's companies—from the Rio Grande.

C.V. SUN. OCT. 21, 1860

We all took a walk this afternoon to the top of the hill & I saw the cave they talk so much about. It is a narrow cleft in the rocks & not ten feet deep. There appears to be water at the bottom.

MON. OCT. 22

We all drove to the Guadalupe to gather pecans. The result of a whole day was not a bushel all told. I am disappointed in the number of trees & quantities of them. We however had a pleasant day of it.

TUES. OCT. 23, 1860

The wagon from S.A. got up yesterday. It was detained through Lt. Harrison's carelessness. We got a few potatoes—& sweet.

Our mail got in at 3½ P.M. I have a letter from Solon dated 3 Oct. He still expects to leave on the 10th or about.

Polly is back from San Antonio.

WED. OCT 24, 1860

We—Dr. Byrne, Margaret & I rode out to Camp Ives on horseback & did

---

troversial John Robert Baylor as agent to the Comanches at the reserve on the Clear Fork of the Brazos. Kenneth Franklin Neighbours, *Robert Simpson Neighbors and the Texas Frontier, 1836–1859* (Waco: Texian Press, 1975), 181, 185, 285.

not get home till after dark. The Captain wished me to inspect his ordnance equipment, condemn it, to get a new supply. He had such a mess that I did not have time & will have to go out tomorrow. Lt. Mower got back at 2 P.M. Lt. Col. Morris & Lt. Washington he met in S.A. The latter came after supplies & the former looked very well. He wants to go out in the spring. It was very dusty at S.A. & no news, except political.

CAMP VERDE THURS. OCT. 25, 1860

I had my horse saddled to go to Ives this morning, but Capt. Caldwell told me of an old order about Ordnance stores. I doubt how far my authority extends & not a note. I will not be there & have written to Capt. Whitely at S.A. to know how to act. I think it the safest way.

I sent a man with our mail to Comfort.

FRI. OCT. 26, 1860

I wrote three letters—to Capt. Stoneman on the Rio Grande, to Major Lowry at the Dolores mine, Vallecillo mine, Mexico & to Col. Kennett Cincinnati.

Capt. Brackett drove in yesterday & we had a talk about his ordnance stores & we have concluded to wait.

SAT. OCT. 27, 1860

Yesterday Margaret & I rode on horseback & saw some Pecan trees. This afternoon we drove down the river & gathered a few. Capt. Brackett rode in as we were at dinner with some papers, he had to deal with Lt. Mower.

Our mail we sent for. I got a letter from Charles. He is going to pay a week's visit to the Wrightsons.

SUN. OCT. 28, 1860

I intended to write some letters to-day, but I have spent most of the forenoon reading newspapers—some I got from Dr. Byrne. He & Polly went hunting Fri. & he shot three Turkeys at a roost. He sent us one, we had to-day for dinner. It is record (game) this year. I read in a Balitmore paper that Philip Arndt's barn & several others in Manheim Pa. were burned the first week this month.

CAMP VERDE TEXAS MON. OCT. 29, 1860

Dr. Byrnes & Polly went Turkey hunting up the creek.

TUES. OCT. 30, 1860

Sharp, one of the men out hunting ducks up the Verde shot a she bear 1½ miles off. We went up & saw her cut up. The Doctor & Polly returned with 13 Turkeys, having got into a large Turkey roost. The Doctor gave us three & we gave one to Capt. Brackett who was in. I was going out but no one was ready to go & the bear was killed.

Yesterday I wrote to Sisters Maria & Juliana & to Charles.

The mail brought me letters from Ehrenberg & Lathrop. The latter has fever at Tubac. Wrote to Ehrenberg.

WED. OCT. 31, 1860

We had muster etc. It rained & we have a cold norther. I was going out to Camp Ives, but it is to unpleasant.

"There appears to be no doubt of Lincoln's election."

———•·••·•———

Fri. Nov. 2, 1860

Yesterday Margaret & I took a short ride on horseback. Weather cool, as well as today.

Dr. Byrne, Mr. Newton & I rode to Camp Ives. I condemned some horses & Qr. M. property. We got back to dinner.

Sun. Nov. 4, 1860

Yesterday we had dinner at 12 & Dr. Byrne, Mr. Newton & I rode out to Mason's Creek after Turkeys. About four miles from here Polly shot a fine gob[b]ler, the only shot anyone had. We stopped at dusk & tried to get a shot at a roost, but they were so shy we could not. We got home at 9½ P.M. It was a beautiful day. We rode 18 or 20 miles. We saw three deer but I did not get a shot.

Before we left the mail got in. Margaret got a letter from Charles & I from Dr. Tripler & Mr. Howe & Mr. Poston. Our company failed to sell their bonds & have leased the mine to Poston for ten years at $10,000 & 15,000$ for 5 more. I am assessed 2,000$ for my share & Colt is not allowed to come in at all. If I understand it right it is a good arrangement, but the information I have is not very definite. Some hard things are said against Mr. Lathrop & I fear with considerable justice. W. Wrightson paid Mr. Poston $300 on my account. Why not $800? I dont know as I had that amount of money in his hands. I fear that he has used it in his business & it was not available. I dont like the way busisnessmen do business. If my account is correct I should have over $850 in W's hands. If it is so I can without much difficulty raise some $2,000.

This is a beautiful day. We had Dr. Byrne, Newton & Polly to dinner.

We yesterday passed a tree with a black berry that Polly called the "Noe." It is the first I have seen & I like the taste.

Mon Nov. 5, 1860

This is the anniversary of St. Clair's defeat.

"On the 5th of Nov. in the year '91, we had a severe engagement near Fort Jefferson."[1]

I have written three letters to-day—to Howe, T. Wrightson & Poston, about our mining company. I will try & furnish all the money required of me—$2,000.

A little rain last night.

I broke the main spring of my watch. It is always getting out of order.

Camp Verde Texas Tuess. Nov. 6, 1860

Our mail went out this morning & we got a return in the afternoon. It did not amount to much. I did not get one private letter. I got an order from Col. Lee about the fight with Indians etc. since a previous order. In Gen. Scott's style. Dr. Foard sent me a N.Y. Herald & the "Billard Cue" a New York paper.

It is Presidential election day.

It is a dull cloudy cold day. Wind North & a little rain.

Wed. Nov. 7, 1860

Heavy rain, thunder & lightening last evening. We had Capt. Caldwell's family, Dr. Byrne & Mr. Newton & played cards last evening.

We got an order to suspend all repairs, after additions & to put horses & mules on half allowance.

It is still cloudy, rainy & unpleasant.

Fri. Nov. 9, 1860

Yesterday was cold, rain, & unpleasant. Spent the evening at Capt. Caldwell's playing cards.

---

[1] Along with a 2,000-man army, Gen. Arthur St. Clair, first governor of the Northwest Territory, blundered into an ambush masterminded by Miami Chief Little Turtle near present-day Fort Wayne, Indiana, on November 5, 1791. General St. Clair had 600 men killed in the worst defeat suffered by the U.S. Army in the Indian Wars. Heintzelman had read a book on the defeat in 1844 and became convinced that Gen. St. Clair, a "gallant officer," was not responsible for the defeat. Clifford H. Richards, *Little Turtle: The Man and His Land* (Fort Wayne: Allen County Historical Society, 1974), 3–7; HJ, Oct. 23, 1844.

SAT. NOV. 10, 1860

This morning Capt. Caldwell's family & ours, with Mr. Newton & Polly the guide went six miles out towards Bandera & gathered Pecans. We got about a bushel & had a pleasant day. Dr. Byrne did not go—said it wont pay.

Our mail was in when we got home. I got letters from Mr. Lathrop—he is bitter & will soon leave. Mr. Galvan & two B'ville newspapers—& Major Ketchum at Ft. Vancouver.

I also got back some papers from S. Antonio. There is an evident effort to find fault with what I do, by Major Vinton. He has now put his foot in & I will make him keep it there.

C. VERDE SUN. NOV. 11, 1860

We had a review this morning, to instruct officers & men. The doctor dont know much about his military duties.

TUES. NOV. 13, 1860

Yesterday was a beautiful day. We rode in the Ambulance to Camp Ives & invited Miss Lacy & Mrs. Newton. Capt. Brackett was at Dr. Ganahls & we drove to Mr. Reeses & got a few sweet potatos & turnips. On our return he was home & Mrs. Thompson & Mrs. Ganahl also. I examined the ordnance stores & we got home about 3 P.M. It rained last night & is cloudy wet & disagreeable today.

It is a year to-day since I left here for the Rio Grande. Our mail got in late. Capt. Caldwell & I are on a court to meet at Ft. Mason on the 26th with all our prisoners & witnesses. Margaret got a letter from Charles & one from Dr. Foard, enclosing a photograph of the Prince of Wales & a needle threader.

Solon writes on the 26th of Oct. that he is better & will get off in about ten days. I also got a letter from Mr. T. Wrightson. He lost $10,000 by Mr. Park but hopes to get some back.[2] He sends me an account & I find he paid my S.P.R.R. & had but $304.70 of my money left. He says he will protect my interest.

I am very much disgusted with the court martial order & fear it will interfere with my leave.

---

[2] John D. Park, a Cincinnati merchant who sold "family patent medicines," was a director of the Santa Rita Silver Mining Company who purchased $30,000 worth of stock in the Sonora Exploring and Mining Company in 1856. North, *Samuel Peter Heintzelman*, 23, 195.

CAMP VERDE TEXAS WED. NOV 14, 1860

Much rain, thunder, lightening & wind last night. Margaret is very much put out about this order & lays it all to me, because I did not make an application for leave long ago. It is very much like "I told you so." She says she wont stay in Texas this winter. I told her she could go out with Solon, if I could not go.

Capt. Caldwell went to Comfort this morning to attend to Aunt Lacey's case. The complaint Cloud made that she is a free cold. woman. Mary went with the Capt. & his children.

THURS. NOV. 15, 1860

A cold windy norther this morning. Pvt. Howe has left for S. Antonio & sent my watch with him to have a new main spring put in.

The Captain got back yesterday before night. I believe he got his matters arranged satisfactorily about Old Lacey. I wrote yesterday to Mr. Lathrop, T. Wrightson & sent a circular of the Odometer to Sanders of Roma Tex.

The sewing machine has got so it wont work.

Capt. Brackett & Mr. Gallager are in. We are to meet & dine at Dr. Ganahl's with Judge Davis & some lawyers from Comfort tomorrow. We were invited before to spend the day there.

It is still cold & uncomfortable.

CAMP VERDE SAT. NOV. 17, 1860

We were looking for the paymaster, but he did not come & at 12 we started (Marg. & Mary) & I for Dr. Ganahls. Judge Davis, & Lawyers Cotter & Cox soon came.[3] Capt. Brackett was there & we spent a pleasant day. We dined late in the afternoon & left at dusk. The ride home was cool.

To-day has been cool. The mail did not bring me a private letter or newspaper. I got some orders. Col. Lee wants to know whether I intend to keep Capt. Brackett at Camp [Ives] or bring him in here & wants to know what horse accommodations I have.

SUN. NOV. 18, 1860

A beautiful day. We had a mutiny of the "Bar" club last night, at Capt. Caldwells. It was his birthday. This morning Capt. Brackett came in & we

---

[3] A. E. Cotten was a twenty-two-year-old Virginia-born attorney. Cox is possibly Samuel Cox, who is listed on the 1850 Bexar County census. 7th and 8th Census, Bexar County.

examined the stables with reference to his moving in. We both have decided that he had better remain where he is.

Capt. Brackett & Capt. Caldwell dined with us.

Mon. Nov. 19, 1860

A warm pleasant day. All the doors & windows open. Capt. Brackett sent his Blk. S. in & I had all the horses shod. Pvt. Howe returned & brought me my watch. It was not the main, but the click spring broken. The repair cost six dollars. My watch, beside being frequently out of order is expensive. I am writing to Lt. Gillam.

We are all going tomorrow evening to see a dance here Mrs. Ganahl's governess is giving to our Sergts.

C. Verde Texas Tues. Nov. 20, 1860

Wind north, cloudy, cool & unpleasant. The morning was pleasant. We had Lt. & Mrs. Mower, Dr. Byrne & Mr. Newton to dinner. It passed off pleasantly.

Our mail came in after dinner. Mr. Lathrop will soon leave for home. I got a letter dated 1st Nov. I also have a letter from Dr. Foard. He is in Phild.—dated Nov. 2, 1860.

There appears to be no doubt of Lincoln's election as President. There is great excitement, but I think all will blow over.

All the garrison, but the Mowers, are invited to Dr. Ganahl's but no one will go but us.

Wed. Nov. 21, 1860

All backed out because the invitation did not suit their views, so that no one went but Margaret, Mary & I to Dr. Ganahl's. We left here about dusk. We met at Dr. G's a Mr. Phips & wife from N. Orleans, living near Comfort. Capt. Brackett & Mr. Gallagher were also there. We had a cup of coffee & then went to see the dance.

The evening passed off pleasantly & it was 2 P.M. before we went to bed. We occupied Mr. G's room. We danced at one end of the room. All went off well except one of our Sergts got a little too much to drink. After they went to their supper we returned to the house & had ours.

The mail got in yesterday. Solon is well & will soon be here. I got a letter from Dr. Foard dated Nov. 4. He is in Phild.

Lincoln is no doubt elected president & South Carolina is going to make a fool of herself. I dont think that the other States will join her in secession.

There will be considerable excitement but I suppose it will subside in a short time.

It rained last night is cold & unpleasant.

CAMP VERDE THURS. NOV. 22, 1860

The paymaster got in yesterday afternoon. He only pays here & at Ives. He let the sutlers pay at other places. He brought an order from Col. Lee letting me know that Major Van Dorn is on the court & should be placed above me. It was not courteous to put me on a court with him. The order is at S.A. for Gen. Twiggs to return to the Dept. He is expected every day. I am glad of it.

Major Macklin thinks there will be a dissolution of the Union. I cant believe it yet. Margaret is very much provoked at this order putting me below Major Van Dorn & says it is my fault as I did not do all I ought. She dont feel well to-day. It rained last night & still continues. We will have a disagreeable journey.

I drew my pay for Oct. $261.80 of Major Macklin. He gave me a check for $300 I sent to Mr. Poston in Tubac & I have another for $51.20 for Mr. Hooper. Major Macklin took dinner with us & left for Camp Ives.

There is more prospects of it clearing off. It is warmer.

Paid William to-day to the 24 of the Month.

FORT MASON TEXAS TUES. NOV. 27, 1860

Spring 19 Miles from Verde Fri. Nov. 23, 1860

Wind north & cold & unpleasant. We left Verde at 9 A.M. with two wagons & about 30 men. At Dr. Ganahl's we met 9 men from Camp Ives. We stopped there near an hour, got a cup of coffee & Dr. G. showed us a shorter road to leave Comfort to the right. The road is tolerably good, with the exception of one or two places.

CHERRY VALLEY SPRING[4] SAT. NOV. 24, 1860

We had a very cold night. Ice before we went to bed & the first I have seen this year.

We only stopped a few minutes at Fredericksburg. I learned the court had adjourned & the man did not know where Judge Davis would be found. We estimated it 12 miles to Fredericksburg so we came 15 miles further. The road is tolerable, one bad hill.

---

[4] Cherry Spring, a small community sixteen miles north of Fredericksburg and ten miles west of Enchanted Rock, had been established in the early 1850s.

COMANCHE CREEK[5] 3 MILES FROM MASON SUN. NOV. 25, 1860

We had a little rain. We crossed the Llano, a fine stream. It was very high when the Verde was last summer. We have a great many pecans. I gathered several quarts in a little while.

FORT MASON[6] MON. NOV. 26, 1860

Major Van Dorn sent a man with a note for us to come to his house—he had a room & plate.

I sent Capt. Brackett's men in to the Post, as their forage was out. It rained in the afternoon & off & on all night but not hard. It rained a little this morning. We got in to this place at 9 A.M.

Major Van Dorn met us very cordially & showed us a comfortable room. We saw several of the officers. At ten our Court met.

The officers are, Major Van Dorn, Maj. Heintzelman, Capts. Caldwell & Johnson, Lts. Shaaff, Phiffer & Porter & Lt. Minter Judge Advocate.[7] Capt. McArthur is the only other officer at the Post.[8] Major Van Dorn has had very little experience as Presd. & Lt. Menton none as Judge Advocate. We have some thirty cases to try & got through three to-day.

All the officers dined at Major Van Dorns at 5 P.M. We had a nice dinner & pleasant time. The sutler Mr. Ward, I saw in San Antonio dined with us.[9]

I wrote to Margaret & it goes off in tomorrow's mail.

The officers have later news than we had at Verde. They say that S. Carolina has seceeded & that others of the Southern States will. It is sad news.

----

    [5] Comanche Creek rises in north central Mason County and flows southeast about twenty miles into the Llano River.

    [6] See footnote 11, September 1859 chapter.

    [7] Richard W. Johnson, a Kentuckian and an 1849 West Point graduate, had been promoted to captain in the 2d Cavalry in December 1856. James Nelson Caldwell was a captain in the 1st Infantry. Charles W. Phifer was a second lieutenant in the 2d Cavalry who became a brigadier general in the Confederate Army. Andrew Parker Porter, twenty-four, from the West Point class of 1856, was also a second lieutenant in the 2d Cavalry. Second Lt. Joseph F. Minter served as quartermaster of the 2d Cavalry from October 1857 to 1861. For Shaaff, see footnote 9, April 1859 chapter. Shaaff's wife, Helen, twenty-one and from Kentucky, and a four-month-old daughter, were at the post. Heitman, *Historical Register*, 273, 577, 715, 788, 798; 8th Census, Mason County.

    [8] Joseph Hunter McArthur, West Point class of 1849, had been promoted to captain in the 2d Cavalry in 1860. Heitman, *Historical Register*, 652.

    [9] Louisiana-born James J. Ward, forty, was the sutler at Fort Mason. Six laundresses were also listed on the 1860 census at the post. 8th Census, Mason County.

Fort Mason Tues. Nov. 27, 1860

It rained last night & is cold & was rainy & unpleasant to-day. We sat till near 3 P.M. & only tired one case. The Judge Advocate is not [an] expert. The room is very uncomfortable & I went & looked at the Mason spring. It is a nice spring but the Post is on a hill & is far off. It is great labor to haul everything up to it. The buildings are small & open. I have not seen any of the ladies yet.

Fort Mason Texas Wed. Nov. 28, 1860

After tea a while Capt. McArthur, Capt. Caldwell & I went & called on Mrs. Lt. Minter. She is not handsome or interesting, at least on a short acquaintance.

We, Capt. C. & I went & called at Lt. Shaaff's & saw him & his wife. She is good looking & agreeable.

The weather cleared off last night & has been pleasant to-day. We tired a case & a half. Our Judge Advocate gets along badly. We have not done half the work we ought to have. We have got rid of some or the worst cases. We, Major Van Dorn, Capts. Caldwell & McArthur & I dined at Capt. Johnson's. His wife looks much older than he but is pleasant & agreeable.

Fort Mason Texas Thurs. Nov. 29, 1860

It has cleared off beautifully & has been quite pleasant to-day. We tried several cases to-day, but it still goes on slowly. Shakespear—one of Capt. Caldwell's men gives a theatrical performance this evening. The Band serenaded last evening.

❦ December 1860 ❦

"South Carolina has actually seceded."

SAT. DEC. 1ST, 1860

Our weather has been delightful the last few days. We get along as slowly as ever with our court. We are now I believe through one over half the cases.

Capt. Caldwell & I dined yesterday at the mess. Lts. Phiffer, Porter & Mr. Ward the Sutler. We had a very fair & pleasant dinner. We dine to-day with Lt. Shaaff.

We finished four cases to-day & have some 12 more. We have done with 17. Capt. Caldwell thinks we will get through on Wednesday. I will be satisfied with Thursday. It is too provoking when I think that an experienced Judge Advocate would have finished in a week.

We expected the Qr.M's mail at 4½ P.M. but it is now after tattoo & he is not here. It is provoking when an important mail is expected & it fails.

We had a pleasant dinner at Mr. Shaaff's. Lt. & Mrs. Minter & Major Van Dorn & Capt. [Mc]Arthur dined with us. I wrote a letter to Margaret & my application to Col. Lee with a private letter. I will send by Sergt. Gutterman who starts for Verde tomorrow. He will put my letter for the Col. in the Post Office at Fredericksburg & it will have three chances a week to get along.

FORT MASON TEXAS SUN. DEC. 2, 1860

The mail did not get in till near day light. I got a letter from Col. Lee, in which he says he learns from Major Macklin that the court interferes with my preparations for leave—that if I will make application it wont detain me long. He then adds he expects Gen Twiggs soon & that he has no doubt he will view my case favourably. I added a line to Margaret & enclose the Col's letter & also wrote to Col. Lee. Sergt Gutterman has left with the letters. I wrote to Mr. Hooker & concluded not to send the check to pay taxes as I left a horse for the purpose.

The Judge Advocate thinks we will be through Tuesday. Some cases cant be tried. It is very windy to-day.

FORT MASON TEXAS MON. DEC. 3, 1860

Wind north yesterday afternoon & appearance of a regular norther, but pleasant to-day.

We finished three cases to-day & part of another—the last. If we had had half an hour more to-day we would be through. We will be through in an hour tomorrow. We will go the short road & hope to be at home the day after tomorrow. It is said it is but fifty miles.

TUES. DEC. 4, 1860

Court adjourned & we were off at 10½ A.M. Last evening we called on all the ladies & bid them good bye. I also called on Mr. Ward the Sutler.

CAMP VERDE TEXAS WED. DEC. 5, 1860

We encamped last night on the Pedernales near Dorses Mill, having come they say 20 miles. We lost the road near the crossing of the Llano, but did not loose much by it.[1] On the 28 Aug. there was a great flood on this river. It was run down when we got into camp. We left at 7½ A.M. & about 10 miles lost our road & came to a ranche on Spring creek. It was only a mile to the road. We here found in a house with one small room three families—3 grown women & near a dozen children.

We reached Kerrsville a little before sundown & home a little before 8 P.M. having been some 12 hours in the saddle. It is called from the Pedernales to Kerrsville 28 miles & I think it it all that & I suppose 10 miles from there to here—or 38 miles making 55 miles in all, a pretty good ride for two days. The road is better than the one we went up on. The hill into the valley of the Guadalupe is by no means a bad one. The road can be shortened some & is the one to travel. This is the route from S. Antonio & the Qr. M. mail to Camp Colorado, should pass this way.

Mr. Lathrop has not arrived. We may expect him any day. He writes that Henry Norton is quite sick & will come out. Poston has not arrived.

This is our wedding day. We have been married sixteen years. A long time when you look forward but nothing when you look back.

The sick man sent from Ft. Mason to our hospital arrived here about

---

[1] The Llano River, with headwaters in Sutton and Edwards Counties, drains a large section of the Edwards Plateau before emptying into the Colorado River fifty miles west of Austin.

dusk yesterday. The Ambulance returns in the morning. I have written to Major Van Dorn. I send him an odometer circular.

Fri. Dec. 7, 1860 C. Verde

I went with Dr. Byrnes, Mr. Newton, Policarpo the guide & Francisco on a bear hunt. We were gone 8 hours & in the saddle 7½. We saw one bear & cub but the dogs were off & they escaped. The country is very rough & difficult. We saw two deer & three turkeys. The weather delightful.

Sat. Dec. 8, 1860

Rain last night & part of the morning & now high wind & flying clouds. Prospect of a norther.

I got Gen. Twigg's order assuming command & Major Nichols has assumed his duties as Adjt. Genl. I got a note from Col. Lee that he would grant my leave, but Gen. Twiggs has arrived. I dont think he will refuse me & so shall continue my preparations. We have sold several things & I have the prospect of the sale of others.

Camp Verde Mon Dec. 10, 1860

Yesterday morning more rain, but pleasant towards night. I wrote to Dr. Foard.

Mrs. Ganahl & Capt. Brackett were in this morning. They have taken several of our things, household. We have now little besides the carriage & horses to sell. Gen Twiggs was to be yesterday in S. Antonio. I may expct my leave on Saturday.

Weather cool & pleasant to-day.

Tues. Dec. 11, 1860

We spent last evening at Capt. Caldwells playing Euchre. They were to come here, but Miss Helen sprained her ankle & could not come out.

Wind north & cold.

I packed one box of books—the R.R. Reports & Jomini.[2] Our mail is in & not a letter. Mr. Lathrop came up with the mail carrier. He looks thin. Henry Norton is much better. They all say in San Antonio I will get my leave. Gen. Twiggs is here.

---

[2] Maj. Gen. Antoine Henri Jomini, who analyzed the Napoleonic Wars in terms of basic principles, wrote *Traite des Grandes Operations Militaires* (1804) and *Precis de l'Art de la Guerre* (1838), both of which were used at West Point. Along with Karl von Clausewitz, Jomini's influcence on the antebellum army was profound.

WED. DEC. 12, 1860

Cold, cloudy & unpleasant. Lt. N. Bowers Top. Eng. arrived from a survey for a road from Camp Wood to this place.[3] Country impracticable.

THURS. DEC. 13, 1860

A pleasant day. The Doctor & Mr. Newton went hunting & brought home a Leopard cat.

Margaret is in a fit again. I dont know what has got in her. These fits come frequently.

I got my leave—2 mos. & permission to apply for six. I sent to Comfort for the mail.

CAMP VERDE FRI. DEC. 14, 1860

We all spent the evening at the Captain Caldwells. There were about a dozen men absent at tattoo & I ordered a garrison court this morning.

We have been very busy all day packing & are nearly done. The weather cold & unpleasant.

SAT. DEC. 15, 1860

Wind north—cold & unpleasant to-day. As soon as guard mounting was over we drove out & bid Mrs. Ganahl good bye & then came by Camp Ives & saw Capt. Brackett. We got home at 2 P.M. & dined at Capt. Caldwell's.

The mail brought Margaret & I letters from Charles. Also Gen. Scotts order about combat etc. of the troops. He mentions my affairs at La Ebonal & Rio Grande City & calls the latter a brilliant affair.

We are now pretty well packed & will leave on Monday.

SUN. DEC. 16, 1860

A cold misty day & now turning into rain. I thought we had but little to-day, but we have been busy all day. I fear that one wagon wont take all our things.

The Doctor & Mrs. Newton are going with us & Polly.

Capt. Brackett & Mrs. Ganahl were here this afternoon.

---

[3] Nicholas Bowen had recently graduated from West Point in July 1860 and was assigned to the Topographical Engineers. Promoted to lieutenant in the Federal Army during the Civil War, Bowen died in 1871. Heitman, *Historical Register*, 233.

CAMPT. ON SAN GERONIMO[4] MON. DEC. 17, 1860

We had rain last night & this morning & a little during the day. Capt. Brackett sent a wagon to San Antonio. Our wagon would not hold all & I put some of our baggage in his.

We got off at 10½ A.M. We have sold nearly everything. Dr. Byrne took my Mexican horse & will pay me $70, what I paid for him in a few months. I have the little poney along.

We got here at 5 P.M. & the wagons at dusk. Mr. Newton & Poly went out & shot four fine Turkeys. Dr. Byrne is also along. Mr. Lathrop rides with them in Polly's ambulance.

SAN ANTONIO TEXAS TUES. DEC. 18, 1860

It rained last night. Margaret, Mary & I slept in the Sibley tent. The other gentlemen slept in the ambulances. It rained a little when we started but cleared off some & has been warm & pleasant. We got here at 3 P.M.

There is a funeral at the House. A gentleman named King of Georgia died here suddenly.

Gen. Twiggs has taken a house. Col. & Mrs. Waite are here. His leave is not out yet & the Gen. wont assign him a post as he says the Union is dissolved. Dr. Abbott is here sick.[5] Dr. Byrne's ordered to Laredo. Capt. King goes to Verde, but Caldwell dont leave. I suppose that Col. Waite will go there with Head Quarters. Col. Lee leaves here on Thurs. to command Mason.

I fear it will be difficult for me to sell my ambulance & horses. There is no business & no money. I will try hard & take the team to the coast & get mules of the Qr. M. for my Ambulance. Mrs. Capt. Arthur Lee is here & will stay the winter.

SAN ANTONIO TEXAS WED. DEC. 19, 1860

A beautiful day. I went & called on Gen. Twiggs & saw him & Major Nichols, the Adjt. Genl. Major Vinton passed & I saw him. I went with him to his office. I asked him for mules to take my ambulance to the coast & he gave them & said he would do all the could for me. Gen. Twiggs is certain the

---

[4] San Geronimo Creek, an intermittent stream, rises in eastern Bandera County and flows south and southwest past the village of San Geronimo twenty-one miles into the Medina River.

[5] This is probably Robert Osborne Abbott, who had been an assistant surgeon in the army since 1849.

Union is gone. I also met Capt. Whiteley & he took Capt. Pitcher & I to see a paper dated in Oct. containing Gen. Scott's "view" on the crisis.[6] He thinks that if the Union will be dissolved there will be several Confederacies. This is a copy of a paper sent to the President & Sec. of War & was sent by Gen. Scott to Mr. Anderson of Ohio now living near here. The paper dont amount to much.

I saw Major Macklin. He has no money & the Quarter Master, after getting notice that he would have money, got notice it would not be sent. It is said Treasury drafts have been protested.

I have got rid of Robucks patent medicine. I left the boxes at P.J. Edwards's drug store.[7]

I have been trying all day to sell my ambulance & horses & think that I will succeed. If not I think I can get $200 for the best horse & then I will sell the other at auction. He was quite stiff & lame this morning. I have no offer for the poney.

I left my Odometer with Hines the Jeweller. It was rusty & he will put it in order.

I wrote to Major Jno. Ford at Austin & to Capt. Caldwell.[8] Capt. Brackett's wagon goes back tomorrow.

I think that Col. Waite, with the Hd. Qrs. will go to Verde & Capt. King's company. They will be crowded, but it will be pleasant there.

I met Col. Lee in his ambulance, on his way to Fort Mason to take command.

----

[6] From Indiana, Capt. Thomas Gamble Pitcher, West Point class of 1845, was a captain in the 8th Infantry. Pitcher became a brigadier general during the Civil War and died in October 1895. Heitman, *Historical Register,* 793.

[7] Illinois native P. J. Edwards, twenty-six, is listed on the Bexar County census as an apothecary. Edwards sold drugs, medicines, chemicals, paints, and perfumery, as well as "Pure Wines and Brandies for Medical Purposes." 8th Census, Bexar County; *Alamo Express* (San Antonio), Feb. 13, 1861.

[8] Writing from Austin, Ford told Heintzelman that although Cortina was near San Luis Potosí, he had been making inquiries about the number of soldiers at Fort Brown and elsewhere on the border. Ford was fearful that Cortina might make "another descent [on] Brownsville." Preoccupied with the growing secessionist crisis in Texas, Ford reported "considerable excitement . . . regarding Lincoln's election," but he did not "think extreme measures will be advocated." Ford went on to say that he was "for the Union as long as we can remain in it as equals, but when the aggressive policy of the Northern States shall have destroyed that equality, and rendered us vassals to the will of a fanatic and irresponsible majority, then they have violated the Constitution and dissolved the Union. Our duty is self protection. The south should be ready to meet the crisis." Ford to Heintzelman, Nov. 20, 1860, HP.

I saw Dr. Abadie this morning. He has a poney. He & Mrs. Abadie, Capt & Mrs. Whitely, Capt. & Mrs. Pitcher, Major & Mrs. Macklin, Major & Mrs. Vinton, etc. called this afternoon. Margaret will have to return some of them, but I dont have time, I dont think.

Major Nichols called. His wife has a sick child & did not go out. Mr. & Mrs. Smyth also called. I cant recollect all. I went to see Vinton this evening, but the parlor & hall were dark & I did not knock.

Dr. Byrne goes to Laredo. Dr. Abbott is here sick in bed, a fever. When he gets better he will probably go to Verde. I called & saw him.

San Antonio Texas Thurs. Dec. 20, 1860

A beautiful day. Mr. Lathrop & I drove the horses up town to try & sell them & the Ambulance. We had no success after spending all the forenoon at it. I can get $200 for the Ambulance, but think it too little. This uncertainty about National affairs has paralized all business. I have left one of my horses with Capt. Reynolds to sell to Major Frenches battery & the other to sell with the Govt. mules on Saturday at auction. The poney I think that Dr. Abadie will take.

I called & saw most of the officers at the office. Mrs. Capt. Reynolds & her daughters, Mrs. Ashe called, but we were out. Margaret & Dr. Bryne went & returned calls. Major Macklin was in this afternoon & Mrs. M. took Margaret out riding.

Gen. Twiggs sent for Col. Wait[e] & he goes to Verde. I have made arrangements & we leave at 8 or 9 in the morning.

I fear the Union is gone. The Southern States appear to be determined & the Blk. Republicans are not disposed to make any concessions—at least until they will be too late.

Indianola Texas Tues. Dec. 26, 1860

Fri. Dec. 21—Left S. Antonio at 10 a.m. Mr. Lathrop, Margaret & Mary in the Ambulance. Major Vinton let me have four mules & I took with me the mule team from Verde. I had to leave boxes 7, 8, 14, 11, & 13 containing table, rocking chair & books. This left as much as our wagon could carry.

Before we left we concluded it best to take $200 I had offered me for the Ambulance & sent it back. I left one horse to be sold at auction & the other for Major Frenches battery. The poney & saddle Major Macklin took with the bridle, at $60. I also left the horses to sell at auction. I am well satisifed with what I have done. I tried to get to Major Vinton's but persons were in all the afternoon & evening.

We had a pleasant day & came as far as the Sulphur Springs—about 30 miles. It was quite dark before the wagon got in. The night was cold & we had the stove up.

SAT. DEC. 22—We started about 8 A.M. & got supper within about 12 miles of Yorktown. The lead mule in the wagon has about given out & the wagon did not get in till after dark. Weather milder.

SUN. DEC. 23, 1860 We got off about the usual time & went within about 16 miles of Victoria & the wagon did not get in until after dark.

MON. DEC. 24—Got to Victoria about 1 P.M. & the wagon at 3 P.M.—very tired. Bought fodder for the mules. A poor camp. We had a Christmas in town. We had a bottle of Cal. sparkling wine.[9]

TUES. 25 DEC. A dull Christmas. We got to the Chocolate & the wagon got in after dark. Little wood & bad water.

INDIANOLA WED. DEC. 26, 1860

Got here about 2 P.M. We had a drizzling rain part of the time & cold & unpleasant. We had considerable cold & unpleasant weather on the road. It has rained all the afternoon. We intended to encamp, but there is no place. We are at the Casino House.[10] There is no steamer in. The Texas should be off the bar, but it is raining & blowing from the Eastward.

We met Lt. Majors here & have put the mules in the yard.[11] Dr. and Mrs. Howard are here. I think I will let them have my Ambulance to go back to S. Antonio.

It is said that Major Anderson has surrendered to South Carolina Fort Moultrie, under orders from Washington.[12] South Carolina has actually

---

[9] Heintzelman was probably at the Globe Hotel. See footnote 13, April 1859 chapter.

[10] The Casino House, one of the largest buildings in Indianola, had been constructed by the German Casino Association. The building was later enlarged to accommodate as many as 400 for theatrical performances, public concerts, public and private dances. Mallsch, *Indianola: Mother of Western Texas*, 224.

[11] James Patrick Major, West Point class of 1856, was a second lieutenant in the 2d Cavalry. He became a brigadier general in the Confederate Army, lived in France for a time after the war, engaged in planting in Louisiana and Texas, and died in May 1877. Warner, *Generals in Gray*, 209–210.

[12] On an island at the mouth of the Cooper River, less than a mile from Charleston, Castle Pinckney had been occupied by Charleston Zouave cadets shortly after South Carolina seceded on December 20, 1860. On the evening of December 26, 1860, a thirty-five year army veteran Maj. Robert Anderson, a Kentuckian and former

seceeded & some other States will soon follow. Some of the Northern fanatics are not disposed out of this country. I have very little hope of a satisfactory adjustment. I think the other States will hold together for the present & we will be retained in service. I can get along for some time with the two month's pay now due me.

STEAMER AUSTIN INDIANOLA BAY FRI. DEC. 28, 1860

Charles's birthday.[13] He is fifteen years of age.

It rained all day yesterday. We packed our luggage & prepared for the Steamer.

In the afternoon Dr. Howard & his wife left in the Ambulance for S. Antonio. It was an excellent opportunity for them & a good chance for me to get it back safe to the purchaser.

I arranged for a fresh mule for the wagon & it left this morning. I sent up a box of bedding to the care of the Qr. M. at San Antonio.

Yesterday was the anniversary of the fight at Rio Grande City, when Cortinas' bands were dispersed.

The steamer Austin came in this forenoon & we went on board at 11½. We left at about 2 P.M. It is a fine pleasant day—quite warm. Our accommodations are good. Lt. Majors the Comm. at Indianola left this morning to fetch his wife at Austin.

NEW ORLEANS MON. DEC. 31, 1860

We left Indianola on Friday at about 2 P.M. with pleasant weather, but we had not been long at sea before the wind changed to the North & it rained & we soon had a heavy sea. Before night Solon, Margaret & Mary were in their berths & did not leave them until we got into the river. We had a fine dinner the first day & all enjoyed it.

I never was on a boat [that] rolled more badly or was more unpleasant. It was cold & wet on deck. She rolled so we could scarcely move about & spilled the dishes off the table. We had over 100 cattle on board & they all went down. Before we got in more than half died & many were thrown overboard. All together I dont think that I ever had a more unpleasant passage.

---

slave-owner, moved his forces from Fort Moultrie, an old fort vulnerable to land attack, across the bay to a more defensible and unoccupied Fort Sumter.

[13] Charles Stuart Heintzelman was born on December 28, 1845, while his father was stationed at Detroit, Michigan. HJ, Dec. 29, 1845; North, *Samuel Peter Heintzelman*, 9.

I got a fall on deck 24 hours before we got in from which I still suffer severely.

We got in here at Breakfast. Whilst we were putting out the cattle, Solon & I went ashore & took an Omnibus to the city. We went to the Qr. M. office & learned that Col. Meyers has resigned & left for Charleston leaving the office in charge of a clerk. We also learned that Major McClune was here & had money, as well as Major Smith.

Major McClune soon came in & I drew my pay for Nov. & Dec.—$502. I also drew my per diem $13 for the court martial at Fort Mason. Major Smith was not in his office.

Major McClure rode with us to the Mint where I drew the gold, as for one of Major Maclins checks. They have notice of more than a million of dollars coming here. On board the Austin the purser would not take a check on the Sub. Treasury in New York or this place. I still keep the $100 on New York.

The friends of the Union are loosing all hope of preserving it. Fort Moultrie is in the hands of the Secessionists & Castle Pinckney. Major Anderson holds Ft. Sumpter so tis said.

The evening papers say that a forced loan has been ordered in South Carolina. If well followed up this will be death to secession.

After I got my pay we went to look at the boats & have selected the Chancellor. A fine boat for Louisville, but not the first class. We save $5 each on the passage. She says go to-day but wont till tomorrow. We thought it preferable to going to a hotel as it saves much expense.

When we got on board it was after dinner so we went ashore & got a room at a restaurant & got a good dinner. We then took a long walk in town.

After tea Mr. Lathrop & I walked to town & went to the St. Charles & called on Major McClure at the St. James, a new Hotel.[14] He was not in. After walking about a little longer & not seeing much, we returned to the boat. The weather is cool & unpleasant, but I think the rain is over. The mud was frozen this .norning.

Thus ends the year full of events.

S.P.H.

---

[14] Legendary St. Charles Hotel, two blocks above Canal Street, was one of the most elegant in the South. Although the original structure had been destroyed by fire, a second building was constructed in 1851 and was used by Federal forces as their headquarters during the Civil War. Following a second fire, the present structure was completely rebuilt in 1896. The more modest two-story James House was located at 2405 Prytania Street. Harnett T. Kane, *Queen New Orleans, City by the River* (New York: William Morrow and Co., 1949), 135.

Bibliography

Manuscripts and Archival Collections

Agricultural Census (1860). Cameron County, Tex. National Archives, Washington.

Battalion Returns. Companies D&H (2d Infantry). Adjutant General's Office. Record Group 94. National Archives, Washington.

Brownsville City Council Minutes (1850–1859). City Secretary's Office, Brownsville.

Cameron County Commissioner's Court Minutes (1848–1862). County Clerk's Office, Brownsville.

Cameron County District Court Minutes (1849–1914). Office of the District Clerk, Brownsville.

Cortina File. Daughters of the Republic of Texas Library at the Alamo, San Antonio.

Despatches from United States Consuls in Camargo, 1869–1880. Records of the Department of State. Record Group 59. National Archives, Washington.

Eighth Census (1860). National Archives, Washington.

Arizona County, N.M.

Bandera County, Tex.

Bexar County, Tex.

Cameron County, Tex.

Hidalgo County, Tex.

Kerr County, Tex.

Mason County, Tex.

Maverick County, Tex.

Starr County, Tex.

Ford, John S. Memoirs. Center for the Study of American History, University of Texas at Austin.

Heintzelman, Samuel Peter. Papers and Journals. Library of Congress, Washington.

Hidalgo County Commissioner's Court Minutes (1852–1912). Rio Grande Valley Historical Collection. University of Texas Pan American Library, Edinburg.

Hidalgo County District Court Minutes (1853–1912). Rio Grande Valley Historical Collection. University of Texas Pan American Library, Edinburg.

Houston, Sam. Papers. Record Group 301. Texas State Archives, Austin.

Kingsburg, Gilbert. Papers. Center for the Study of American History, University of Texas at Austin.

Letters Received. Adjutant General's Office. Record Group 94. National Archives, Washington.

Letters Received. United States Military Academy, West Point.

Post Returns. Adjutant General's Office. Record Group 393. National Archives.

Camp Verde, Tex.

Fort Brown, Tex.

Fort Duncan, Tex.

Fort Yuma, Cal.

Ringgold Barracks, Tex.

Regimental Returns. Adjutant General's Office. Record Group 94. National Archives.

2d Infantry

3rd Infantry

San Roman, José. Papers. Center for the Study of American History, University of
    Texas at Austin.
Seventh Census (1850). National Archives, Washington.
Bexar County, Tex.
Cameron County, Tex.
San Diego County, Cal.
Starr County Commissioner's Court Minutes (1852–1923). Rio Grande Valley
    Historical Collection. University of Texas Pan American Library, Edinburg.
Texas Adjutant General's Records. Texas State Archives, Austin.
Third Census (1810). National Archives, Washington.
Lancaster County, Pa.
West Point Application Papers of Samuel Peter Heintzelman, Adjutant General's
    Office. Record Group 94. National Archives, Washington.
West Point Application Paper of Charles Heintzelman, Adjutant General's Office.
    Record Group 94. National Archives, Washington.

BOOKS

Altshuler, Constance Wynn, ed. *Latest From Arizona: The Hesperian Letters,
    1859–1861.* Tucson: Arizona Pioneers' Historical Society, 1969.
Austerman, Wayne. *Sharps Rifles and Spanish Mules: The San Antonio–El Paso Mail.*
    College Station: Texas A&M University Press, 1985.
Bay, Betty. *Historical Brownsville: Original Townsite Guide.* Brownsville, Tex.:
    Brownsville Historical Association, 1980.
Bauer, K. Jack. *The Mexican War: 1846–1848.* New York: Macmillan Publishers, 1974.
Brooks, Nathan Covington. *A Complete History of the Mexican War, 1846–1848.*
    Chicago: Rio Grande Press, 1965.
Creola Blackwell, transcriber. *Samuel P. Heintzelman's Journal: 1851–1853, Fort Yuma.*
    Yuma: Yuma County Historical Society, 1989.
Chatfield, W. H. *Twin Cities of the Border and the Country of the Lower Rio Grande.* New
    Orleans: E. P. Brandao, 1893.
Cheeseman, Bruce S., ed. *My Dear Henrietta: Hiram Chamberlain's Letters to His
    Daughter, 1846–1866.* Kingsville, Tex.: King Ranch, 1993.
Clarke, Dwight L. *Stephen Watts Kearny: Soldier of the West.* Norman: University of
    Oklahoma Press, 1961.
Coker, Caleb, ed. *The News from Brownsville: Helen Chapman's Letters from the Texas
    Military Frontier, 1848–1852.* Austin: Texas State Historical Association, 1992.
Copeland, Fayette. *Kendall of the Picayune.* Norman: University of Oklahoma Press,
    1943.
Cude, Elton R. *The Wild and Free Dukedom of Bexar.* San Antonio: Munguia Printers,
    1978.
Cullum, George W. *Biographical Register of the Officers and Graduates of the U.S.
    Military Academy at West Point, N.Y. From its Establishment, in 1802, to 1890.*
    Cambridge: Riverside Press, 1891.
Daddysman, James W. *The Matamoros Trade: Confederate Commerce, Diplomacy and
    Intrigue.* Cranbury, N.J.: University of Delaware Press, 1984.

Davis, William C. *Battle at Bull Run: A History of the First Major Campaign of the Civil War.* Baton Rouge: Louisiana State University Press, 1977.

De Cordova, J. *Texas: Her Resources and Her Public Men.* Waco: Texian Press, 1969.

De León, Arnoldo. *They Called Them Greasers: Anglo Attitudes Towards Mexicans in Texas, 1821–1900.* Austin: University of Texas Press, 1983.

———. *Mexican Americans in Texas: A Brief History.* Arlington Heights, Ill.: Harlan Davidson, 1993.

———. *The Tejano Community, 1836–1900.* Albuquerque: University of New Mexico Press, 1982.

Dobie, J. Frank. *A Vaquero of the Brush Country.* Reprint. Austin: University of Texas Press, 1965.

Edwards, William B. *The Story of Colt's Revolver: The Biography of Col. Samuel Colt.* Harrisburg, Pa.: Stackpole Co., 1957.

Eleventh Annual Reunion of the Association of the Graduates of the U.S. Military Academy at West Point, New York, June 17, 1880. East Saginaw, Mich.: E. W. Lyon, 1880.

Emmett, Chris. *Texas Camel Tales: Incidents Growing up Around an Attempt by the War Department of the United States to Foster an Uninterrupted Flow of Commerce through Texas by the Use of Camels.* Reprint. Austin: Steck-Vaughn, 1969.

Folkman, David I, Jr. *The Nicaragua Route.* Salt Lake City: University of Utah Press, 1972.

Ford, John Salmon. *Rip Ford's Texas.* Ed. Stephen B. Oates. Austin: University of Texas Press, 1963.

Frazer, Robert W. *Forts of the West.* Norman: University of Oklahoma Press, 1965.

———. *Forts and Supplies: The Role of the Army in the Economy of the Southwest, 1846–1861.* Albuquerque: University of New Mexico Press, 1983.

———, ed. *Mansfield on the Condition of the Western Forts, 1853–54.* Norman: University of Oklahoma Press, 1963.

Freeman, Douglas Southall. *R. E. Lee, A Biography.* New York: Scribner's Sons, 1934.

Garza, Israel Cavazos. *Diccionario Biografico de Nuevo León.* Monterrey: Universidad Autonoma de Nuevo León, 1984.

Goldfinch, Charles W., and Jose T. Canales. *Juan N. Cortina: Two Interpretations.* New York: Arno Press, 1974.

Grimm, Agnes. G. *Llanos Mesteñas, Mustang Plains.* Waco: Texian Press, 1972.

Hall, Martin H. *Sibley's New Mexico Campaign.* Austin: University of Texas Press, 1960.

Hazen, William B. *A Narrative of Military Service.* Reprint. Huntington, W.Va.: Blue Acorn Press, 1993.

Hebert, Rachel Bluntzer. *The Forgotten Colony: San Patricio de Hibernia.* Burnet, Tex.: Eakin Press, 1981.

Heitman, Francis B. *Historical Register and Dictionary of the United States Army, From its Organization, September 29, 1789, to March 2, 1903.* 2 vols. Washington, D.C.: Government Printing Office, 1903.

Hennessy, John J. *Return to Bull Run: The Campaign and Battle of Second Manassas.* New York: Simon and Schuster, 1993.

Hesseltine, William B., and Hazel C. Wolf. *The Blue and the Gray on the Nile.* Chicago: University of Chicago Press, 1961.

Hughes, W. J. *Rebellious Ranger: Rip Ford and the Old Southwest.* Norman: University of Oklahoma Press, 1964.

Hunter, J. Marvin. *Old Camp Verde: The Home of the Camels.* Bandera, Tex.: n.p., 1948.

Jackson, Jack. *Los Mesteños: Spanish Ranching in Texas, 1721–1821.* College Station: Texas A&M University Press, 1986.

Jenkins, John H., ed. *Robert E. Lee on the Rio Grande: The Correspondence of Robert E. Lee on the Texas Border, 1860.* Austin: Jenkins Publishing Co., 1988.

Johannsen, Robert W. *To the Halls of the Montezumas: The Mexican War in the American Imagination.* New York: Macmillan Publishers, 1974.

Kearney, Milo, and Anthony Knopp. *Boom and Bust: The Historical Cycles of Matamoros and Brownsville.* Austin: Eakin Press, 1991.

Kearney, Milo, ed. *Studies in Brownsville History.* Brownsville, Tex.: Pan American University at Brownsville, 1986.

———, ed. *More Studies in Brownsville History.* Brownsville, Tex.: Pan American University at Brownsville, 1989.

———, ed. *Still More Studies in Brownsville History.* Brownsville, Tex.: University of Texas at Brownsville, 1991.

Kelly, Pat. *River of Lost Dreams: Navigation on the Rio Grande.* Lincoln: University of Nebraska Press, 1986.

Klement, Frank L. *The Copperheads in the Middle West.* Chicago: University of Chicago Press, 1960.

Larralde, Carlos. *Mexican American Movements and Leaders.* Los Alamitos, Calif.: Hwong Publishing Co., 1976.

Lea, Tom. *The King Ranch.* 2 vols. Boston: Little Brown and Company, 1959.

Lyon, William H. *Those Old Yellow Dog Days: Frontier Journalism in Arizona, 1859–1912.* Tucson: Arizona Historical Society, 1994.

McFeely, William S. *Frederick Douglass.* New York: W.W. Norton, 1991.

Malsch, Brownson. *Indianola: The Mother of Western Texas.* Austin: State House Press, 1988.

Marszalek, John F. *Sherman: A Soldier's Passion for Order.* New York: Free Press, 1993.

Martin, Douglas D. *Yuma Crossing.* Albuquerque: University of New Mexico Press, 1954.

Metz, Leon. *Border: The U.S.-Mexico Line.* El Paso: Managan Books, 1989.

Moneyhon, Carl, and Bobby Roberts. *Portraits of Courage: A Photographic History of Louisiana in the Civil War.* Fayettville: University of Arkansas Press, 1990.

Moneyhon, Carl H. *Republicanism in Reconstruction Texas.* Austin: University of Texas Press, 1980.

Montejano, David. *Anglos and Mexicans in the Making of Texas, 1836–1986.* Austin: University of Texas Press, 1987.

Nelligan, Mary H. *Custis-Lee Mansion: The Robert E. Lee Memorial.* Washington, D.C.: National Park Service, 1962.

North, Diane M. T. *Samuel Peter Heintzelman and the Sonora Exploring and Mining Company.* Tucson: University of Arizona Press, 1980.

Olliff, Donothon C. *Reforma Mexico and the United States: A Search for Alternatives to Annexation, 1854–1861.* University, Ala.: University of Alabama Press, 1986.

O'Neil, James Bradas. *To Die But Once: The Story of a Tejano.* New York: Knight Publications, 1935.

Pierce, Frank Cushman. *A Brief History of the Lower Rio Grande Valley.* Menasha, Wis.: George Banta Publishing Co., 1917.

Pingenot, Ben E., ed. *Paso del Aguila: A Chronicle of Frontier Days on the Texas Border as Recorded in the Memoirs of Jesse Sumpter.* Austin: Encino Press, 1969.

Pirtle, Caleb, III, and Michael F. Cusack. *The Lonely Sentinel, Fort Clark: On Texas's Western Frontier.* Austin: Eakin Press, 1985.

Pitt, Leonard. *The Decline of the Californios: A Social History of the Spanish-Speaking Californians, 1846–1890.* Berkeley: University of California Press, 1971.

Randall, Ruth Painter. *Colonel Elmer Ellsworth: A Biography of Lincoln's Friend and First Hero of the Civil War.* Boston: Little, Brown and Co., 1960.

Richter, William L. *The Army in Texas during Reconstruction.* College Station: Texas A&M University Press, 1987.

Rister, Carl Coke. *Robert E. Lee in Texas.* Norman: University of Oklahoma Press, 1946.

Robertson, Brian. *Wild Horse Desert: The Heritage of South Texas.* Edinburg, Tex.: New Santander Press, 1985.

Rodríguez, José Policarpo. *The Old Guide: Surveyor, Scout, Hunter, Indian Fighter, Ranchman, Preacher.* Dallas, n.d.

Roland, Charles P. *Albert Sidney Johnston: Soldier of Three Republics.* Austin: University of Texas Press, 1964.

Rosenbaum, Robert J. *Mexicano Resistance in the Southwest, "The Sacred Right of Self-Preservation."* Austin: University of Texas Press, 1981.

Sacks, B. *Be It Enacted: The Creation of the Territory of Arizona.* Phoenix: Arizona Historical Foundation, 1964.

Sandwich, Brian. *The Great Western: Legendary Lady of the Southwest.* El Paso: Texas Western Press, 1991.

Sayner, Donald B., and Robert P. Hale., comps. *Arizona's First Newspaper: "The Weekly Arizonian."* Tucson: Arizona Historical Society, n.d.

Sears, Stephen W., ed. *The Civil War Papers of George B. McClellan: Selected Correspondence, 1860–1865.* New York: Ticknor and Fields, 1989.

———. *George B. McClellan: The Young Napoleon.* New York: Ticknor and Fields, 1988.

——— *To the Gates of Richmond: The Peninsula Campaign.* New York: Ticknor and Fields, 1992.

Sherman, John. *John Sherman's Recollections of Forty Years in the House, Senate, and Cabinet: An Autobiography.* Chicago: Werner Co., 1895.

Simpson, Harold B. *Cry Comanche, The 2nd U.S. Cavalry in Texas, 1855–1861.* Hillsboro: Hill College Press, 1979.

Sixty-Seventh Annual Report of the Association of Graduates of the United States Military Academy at West Point, New York, June 11, 1936. Newburg, N.Y.: Moore Printing, 1936.

Smith, Thomas Tyree. *Fort Inge: Sharps, Spurs, and Sabers on the Texas Frontier, 1849–1869.* Austin: Eakin Press, 1993.

Sonora and the Value of its Silver Mines, Report of the Sonora Exploring and Mining Co., Made to the Stockholders, December, 1856. Cincinnati: Railroad Record Print, 1857.

Stratton, R.B. *Captivity of the Oatman Girls.* Lincoln: University of Nebraska Press, 1983.

Stillman, Devereux. *Charles Stillman, 1810–1875.* New York: 1956.

Swift, Roy L. *Three Roads to Chihuahua: The Great Wagon Roads that Opened the Southwest, 1823–1883.* Austin: Eakin Press, 1988.

Thomas, Stephen. *Fort Davis and the Texas Frontier: Paintings by Captain Arthur T. Lee, Eighth U.S. Infantry*. College Station: Texas A&M University Press, 1976.

Thompson, Jerry. *Sabers on the Rio Grande*. Austin: Presidial Press, 1974.

———. *Henry Hopkins Sibley: Confederate General of the West*. Natchitoches: Northwestern State University Press, 1987.

———. *Juan N. Cortina and the Texas-Mexico Frontier, 1859–1877*. El Paso: Texas Western Press, 1994.

Thrapp, Dan L., ed. *Encyclopedia of Frontier Biography*. 3 vols. Spokane: Arthur H. Clark Co., 1990.

Twelfth Annual Return of the Graduates of the U.S. Military Academy, June 9, 1881. East Saginaw: E.W. Lyon, 1881.

Tyler, Ron C., et al., eds. *The New Handbook of Texas*. 6 vols. Austin: Texas State Historical Association, 1997.

Tyler, Ronnie C. *Santiago Vidaurri and the Southern Confederacy*. Austin: Texas State Historical Association, 1973.

Utley, Robert M. *Frontiersmen in Blue: The United States Army and the Indian, 1848–1865*. New York: Macmillan, 1962.

Vayssade, Martin Reyes, comp. *Cartografía Historica de Tamaulipas*. Ciudad Victoria: Instituto Tamaulipeco de Cultura, 1990.

Vezzetti, Robert B., and Ruby A. Wooldridge. *Brownsville: A Pictorial History*. Virginia Beach, Va.: Donning Co., 1982.

Wagoner, Jay J. *Early Arizona: Prehistory to Civil War*. Tucson: University of Arizona Press, 1954.

Warner, Ezra J. *Generals in Blue: Lives of the Union Commanders*. Baton Rouge: Louisiana State University Press, 1977.

———. *Generals in Gray: Lives of the Confederate Commanders*. Baton Rouge: Louisiana State University Press, 1959.

Watkins, Clara. *Kerr County, Texas, 1856–1976*. Kerrville, Tex.: Hill Country Preservation Society, 1975.

Weaver, Bobby D. *Castro's Colony: Empresario Development in Texas, 1842–1865*. College Station: Texas A&M University Press, 1985.

Webb, Walter Prescott. *The Texas Rangers: A Century of Frontier Defense*. 2d ed. Austin: University of Texas Press, 1965.

—————, H Bailey Carroll, and Stephen Branda, eds. *Handbook of Texas*. 3 vols. Austin: Texas State Historical Association, 1952, 1976

Weber, David J. *Richard H. Kern: Expeditionary Artist in the Far Southwest, 1848–1853*. Albuquerque: University of New Mexico Press, 1985.

Welcher, Frank J. *The Union Army, 1861–1865: Organization and Operation*, Volume I, *Eastern Theater*. Bloomington: Indiana University Press, 1989.

Williams, Amelia W., and Eugene C. Barker. *The Writings of Sam Houston, 1813–1863*. Austin: Jenkins Publishing Co., 1970.

Woodman, Lyman L. *Cortina, the Rogue of the Rio Grande*. San Antonio: Naylor Co., 1950.

Woodward, Arthur, ed. *Journal of Lt. Thomas W. Sweeny, 1849–1853*. Los Angeles: Westernlore Press, 1956.

Wooster, Robert. *Soldiers, Sutlers, and Settlers: Garrison Life on the Texas Frontier*. Texas A&M University Press, 1987.

Wright, Marcus J., comp. *Texas in the War, 1861–1865*. Ed. Harold B. Simpson. Hillsboro, Tex.: Hill Junior College Press, 1965.

ARTICLES

Baldridge, Lillian W. "Cattle Bandit Extraordinary." *Cattlemen* 34 (June, 1947), 20, 58–63

Bridges, C. A. "The Knights of the Golden Circle: A Filibustering Fantasy." *Southwestern Historical Quarterly*, 44 (Jan., 1941), 287–302.

Broussard, Edward J. "The Origins of the McLane-Ocampo Treaty of 1859." *Americas*, 14 (Winter, 1958), 223–246.

Champion, A. A. "The Miller Hotel in the Antebellum Period." In *More Studies in Brownsville History*. Ed. Milo Kearny. Brownsville: Pan American University at Brownsville.

Crenshaw, Ollinger. "The Knights of the Golden Circle: The Career of George Bickley." *American Historical Review*, 47 (Oct. 1941), 23–50.

Crimmins, M. L. "An Episode in the Texas Career of General David E. Twiggs." *Southwestern Historical Quarterly*, 41 (Oct., 1937), 167–173.

Darrow, Caroline Baldwin. "Recollections of the Twiggs Surrender." In *Battles and Leaders of the Civil War*. Vol. 1. New York: Yoseloff and Co., 1956.

Davenport, Harbert. "General José María Jesús Carbajal." *Southwestern Historical Quarterly*, 55 (Apr., 1952), 475–483.

Duffen, William A., ed. "Overland Via 'Jackass Mail' in 1858: The Diary of Phocion R. Way." *Arizona and the West*, 2 (Spring-Winter, 1960), 35–54, 147–164, 279–293, 353–371.

Dunn, Roy Sylvan. "The KGC in Texas, 1860–1861." *Southwestern Historical Quarterly*, 70 (Apr., 1967), 543–573.

Elliott, J. K. "The Great Western: Sarah Bowman, Mother and Mistress to the U.S. Army." *Journal of Arizona History*, 30 (Spring, 1989), 1–26.

Ellis, Richard E. "Duff Green." In *Encyclopedia of Southern History*. Baton Rouge: Louisiana State University Press, 1979.

Glavecke, Adolphus. "The Story of Old Times." In W. H. Chatfield, *Twin Cities of the Border and the Lower Rio Grande*. New Orleans: E. P. Brandao, 1893.

Fornell, Earl W. "Texans and Filibusters in the 1850s." *Southwestern Historical Quarterly*, 59 (Apr., 1956), 411–428.

Heiges, George L. "Gen. S. P. Heintzelman Visits his Hometown of Manheim." *Journal of Lancaster County Historical Society*, 68 (1964), 85–109.

Hingo, Don. "Texas' First Aristocracy: Robber or Robin Hood." *Houston Genealogical Journal*, 7 (No. 2, 1989), 62–65.

Hostetter, A. K. "Major Samuel Peter Heintzelman." *Historical Papers and Addresses of Lancaster County Historical Society*, 17 (No. 2, 1913), 57–78.

Hunter, J.T. "Captain J. T. Hunter Tells of the Cortina War." *Hunter's Magazine*, 2 (Nov., 1911), 3–8.

Kroeker, Marvin E. "William B. Hazen." In *Soldiers West: Military Biographies from the Military Frontier*. Lincoln: University of Nebraska Press, 1987.

Long, J. W., Jr. "The Origin and Development of the San Juan Island Boundary Controversy." *Pacific Northwest Quarterly*, 43 (Fall, 1952), 187–213.

Poston, Charles D. "In Memoriam: Major-General Samuel P. Heintzelman." In *Arizona Weekly Star* (Tucson) (May, 1880).

Rippy, J. Fred. "Border Troubles Along the Rio Grande, 1848–1860." *Southwestern Historical Quarterly*, 23 (Oct., 1919), 91–111.

Sacks, B. "Charles Debrille Poston: Prince of Arizona's Pioneers." *The Smoke Signal*, 7 (Spring, 1963), 1–12.

———. "The Creation of the Territory of Arizona." *Arizona and the West*, 5 (Spring–Summer, 1963), 29–62.

———. "Sylvester Mowry: Artilleryman, Libertine, Entrepreneur." *American West*, 3 (Summer, 1964), 14–25, 79.

Secrest, William B. "Wozencraft." *Real West*, 24 (Oct.–Dec., 1981), 6–13, 56, 36–40, 54.

Shearer, Ernest C. "The Carvajal Disturbances." *Southwestern Historical Quarterly*, 55 (Oct., 1951), 430–451.

Shook, Robert W. "The Battle of the Nueces, August 10, 1862." *Southwestern Historical Quarterly* 66 (July 1962), 201–230.

Thomas, Emory M. "Battle of Glendale." In *Historical Times Illustrated Encyclopedia of the Civil War*. New York: Harper & Row, 1986.

Thompson, Jerry. "The Many Faces of Juan Nepomuceno Cortina." *South Texas Studies*, (1991), 85–98.

Von Schweinitz, Helga. "Hermann Ehrenberg, Fighting for Texas." *True West*, 33 (Apr., 1986), 22–26.

Weisinger, Sidney R. "Globe House." *Victoria Advocate*, (Feb., 1974).

Wert, Jeffry D. "Battle of Malvern Hill." In *Historical Times Illustrated Encyclopedia of the Civil War*. New York: Harper & Row, 1986.

———. "Engagement at Oak Grove." In *Historical Times Illustrated Encyclopedia of the Civil War*. New York: Harper & Row, 1986.

Winfrey, Dorman H. "Fort Clark." In *Frontier Forts of Texas*. Waco: Texian Press, 1968.

NEWSPAPERS

Brownsville: *American Flag, Bandera Americana, Daily Ranchero, Daily Ranchero and Republican, Fort Brown Flag*

Corpus Christi: *Ranchero*

Clarksville: *Northern Standard*

Dallas: *Dallas Herald*

Galveston: *Galveston News, Tri-Weekly News*

Houston: *Tri-Weekly Telegraph*

New Orleans: *Daily Delta, Daily True Delta, New Orleans Bee, New Orleans Daily Picayune, New Orleans Picayune*

New York: *Frank Leslie's Illustrated Newspaper, New York Herald , New York Times*

San Antonio: *Alamo Express, Daily Herald, Ledger*

San Diego: *San Diego Herald*

San Francisco: *Alta California*

Tubac: *Weekly Arizonian*

Tucson: *Arizona Weekly Star*

Victoria: *Victoria Advocate*

Government Publications

Emory, William H. *Report of the United States and Mexican Boundary Survey, Made Under the Direction of the Secretary of the Interior.* 34th Cong., 1st sess.

Ives, Joseph Christmas. *Report upon the Colorado River of the West, explored in 1857 and 1858 by Lt. Joseph C. Ives, Corps of Topographical Engineers, under the direction of the Office of Exploration and Surveys, A.A. Humphreys, Captain Topographical Engineers, in charge.* Washington: Government Printing Office, 1861.

U.S. Congress. House. "Difficulties on the Southwestern Frontier." 36th Congress, 1st sess.

Reports of the Committee of Investigation sent in 1873 by the Mexican Government to the Frontier of Texas. New York: Baker and Godwin, 1875.

U.S. Congress. House. "Message from the President of the United States transmitting report in regard to Indian Affairs on the Pacific." 34th Cong., 3d sess.

U.S. Congress. House. "Troubles on Texas Frontier." 36th Cong., 1st sess.

U.S. Congress. House. "Reconnaissance of Routes from San Antonio to El Paso." 31st Cong., 1st sess.

U.S. Congress. House. "Texas Frontier Troubles." 44th Cong., 1st sess.

U.S. Congress. Senate. "Hostilities on the Rio Grande." 36th Cong., 1st sess.

War of the Rebellion: A Compilation of the Official Records of the Union and Confederate Armies. 128 vols. Washington: Government Printing Office, 1889.

Unpublished Material

De Blasio, Mario. "Sonora Exploring and Mining Co., 1856–1861." M.A. thesis, University of Arizona, 1949.

Douglas, James Ridley. "Juan Cortina: El Caudillo de la Frontera." M.A. thesis, University of Texas, 1992.

Gray, Leroy P. "The Economic History of the Lower Rio Grande Valley, 1820–1875." Ph.D. diss., Harvard University, 1942.

Gray, Ronald Norman. "Edmund J. Davis: Radical Republican and Reconstruction Governor of Texas." Ph.D. diss., Texas Tech University, 1976.

Hargett, Janet Lee. "Louis John Frederick Jaeger: Entrepreneur at Yuma Crossing." M.A. thesis, University of Arizona, 1967.

Heidler, Jeanne Twiggs. "The Military Career of David Emanuel Twiggs." Ph.D. diss., Texas Christian University, 1987.

Lackman, Howard. "George Thomas Howard, Texas Frontiersman." Ph.D. diss., University of Texas, 1954.

Marcum, Richard T. "Fort, Brown, Texas: A History of the Border Post." Ph.D. diss., Texas Tech University, 1964.

Sellers, Rosella A. "The History of Fort Duncan, Eagle Pass, Texas." M.A. thesis, Sul Ross College, 1960.

Thompson, James Heaven. "A Nineteenth Century History of Cameron County, Texas." M.A. thesis, University of Texas, 1965.

Index

Eagle, Robert Nelson: 224
East Pascagoula, Mississippi: 10
Edinburg, Texas: 138, 151, 221, 112, 222,
    226–228
Edwards County, Texas: 299
Edwards, P. J.: 303
Edwards Plateau, Texas: 77, 299
Ehrenberg, Hermann Vollrath: 12, 52, 92,
    264, 278
El Alamo, Nuevo León: 166, 169–170
El Capitan Peak, Texas: 16
El Ebonal, Texas: skirmish at, 3, 139
El Paso, Texas: 13, 49
El Paso Road, Texas: 20
Emory, William Helmsley: 56, 108, 159
Enchanted Rock, Texas: 295
Escandon, José de: 163, 231
Espíritu Santo Grant, Texas: 18, 138
Evans, Nathan George: 286

F

Fair Oaks, Virginia: battle of, 96
Falcón, Ramón: 193
Falcon Reservoir, Texas and Tamaulipas:
    163
Fannin County, Texas: 176
Fannin, James: 92
Fauntleroy, Thomas Turner: 206
Fayetteville, Arkansas: 16
Fenn, F. F.: 223
Fireman's Cemetery, New Orleans: 60
First Bull Run, Virginia: Battle of, 2, 39, 47
Fitzgerald, Edward H.: 65
Fitzpatrick, Richard: 149, 180, 194, 221,
    236
Flores, Inocéncia: 159
Floyd, John B.: 16, 28, 194, 208, 217
Foard, Andrew Jackson: 76, 91, 95, 104,
    120, 124, 185, 255, 263, 267, 273, 270,
    275
Ford, John Salmon: 125, 140–143, 147,
    156–158, 174, 179, 195, 202, 219, 242,
    244, 246
Forest Lawn Cemetery, Buffalo, New York:
    5
Forrest, Edwin: 5
Fort Atkinson, Nebraska: 81
Fort Belknap, Texas: 16
Fort Brown, Texas: 20, 40, 131–138,
    143–149, 178–221, 230–243, 281, 303.
    See also Brownsville

Fort Buchanan, Arizona (New Mexico
    Territory): 15
Fort Chadbourne, Texas: 16, 90
Fort Clark, Texas: 25, 71, 82, 94, 200, 278
Fort Cobb, Oklahoma: 99
Fort Columbus, New York: 36
Fort Craig, New Mexico: 150
Fort Davis, Texas: 281
Fort Duncan, Texas: 17, 20, 25, 68–69,
    Heintzelman at, 78–82; 84, 94, 118, 156,
    223–224, 281
Fort Gratiot, Michigan: 6
Fort Inge, Texas: 69, 78, 82, 281
Fort Kearny, Nebraska: 54
Fort Leavenworth, Kansas: 31, 281
Fort Lyon, Virginia: 43
Fort Mason, Texas: 62, 106, 292, 299
Fort McIntosh, Texas: 25, 137, 173, 200,
    281
Fort Merrill, Texas: 34, 118, 120, 122
Fort Monroe, Virginia: 31, 111
Fort Moultrie, South Carolina: 281, 283
Fort Quitman, Texas: 218
Fort Riley, Kansas: 83
Fort Smith, Arkansas: 16
Fort Snelling, Minnesota: 97
Fort Stockton, Texas: 251, 281
Fort Sumter, South Carolina: 36
Fort Yuma, California: 11, 14, 56, 70, 281
Fox, John: 32, 131
Franklin (El Paso), Texas: 16
Franklin, William B.: 45
Fredericksburg, Texas: 73, 295
Fredericksburg, Virginia: 104
Freedom, Pennsylvania: 203
Freiburg, Saxony: 72
French, William Henry: 171–172
Frio River, Texas: 25, 77
Futhey, John S.: 107, 124, 277
Futhey, Juliana: 107

G

Gadsden Purchase: 13, 56
Galvan, Jeremiah: 25, 40, 46, 147, 197, 278,
    202, 207, 210, 215, 217, 220, 230, 236,
    239, 252, 292
Galveston, Texas: 50–52, 61
Galveston *Daily Civilian*: 28
Gambier, Ohio: 271–272
Ganahl Charles de: 89, 92, 98, 101–102,
    107, 118, 259, 263, 272, 285–186, 294